The Underside of Modernity

The Underside of Modernity:

Apel, Ricoeur, Rorty, Taylor, and the Philosophy of Liberation

Enrique Dussel

Translated and Edited by
Eduardo Mendieta

HUMANITIES PRESS
NEW JERSEY

First published 1996 by Humanities Press International, Inc.
165 First Avenue, Atlantic Highlands, New Jersey 07716

This English translation © 1996 by Humanities Press International, Inc.

Library of Congress Cataloging-in-Publication Data
Dussel, Enrique D.
 [Essays. English. Selections]
 The underside of modernity : Apel, Ricoeur, Rorty, Taylor, and the philosophy of liberation / Enrique Dussel ; translated and edited by Eduardo Mendieta.
  p. cm.
 Includes bibliographical references and indes.
 ISBN 0-391-03932-6 (cloth)
 1. Philosophy. 2. Ethics. 3. Liberty. 4. Dussel, Enrique D. Modern—20th century. 8. Liberation theology. I. Mendieta, Eduardo. II. Title.
B1034.D872E5 1996
190'.9'04—dc20   95-32838
                                                                                   CIP

All rights reserved. No part of this publication may be reproduced
or transmitted, in any form or by any means, without written permission.

Printed in the United States of America

Contents

Foreword   vii
Acknowledgments   xii
Editor's Introduction   xiii

PART ONE

1. LIBERATION PHILOSOPHY FROM THE PRAXIS OF THE OPPRESSED   2
   - 1.1 Demarcation of Liberation Philosophy: Beyond Eurocentric Developmentalism   3
   - 1.2 Liberation Philosophy and Praxis: Categories and Method   5
   - 1.3 Horizons and Debates of Liberation Philosophy   7
   - 1.4 Pertinence of Economics   12
   - 1.5 Paths Opening Up to the Future   14
2. THE REASON OF THE OTHER: "INTERPELLATION" AS SPEECH-ACT   19
   - 2.1 Point of Departure   19
   - 2.2 Interpellation   21
   - 2.3 The Reason of the Other: Exteriority and the Community of Communication   27
   - 2.4 From Pragmatics to Economics   32
3. TOWARD A NORTH-SOUTH DIALOGUE   49
   - 3.1 State of the Question   49
   - 3.2 Toward the Origin of the "Myth of Modernity"   51
   - 3.3 Exteriority-Totality, "Lebenswelt"-System   53
   - 3.4 Communication Community and Life Community   54
4. FROM THE SKEPTIC TO THE CYNIC   64
   - 4.1 The Skeptic and the Ultimate Grounding of Discourse Ethics   65
   - 4.2 The Cynic and the Power of Strategic Rationality as Criticized by Liberation Philosophy   67
   - 4.3 The Skeptic as a Functionary of Cynical Reason   70
5. HERMENEUTICS AND LIBERATION   74
   - 5.1 Following Ricoeur's Philosophical Project Step by Step   74
   - 5.2 Toward a Latin-American Symbolics (up to 1969)   77
   - 5.3 Origins of Liberation Philosophy (1969–76)   79

	5.4	From Hermeneutical Pragmatics to Economics	83
	5.5	A Philosophy of "Poverty in Times of Cholera"	88
6	A "CONVERSATION" WITH RICHARD RORTY		103
	6.1	Different Original Situations	103
	6.2	Rorty's Philosophical Project	106
	6.3	Rorty's Pragmatism and Liberation Philosophy	113
7	MODERNITY, EUROCENTRISM, AND TRANS-MODERNITY: IN DIALOGUE WITH CHARLES TAYLOR		129
	7.1	The Project of the Historical Reconstruction of Modernity	129
	7.2	Taylor's Ethics of the Good	138
	7.3	Conclusions	147

PART TWO

8	RESPONSE BY KARL-OTTO APEL: DISCOURSE ETHICS BEFORE THE CHALLENGE OF LIBERATION PHILOSOPHY		163
	8.1	The Prehistory of the Contemporary Discourse	163
	8.2	The Themes of the Dusselian Challenge	164
	8.3	European Perspectives on the Collapse of Marxism-Leninism	167
	8.4	Methodological Gains of the Theory of Dependence	172
	8.5	The Skeptical-Pragmatic Problematization of the Grand Theories of Political Development	177
	8.6	The Ethically Relevant Facts of the Relationship between the First and Third World	180
9	RESPONSE BY PAUL RICOEUR: PHILOSOPHY AND LIBERATION		205
10	RESPONSE BY ENRIQUE DUSSEL: WORLD SYSTEM, POLITICS, AND THE ECONOMICS OF LIBERATION PHILOSOPHY		213
	10.1	The World System as a Philosophical Problem	214
	10.2	The Pretention to Globality and the Fundamental Insight into the Question of Dependence	217
	10.3	Why Marx? Toward a Philosophical Economics	219
	10.4	There Is No Economics without Politics nor Politics without Economics	227

Bibliography 240
Index 245

Foreword

This book gathers some of the essays which are fruits of recent debates and dialogues that have only just begun. The Philosophy of Liberation that I practice, not only in Latin America, but also regarding all types of oppression on the planet (of women, the discriminated races, the exploited classes, the marginalized poor, the impoverished countries, the old and homeless exiled and buried in shelters and asylums, the local religions, the homeless and orphaned children (a lost generation) of inhospitable cities, the systems destroyed by capital and the market . . . in short, the *immense majority of humanity*), begins a dialogue with the hegemonic European-North American philosophical community. The works here presented all gravitate around one central theme: eurocentrism and the invisibility of "economics" that in turn prevent the development out of poverty of the *greater part of humanity* as a fundamental philosophical and ethical theme.

In the first part of this book, in fact, the essay "Liberation Philosophy from the Praxis of the Oppressed" was presented at the First International Congress of Latin American Philosophy that took place in the city of Juárez (Mexico), May 1990, and in which I situated some issues in debate from the perspective of my re-interpretation of Marx's work, and from my critique of machismo, a problem that I began to reformulate in this work and which will be the object of future explicit studies in *Ethics of Liberation*, under redaction.

On 25 November 1989, two weeks before the so-called fall of the Berlin Wall—news of which I received on 9 December from Agnes Heller before I was to give a lecture on "The Four Redactions of *Capital*" at the New School for Social Research in New York—I delivered a work in German on the "Introduction to Apel's *Transformation of Philosophy* and Liberation Philosophy,"[1] which had been requested by Raúl Fornet-Betancourt of Aachen, in order to initiate a dialogue with Apel's discourse ethics from the perspective of liberation philosophy. This was only a beginning.

In another work, therefore, which is here the second essay, "The Reason of the Other: 'Interpellation' as Speech Act," I presented the clarification and development of my position in Freiburg. This work was presented originally in March of 1991 at a seminar organized in Mexico. The last part of this essay, and the latter sections of the work dedicated to a dialogue with Ricoeur, share some similarities given that my intention was to note the urgency of a return, "against fashion," to the philosophical and critical discourse of Marx (which I articulated without contradiction in my interpretation of several volumes with respect to Levinas and as a function of a philosophical discourse on the liberation of the poor of the earth).

The third work, "Toward a North-South Dialogue," was presented in German on 14 March 1992, in Bad-Homburg (next to Frankfurt), on the occasion of Karl-Otto Apel's seventieth birthday, and was later published by Suhrkamp in a *Festschrift* for Apel.

The fourth work, "From the Skeptic to the Cynic," was presented in German at a conference which took place in Mainz, 11 April 1992, as the third stage in the dialogue that had begun in Freiburg in 1989.

The fifth work, in French, "Hermeneutics and Liberation," requested by Domenico Jervolino, professor at the University of Naples, was a lecture that served as the basis for a dialogue with Paul Ricoeur, which took place in the university on 16 April 1991. I had already spoken with Ricoeur on the theme in January of 1990 in Rome, on the occasion of a seminar on ethics which had taken place at the Lateranense University, and during a trip I made to Chicago to meet and talk at length during a most amicable evening with my old professor from the Sorbonne.

The sixth work, "A 'Conversation' with Richard Rorty," I prepared in order to be able to exchange some ideas with Rorty on the occasion of his visit to us in Mexico, 2–5 July 1991. We were only able to converse a little with Rorty. However, given that I had read his work expressly for this encounter, this was enough in order to understand better his thought "in action," personally. To the question whether "the exploitation of Latin America, or of poor North-Americans, is a fact *caused* by capitalism?," Rorty answered: "I do not know!" He exclaimed doubtfully, "Is there in any event a system without exploitation?"—which contained, without him noticing it, an affirmative answer to my question.[2]

The seventh work, "Modernity, Eurocentrism" and Trans-Modernity," I wrote when Charles Taylor had been invited to hold a seminar in Mexico, in 1992 (but which was later postponed). The philosopher of the "ethical life" and "authenticity," who has so many merits for cultures which would like to affirm their identity, I had to submit to some critiques which nevertheless do not diminish his historical work.

In the second part, the eighth work is the first written entry of Apel in the debate—since in 1991, in Mexico, Apel had made only an extemporaneous presentation, situating himself still at the level of a clarification of context and methodology, and manifesting in his critique, in any event, an extremely open position toward the problem of the South. This work has been included here in order to give greater clarity to the breadth and depth of the debate.

Ricoeur's answer, the ninth work, "Philosophy and Liberation," delivered at the meeting that took place in Naples, consists in admitting, in certain way, the lack of an economics in his own discourse, but concerns itself primarily with demonstrating the danger of an economics without politics.

It is for this reason that in the tenth contribution, "On World System, Politics, and the Economics of Liberation Philosophy," I began an answer, initially to Ricoeur—the logic of the argumentation required it so—in order to later focus almost exclusively on Apel.

I hope that this debate will help the reader to understand better the meaning of a Philosophy of Liberation, such as I personally practice.[3] I think this is a new stage for the Philosophy of Liberation. It would seem as though its stage of hidden and criticized gestation has ended and the public debate has began, beyond the boundaries of the Latin American horizon. This was necessary in order to better discover and elaborate its own architecture. However, this was equally necessary in order to make it known within the context of the contemporary discussion; because, it is my opinion, it has very good reasons to contribute in favor of the oppressed, exploited, and dominated, especially in favor of the impoverished peoples of the peripheral nations of capitalism, who live under a neo-liberal hegemony of economies of free competition (as Friedrich Hayek would say), where, soon and not too far from the "Fall of the Berlin wall" (1989), the true meaning of the New World order, inaugurated with the "cruelty" (to talk as Rorty) of thousands of tons of bombs thrown on an innocent people—since the madness of Saddam Hussein and the people of Iraq have to be distinguished—will be seen. It is necessary to ethically demonstrate, in a time of confusion, how the same principles should reign concerning the rights of the people of Kuwait, as well as the rights of Panama or Grenada, and not simply to allow the invasion of the Persian Gulf by the great American power, and to legitimate its violent and destructive action against Iraq simply because it is a lesser power and because it threatened the center of petroleum supply for the capitalist world (a "great word" for Rorty, but a necessary one for the clarification of the oppression of poor peoples).

The Philosophy of Liberation, thus, opens itself up to new themes from the same *punto de partida* (point of departure): the "interpellation" of the oppressed (be they poor, women, children, elderly people, the discriminated-against race, the peripheral nation) that pragmatically irrupts (in the sense of Austin) within the horizon of the Totality (in the sense of Levinas) dominated by the hegemonic reason, or what we have began to call recently *cynical reason* (which Rorty does not criticize because he refuses to enter into discussion). The Philosophy of Liberation affirms decisively and unequivocally the communicative, strategic, and liberating importance of "reason" (with Habermas and Apel). It denounces eurocentrism and the pretension to universality of modern reason (with the postmoderns, but for other "reasons"), and commits itself to the reconstruction of a critical philosophical discourse that departs from the

"Exteriority" (with Marx and Levinas, for example) and assumes a practico-political "responsibility" in the "clarification" of the liberating praxis of the oppressed. Neither abstract universalistic rationalism nor irrationalist pragmatism: transcendence and synthesis of a liberating *historical reason*, critique of the pretension to universality of particular reason, and affirmation of the rational novelty of future totalities constructed by the erotic, pedagogic, political, and even religious praxis of the *oppressed* (women, children, popular cultures, classes, national exploited groups, and the alienation of many in the fundamentalism that is in fashion). In this sense, yes, the Philosophy of Liberation is a particular language and a meta-language (a "language game") of the "languages of liberations." The philosophy of feminist liberation, the philosophy of political-economic liberation of the poor (as persons, groups, classes, popular masses, and peripheral nations), the philosophy of cultural liberation of youth and peoples (from the educational systems and hegemonic media), and even the philosophy of religious and anti-fetishist, or anti-racist, liberation are all concrete levels of the Philosophy of Liberation. Rorty would be scandalized by this great "meta-narrative" of "great words"; but at least I believe he accepts the importance of poetry and propheticism. The Philosophy of Liberation pretends, and I have been saying it for more than twenty years, being a "proteptics" ("exhortation" to the transformation of critical thinking) that should create ethical conscience, promote solidarity, clarify and ground the responsible demand to engage and commit oneself organically (as Gramsci would say) in the movement of the praxis of liberation of the oppressed—whatever the level of oppression. It is a great moment in the history of Reason as communication (Habermas), as community (Apel), as solidarity (Rorty), as positive hermeneutics of the symbolics of the oppressed (to which Ricoeur contributes elements but does not develop the theme) . . . not forgetting, which appears to be always forgotten, that it is the oppressed herself or himself—themselves (child, women, "pueblo")—who are the *historical subjects of their own liberation*: a subject that philosophy cannot pretend to replace but instead, with clear conscience, in which philosophy plays a function of solidarity of "second act"—a reflection (the a *posteriori*) about praxis (the a *priori*).

A last comment about the language used in this work is in order. All of these texts must be placed within their respective debates and their diverse languages. It is for this reason that far too frequently there appear within parentheses, or the text itself, words in their original languages, or, in the notes, suggestions for translations or for oral conversation. Forgiveness is requested from the reader. We have left the texts just as they were prepared in order to retain their provisional character, as materials for future development, and in order to remember the expressions and style of the authors with whom these dialogues were held. There are, as well, many repetitions because each text had to explain everything to the new interlocutor. Finally,

I would like to thank Eduardo Mendieta for the great labor he has undertaken in gathering and translating these texts, certainly an authentic promise for the irruption of Hispanic philosophy in the United States.

Enrique Dussel

Notes

1. This has been published in Raúl Fornet-Betancourt, ed., *Ethik und Befreiung* (Aachen: Augustinus Buchhandlung, 1990); pp. 69–97; in Spanish, it has appeared in Raúl Fornet-Betancourt, Enrique Dussel, and Karl-Otto Apel, eds., *Fundamentación ética y filosofía de la liberación* (México: Siglo XXI, 1992), but has not been included in here.
2. If "one does not know" whether capitalism is the cause of exploitation, but one affirms (given that the question is a rhetorical device in this question) that there is no system without exploitation (that is, in all systems there is exploitation), the next question then would be: "How is it that you have not asked yourself, or have not interested yourself, in knowing what is the cause of exploitation in *this system*, the capitalist system?" given that there must be one since it is *a* system and it cannot lack some type of exploitation. There is no room here for the evasive: "I do not know," Instead, one has to be in solidarity and attempt to "clarify" *the cause* of their suffering. This it is my opinion, is the objective of a pragmatic philosophy, at least in the sense of Dewey's or Cornel West's vision.
3. See my old work *Philosophy of Liberation* (Maryknoll: Orbis Books, 1985).

Acknowledgments

I would like to express my deepest gratitude to Stephen Eric Bronner, who has been an inspiration and a mentor. Enrique Dussel was kind to read over my translation and make comments. Prof. Karl-Otto Apel was also very generous with his time. He checked and made suggestions on my translation of his work. I have been fortunate to have received institutional support, without which this project would not have been possible: the New School for Social Research, and in particular Elizabeth Brewer; the DAAD (Deutscher Akademischer Austauschdienst); and the University of San Francisco, where I held the Irvine Fellowship in philosophy, which allowed me the time to complete the research for the introduction and to revise the final manuscript. At the University of San Francisco, I am very thankful for all the support and encouragement I received from Gerardo Marín and the Dean of Arts and Sciences, Stanley Nel. I also want to thank Prof. Jürgen Habermas and my colleagues in the Habermas colloquium at the Goethe University of Frankfurt, where most of the work for this book was carried out, especially Pere Fabra, Luis Sánchez, Amós Nascimento, Juan Carlos Velasco, Max Pensky, Christina Lafont, Anna Riek, Peter Niesen— a global philosophical community. Finally, I am very thankful to Keith Ashfield of Humanities Press for his confidence, patience, and encouragement, and Cindy Kaufman-Nixon, who took special care of this manuscript. I would also like to thank William Zeisel for his work on this manuscript and my research assistants, José Espinoza and Maria José Perry.

Eduardo Mendieta
University of San Francisco

Editor's Introduction

In Marxist, theological, or Latin American studies circles Enrique Dussel would not need any introduction. Unfortunately, this is not the case in philosophical circles, although Dussel himself was trained primarily as a philosopher. There are several reasons for this distorted reception of what is undoubtedly one of the most impressive—in its breadth, depth, and sheer quantity—creative and synthesizing philosophical, historical, cultural, and theological minds to come out of Latin America in the last thirty years. First, and above all, Dussel is a Latin American philosopher writing in what is today a "barbaric" language, Spanish. This, however, translates into two strikes against him; that is, he is neither from one of the cultural "centers" authorized to produce and disseminate the latest philosophical fashions, nor are his works known or translated (except for a few exceptions). The marketplace of ideas remains bewitched by the linguistic prolixity and seductiveness of playful and sensual French or the Teutonic seriousness and finality of German. Second, for political, cultural, and historical reasons, Dussel, as one of the main representatives and articulators of Liberation Theology, has been unequivocally ghettoized and relegated to the "safe" area of theological studies. Politically, liberation theology has always been suspect to both Washington and Rome. Perhaps we need to remind ourselves of President Reagan's official condemnation of Liberation Theology. Culturally and historically, North American philosophers have for the most part lacked sensivity toward the interpenetration of religion, society, politics, and philosophy,[1] *pace* Robert Bellah, Harold Bloom, and Cornel West, and *pace* the unquestionably important, almost fundamental role religion played in the thinking of the founders of a distinctly North American philosophical tradition (think for instance of Royce, Peirce, Dewey). As an illustrative analogy, the curious reception Cornel West's work has had in the recent past in the United States, which for a long time remained in the shadow of religious and theological faculties, is indicative of the same schizophrenic attitude. Third, as a "third world" Marxist—Dussel Marxism not only advocates a unique but has, over the last fifteen years, established himself as one of the foremost exegetes, critics, and analysts of Marx's *œuvre*—and philosopher who takes seriously the "dependency" theories of social scientists, he has been taken, when heard, to be talking at the beat of an "unfashionable," anachronistic, and superseded "language game." Fourth, and perhaps this goes without saying, the philosophical disciplines remain, for the most part and with some rare exceptions, imprisoned by their deeply entrenched eurocentrism. In the following introduction, therefore, I hope to address this unfortunate state of affairs by providing some very general and schematic markers in Dussel's life, his intellectual development (I), and the development of Liberation Philosophy (II). I will conclude with some remarks on the essays here collected concerning their place within a Liberation Philosophy discourse and their possible impact within the philosophical discourse of the global community of philosophers and social scientists (III).

I. Biographical Sketch

In accordance with one of the main tenets of Dussel's philosophical system, a philosopher's life, as well as that of any other human being, cannot be cogently understood if it is not related to the concrete historical period(s) through which that life extends. Moreover, the historical context of a person's life, as Dussel never tires of emphasizing, is always entwined with its location in the social space (or geopolitical space) that constitutes the spatial referent of all historical events. The historical time of someone in Paris or New York is very different from that of someone in New Delhi or Bogotá by virtue of their place in a geopolitical space. Dussel's life, therefore, is punctuated as much by what has happened in historical time as by where he was when something happened. I will divide Dussel's life into four periods, following Dussel's own chronology as well as that of other Dussel scholars. I will, however, follow this division not merely because it fixes certain dates and places, but also because it refers to particular stages in the evolution of the conceptual architectonic of Dussel's system which bear the imprint of their spatial and temporal referents. These periods will refer specifically to areas of research and particular philosophical approaches that reflect shifts in space as well as shifts in historical time.[2]

The Formative years (1934–57). Enrique Dussel was born in 1934, in La Paz, a small village about 150 km from Mendoza, a major city in Argentina. His great grandfather was of German provenance and his father was the village doctor. He grew up without hardship but exposed to the general penury and hunger of his people. During his youth, Dussel was involved in the Catholic Action movement. He also was extensively involved in university student politics. He became president of the student federation of the University of Mendoza. His formation, reflecting the rather classical character of university education at the time, was primarily in Thomism. It was during this period of his education that Dussel was exposed to the category of analogy and its central role in medieval philosophy. He obtained his philosophy licentiate with a thesis on "the concept of the common good from the pre-

Socratics to Aristotle" (1957). These are the years of a young, village intellectual, moving back and forth between the country and the city.

The Years of the Discovery of Latin America (1957–67). In 1957, after completing his licentiature, Dussel traveled to Spain to continue his philosophical studies. In Spain he received a doctorate in philosophy with a 1,200-page dissertation on "The Concept of the Common Good in Charles de Konick and Maritain." During this time he came under the influence of Xavier Zubiri, a member of the "Madrid School" that gathered around Ortega y Gasset. It is from the distant perspective of Europe, as a foreigner in the colonizing land, that Dussel discovered "Latin America." This discovery, as he understood it at the time, called for an archeological recovery of the "ethical-mythical sources" of Latin America, as well as the development of a universal historical perspective within which to place the life world of Latin America. From 1959 to 1961, after finishing his doctorate in philosophy, and having come under the influence of Paul Gauthier, Dussel moved to Israel to live in a kibbutz. During this period Dussel inmersed himself in the Semitic roots of Christianity, learned Hebrew, and explored the spiritual dimensions of poverty. From the colony, to the center, and then to another historical and spatial periphery, Dussel moved through the layers of a space filled with historical consequences and memories. It is during this period that he began a trilogy on the three different ethical-mythical cores from which our modern Latin American cultures descend, that is, the Semitic, the Greco-Roman, and the Christian "mythical-ethical cores." In 1961, he wrote his *Semitic Humanism,* followed in 1963 by *Hellenic Humanism.* This trilogy was concluded in 1968 with *Dualism in the Anthropology of Christendom.* The trilogy was methodologically motivated by Paul Ricouer's symbolics and hermeneutics, especially as these were articulated in his *Symbolism of Evil.* The theme was the phenomenological elucidation of the worldviews disclosed in the particular symbols that different cultures use to give meaning and guide their life worlds. After Israel, Dussel returned to Europe, this time to France and Germany, to continue his studies. In 1964, in Mainz, he wrote *Hypotheses for a History of the Church in Latin America.* This work later became influential in the development of Liberation Theology, and in particular the critiques of European ecclessiology (Boff, for instance). During this period he received his second doctorate, in history, from the Sorbonne with a dissertation on the defense of the indians in the Christian Church in the New World, published as *Les Eveques Hispano-Américains. Défenseurs et evangélisateurs de l'Indien 1505–1620* (1970). In Dussel's intellectual biography, this period is particularly important because he discovered Latin America as a horizon of meaning and understanding that must be understood from within and from without, according to its own symbolics, and according to its place in world history.

The Beginning of Liberation Philosophy (1967–75). After ten years of absence, Dussel returned to Argentina in 1967. He became a professor of philosophical anthropology and later of philosophical ethics at the National University of Cuyo. From 1967 to 1969, Dussel travelled throughout Latin America lecturing on the history of Latin America, its place in world history, and its intellectual, philosophical, and spiritual sources. Dussel himself points to 1969 as a determining moment in the emergence of a new phase of his thinking, for it was during this year that he attended a conference of sociologists in Argentina and was introduced to "dependency theory." However, as he himself has pointed out in many other places, his openness to "new approaches" could not have been possible without the continuous dialogue, debate, and exchange that took place during the two years he had been back in Latin America. Another very important discovery of this period was that of Emmanuel Levinas's work, which "woke him up from his ontological sleep (as much Heideggerian as Hegelian)." Indeed, if the prior period was one of "reconstruction" and "discovery," this period was one of "destruction" and "building anew." From 1969 onwards, Dussel set out to develop the categories of a uniquely Latin American philosophical perspective, which required the "dismantling" and "recuperation" of the categories that made possible the elaboration of a Latin American emancipatory discourse. This project, it should be kept in mind, only makes sense against the background of the influential debate between Leopoldo Zea and Salazar Augusto Bondy.[3] By early 1970, after in-depth studies of Hegel, Heidegger, and Levinas, and with all of his historical works on Latin America in his bag, Dussel discovered and elaborated the main tenets of a liberation ethics: ethics is *prima philosophia* (in Levinas's and Apel's sense[4]) and its method is not the dialectic (whether in its cosmological, ontological, or egological versions) but the analectic of Otherness (the rupture into and transformation of totalized life worlds by the creative and appellant epiphany of the Other, not as mere *difference* but as the truly *distinct*, as wholly Other).[5] In the spring and summer of 1970, he lectured on ethics and began work on what became a five-volume ethics. During this time he also lectured throughout Latin America on "Ethics, History and the Theology of Liberation."[6] These early years of the ferment of Liberation Philosophy were also some of his most prolific.

This period of gestation and elaboration, however, cannot be understood without the political background against which Dussel and his Argentinian colleagues worked. The late sixties and early seventies were the period of Latin American "populisms," partly inspired by the Cuban revolution, partly inspired by the bourgeois anti-imperialistic movements, of which Peronism was one instance (see chapter 10, below). Right-wing and left-wing Peronism waged war on the Argentinian national landscape, and liberation philosophers were caught in the middle. In 1973, Dussel was the target of a bomb attack in his house. By 1975, after years of persecution and threats, and finally being expelled from the National University of Cuyo, he took his family out of the country. In 1975, Dussel began his exile in Mexico, and a new stage in the development of liberation philosophies was initiated.

Toward a "Transcendental Economics" and Mexican Exile 1975–Present. In Mexico, Dussel wrote what is perhaps the most systematic, broad, and rigorous presentation of the basic propositions of Liberation Philosophy. Unfortunately, many people come to this book without realizing that it is in fact the summary of his five volumes on ethics, his works on Hegel and Levinas, and his numerous historical writings. *Philosophy of Liberation* is a work which also tries to give an overview of a fairly sophisticated and developed philosophical discourse. What is distinctive about this stage is not only that Dussel was in exile in Mexico, but that, partly inspired by the failures of populism (see chapter 10 below), the criticism and debates about the categories of class and people as foundations for any philosophy, and the need to translate dependency theory into a philosophical formulation, Dussel began an in-depth study of Marx. As a by-product of his *Widerholung* of the tradition, Dussel discovered a "warm current," to use Ernst Bloch's term,[7] that is linked to left Hegelianism, but which in Dussel's terms has to do more with the Semitic aspects of the thought current, in which we can find medieval mystics, Feuerbach, Schelling, Marx, Rosenzweig, Buber, and Levinas. In contrast to the dialectic of a cosmos, being, or consciousness that ascends to unity, autonomy, divine passivity, or self-determination so as to return to itself—where the other of itself is left out as a residue of the true process (the dialectic) as the non-being, the particular, the unknown and worthless—the "warm current" of dialogic, apophantic, creative, analogical thinking moves from the otherness of the other, which always remains beyond the totalized totality. The moment of transformation, of creative irruption into the frozen and stabilized totality, arrives from beyond the horizon of this totality. This is the metaphysical "exteriority" of the Other. Dussel discovered how Marx, not just the young Marx but also, and especially, the older Marx, belongs to this tradition. And while Dussel's works, up through his 1975 *Philosophy of Liberation*, elaborate ethics as first philosophy, it is only after 1975 that this ethics obtained a substantive, practical dimension through the incorporation of Marx into the understanding of a human being's being-in-the-world. Levinas's categories of the Other, the face-to-face, the offering, and so on, will obtain "materiality," "carnality," through their Marxist transformation. The Other will become the dispossessed, the paupers, the ones without anything but their own flesh. The face-to-face will became the fundamental practical-ethical encounter. A Marx seen not just as a Hegelian, but primarily as a Schellingian, in the tradition of Buber, Rosenzweig, Levinas, became the point of departure for the formulation of a "transcendental economics."[8] Transcendental refers in Dussel's philosophy to, on the one hand, the transcendence of the Other, the exteriority of the dispossessed, and, on the other hand, to the "conditions of possibility" which have been hermeneutically, linguistically, and pragmatically transformed by Karl-Otto Apel.[9] As a reference to the exteriority of the Other, Dussel's transcendental economics points to the poverty of the worker, or pauper, who is the sole creative source of value. As a reference to the conditions of possibility, Dussel's transcendental economics refers to the conditions of the preservation of life as such, the one true condition of possibility for everything else. "Transcendental economics" can be seen as product of the marriage between Levinas's critique of ontology and Marx's critique of capitalism. It is an approximation to writing the *Critique of Practical Reason*, for which Marxism and apophantic metaphysics are already close to being a *Critique of Pure Reason*, to paraphrase Ernst Bloch.[10]

This is not only a new stage in Liberation Philosophy, but also one in the development of world philosophy. This may be the case not only because Liberation Philosophy takes itself to be a particular philosophical discourse that unmasks the false universality of eurocentric philosophical discourses (of modernity as well as postmodernity), but also, and as its corollary, because Liberation Philosophy at the same times claims to have elucidated the parameters of all contemporary philosophical thinking, namely, their forming part and taking place within a "world system." In fact, just as Apel, Habermas, Ricoeur, Taylor, Rorty et al. claim that philosophy has made a "linguistic," "pragmatic," "hermenutical," "post-metaphysical" turn, where the locus of universal philosophical claims is language and not being or consciousness, Dussel assents but adds the severe proviso that philosophy has made this turn but not sufficiently, or not in earnest and in accordance with the deepest insights of the triple paradigm shift. It is the role of a "transcendental economics" to not only make good on the promises of the three different moments of the linguistic turn, but also to make good on Marx and the promise that he still holds out for the Third World.

II. Historical Sketch of Liberation Philosophy

Just as the history of contemporary neo-pragmatism, which is espoused in one way or another by Rorty, Bernstein, Fraser, and West, has a pre-history that dates back to the early 19th century, but which has a more immediate history in the late sixties,[11] Liberation Philosophy has a pre-history which at least dates back to the 16th century (de las Casas, Montesinos, and others) and the 18th and 19th century (Bolívar, Santander, and others) with the development of emancipatory discourses that legitimated the movements of independence and liberation from Spain, England, Portugal, etc., but which has its most immedi-

Editor's Introduction

ate historical antecedents in the late sixties and early seventies (see chapter 1).

Following Raúl Fornet-Betancourt, but adding some other elements, I will suggest that there are at least eight factors that must be considered when trying to understand the emergence of liberation philosophy:[12]

1. The Cuban Revolution (1959) and its significance for Latin America.[13]
2. The second general assembly of CELAM in Medellín (Colombia) in August 1968.[14]
3. The development of Latin American Liberation Theology (1968–72); the appearance of its "manifesto," Gustavo Gutiérrez's *A Theology of Liberation*.[15]
4. The polemic between Augusto Salazar Bondy and Leopoldo Zea (1969–70) concerning the possibility of an authentic Latin American philosophy.[16]
5. The renaissance of Latin American "populisms," and Argentina's case in particular (1970–75).
6. The development of dependence theory.[17]
7. The global events that go by the name 1968.[18]
8. Globalization of finance capital, a new phase in "Late Capitalism".[19]

The Cuban Revolution was, and continues to be, a source of inspiration for Latin Americans. The possibilities and limits of any possible revolutionary movement in Latin America were exemplified by the triumph and ultimate constraint of this great challenge to the imperialist hegemony the United States exercised over the whole continent. The Cuban Revolution meant the possibility of a unique Latin American path toward political emancipation that navigated between the populisms of some of the most reactionary dictatorships the history of Latin America has seen and the violence of the "national security" states that became the rule after the fifties, partly as a reaction to the threat of communism, but based mostly in an ideology of top-down political modernization (yet another aspect of *desarrollismo*). As Martin Luther King, Jr., galvanized African-Americans in the late fifties and early sixties in the United States, and today has become an icon of hope and transformation, Che Guevara was the prototype of the new Latin American man. Even today there is no Latin American city without a mural of Che Guevara.

As important as Vatican II was for the general transformation of Catholicism in the beginning of the second half of the 20th century, it was not until Medellín that Latin American bishops appropriated Vatican II for their churches. The documents that came out of this conference have been appropriately called the Vatican II of Latin America.[20] In general terms the conclusions reached at this conference opened the way and laid the foundations for the "church of the people" and its concomitant, a theology of liberation.

Gustavo Gutiérrez gave the clearest formulation of the consequences of both

Vatican II and the second general assembly of Latin American bishops. In *A Theology of Liberation*, Gutiérrez began the paradigm shift that would take Latin American theology away from abstract philosophy to the social sciences, away from the fallacy of *desarrollismo* to a historical theology of "liberation," away from the conceptual naivete and self-deceiving autonomy of European theological discourse to self-concious, self-critical, engaged theological reflection. It is not without justification that Liberation Theology has been called a second Reformation.

While Latin American theologians were developing a unique theological discourse that would be true to the social reality from which it arises and of which it is a critical commentary, philosophers were trying to come to terms with the inauthentic state of Latin American philosophy. Augusto Salazar Bondy asked whether *there exists a Latin American Philosophy*, to which he answered negatively. Bondy saw the Latin American state of oppression, under-development, and dependency as the conditions for the impossibility of a truly authentic Latin American philosophy. Thus, for Bondy, an authentic Latin American philosophy could only appear in the form of a liberation philosophy, a philosophy which begins with the Latin American reality of oppression and dependence. Zea, in contrast, argued that Latin American philosophy was, by virtue of its having arisen from Latin American reality, already truly Latin American and thus could not be any less authentic than it was. Latin American philosophy, whether in the form of exegesis, critique, or creative intervention vis-à-vis European philosophy, was philosophy as such (*sin más*). For Zea, Bondy's denial of the Latin American past was a tremendous failure which vitiated his own project of a liberation philosophy. In contrast, Zea called for the development of a Latin American philosophy of history, one which would place Latin America within universal history.

After the Cuban Revolution, and in conjunction with the ascendancy of home-grown bourgeoisies, populism made a reappearance in Latin America, especially in Chile and Argentina. It is against the background of these populist political movements that we must understand both the revival of the Catholic Church through its *comunidades de base* and the philosophical debates about an authentic Latin American philosophy. It is with reference to the same context that the important debates between liberation philosophers about whether "class" or "people" were better analytical categories must be seen to reflect the ambiguities and dangers of applying European categories to a different social reality. Still, what is central about these populisms is that they gave occasion for much hope as well as reason for much disappointment about what the "people" could do and, in effect, would do.

From the standpoint of the so-called autonomy of philosophical thinking, however, it was the development of dependence theory which catalyzed the development of Liberation Philosophy. While philosophers had already begun to orient themselves to the social sciences, just as the theologians were doing, partly as a consequence of the influences of hermeneutics and Frankfurt-school critical theory, it was dependence theory that caused the major caesura in philosophy. Dependence theory provided the fundamental conceptual framework within which Latin American under-development and dependency could be understood. Liberation Philosophy translated it into philosophical categories. Dussel's early works reflect this clearly. Through Zea, Bondy, Scannone, Dussel, et al., dependence theory became a philosophy of history, a metaphysics of exteriority, an ethics of liberation, and so on. Just as the convergence between Wittgenstein, Heidegger, Peirce, Searle, and Austin created the rupture in the self-understanding of (Euro-North Atlantic) philosophy that goes by the name of "linguistic turn," the convergence of the works of Wallerstein, Frank, Cardoso, Faletto, and Amin[21] created an "epistemological break" in the reflection of Latin American philosophers. Everything from now on was seen differently.

Mexico City, New York, Berlin, Paris, all across the world students were "liberating" universities, intellectuals were on the side of the people, cities were in flames, and the streets were barricaded. The year 1968 saw a global phenomenon that pointed to a transformation not just in the nature of capital, now in the process of complete globalization, but also in the consciousness of First World and Third World peoples. The year 1968 was as much about the critique of imperialism, racism, and sexism within industrialized nations as it was about the affirmation of Third World peoples' autonomy, identity, will to freedom, and liberation. A global, non-Euro-North American history of philosophy would have to look at the resurgence of pragmatism and the development of an autochthonous black liberation theology, for instance, after the late sixties, as a parallel process to the emergence of Liberation Theology and Liberation Philosophy in the southern cone of the continent.

III. The Impact of These Essays

This book reflects both Dussel's coherent and systematic philosophical positions and how his ideas have developed in a constant dialogue. The book is thus divided into two sections. The first gathers Dussel's original contributions to what were sometimes first encounters, but were more frequently already ongoing debates. The second section gathers responses by Karl-Otto Apel and Paul Ricoeur, as well as Dussel's own rebuttals. The first four chapters reflect clearly Dussel's and Apel's philosphical *Auseinandersetzung*. The rest stand as confrontations with the philosophical propositions of individual thinkers from the standpoint of an overall argumentative strategy. It is precisely this argumentative strategy and philosophical position that gives coherence to this book.

In the first essay, Dussel discusses the present status of Liberation Philosophy from the standpoint of a global history of Liberation Philosophy and the tasks that lie ahead for it. Dussel suggests here a periodization that recuperates the earliest, and sometimes unfairly forgotten, manifestations of liberation thinking within Latin America and Europe as nascent center. Liberation Philosophy has as its earliest antecedents the philosophy of the critique of the conquest of Amerindia (1510–53) and the philosophy of colonial liberation (1750–1830). To the period of the critique of the conquest of Amerindia belong Montesinos, Mendieta, Vittoria, and de las Casas. With them, in fact, begins the true counter-discourse of modernity. The historical and philosophical antecedent of the struggles for justice and political autonomy that will give rise to the differentiation among the state, civil society, the Church, and the emergence of something like a *Rechtstatt* are for the most part dated in the 17th and 18th centuries by thinkers like Weber, Parsons, Habermas, Rorty, Taylor, even Ricoeur. This, however, reflects not only a false chronology but also an inappropriate focus on central Europe (France, Germany, etc.) as the center or loci of true political development.[22] In recuperating these "forgotten" discourses for liberation philosophy, Dussel also redeems them for the counter-discourses of modernity, the counter-discourses that give any emancipatory and normative content to modernity as a project. In general, however, this first essay is a very clear, succinct introduction to the main philosophical and historical sources of liberation philosophy, as well as to its most pressing problems and tasks.

The second, third, and fourth chapters are direct confrontations with Karl-Otto Apel's transcendental pragmatics and discourse ethics. The first part of chapter 2 presents a brief but very accurate sketch of Apel's *Denkweg*.[23] Dussel also clarifies the status of Liberation Philosophy vis-à-vis postmodernism, a clarification which was needed due to Apel's initial perception of liberation philosophy as a type of postmodern discourse. Interestingly, while Dussel himself already in the early seventies talked of liberation philosophy as a type of postmodern philosophy, inasmuch as it saw itself overcoming the philosophy of consciousness or its egological dialectic, more recently, since the vogue of postmodernity brought on by the Lyotard et al., Dussel has opted for a different descriptive term: trans-modernity. The term trans-modernity underscores that Liberation Philosophy is not about either negating modernity or blithely accepting it, but about transcending it anadialectically; that is, to think the couplet modernity and postmodernity not just from within, but also, and especially, from the perspective of its *reverso*, its underside, its occluded other.

This chapter will also be particularly important in what it contributes to the further clarification of the foundations of a post-linguistic paradigm of philosophy. One of the central problems in the speech-act theory has been the status of statements which do not fit easily into either the perlocutory or illocutory categories, such as is the the case with interpellation. In this second chapter, Dussel proceeds to elaborate "interpellation," which in his case assumes the primordial character of a moral appellation, as a *sui generis* speech act. Interpellation as such, instead of pointing to the positive description of its background assumptions (i.e., either the ideal communication community or the ideal speech situation of Apel and Habermas, respectively), points to the negative (*via negativa*) deliniation of the conditions which are required but never given that would make the speech act both understandable and acceptable. At stake, however, in Dussel's problematization of interpellation is the same problem that has been raised by Charles Taylor, Martin Seel, and Karl-Otto Apel with respect to the constitution of meaning and the justification of validity. In other words, the problem of *Welterschließung* (world-disclosure). The question raised by this term is: How does the "new" disclose itself or is allowed to be disclosed within an already given horizon of meaning?[24] Dussel's question, then, is: How are new moral-ethical claims allowed to shatter and re-constitute perspectives that do not allow for them (examples: responsibility for the past, for future generations, for nature, for the genetic integrity of species, etc)?

Chapter 3, written on the ocassion of Apel's seventieth birthday, sets out to clarify some of the conditions of possibility for a mutually fruitful dialogue between First World and Third World philosophers. Central to this encounter is the critique of a eurocentric conceptualization of modernity, the assumption of a new category of social analysis (the "world-system"), and the translation of the linguistic turn into a "transcendental economics." In the next chapter, Dussel, again trying to assimilate Apel's conceptual gains and advances, profiles a division of labor between discourse ethics and liberation ethics. Whereas the former deals with the skeptic, the latter deals with the cynic. Each one represents a respective rhetorical figure. Each one represents a set of very different, but complementary, challenges. While the skeptic accepts the other as a dialogue partner, the cynic negates such encounter. Discourse ethics and liberation ethics meet at the point where the skeptic and the cynic turn into each other, namely, at the boundary, at the shady area of the exceptional, the extraordinary, the extreme situation of moral denial and ethical irresponsibility. Another way of looking at this problem will be presented in the seventh chapter, on Taylor.

The fifth chapter is significant for an understanding of both the hermeneutical origins of Liberation Philosopy and its revisioning of hermeneutics. After a careful reconstruction of Ricouer's intellectual biography and comparison with the evolution of Liberation Philosophy, Dussel proceeds to argue for the need to develop an "economics of symbolics" or an "economic semiology," that is, a hermeneutics or semiology that takes into account seriously the economic dimensions of the symbolic constitution and appropriation (and disappropriation for others) of the world. In the next chapter, Dussel enters into a similar dialogue with Rorty. In contrast to the general and frequently vicious and contentious character with which Rorty's work is dealt, Dussel proceeds to demonstrate and apprecipate its importance. Rorty's skepticism vis-à-vis analytic philosophy is extremely healthy for Latin American philosophy departments, where analytic philosophy still reigns supreme. Furthermore, just as Rorty's work has led to a broader perspective within North American philosophy circles that sees both ordinary language philosophy and continental hermeneutical philosophy as aspects of the same project (a project which was in fact began by Apel in the early sixties[25]), his work may lead to the thawing of relations between the analytic and the continental-oriented institutes, faculties, and schools, within Latin American philosophical circles. All of that granted, Dussel points out a very serious aporia in Rorty's discourse. On the one hand, he is open, and is properly praised by Dussel for being so, to the "prophetic" voices of feminists and even African Americans,[26] but, on the other, he seems to be closed to the possibility that Third World countries may raise similar prophetic voices. In Dussel's view, Rorty seems to be too preocuppied with a discussion about "language" and not enough about what language should be talking, namely, the realities of suffering and oppression that only seem to be voiced in terms of the "great narratives" of liberation that Marxist discourses still make possible.

Chapter 7 is a significant intervention in the debate between universalists and communitarians, or between neo-Kantians and neo-Hegelians.[27] Beyond, however, being an innovative intervention in this debate, it is also a contribution to moral theory in general. After a careful analysis of Taylor's project of a reconstruction of the sources of the modern self, Dussel points out a series of extremely deleterious biases and occlusions that threaten the reach and validity of such a project. Against Taylor's focus on the Greeks as the great grandfathers of our concepts of autonomy, authenticity and self-actualization, Dussel points out that the notions of individuality and self-responsibility ought to be dated, more appropiately, as far back as Egyptian burial practices and even the more ancient Mesopotamian practices of responsibility for one's fellow human being (*Code of Hammurabi*). Similarly, just as Apel and Habermas are faulted for identifying modernity with the Renaissance, the Reformation, and the French Revolution—thus following Hegel—without noting that in many cases these are but consequences of more fundamental and determining events, such as the "discovery" of the New World and the installation of Europe as center of a "world system," Taylor is also found to be affected by this type of eurocentrism. However, in terms of moral theory, Dussel suggests that liberation ethics articulates itself as a *tertium quid* between neo-Kantian proceduralism and neo-Hegelian substantive ethical life. As a third path, or approach, liberation ethics elucidates, on the one hand, that within all types of Kantian proceduralism there is always someone affected who has not formed part of the discussion of validation and universalization of norms, which Dussel calls the *principium exclusionis*, and, on the other, that within all ethical projects that depart from some substantive principles of a given life world or form of life there is always someone who is oppressed, which Dussel calls the *principium oppressionis*. Dussel, again, underscores how liberation ethics and discourse ethics, whose relationship is now mediated vis-à-vis Taylor's ethics of authenticity, meet and part ways at the intersection of exceptional moral situations, which are the exception for "developed" societies but are the rule for "under-developed" societies.[28]

The second part of the book gathers the most immediate answers and rebuttals by Apel, Ricouer, and Dussel.[29] In his answer to Dussel, Apel takes the opportunity not only to address certain confusions and uncertainties about the reception of discourse ethics, but also, and especially, takes this as an opportunity for an extremely fruitful exchange. Apel takes Dussel's challenges and translates them into direct modifications of the architectonic of discourse ethics. Apel, for instance, considers Dussel's challenge to be not just morally justifiable and appropriate but also extremely important and revealing from a methodological perspective. Indeed, Apel appropriates Dussel's imputations of eurocentrism for a clarification of his own *Selbsteinholungsprinzip*,[30] which demands an internal account of the logic and validity of one's normative stand. Apel, thanks to Dussel, realizes that most discourses of the human sciences, in particular the economic sciences, have failed to take into account the world-system perspective and the development of under-development (in Andre Gunder Frank's phrase). In this sense, Apel concludes that even if dependency theory, as well as Dussel's appeal to Marx, are found wanting in terms of a series of empirical qualifications, they nevertheless present a series of extremely important methodological and normative challenges.[31]

Ricouer's answer, based on the transcript of his oral answer to Dussel, is a wonderfully succinct description of the "normative goals and contents" of the project of modernity. First, Ricoeur acknowledges the variety of contexts from which most discourses of liberation emerge. More precisely, for Ricoeur, while Europe's background is the struggle against totalitarianism in its two variants, fascist and communist, Latin America's context is one of direct confrontation with the United States. These different "points of departure" may make them incommensurable or incommunicable. Second, Ricoeur wants to acknowledge the rich and valuable inheritance bequeathed to us by the historical experience of the West. In Hegelian fashion, Ricoeur sees this tradition as being about political and ethical freedom. This tradition has agglutinated and appeared under three different aspects: the critique of the sovereign and sovereignty; the crisis of the concrete universal—which Ricoeur very suggestively correlates to the emergence of hermeneutics and the transition to a philosophy of language—and the development of a system of law with its corresponding infrastructure.

In his rebuttal to Apel and Ricoeur, Dussel returns to some of the central themes that run through all the essays gathered here. First, against Ricoeur's claim that the European experiences of totalitarianism may be incommunicable to a substantially different situation, Dussel articulates from a "world perspective" the interconnection between Latin American or peripheral populism (or bourgeois nationalisms) and the European or central nationalistic movements (fascism and nazism). From a world-system perspective, both movements are trying to gain control of national capital in a situation of the growing globalization of capital. In response to Apel, Dussel underscores again the importance of Marx for Latin American social-scientific and philosophical discourses. It is through a rediscovered, or for the first time truly discovered, Marx (given the incredible amount of material that has been published over the last twenty-five years) that a philosophy in a planetary and non-eurocentric key can evade either extreme politicism, or insufficient globalization and concretization. Here again are profiled two of the central theses of this book, and of Dussel's most recent work, namely, that eurocentrism must be taken seriously as a *philosophical* problem, and that philosophy must abandon no longer appropriate or useful notions or categories of universal history; instead it must appropriate for its methodology the more concrete methodological approach of the world-system.[32] Insofar as Dussel's articulation of Liberation Philosophy raises these questions, Liberation Philosophy de-centers itself in order to make a global or planetary (not universal) claim. It ascends from its particularity to globality. This is a new phase of Liberation Philosophy, and, it is to be hoped, the beginning of a global philosophy as well.

Eduardo Mendieta
University of San Francisco

Notes

1. For a discussion of the nexus betweeen these different spheres, see Enrique Dussel, *A History of the Church in Latin America: Colonialism to Liberation (1492–1979)*, trans. Alan Neely (Grand Rapids, Michigan: William B. Eerdmans Publishing Company, 1981).
2. I developed the biographical sketch from the following sources: Roberto S. Goizueta, *Liberation, Method and Dialogue: Enrique Dussel and North American Theological Discourse* (Atlanta, Ga.: Scholars Press, 1987), especially the introduction, pp. xviiff; Hans Schelkshorn, *Ethik der Befreiung: Eiführung in die Philosophie Enrique Dussels* (Freiburg: Herder & Co., 1990), especially sec. 1.2, pp. 16ff; the biographical essay by Germán Marquínez A., "Enrique Dussel: filósofo de la liberación

latinoamericana" in Enrique Dussel, *Introduccion a la filosofía de la liberacion*, 3d ed. (Bogotá: Editorial Nueva América, 1988), pp. 5–51; Enrique Dussel, "Liberación Latinoamericana y Filosofía" in *Praxis Latinoamericana y Filosofía de la Liberación* (Bogotá: Editorial Nueva América, 1983), pp. 9–19; Luis Sánchez, "Dussel, Enrique" in F. Maffé, ed., *Dictionnaire des Oeuvres Philosophiques*, Vol. 2 (Paris: PUF, 1992), col. 3196. See also in this book chapters 1, 5, and 10. In chapter 10, Dussel speaks of six moments. These moments or phases, however, occur within the four periods that he originally set up; these are the ones I have decided to appropriate for my own sketch. See also my reviews of Schelkshorn's work on Dussel and Dussel's collection of essays on the history of philosophy in general and liberation philosophy in particular in *Journal of Hispanic/Latino Theology*, Vol. 3, 1 (August 1995), pp. 62–63, 71–75.
3. See Leopoldo Zea, *La filosofía americana como filosofía sin más* (Mexico: Siglo XXI, 1969); Leopoldo Zea, *El Pensamiento Latinoamericano*, 3d. ed. (Mexico: Ariel, 1976), especially Chapter V of the third part. Raúl Fornet-Betancourt, *Philosophie und Theologie der Befreiung* (Frankfurt: Materialis Verlag, 1987), especially Chapter 2, section II. Ofelia Schutte, *Cultural Identity and Social Liberation in Latin American Thought* (Albany: SUNY, 1993), pp. 73ff.
4. See Levinas, *Totality and Infinity* (Pittsburgh: Duquesne University Press, 1969) pp. 72ff, pp. 302ff. Karl-Otto Apel, *Towards a Transcendental Semiotics* (Atlantic Highlands: Humanities Press, 1994) pp. 112ff., and *Diskurs und Verantwortung* (Frankfurt: Suhrkamp Verlag, 1988). See also Adriann T. Peperzak, ed., *Ethics as First Philosophy: The Significance of Emmanuel Levinas for Philosophy, Literature and Religion* (New York: Routledge, 1995).
5. A frequent criticism against Dussel is that he is not really developing a Latin American liberation philosophy because he remains as fixated on European philosophical discourses as the most naive eurocentrist. This criticism is not only unfounded, but also blind to the dialectic of ideas. It is unfounded because Dussel has pursued one of the most extensive analyses of Latin American autochthonous critical and emancipatory thinking—Leopoldo Zea and Francisco Miró Quesada being some of the other most important historians of ideas in Latin America. His histories of the church, theology, and philosophy in Latin America are compendiums and encyclopedias of occluded and forgotten popular knowledge. His histories are always histories from the "underside," from the side of the oppressed. This criticism, furthermore, is blind to the dialectic of ideas by pretending that there has not been a co-determination of both center and periphery. Latin America is as much what it is and what is not in the eyes of European philosophers (think of Hegel and Marx), as Europe is what it is and is not in the eyes of Caliban the savage, the primitive.
6. These lectures have appeared as *Ethics and the Theology of Liberation*, trans. Bernard F. McWilliams (Maryknoll: Orbis Books, 1978).
7. On Ernst Bloch's notions of "warm" and "cold" currents, see "Avicenna und die Aristotelische Linke", in *Das Materialismusproblem—seine Geschichte und Substanz. Gesamtausgabe. Volume 7* (Frankfurt: Suhrkamp, 1977), pp. 479–546.
8. See chapter 10 especially for a clarification of this term. See also Enrique Dussel, *Las metáforas teológicas de Marx* (see my review of this book in *The Journal of Hispanic/Latino Theology*, 2, 3, February 1995, pp. 67–71), as well as the five volumes of commentary, reconstruction, and critiques of Marx that Dussel published over the last decade (see Bibliography). See also Enrique Dussel, *Historia de la Filosofía y Filosofía de la Liberación*, especially part two, which gathers a series

of preliminary studies on Marx. With respect to the relationship between Marx and what I have here called the warm current, see chapter 10, below.
9. See Karl-Otto Apel, *Towards a Transcendental Semiotics*.
10. The citation reads: "Man kann darum sagen, daß gerade die scharfe Betonung aller (ökonomisch) determinierenden und die vorhandene, aber noch im Geheimnis bleibende Latenz aller transzendierenden Momente den *Marxismus in die Nähe einer Kritik der reinen Vernunft rückt, zu der noch keine Kritik der praktischen Vernunft geschrieben worden ist.* Die Wirtschaft ist hier aufgehoben, aber die Seele, der Glaube fehlen, dem Platz gemacht werden sollte...." Ernst Bloch, *Geist der Utopie*, 1924, 2nd rev. ed. (Frankfurt: Suhrkamp Verlag, 1964), p. 290.
11. See Cornel West, *The American Evasion of Philosophy: A Genealogy of Pragmatism* (Wisconsin: University of Wisconsin Press, 1989). See also Richard Rorty, *Consequences of Pragmatism* (Minnesota: Minnesota University Press, 1982).
12. Fornet-Betancourt, *Philosophie und Theologie der Befreiung*. See also Jorge J. E. Gracia, guest editor, *The Philosophical Forum: A Quarterly*, XX, 1–2, Fall-Winter 1988–89, special double issue: "Latin American Philosophy Today." This volume has essays by Leopoldo Zea, Horacio Cerutti-Guldberg, Ofelia Schutte, David Sobrevilla, Adolfo Sánchez Vázques, Jorge J. E. Gracia, and Iván Jaksic. Gracia's and Cerutti-Guldberg's essays are particularly important for an understanding of the history of Latin American liberation philosophy.
13. See Jorge G. Castañeda, *Utopia Unarmed: The Latin American Left after the Cold War* (New York: Vintage Books, 1994), for a recent critical but fairly accurate assessment of Cuba's role in the history of Latin America.
14. See Christian Smith, *The Emergence of Liberation Theology: Radical Religion and Social Movement Theory* (Chicago: The University of Chicago Press, 1991), pp. 111ff. This is one of the best socio-political analyses of the emergence of Liberation Theology in Latin America. See also Daniel H. Levine, *Popular Voices in Catholicism* (Princeton: Princeton University Press, 1992).
15. Gustavo Gutiérrez, *A Theology of Liberation: History, Politics, and Salvation*, trans. Sister Caridad Inda and John Eagleson (Maryknoll: Orbis Books, 1988), originally published in Spanish in 1971 and translated into English in 1973. For a survey of the significance and impact of Gutiérrez, see Marc H. Ellis and Otto Maduro, eds., *The Future of Liberation Theology: Essays in Honor of Gustavo Gutiérrez* (Maryknoll: Orbis Books, 1989).
16. Augusto Salazar Bondy, *¿Existe una filosofía de nuestra América?* 11th ed. (México: Siglo XXI editores, 1988); originally published in 1968. For Zea's response see his *La filosofía americana como filosofía sin más*; see other works cited in note 3.
17. It is not be noted that the development of dependence theory coincided with the ultimate failure of the "Alliance for Progress," which was founded in 1961 by President John F. Kennedy. See Christian Smith, *The Emergence of Liberation Theology: Radical Religion and Social Movement Theory*, pp. 111ff. For an analysis of the centrality of dependency theory in the development of Liberation Philosophy as critical theory, see Stephen T. Leonard, *Critical Theory in Political Practice* (Princeton: Princeton University Press, 1991), pp. 96ff. His analysis of Liberation Theology as critical theory is also extremely insightful. In general, my approach to Liberation Philosophy is very similar to Leonard's, i.e., I would like to see it not "just" as a Third World theory of emancipation but also, and above all, as part of a global (planetary in Dussel's and Apel's sense) critical theory. In other words,

Liberation Philosophy is the critical theory of the Third World, just as critical theory is the Liberation Philosophy of the First World. Evidently, their different "points of departure" and "problematics" require that they use different analytical tools. Yet, they share the same "practical intent": liberation, emancipation, redemption, justice, solidarity.

18. The literature on 1968 is immense, but with respect to the development of Third World philosophies, changes in the global system, and the "explosion of the Third World" by means of which the "natives" become "human," see Fredric Jameson, "Periodizing the 60s (1984)" in Fredric Jameson, *The Ideologies of Theory. Essays 1971–1986. Volume 2. Syntax of History* (Minneapolis: University of Minnesota Press, 1988), pp. 178–208. It is interesting to note that Dussel at times refers to Liberation Philosophy as a philosophy of/from/about barbarity. Zea also speaks of the discourse from/of barbarity and margination; see his *Discurso desde la Marginación y la Barbarie* (Barcelona: Editorial Anthropos, 1988).
19. See Paul Kennedy, *Preparing for the Twenty-First Century* (New York: Vintage Books, 1993). On transformation of the capitalist economic world-system and its ideological effects see James O'Connor, *Accumulation Crisis* (New York: Basil Blackwell, 1984).
20. Enrique Dussel, *A History of the Church in Latin America: Colonialism to Liberation (1492–1979)*, p. 147.
21. See Anthony Brewer, *Marxist Theories of Imperialism: A Criticla Survey* (London and New York: Routledge & Kegan Paul, 1980), part III, for a survey of some of these authors. See Apel's superb discussion of the importance of dependence theory in his anwer to Dussel, chapter 8. See also Fornet-Betancourt's *Philosophie und Theologie der Befreiung*, pp. 66, and Schelkshorn's *Ethik der Befreiung*, pp. 20ff. See also Andre Gunder Frank," Latin American Development Theories Revisited: A Participants Review" in *Latin American Perspectives*, 19, Issue 73, No. 2, Spring 1992, pp. 125–39.
22. See the extremely important works by Lewis Hanke, *The Spanish Struggle for Justice in the Conquest of America* (Philadelphia: University of Pennsylvania Press, 1949), *All Mankind Is One: A Study of the Disputation Between Bartolomé de las Casa and Jaun Ginés Sepúlveda in 1550 on the Intellectual and Religious Capacity of the American Indians* (De Kalb: Northern Illinois University Press, 1974). See also the classic Silvio Zavala, *La filosofía política en la Conquista de América* (México: Fondo de Cultura Económica, 1947). Gustavo Gutiérrez, *Las Casas: In Search of the Poor of Jesus Christ*, trans. Robert R. Barr (Maryknoll, New York: Orbis Books, 1993).
23. This is a summary of a larger essay which has appeared in Spanish as "La Introducción de la 'Transformación de la Filosofía' de K.-O. Apel y la Filosofía de la Liberación (Reflexiones desde una Perspectiva Latinoamericana)" in K.-O. Apel, E. Dussel, Fornet-Betancourt, eds. *Fundamentación de la ética y Filosofía de la liberación*, pp. 45–104. Given the dearth of secondary, and even primary, materials on Apel, all of these are extremely welcome scholarly contributions.
24. I would like to underscore that this is central problem as much in Apel's transcendental semiotics as it is in Habermas's theory of communicative action. Note, for instance, on page 339 of *The Philosophical Discourses of Modernity*, Habermas talks about *two axes* around which the value spheres have differentiated: the axis of *Welterschließung*, or world-disclosure, which has to do, as Habermas points out, with the disclosure of the new, the transformative that takes place in language through art, literature, and art criticism; and the axis of intra-mundane learning

processes, where we deal with culture, society, and our own selves from the standpoint of the development of subsystems of management or personal, cognitive, and moral competencies. The former has do with creativity and the co-constitution of the world in and through language. The latter has do with language as a "problem-solving tool." It has to be noted that Habermas is developing this new line of argumentation as a way to counteract the challenges of postmodern criticism that accuse him of totally leveling off or excising the dimension of creative aesthetic experience. Habermas, however, wants to do this without losing the problem-solving capacity of language. Note Thomas McCarthy's comments in the introduction, p. xiii, as well as Habermas's further comments in pages 114–16. See "Question and Counterquestions" in Richard Bernstein, ed., *Habermas and Modernity* (Cambridge: The MIT Press, 1985), pp. 202–03. See also "A Reply" in Axel Honneth and Hans Joas, eds. *Communicative Action: Essays on Jürgen Habermas's The Theory of Communicative Action*, trans. Jeremy Gaines and Doris L. Jones (Cambridge: The MIT Press, 1990), pp. 221–22. It would be interesting to explore whether these parallelisms map over to the distinction between life-world and system. Compare with the tables in "What Is Universal Pragmatics?" in Jürgen Habermas, *Communication and the Evolution of Society*, trans. Thomas McCarthy (Boston: Beacon Press, 1979), p. 58, and Table 16 in Jürgen Habermas, *The Theory of Communicative Action. Vol. 1: Reason and the Rationalization of Society*, trans. Thomas McCarthy (Boston: Beacon Press, 1984), p. 329.

Axis	Value Spheres	Linguistic Function	Moment or Interests	Validity Claim
Welterschliessung: world-disclosure	*Questions of taste:* art, literature, criticism	Subjective expression	Expressive	Truthfulness
Intra-mundane learning processes	*Problem-solving discourses:* 1. Truth 2. Justice 3. Morality	1. Representation	1. Cognitive-Instrumental	Truth
		2. and 3. Interpersonal relationships	2. and 3. Moral-practical	Appropriateness or Rightness

For Karl-Otto Apel's position on this problem, see "Sinnkonstitution und Geltungsrechtfertigung. Heidegger und das Problem der Transzendentalphilosophie" in Forum für Philosophie Bad Homburg, eds. *Martin Heidegger: Innen- und Außensichten* (Frankfurt: Suhrkamp, 1989), pp. 131–75. See Maria Lafont, *Sprache und Welterschließung: Zur linguistischen Wende der Hermeneutik Heideggers* (Frankfurt: Suhrkamp, 1994), *La razón come lenguage. Una revisión del giro lingüístico en la filosfía del lenguaje alemana* (Madrid: Visor, 1993), as well as her essay "Welterschließung und Referenz" in *Deutsche Zeitschrift für Philosophie*, 41/3, 1993

491–507. Martin Seel, *Die Kunst der Entzweiung. Zum Begriff der äesthestichen Rationalität* (Frankfurt: Suhrkamp, 1985). See also Albrecht Wellmer's important discussion on truth and fallibility with respect to the Habermasian speech-act theory: "What Is a Pragmatic Theory of Meaning? Variations on the Proposition 'We understand a Speech Act When We Know What Makes It Acceptable'" in Axel Honneth, Thomas McCarthy, Claus Offe, and Albrecht Wellmer, eds. *Philosophical Interventions in the Unfinished Project of Enlightenment*, trans. William Rehg (Cambridge: The MIT Press, 1992), pp. 171–219.

25. See Karl-Otto Apel, *Transformation der Philosophie*, 2 vols (Frankfurt: Suhrkamp Verlag, 1973).
26. See Richard Rorty, "The Professor and the Prophet" in *Transition*, 52, 1991, pp. 70–78, for a very appreciative review of Cornel West's work.
27. See Seylar Benhabib and Fred Dallmayr, eds., *The Communicative Ethics Controversy* (Cambridge: The MIT Press, 1990); Michael Kelly, ed., *Hermeneutics and Critical Theory in Ethics and Politics* (Cambridge: The MIT Press, 1990); David Rasmussen, ed. *Universalism vs. Communitarianism: Contemporary Debates in Ethics* (Cambridge: The MIT Press, 1990).
28. I treated this theme in my essay "Discourse Ethics and Liberation Ethics: At the Boundaries of Moral Theory," *Philosophy and Social Crititicism*, 21:4, July 1995, pp. 111–26.
29. The essay here included is an extensively revised and expanded version of Apel's German version of the first part of his answer to Dussel. Apel has written a second part which I have already translated and is forthcoming in *Philosophy and Social Criticism*, vol. 22, no. 2, pp. 1–25. Dussel also has a second rebuttal: "La Ética de la Liberación ante La Ética del Discurso," which is forthcoming in a *Festschrift* for Helmut Peukert edited by Edmund Arens. The most competent and thorough study of the debate between Apel and Dussel is a recent doctoral dissertation by Hans Schelkshorn, *Diskurs und Befreiung: Studien zur philosophischen Ethik von Karl-Otto Apel und Enrique Dussel* (University of Vienna, March 1994), 448 pages.
30. For elaboration on this see Karl-Otto Apel *Ethics and the Theory of Rationality. Selected Essays. Volume Two* (See Bibliography), and "The Rationality of Human Communication: On the Relationship between Consensual, Strategic, and Systems Rationality" in *Graduate Faculty Philosophy Journal*, 18, 1, 1994, pp. 1–25.
31. Apel's more recent works reflect the insights he has gained from his encounter with Dussel; see "Institutionsethik oder Diskursethik als Verantwortungsethik? Überlegungen zur Wirtschaftsethik" in J. P. Harpes, ed., *25 Jahre Diskursethik. Anwendungsprobleme der Diskurethik* (forthcoming).
32. For Dussel's most recent discussions of the relationship between world-system and philosophy, see: "The 'World-System': Europe as 'Center' and Its 'Periphery.' Beyond Eurocentrism." Lecture presented at the Seminar on Globalization, Duke University, November 1994, Eduardo Mendieta and Pedro Lange-Churión, eds., *Latin America and Postmodernity: A Reader* (Atlantic Highlands: Humanities Press, forthcoming). See also the recent work by Walter D. Mignolo, *The Darker Side of the Renaissance: Literary, Territoriality and Colonization* (Ann Arbor: The University of Michigan Press, 1995).

Part One

1

Liberation Philosophy from the Praxis of the Oppressed

It was twenty years ago, toward the end of the decade of the sixties, that Liberation Philosophy emerged in Latin America; in Argentina at first, but slowly in the entire continent, and later in other places in the peripheral world and, even still, in some of the developed countries.

The critique of the conquest (1510–53) may be considered as the first, implicit, Liberation Philosophy. The second was the philosophical justification of the first emancipation (1750–1830). The third Liberation Philosophy is being articulated now (since 1969). Its antecedents can be searched for in José Carlos Mariategui, in the twenties, or in the Cuban Revolution of 1959. The first explicit phase takes place from 1969 to 1973, the stage of constitution.[1] The second phase takes place from 1973 to 1976, the stage of maturation. The third stage takes place until 1983, the stage of persecution, debate, and confrontation. And the fourth, up to the the present, is the stage of growth and response to new problematics.[2]

In fact, although during the last two decades many new events have taken place, the original hypotheses have not being modified, but have been deepened and developed. On the other hand, neither have they been contradicted. Instead, they have been ignored—the non-rational tactic of domination. Meanwhile, in Latin America analytical philosophy and positivist epistemology have lost their sectarian elan[3]; Stalinist marxism has almost disappeared; the historicist latinamericanist philosophy has had to nourish itself on a greater methodological rigor. All of this has strengthened the philosophical "tradition" out of which Liberation Philosophy emerged. And because of this, today, in the last decade of the 20th century, it can grow with an unprecedented clarity. Above all, the *reality* out which such a philosophy emerged is today more pressing than ever before in its continuous and maddening spiral of underdevelopment: the *misery*, the poverty, the exploitation of the oppressed of the global periphery (in Latin America, Africa, or Asia), of the dominated classes, of the marginalized, of the "poor" in the "center," and the African-Americans,

Hispanics, Turks, and others, to whom we would have to add women as sexual objects, the "useless" aged gathered in misery or in asylums, the exploited and drugged up youth, the silenced popular and national cultures and all the "wretched of the earth," as Franz Fanon put it, who wait and struggle for their liberation.

1.1 Demarcation of Liberation Philosophy: Beyond Eurocentric Developmentalism

The philosophical "language" of Liberation Philosophy, in its origin, has to be inscribed within the hermeneutic and dialogical phenomenological tradition. The point of departure was the "late Heidegger,"[4] which involved making reference to the Husserl of the *Lebenswelt* (world of daily life) and the *Krisis*,[5] who nevertheless was still too much within the "paradigm of consciousness." Gadamer and Merleau-Ponty, and even still Ricoeur of that period, should also be inscribed within that current. The early Marcuse, still a representative of this current, allowed us to "politicize" ontology.[6] Ernst Bloch opened up the future and utopian horizons (however, it is still not yet exactly a "pro-ject" [*Entwurft*] of liberation). But it was departing from the critique of the "negative dialectics" (from Hegel[7] to Adorno), and partly due to the rediscovery of the concept of the "dialectic" by Sartre,[8] that we could understand the importance of the "old Schelling." It was he who superseded the Hegelian "negative dialectics" from the *positivity* of the exteriority of the "Lord of Being."[9] It was thus that the reflection of a "community of philosophers" (Argentinean, at the end of the decade of the sixties),[10] situated within a society oppressed by a peripheral military dictatorship, militantly articulated by popular movements (also populists) who struggled for their liberation, made the importance of Emmanuel Levinas's thought evident; but not only and not mainly in the matter of the "Other" as *language* (although still always), but instead essentially as the *poor*: as the wretched one who suffers traumatically in her corporeality the oppression and exclusion from the "benefits" of the totality.[11] The *poor* as "the Other": as peripheral Latin America, as oppressed classes, as woman, as youth.

Twenty years later, unfortunately, the "reality" has dramatically and contradictorily been accentuated in its injustice. The European-North American "community of philosophers" has undertaken other themes, and Liberation Philosophy cannot prevent a confrontation with them. Now, the "Other" is the "other face" of modernity.[12] Latin America is neither pre-, anti-, nor post-modern; and, for that reason, we cannot "realize" fully an incomplete modernity (as Jürgen Habermas suggests optimistically[13]), because as the slave (before the "Lord" of slavery) we have "paid" with our misery, with our "non-Being" (since 1492 as colonial world, first, and since 1810 as neocolonial world); for the "Being," the primitive accumulation and successive supersessions of the "happy" capitalism of the center, and even of those who are so-called delayed (the "developmentalist" notion of *Spätkapitalismus*, conceals the "exploited capitalism," and because of that the underdevelopment of the periphery).

The postmodern critiques of modernity can be of great use to Liberation Philosophy, as Heidegger's and Wittgenstein's critiques of modern metaphysics were,[14] but they are not sufficient. Richard Rorty's neo-pragmatism, for instance, is useful for an integral critique of the analytic "style" of thinking (which since the 18th century had been epistemological but which became positivist within the Anglo-Saxon tradition -with Frege, Carnap, and Popper) which is so prevalent in Latin American universities. Interestingly, while influenced by Heidegger and Levinas, I had already begun, in the sixties, a critique of modernity's imposition of a philosophy of *enlightenment*, that is, of "representation" and the "subjectivity" of the cogito. Michael Foucault, especially in his masterful *Archeology of Knowledge*,[16] that no longer intends "com-prehension" but instead the archeological "destruction" of subjectivity, where the "false continuity" is not attempted to be seen but instead the "fissure," can help us, for instance, as a way, as a method to "re-trace" the history of "eurocentrism" or the "developmentalist" fallacy, present still in him and all of modern philosophy, and in order to describe the origin of our peripheral consciousness as a "fissure" of the Exteriority (since Liberation Philosophy is one of these historical "ruptures"). The same can be said of the attempts of Jacques Derrida,[17] Jean-François Lyotard,[18] or Gianni Vattimo.[19] Like Friedrich Nietzsche,[20] they help us as "destroyers" but little as "re-constructors," where liberation as praxis is always "constructive" of novelty (rationally prudent and consensual, realizable utopia, hopeful negativity in the possibility of the "new": How can the hungry not *hope* to eat tomorrow?).

Similarly, the critique of metaphysics by Popper or Wittgenstein—especially the "late"—demanding a precision of language[21] that denies the overcoming of certain limits naive metaphysics had already jumped over, is compatible with the de-constructive task of Liberation Philosophy. But, again, neither its arguments nor its "closed door" to every realization of any actualizable utopia can be seriously considered by any of us. On the contrary, the epistemology that always already presupposes an *a priori*, a "community of scientists"—like that of Peirce or Kuhn—retraced and radically transformed at the hands of Karl-Otto Apel, can be a valid point of departure for the contemporary stage of Liberation Philosophy. Now, however, taking into account that the "communication community" has to be extended not only to humanity in general, but also to the historical subject of the process of liberation, the "we" (a "Thou" which is exterior to the dominating "us") of the "people," as a social block of the oppressed, women, the youth, and others, and, because of that, "transcendental pragmatics," ought to be superseded, overcome, and preserved, in a "transcendental *economics*," as we will see later on.

Habermas's defense of modernity, in the work already cited, and in others, is equally helpful because it prevents us from falling into populist, folklorist, fascist irrationalism;[22] but this is still not enough. The ambiguity of the realization of modernity, on the part of the "open society" of *late* capitalism, finds itself limited by what we call the developmentalist fallacy. That is, it would like to extrapolate, to impose the model (and the philosophy that derives from it) of late and central capitalism, in the very same straight line of development without discontinuity, on peripheral capitalism (of Africa, Asia, and Latin America; or in other words, to more than 80 per cent of global capitalism, if we take its population numerically), underdeveloped and, as is said in such developmentalist ideology, "delayed." The "delay" of peripheral capitalism is a "before" with respect to the "after" of "late" capitalism. What is not taken into account, in this eurocentric ideology, is that there is no such "before." Since 1492, the periphery is not a "before," but an "underneath": the exploited, the dominated, the origin of stolen wealth,' accumulated in the dominating, exploiting "center." We repeat: the developmentalist fallacy thinks that the "slave" is a "free lord" in his youthful stage, and like a child ("crude or barbarian"). It does not understand that the slave is the dialectical "other face" of domination: the as-always, the "other-part" of the exploitative relation. The peripheral world will never be able to be "developed," nor "center," nor "late." Its path is another. Its alternative is different. Liberation Philosophy gives expression to this "dis-tinction."[23]

Since the fall of the Berlin Wall (November 1989), and thanks to the process of *perestroika*, the "democratic" alternatives of a socialism of liberation in the periphery manifest themselves with greater clarity as never before. Although the periphery of capitalism suffers with greater force the lashing of imperialism, a utopian critique, more necessary than ever before, of inhuman, unjust capitalism (and where the "free market" allows it, of the competition of the *homo homini lupus*, where only the the stronger, more developed, more militarized, more violent triumph) profiles itself in the horizon. The irrationality of capitalism is suffered by its periphery (a point which Marcuse could not fathom, and which Habermas ignores completely). This is the central theme of Liberation Philosophy.

1.2 Liberation Philosophy and Praxis: Categories and Method

Liberation Philosophy moves in the dialectic or the "passage" that departs from a given or established system (be it political, erotic, pedagogical, fetishist, economic, etc.), and that enters into the depth of a future system of liberation. The dialectical passage moves between an order and another, and all the problematic of the rupture within the old (1); order as system of domination, by the *praxis of liberation* itself (2); and of the constructive moment of the *new* order (3)

Old order (1) → *Passage* of liberation (2) → *New* order (3)

What is of interest, therefore, is not so much the "reform" of the "open society" (the ruling Totality), as its liberating "overcoming." Therefore we must define clearly the *negative* category—with respect to the ruling Totality as in (1)—that allows the act of "superseding" which is implicit to liberation.

The Latin American "reality" of misery, of classes and peoples exploited by capitalism, of the women oppressed by machismo, of the dominated youth and popular culture, is the starting point and the criterion for the choice or construction (if this was not available) of a method and the pertinent categories for a philosophical reflection on such "reality." In our work *Liberation Philosophy*, we have attempted a description of some of the essential categories (Proximity, Totality, Exteriority, Alienation, Liberation, etc.)[24] that in our judgment remain the same and are still necessary for the analysis of the "praxis of liberation" of the oppressed.

Inasmuch, then, as we have to take seriously the Totality (as any ontology), and the "institutionalization" of Mediation (as much technological as scientific or mundane), Liberation Philosophy cannot negate the determining place of "rationality," even in the Habermasian sense. Concerning this point, therefore, it cannot be postmodern. Inasmuch as the institutionalization may be dominating, the negation of the being of another person, the critique of the Totality is now an essential moment of Liberation Philosophy. However, it is necessary to know "from where" the critique is announced. It can neither be nihilist nor a mere return to the past (as is the case with Nietzsche), nor simply a negation of all rationality (like Rorty). Unlike Schelling, it will not depart from the "Other of Reason" but instead from the "Other" of the *dominating*, oppressing, and totalitarian totalizing reason. That is, it will not depart from the dominating moment of rationality. Furthermore, when "critique" departs from the Exteriority of the exploited and excluded poor (excluded from the distribution of life), from women as sexual object, and so on (that is, from the "positivity" of the reality of the Other, who is non-being for the system, the one who is negated), the critique and the praxis that precedes it and is its concomitant, it is not only the negation of the negation (negative dialectics) but also the affirmation of the Exteriority of the Other, the source (*Quelle*)—and not the foundation (*Grund*)—"from where" the critique departs (from the "living labor" facing capital, as in Marx; from the active subjectivity of feminine corporeality as constitutive of Eros and not as "object"; as the trans-Oedipal subjectivity of youth, from popular culture as creator of a "new" ideology and symbols). From the "positivity" of this affirmation can the "negation of the negation" be performed. Liberation Philosophy, in this sense, is a positive philosophy. This movement beyond mere negative dialectics we have called the "analectical moment" of the dialectical movement—essential and belonging to liberation as affirmation of a "new" order, and not merely as negation of the old.[25]

Hence, utopia is not the fruit of a mere "creating imagination" which sets out from out of the Totality (from Marcuse to Bloch), but instead and above all, is the affirmation of "that-which-has-no-place" (*ouk-tópos*): the poor, the "castrated" women, the alienated Oedipus, the exploited people, the capitalist peripheral nations. "Ouk-topias" (which have no place in the dominating totality) are the non-beings, who nevertheless have *reality*. There is no need to create future projects, products of pure imagination and fantasy that are only "possible" for the ruling order. It has to be known how to discover in the transcendental exteriority of the oppressed the *actual* "presence" of utopia as actual reality of the impossible, which is impossible for the system of domination without the help of the Other. Hence the sense of "analogy" of a new order of liberation—which is not simply a "metaphor" of the given, as Ricoeur would say, but as an "analogical"[26] impossibility for the Totality without mediation of the irruption of the Other. From this comes the specific meaning of a "project of liberation."[27]

1.3 Horizons and Debates of Liberation Philosophy

Liberation Philosophy affirms that ethics (and therefore politics, as first horizon) is *prima philosophia*. Philosophy begins with reality, and human reality is practical, always already *a priori* person-to-person relationships in a communication community (of language and life), presupposed in reality (objectively) and transcendentally (subjectively). Therefore, prior to nature, the other is always already encountered, vitally and pragmatically.

The first practical communicative horizon of constitution we have denominated "politics."[28] By politics I understand the relation, person-to-person, at the level of equality, of fraternity, of solidarity. Every political "system" (Niklas Luhmann) is a totality of institutions that have to articulate themselves as natural:

> The *natural* distribution is neither just nor injust; nor is it unjust that men are born into society at some particular position. *These are simply natural facts.*[29]

So we are told by John Rawls. For him, it is "natural," not "historical," to be born bourgeois or a wage earner. He confuses the mere "being born" (which certainly is natural) with the being born bourgeois, owner of an "initial" capital. This hereditary property is an historical "institution" and can be perfectly unjust. Marx had already analyzed this "paradise of natural rights" when he wrote:

They contract as *free persons*, who are equal before the law. Their *contract* [anticipating contemporary contractualists] is the final result in which their joint will finds a common legal expression. *Equality*, because each enters into relation with the other, as with a simple owner of commodities, and they exchange equivalent for equivalent.... The only force bringing them together, and putting them into relation with each other, is the selfishness, the gain and the private interest of each. Each pays heed to *himself only*, and no one worries about the *others*. And precisely for that reason, either in accordance with the pre-established harmony of things, or under the auspices of an omniscient providence, they all work together to their mutual advantage, for the common weal, and in the common interest.[30]

Marx had anticipated, even in its smallest details, the liberal argumentation of Rawls. He knows well that both parties of the contract find themselves in radically different situations of non-equivalence: one is violently compelled to sell herself, alienate her corporeality and personality for a given time. The other, in contrast, buys and uses the Other as mediation of its project (valorization of value). "Initial" historical injustice. This is a political, practical "system" which determines the social life of the citizens of a democracy.

Liberation Philosophy will ask itself always, first, who is situated in the Exteriority of the system, and *in the system* as alienated, oppressed. Within the regimes of "formal" democracy—bourgeois, and within the "late" capitalism of the center—it is asked after the rights of minorities. In reality, in the nations of peripheral capitalism, underdeveloped and exploited, the oppressed classes, the marginal ones, the ethnic groups and other groups constitute the greater "social block of oppressed," the *people*. This "people" (as a political category) is excluded from the "formal" democracies (and it is the manipulated "majority" of an institutionalization of the State that makes do, in fact, without the popular will). "Politicism" (as attempted in the "modernization" of peripheral nations, mimetically imitating the Habermasian proposals, for example) does not understand the importance of the economical (not as a juxtaposed "system" but as an essential constitutive moment of the *Lebenswelt*, of the political and the social). The failure of the solely *formal* democracies (such as those of Alfonsín o Menem in Argentina, Alán Garcia in Perú, since 1983), shows that "democratic" politics without "economic" consciousness is a fictitious formality of false and reductive "rationality."

Analogously, populism uses the category "people" in order to affirm the peripheral "nationhood," but hegemonized by the interests of national bourgeoisies and therefore within global capitalism, pretending some sort of national "autonomy" under the control of some national peripheral bourgeoisie. These projects have failed. The bourgeoisies of the central countries have organized a structural transference of value from the periphery to the centers, using the same bourgeoisies of peripheral countries as a mediation. Liberation Philosophy rejects populism (be it Vargista, Peronista, Cardenista, Ibañista,) which was the best hope of the peripheral bourgeoisie and the only democratic and nationalist example, in favor of the "popular." A politics hegemonized by the "social block of the oppressed" (working and farmer classes, radicalized petit bourgeoise marginalized classes, ethic groups, etc), and departing from such a "historical" subject (when the social block organizes and becomes a subject), only this, then, can be of liberation. Liberation Philosophy has debated at great extent this central question.[31]

The economic crisis of real socialism, and its political democratization through the process of "perestroika," opens up new possibilities to a praxis of liberation. The alternative of a democratic socialism is now possible. Sandinismo, which is not Leninist in its "democratic centralism," is not an ideology about the national, the popular, or the religious, nor is it Stalinist over the control of a competitive market. And although it might have been temporarily defeated in the voting polls, it is all the same a point of reference for Liberation Philosophy (a concrete historical, political "subject" in Latin America).[32]

The second practical horizon (and not second because it is after, but always synchronously co-existing) is the relation women-men, the "erotics."[33] Now the other of the machist Totality is the woman. The constitutive *ego* is a "phallic ego," as Lacan would say. Freud may be re-read as the one who analyzes and diagnoses the Machist Totality, when he says that sexuality is "the masculine but not the feminine; the opposition is announced: masculine genitality or castration. . . . The masculine comprises the subjects, the activity and the possession of the phallus. The feminine constitutes the object and passivity."[34] Freud contributes categories that need to be de- and re-constructed. In any event, the Latin American erotics of liberation is far more complex than that of the European Oedipus. The conquering masculinity (which is epitomized in Hernán Cortés) rapes the Indian woman (Malinche); Oedipus is the Latin American mestizo child. Phallocracy becomes conquest, plutocracy, and social domination. This is the machist culture of hypocrisy and the mystification of women's domination. Because of this, women's liberation has been a central theme of Liberation Philosophy since the beginning of the decade of the seventies.

However, retractions have to be made, especially when taking into account the conservatism of the general Latin American consciousness and, in particular, that which existed at the beginning of the seventies. A first; central theme is that of abortion. In this limiting situation, philosophy finds itself before a true rational dilemma: two absolute rights confront each other. The right of women over their own persona, their carnality, their corporeality (above everything else, over that which takes place in "their own bodies"). And the right of the new being, the fetus, to live. Before such a dilemma, which rationally cannot be solved *a priori*, the old doctrine of "the least evil" ought to be adopted. In each case, when the circumstances are well defined, it would be an act of responsible liberation and ethics by women—and, of course, solidaristically, by the responsible male—to decide such a situation. Whether or not the fetus is separated from the maternal uterus is an ethical act whose *responsibility* is a contribution of the female human "subject," and of the male in solidarity, since the event takes place in her own body, in her own being. Evidently, there are ethical criteria (such as that the person never be a means but always a end in itself, as in the case of the fetus) that woman also has to respect—for her who has to responsibly decide with justice and equanimity.

In the second place, the grave problem of homosexuality. Again, a conservative mentality prevents seeing the question with clarity. The human person whose sexuality is directed toward the same sex (leaving aside here the cause, whether it is natural, psycho-pedagogical, or psycho-pathological) ought to be respected in the dignity of the person. The ethics of erotics ought to overcome sexuality in order to arrive at the person itself of the Other. A sexual relationship is just if it respects, in justice, the person of the Other. In a homosexual relationship such respect is not impossible. A Liberation Philosophy which thinks and formulates the liberation of women from the machist totality that alienates the Other/woman, and therefore exalts heterosexuality as the full relation of complementarity, solidarity, and love for dis-tinction and justice, can not disallow the possibility of respect for the Other even in the case of the same-sex erotic relationship (homosexuality in the hetero-personality). Again, as in the prior case, it would be a question, if no solution appears, of choosing the "lesser of evils," meaning that only the conscience of the participants ought to decide responsibly. An erotics that only preserves certain "traditional" abstract principles immolates millions of persons whose homosexuality is not yet adequately diagnosed in its causes. This type of erotics would reduce itself in reality to a mere "objectivist" morality that, in attempting to save the customs of a given society (which in reality are historical and relative), would destroy the person (it would, in other words, be an anti-ethical and anti-moral criterion).

These two questions demonstrate the coherence of Liberation Philosophy. Since the personhood of the Other is the absolute criterion of both ethics and liberation, it is necessary to demonstrate in both cases (the dignity of women, the right over her body, and the right of the fetus to life; the dignity of the person over the determination of his sexuality) the primacy of the criterion, even if the situations are culturally and socially new.

The third practical horizon is that of "pedagogy."[35] The political equality of person to person and the erotic relation women-men are now lived through by the adult, parents, institutions, the State, the means of communication, with respect to the child, the youth, the people as *subject of culture*. This is the question of cultural reproduction.[36] Now, the hegemonic educational totality can also dominate the Other, as object of the "Lectern" (Paulo Freire) who simply repeats or "re-remembers" (Socrates) the old. All re-remembering is a pedagogy of domination because the "new" that is brought into the "world" by the youth can not be remembered, but must be discovered with respect to the novelty of the Other. The pedagogy of liberation is cultural revolution, and in the peripheral countries of capitalism it is a revolution of popular culture, where the autochthonous and one's own (Amerindian, African, Asian, etc.) ought to be developed into a modern culture (albeit not of a modernity). Neither folklorism nor eurocentric rationalism: liberating reason, (*liberationis ratio*) which discovers a new "objectivity", has as its function to unify the historical "tradition" of a people with the necessary technological (but adequate) and scientific development (according to the real exigencies of the nation, and not simply imitating foreign models).

A fourth practical horizon, intimately linked to the prior ones, is the one we have denominated anti-fetishist—the traditional question of the Absolute (Hegel), or of theodicy (Leibniz). Liberation Philosophy affirms that all Totalities can be fetishized: the political as in the empires or the State; as historical manifestations of the divinity; the erotic, as in fetishist machismo; pedagogy, because ruling ideology is a historical manifestation of the divine, such as the "Western and Christian civilization" or the *American way of life*. All critique, then, ought to begin by negating the divinity of the fetishized absolute which negates the possibility of human realization. Atheism as negation of the negation of the person (Feuerbach) is the first thesis of Liberation Philosophy. But, from a rational point of view (and from the popular cultures of peripheral nations), one can, however, affirm the Absolute only in the case that it would ground, justify, or give hope (Bloch) to the oppressed in their process of liberation. Symbolically, the Pharaoh-god justified domination; the Yahweh of the slave of Egypt, led by Moses, gave motives for liberation. These symbolic structures (as in Ricoeur's "The symbols that make one think!") are metaphors of a rational discourse: if there is an absolute, it ought to be Other than every historical system (otherwise such a system would be unsurpassable, it would be an end of history). The negation of the divinification of every Totality (the anti-fetishism of Marx with respect to capitalism), as negation of the negation of the human person, is the negative and correlative moment of its affirmation. If there is an absolute, it cannot be but the Other of every system, as the breath of life of all that lives.[37] In this case, religion becomes a fundamental moment of the praxis of liberation. It is not necessary to negate the popular religions of the peripheral world (especially in Africa and Asia, but in Latin America as well). It is necessary to negate the moments that negate the person, and to develop the moments that justify liberation. It is a hermeneutical task (of "tradition") to discern (introjected by the dominators in said "traditions") in these religions their regressive elements and to empower the creative moments of human affirmation. If there is an Absolute, it cannot but affirm and develop the person in justice, autonomy, and freedom.

On this point Liberation Philosophy is inscribed within the popular traditions of the peripheral world and in the philosophical schools of Hamann, Schelling, Schleiermacher, Dilthey, Gadamer, Ricoeur and Levinas, without leaving to the side Kierkegaard, Marx, or Bloch. The hermeneutics of the symbol, politics and economics as cults, the utopian hope as horizon of popular praxis of liberation—this is an entirely new project for the "majority" of humanity (which lives in the South, which dances in Africa; which contemplates in suffering in Asia, and venerates its traditions in Latin America). Secularization is the false name of fetishism; and the atheism of the left was a first dialectical moment, whose second moment is the affirmation of the absolute as liberation. Forgetting the second moment has distanced the left from the peoples who explain their daily lives, in the *Lebenswelt*, with symbols, rituals, and cults.

1.4   Pertinence of Economics

We speak of "economics," and not of economy, as the moment in which praxis and poiesis, in a concrete synthesis, are articulated in order to constitute the practical-productive level par excellance.[38]

If Liberation Philosophy departs from the reality of misery, poverty, exploitation, then the relation person-to-person (practical) is always already *a priori* institutionalized and reproduced historically from a given economic structure, as practical (social relation) and productive (technological) presupposition. Stalinist "economism," understood at the economic level as infrastructural base that determines the superstructure (the political and ideological), and "politicism" (of a Habermasian type, for instance), which gives absolute priority to the social or political relations over and above economics (relegated to a juxtaposed and secondary "system"), imagines that "democracy," legitimation, and other essential levels of human survival are fundamental. However, it is forgotten that corporeality (which is hungry, and lives in misery, in the unjust distribution and productivity of "majority" of humanity in the periphery) points to a relationship to the "products" of technological labor, which fulfill the needs of life. We are living beings who have a *logos*, that is, the *logos* is a function of life and not vice versa. Human life, its corporeality, is not only the condition of possibility but the being itself and human existence as such. Reason (*logos*) is a moment of human life, and not life of reason. Still, to be a corporeality, to have needs (to eat, drink, dress, have a roof, need culture, technology, science, art, religion and other things) is a practical moment because *a priori* we are part of a community, and productive because "bread" is eaten, and "clothing" is for dressing, as products of human labor. This articulation of the practico-productive is economics; it is ethics, anthropological realization par excellance. Marx presented all of this with a clarity and pertinence never equaled. Today, this clarity and pertinence are necessary more than ever for the "majority" of humanity, who live in misery in the peripheral world, where capitalism, more than socialism, has utterly failed.

If the "paradigm of consciousness" (from Descartes through Husserl) has been subsumed by the "paradigm of language" (as Apel demonstrates), this paradigm itself has to be subsumed in the "paradigm of life," the life of the human community (a prudential and consensual practical moment, the grounding of politics) as "participation" and "communication" of the product of social labor (production, distribution, exchange, and consumption). Again at this level, the Totality (Capital) can exclude (as *pauper*, as Marx would say), or exploit, alienating the Other: the "living labor," the poor person in his needy, hungry corporeality. This exteriority of the Other, of "living labor," accepts a contract for the sale of its "creative source of value" from the nothingness of capital, for example, and is subsumed (alienated) in the salary system, as creator of surplus. Liberation here means not only to subvert the practical-social relation (communicative action, political institution, ethical injustice), but also to locate oneself in a different manner in the productive relation of work itself (subsequent and necessary technological revolution). In no other moment can the categories of Liberation Philosophy be manipulated with greater clarity and pertinence. Furthermore, in this "circuitous route," philosophy describes (at ethical, anthropological, ontological, and transcendental levels) the "reality" of the misery in which the Latin American peoples find themselves. "Economics" has a non-substitutable pertinence, because in it the *practical* (politics, erotics, pedagogy, anti-fetishism) and the *productive* relations (ecological, semiotic-pragmatic or linguistic, poietic-technological or of design, aesthetic or of art) are made *concrete*.

The just and urgent claims of ecology can be united to the claims for justice by the exploited person. Earth and poor humanity are exploited and destroyed simultaneously, by a capitalism whose criterion of the subsumption of technology is the growth of the rate of profit, and by a productivist Stalinism whose criterion was the growth of the rate of production, both of which are anti-ecological and anti-human systems. It is time to recuperate, from Marx, the ecological sense. Neither the Earth nor the human person have any "exchange value," because the first can produce values of use and the second values of exchange, but neither is a "product" of human labor, only the substance or creative source of exchange value. The "dignity" of the Earth and the person are two points of reference of the ecologism of Liberation Philosophy (and of Marx). Technology, destructive of nature, is a moment of capital (a social relation which has as its ultimate goal the valorization of value). Frequently, the ecological movements of the center do not acknowledge the essential relation between ecology and capitalism (or productive Stalinism).[39]

1.5 Paths Opening up to the Future

Liberation Philosophy has urgent tasks. I would like to indicate some of them.

Liberation Philosophy has now two lines of argumentation. These developed out of the continental philosophy of the phenomenological, ontological, and hermeneutical traditions, on the one hand, and out of the economic thought in the current of Marx, on the other hand. Now, Liberation Philosophy has to develop more precisely the "paradigm of language" required by the praxis of liberation. Some liberation philosophers are already engaged in this task. But, in the same line of development, it is necessary to continue the debate with "discoure ethics" (of Karl-Otto Apel and Jürgen Habermas), from the Exteriority of the Other, of the "poor," who is not assigned any role within the "communication community" (already excluded from participating in her corporeality with food, clothing, education, and in justice, and not only in argumentation). It will be necessary to describe a transcendental economics (beyond transcendental pragmatics).

Politically, taking in its gravity the Latin American situation, a crisis augmented by the electoral defeat of Sandinismo, in February 1990, it is necessary to clarify and to deepen philosophically the necessity of a national, social, cultural, and economic revolution, from the perspective of a real democracy which would take into account the structural transference of value that originates in peripheral capitalism (which has to be superseded as *conditio sine qua non* for any possible future liberation).

After the fall of the Berlin Wall, Liberation Philosophy, going beyond post-Marxism (but returning to Marx "himself") and post-modernity (from the "other face" of modernity), developed a *positive* discourse from out of misery (where its negativity is negated), and affirmed the real and necessary process of liberation of the great majority of humanity: trans-modernity as a future-oriented project.

Notes

1. See Eduard Demenchonok, "La Filosofía de la Liberación latinoamericana" in *Ciencias Sociales* (Moscow), 1, 1988, pp. 123–40; Horacio Cerutti, "Actual Situation and Perspectives of Latin American Philosophy of Liberation" in *Philosophical Forum* (New York), 1–2, 1988–89, pp. 43–61. See also my essay "Retos actuales a la Filosofía de la Liberación en América Latina" in *Libertacao/Liberación* (Porto Alegre), 1, 1989, pp. 9–29 (also published in *Lateinamerika* [Rostock], 1, 1987, pp. 11–25), where I present the chronology delineated above. In addition see "Una década argentina (1966–1976) y el origen de la Filosofía de la Liberación" in *Reflexao* (Campinas), 38, 1987, pp. 20–50; and to situate Liberation Philosophy within the history of Latin American philosophy, see my "Hipótesis para una historia de la filosofía latinoamericana" in *Ponencias*, II, Congreso Internacional de Filosofía

Latinoamericana, USTA, Bogotá, 1982, pp. 405–36; and "Praxis and Philosophy. Provisional Thesis for a Philosophy of Liberation" in *Philosophical Knowledge* (Washington: University Press of America, 1980), pp. 108–18; also *Praxis latinoamericana y Filosofía de la liberación*, pp. 21–45, section 1 ; and "Histoire et Praxis (Orthopraxis et Objectivité)" in *Revue de l'Université d'Ottawa*, 4, 1985, pp. 147–61. See especially the work of Hans Schelkshorn, *Ethik der Befreiung. Einführung in die Philosophie Enrique Dussels* (Freiburg: Herder, 1992); Christofer Ober, *System, Lebenswelt und Exteriorität. Eine Auseinandersetzung mit den Ethiktheorien von Alfons Auer, Niklas Luhmann, Jürgen Habermas und Enrique Dussel* (Doctoral thesis: Universität Tübingen, 1989); and by same author, *Die ethische Herausforderung der Pädagogik durch die Existenz des Anderen. Ueberlegung zum Verhältnis von Pädagogik un Ethik in Auseinandersetzung mit den Ethiktheorien von Jürgen Habermas und Enrique Dussel* (Institut für Erziehungswissenschaften und am philosophischen Seminar, Universität Tübingen, 1990); Ingrid Schraner, *Überlegungen zum doppelten Aufgabenbereich der Wirtschaftsethik* (Tübingen: Universität Tübingen, 1986); Anton Peter, *Der befreiungstheologie und der transzendental-theologische Denkensatz. Ein Beitrag zum Gespräch zwischen Enrique Dussel und Karl Rahner* (Freiburg: Herder, 1988).
2. During the XVIII World Congress of Philosophy (Brighton, 1988), a panel was organized on "Identity and Liberation" with participants from Africa and Asia. In April of 1991, a first colloquium on Liberation and Philosophy, North-South Dialogue, was organized, in which Paul Ricoeur participated. In Louvain, inspired by Liberation Philosophy, an *Encyclopedia of Latin American Philosophy* is being prepared.
3. Critiques like those of Rorty and Feyerabend have a lot to do with this change.
4. See Dussel, *Para una ética de la liberación latinoamericana*, 3 Vols., (Buenos Aires: Siglo XXI, 1973) 1, Chap. 1–2.
5. See Dussel, *Para una de-strucción de la historia de la ética* (Mendoza: Ser y tiempo, 1972).
6. Especially Herbert Marcuse, *One Dimensional Man* (Boston: Beacon Press, 1964), which had such a profound effect on the movements of 1968, even in Latin America.
7. See my *Método para una filosofía dela liberación*: Superación analectica de la dialectica Hegeliana (Salamanca: Sígueme, 1974).
8. Especially in Sartre's *Critique of Dialectical Reason*, trans. Alan Sheridan-Smith (London: New Left Books, 1976).
9. This was the background thesis of my work already mentioned (Método para una filosofia) without knowing, but anticipating, against Habermas.
10. As example see the collected work *Hacia una filosopia de la Liberación* (Bueno Aires: Bonum, 1973).
11. With respect to this see Chap. 3 of Vol. 1 of my *Para una ética de la liberación latinoamericana*.
12. See "La Modernidad y la falacia desarrollista: el eurocentrismo" in R. Fornet-Betancourt, ed., *Diskursethik oder Befreiungsethik* (Aachen: Augustinus Buchhandlung, 1992)
13. In his excellent work *The Philosophical Discourse of Modernity: Twelve Lectures*, it is interesting that with respect to "Ein anderer Ausweg" (Chap. XI, pp. 294ff), Habermas refers to the work of Hartmut and Gernot Böhme, *Das Andere der Vernunf*. On the contrary, the Other of Liberation Philosophy is not only the other of Reason but the Other of the "life community," who in her corporeality suffers being poor. Furthermore, this Other is not irrational but is in opposition

to the dominant reason ("hegemonic" as Gramsci would say), and that establishes a liberating reason (new and future rationality). We can accept neither the oppressing reason of terror nor nihilist irrationalism. The "poor" has to be "intelligent" (like the Sandinistas, besieged by the "democratic" empire; like the mouse in the paws of the cat, where the least of "irrational" errors would threaten its survival. The cat can be "nihilist" like G. Vattimo, skeptical like R. Rorty, playful like the "language games," *Homo ludens*; while the one that cries out "I am hungry! Don't torture me!" does not play, but dies in her traumatized corporeality. But she has to plan, with *phronesis*, rationally, how she will eat tomorrow, how to structure a system in which torture will disappear). Habermasian, Apelian "rationalism" are welcome, but not as eurocentric "oppressing rationality."
14. As is exemplarily demonstrated by Karl-Otto Apel, *Transformation der Philosophie*, 2 vols. (Frankfurt: Suhrkamp Verlag, 1973).
15. I am thinking of Richard Rorty, *Philosophy and The Mirror of Nature* (Princeton: Princeton University Press, 1979); *Consequences of Pragmatism* (Minnesota: Minnesota University Press, 1982); *Contingency, Irony and Solidarity* (New York: Cambridge University Press, 1989). Concerning my positions on these themes see my *Philosophy of Liberation*, (Maryknoll: Orbis Books, 1985) 1.1.5; *Para una ética de la liberación latinoamericana*, Chap. 3, paragraph 36, V. II, pp. 156ff: "El mètodo analèctico y la filosofía latinoamericana," where I wrote: "El Otro está màs allá del pensar, de la com-prensiòn, de la luz, del lógos; màs allá del fundamento, de la identidad: es un an-arjòs" (The Other is beyond thinking, comprehension, the light, the logos; it is beyond the grounding, identity: it is an an-arjós") (p. 161).
16. Above all in the *Archeology of Knowledge*, where what are important are the concepts of "discontinuity, of rupture, of umbral, of limit, of transformation." In some way, the Other is the principle of discontinuity; it is the origin of change and transformation. Liberation Philosophy can learn from him although critically.
17. See Jacques Derrida, *Speech and Phenomena: and other Essays on Husserl's Theory of Signs*, trans. David B. Allison (Evanston: Northwestern University Press, 1973); *Writing and Difference*, trans. Alan Bass (Chicago: The University of Chicago Press, 1978); *Of Grammotology*, trans. Gayatri Chakravorty Spivak (Baltimore: Johns Hopkins University Press, 1976).
18. Jean-François Lyotard, *The Postmodern Condition: A report on Knowledge*, trans. Geoff Bennington and Brian Massumi (Minneapolis: University of Minnesota Press, 1984).
19. Gianni Vattimo, *The End of Modernity: Nihilism and Hermeneutics in Postmodern Culture*, trans. Jon R. Snyder (Baltimore: Johns Hopkins University Press, 1988).
20. With respect to Nietzsche see my works *Para una ética de la liberación* and *Para una De-struccíón de la historia de la ética*, already cited, which relate the thought of the great nihilist to a eurocentric return to the pretentious Aryan authenticity of war, of domination.
21. See the work of Liberation Philosophy by Franz Hinkelammert, *Crítica de la razón utópica* (San José, Costa Rica: Del, 1984), especially elaborated against Popper, and against Hans Albert. See Chap. V: "La metodología de Popper y sus análisis teóricos de la planificación, la competencia y el proceso de institucionalización," where he concludes: "Thus, Popper neither overcomes nor attains a critique of utopia. What he does is to transform it from a utopia of human liberation—a utopia of praxis—into an utopia of technological progress: there are no goals that this technical progress cannot attain. He translates the utopian strength of technology and the objective inertia of its progress, thus making it act against human

freedom. Heaven on earth is not precisely what Marx promises; it is Popper who promises it, integrating with it its own myth of immortality in the hióstasis of late capitalism" (p. 191). Hinkelammert's critique is unquestionably deeper than that developed by Apel, who, nevertheless, has held an exemplary position on this question.

22. See the biased critique, by Horacio Cerutti, *Filosofía de la liberación latinoamericana* (México: FCE, 1983). Concerning this work see "Filosofía de la Liberación en América. Diez años después," en *Cristianismo y Sociedad*, 80, 1984, issue dedicated to this theme.
23. On the category of "dis-tinction" (Derrida's "différance") see my *Filosofía de la Liberación* 2.4.3–2.4.4, 4.1.5.5; in *Para una ética de la liberación*, Chap. 6, paragraph 37, v. II. With respect to the analysis of the "developmentalist ideology" see Franz Hinkelammert, *Dialéctica del desarrollo desigual* (Santiago de Chile: CEREN, 1970).
24. See *Filosofía de la Liberación*, Chapter 2. The same can be considered in my *Para una ética de la liberación*, through the five books (Vols.I and II [Buenos Aires: Siglo XXI, 1973]; Vol. III [México: Edicol, 1977]; Vols. IV–V [Bogotá: USTA, 1979–1980]). Totality since Aristotle (*tò hólon*), Thomas Aquinas (*ordo*), Hegel (*Totalität*), Marx and Heidegger (*Ganzheit*) up to Lukács, as the point of departure of all ontology, is questioned for the first time by Schelling, and later through Levinas's concepts of "proximitè" or "exteriorité", positions that are subsequently radicalized by Liberation Philosophy. Against Levinas, this philosophy affirms the possibility of a "political liberation" that is beyond the horizon of the Totality (that is to say, the institutionalization of a new future Totality, although it might still be ethically ambiguous; or, in other words, inevitably and in the long range, a new system of domination).
25. From Latin American misery, *machismo*, the oppression of woman, and from the overcoming of a Schelling (certainly taking into account the romantics, especially Hamann), and with respect to Hegel (out of the Schelling lecture of 1841 on the "Philosophy of Revelation," see my work *Método para una filosofía de la Liberación*, pp. 115ff) a path opens up that will follow and deepen with Feuerbach, Kierkegaard, or Marx; and, in another tradition, Franz Rosenzweig and Martin Buber, and even Levinas; and, as convergence of both, and from the periphery, Liberation Philosophy. The European antecedents of Liberation Philosophy, as it can be seen, are "anti-hegemonic," as Gramsci put it; marginal, peripheral, "edifying," as Rorty would christen them.
26. See my article "Pensée analytique en Philosophie de la Libération" in *Analogie et Dialectique* (Geneva: Labor et Fides, 1982), pp. 93–120.
27. See my *Para una ética de la liberación*, Chapter V, paragraph 30, V. II, pp. 97 ff. This is the question of the "meta-physical" or "trans-ontological" project (that neither Heidegger nor Habermas nor Levinas can formulate). It is not the project of either a "real communication community" or and "ideal," for Apel, but of the "historical-possible," as mediation between both. It is not "Being" as the grounding of the ruling Totality, but the "Being-future" of the Totality constructed in the process of liberation.
28. See *Filosofía ética latinoamericana*; Chap. 3.1 of *Philosophy of Liberation* is dedicated to this theme.
29. Rawls, *A Theory of Justice* (Oxford: Clarendon Press, 1972) paragraph 17, p. 102 (emphasis added). Rawls even maintains, further, that: "No one deserves his greater natural capacity nor merits a more favorable starting place in society. But it does not follow that one should eliminate these distinctions" (p. 102). It is evident that no recently born person deserves anything because, obviously, they were "no

one." But this does not mean that initial differences are not injust and that therefore they ought not to be eliminated *a posteriori*. It is a liberal conservatism in the name of a hegemonic reason.
30. Marx, *Capital*, 1, p. 280. Emphasis added.
31. The debate concerning populism has been central to the history of Liberation Philosophy. This problem was formulated in the critiques of Osvaldo Ardiles of the position of Mario Casalla (*Razón y Liberación* [Buenos Aires: Siglo XXI, 1973]). Alberto Parisi analogously refered to the themes (*Filosofía y Dialéctica* [México: Edicol, 1979]). Horacio Cerutti and Brazilian philosophers have taken up the theme.
32. On the critique of real socialism's utopian perfect planning see Franz Hinkelammert, *Critica de la razon utópica* Chap. IV, "El marco categorial del pensamiento soviético" (pp. 123ff).
33. See *Filosofa ética de la liberación*, Chap. VII: "La erótica latinoamericana" (México: Edicol, 1977), pp. 50–123.
34. See *Drei Abhandlungen zur Sexualtheorie* in *S. Freud Studienausgabe*, Vol. V (Frankfurt: Fischer, 1972), p. 88.
35. See "La pedagógica latinoamericana" in *Filosofía ética de la liberación*, Vol. III, pp. 126ff; and *Filosofía de la Liberación*, Chap. 2.3, where the question of Oedipus/ Elektra and the children of couples is treated.
36. See my article "Cultura lationamericana y Filosofía de la Liberación" in *Latinoamrica* (México), 17, 1985, pp. 77–127 (and in *Casa de las Américas* [La Habana], 155–56, 1986, pp. 68–73).
37. See *Philosophy of Liberation*, Chap. 3,4; and the entire fifth volume of *Filosofía ética latinoamericana*
38. On this theme see *Philosophy of Liberation*, Chap. 4.4; in *Filosofía ética de la liberación*, there is in every chapter an economics: economy of erotics (paragraph 45), economics of pedagogy (paragraph. 51), economics of politics (paragraph. 57), anti-fetishist economics (the cult) (paragraph 64). In addition see my works of commentary on Marx: *La producción teórica de Marx. Un comentario de los Grundrisse*; *Hacia un Marx desconcido. Un comentario a los Manuscritos del 61–63*; *El Ultimo (1863–1882) la liberación latinoamerican* (Mexico: Siglo XXI, 1990). Through all of these works I have transversed the "long path" of which Ricoeur speaks, not of linguistics but of economics. In the debate with Apel see point 4.3: "De la comunidad de Comunicación del lenguaje a la comunidad de vida" in "La Introducción a la *Transformación de la filosofía* de K.-O. Apel y la Filosofía de la Liberación" in Karl Otto Apel, et al., eds:, *Fundamentación de la ética y filosofía de la liberacion* (Mexico: Siglo XXI, 1992) pp. 83–95.
39. See Enrique Dussel, *Filosofía de la Producción* (Bogotá: Nueva América, 1983) and my edition and introduction to the *Cuadernos tecnológico-históricos de Karl Marx de 1851* (Puebla: Universidad de Puebla, 1984).

2

The Reason of the Other: "Interpellation" as Speech-Act

The philosophy of Karl-Otto Apel is extremely suggestive and healthy for Latin America for many reasons, but I wish to underscore the most important among them: its subsumptive criticism of the analytical philosophy of language. To dialogue with this philosophy is a demanding experience, as this must be undertaken with a creative purpose.

2.1 Point of Departure

2.1.1 The Course of K.-O. Apel's Philosophy

Since his habilitation thesis,[1] the philosophy of language has been Apel's prefered thematic. In the *Transformation der Philosophie*[2] Apel compiles articles where one may observe his new path. From a hermeneutic position, at that time phenomenological and even Heideggerian-Gadamerian, going through Charles W. Morris, Wittgenstein's criticism is conciliated with Heidegger,[3] where the "analysis of language" is subsumed. From approximately 1970, with Peirce's critique of Kant's solipsism[4] and with the discovery of the "community of communication" as a transcendental[5] and ethical[6] presupposition of all possible "linguistic games" or argumentation, there emerges the "last Apel." Step by step, in dialogue with the philosophy of science, Apel opens a new discussion concerning a typology of rationality, and defines the subject of the possibility of an "ultimate foundation of ethics"[7] in a growing confrontation with Habermas.

A new moment, starting from the pragmatic turn,[8] where the thematic of "transcendental pragmatics" had originated, is constituted by the problem of "transcendental semantics," which is in dialogue with semanticist intentionalism, that is to say, with reference to the intentional state of the second Searle.[9] At the same time, there emerges the need for a mediation between the basic norms of discourse ethics and the problem of its application (*Anwendungsproblem*), that is, the problem of an ethics of responsibility,[10] in order to be *a posteriori* capable of being responsible for the consequences of the acts of those "affected" by the "agreements" reached discursively. To end, Apel has undertaken the possibility of a macro-ethics for humankind.[11]

If in the sixties and seventies his opponent was the Popperian reductivist epistemology or an analytical abstract philosophy of language, in the style of the first Wittgenstein, who had only arrived at the *linguistic turn*, Apel later moved against those having discovered pragmatics, returned to a pre-communicative position. In addition, during the mid-eighties, Apel's discourse was more oriented to a confrontation with postmodern thought—Derrida, Lyotard, and especially Rorty—which he considered radical opponents of rationality. The *Philosophy of Liberation*, inspired by Latin American reality and also by Levinas's philosophy, could, for example, be regarded by Apel as a peripheral representative of such postmodernity. Let me elaborate.

2.1.2 Latin American Philosophy of Liberation

Without assuming the representation of a broad movement, the Philosophy of Liberation, which I have practiced since 1969, sets out from our particular regional reality: the increasing poverty of the majority of the Latin American population;[12] dependent capitalism, which transfers value to central capitalism;[13] the growing consciousness of the impossibility of an autonomous philosophy under these circumstances;[14] the existence of different types of oppression, which demands not only a philosophy of "freedom" but also a philosophy of "liberation" (as an action, as a praxis, the starting point of which is oppression, and its goal, *télos*, liberty from such oppressions as ancestral *machismo*, for example, in the case of women's oppression).[15]

Philosophically, starting from Heideggerian phenomenology and the Frankfurt school at the end of the sixties, the Philosophy of Liberation was inspired by the thought of Emmanuel Levinas, because it allowed us to clearly define the position of "exteriority" (as a philosophy, as popular culture, as the Latin American economy with respect to the United States, Japan, or Europe) as "poor", that is to say, from an anthropological and ethical economical level,[16] and in regards to a hegemonic "totality"[17]—political-authoritarian, economic-capitalist, erotic-*machismo*, cultural-imperialistic, fetishist religion, and so on. We were conscious of being the "other face" of modernity. Modernity was born in 1492 with the "centrality" of Europe eurocentrism originated when Europe was able to dominate the Arab world, which had been the center of the known world up to the 15th century). The "I," which begins with the "I conquer" of Hernàn Cortés or Pizarro, which in fact precedes the Cartesian *ego cogito* by about a century, produces Indian genocide, African slavery, and Asian colonial wars. The majority of today's humanity (the South) is the other face of modernity; it is neither pre- nor anti- nor postmodern, nor can this South "end" or "realize" such a modernity as Habermas pretends. In 1976, when I wrote the *Philosophy of Liberation*, before the European movement called postmodern,[18] I criticized modernity, inspired in the use of this concept by the late Heidegger.[19] We are not, as periphery, the Other *than reason*.[20] We pretend to validly express the reason of the Other, that of the genocidally murdered Indian, of the African slave reduced to merchandise, of women as sexual objects, of the child pedagogically dominated ("the lectern" objects as Paulo Freire defines them). We pretend to be the expression of reason, a reason of one who places him/herself beyond eurocentric, machist, pedagogically dominated, culturally manipulated, religiously fetishist reason. We propose a Philosophy of Liberation of the Other[21] that is beyond the horizon of the economic-political-hegemonic world (fratricide), of the eurocentric communication community (filicide), of the phallic eroticism which castrates women (uxoricide) and last but not least, the subject which uses nature as an exploitable mediation for the valorization of the value of capital (ecocide).

2.2 Interpellation

Our argumentative strategy will start from the most relevant of Apel's thought. This is located within the horizon of a transcendental philosophy of language.

In fact, Apel clearly points out how a mere "sentence" (p), the object of the post-linguistic-turn philosophy since Frege or the first Wittgenstein, remains subsumed in the "speech act" ($F \vdash p$), the pragmatic turn. Schema 1 offers the possibility of visualizing the problem. We have chosen a speech act which gives us the possibility to place the subject we pretend to expose from the perspective of a Philosophy of Liberation.

Schema 1. Sentence and the speech Act

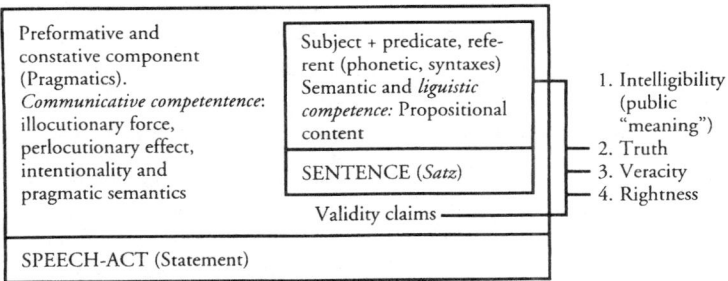

Our discourse starts, at least pedagogically, in an abstract form, from the Levinasean intuition that the "Other" (*Autrui*) is the *original* source of all possible discourse, which is essentially an ethical relation and "appeals" from the "exteriority." It means the irruption of the Other, of the poor (of the dominated woman, etc.) which "appears" *in* the "communication community" of current institutionalism, of the "totality," claiming and demanding justice.[22]

The initial "sentence" with its "propositional content" could thus be approximately stated:

1. *This is an act of justice.* Several speech acts can be expressed from this sentence. One of them could be developed as follows:

2. *You must fulfill the act of justice for me.*[23] Even more developed and if item 2 is not fulfilled, it could be stated:

3. *I accuse you for the justice you should have given me.*[24] The speech act to be taken into account, which may now seem incomprehensible, can thus be stated:

4. *I interpellate*[25] *to you for the act of justice you should have fulfilled for me.*

Since we are dealing with a speech act that is intentionally very peculiar and not with a mere sentence [object of theoretical or analytical understanding (*Verstand*)], we are located at an ethical level, or one of practical reason, the level of the "face-to-face," as Levinas would say, where two persons face each other without external mediation, except for the linguistic one. This is an encounter that takes place also through the immediate corporeality of both: proximity.[26]

2.2.1 Exteriority and Interpellation

We wish to distinguish interpellation from other speech acts, such as ordering:

5. *I order you to fulfill an act of justice for me.* Ordering may be followed by a sanction if the command was not fulfilled. I would also like to distinguish it from those speech acts such as asking or begging:

6. *I ask you to fulfill an act of justice for me.* This is a speech act which may be followed by remorse for an act of unfulfilled mercy, if the asking or begging is not accepted. Or that of demanding:

7. *I demand that you fulfill an act of justice for me.* Or even, and repeating item 2. in another way:

8. *It is your obligation to fulfill the act of justice for me.*

Which may be followed by various possibilities; one of which we will analyze next. In any event, in each of these cases, the speaker (S) places himself in a different position in front of the hearer (H). In a command (5.) S is the authority (from top to bottom) and H must obey (the arrow a of Schema 2). By begging, S is in a dependent position, while H now has the power of decision (6.; arrow b). Regarding the demand, S, from the current institutionalism, has the right to expect a (the perlocutionary effect) from H (that is to say, the fulfillment of the act of justice) (arrow c). In the "obligation" position (8.), S assumes a position of right (another way for arrow a). We would still propose one last case, interpellation in its normal sense:

9. *I appeal for the act of justice (I ordered, asked, demanded) you should have fulfilled for me.*

In this case, based on current norms, S makes H accountable (in the "totality" of the life-world (Lebenswelt) or even on the economic, political, "systems," etc.) (arrow *c*).

Schema 2. Intra- and Extra-Institutional Speech Acts

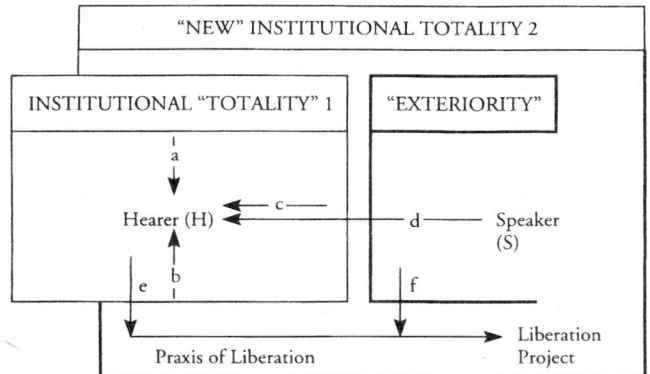

Explanation of schema: a, "command" speech act; b, 'begging"; c, "demand," "recrimination," etc.; d, "inter-appellation." Arrows e (from *H*) y f (from *S*) are the praxis which join in the construction of a Liberation Project (*Entwurf*) ("new" institutional moment 2).

The speech act which I call interpellation, and which I formulated in 4., is the one privileged by Emanuel Levinas but placed by him *before* his linguistic explanation, in the prior silence of the expression (according to the "principle of expressability"[27] developed by Searle).

By interpellation, then, I will understand a preformative, *sui generis* statement uttered by someone (*S*) which is, regarding a listener (*H*), "out" or "beyond" (in this sense, transcendental) the horizon or institutional frame, normative for the ruling "system," beyond the Husserlian-Habermasian *Lebenswelt* or the Hegelian *Sittlichkeit*, which acts as the totality[28] for Levinas. Searle is referring to the subject when he writes:

> Proudhon said: *Property is a theft*. If one tries to consider this as an *internal* observation, then it is non-sensical. It is meant as an *external* observation which attacks or rejects the institution of private property.[29]

For now, I only need this simple description of what is "outside" the institution. Marx refers to this type of situation in the following example:

> To speak here of natural justice, as Gilbart does ... is nonsense.... This content is just whenever it corresponds, is appropriate, to the mode of production. It is unjust wherever it contradicts that mode. Slavery on the basis

of capitalist production is unjust; likewise fraud in the quality of commodities.[30]

For Marx, bourgeois "morals," or "right," justifies "from inside" that which applies to its own principles. Slavery is unjust for the bourgeois or socialist order; it is just for the slavery order. Salaried labor is unjust for Marx or in the socialist regimes, insofar as it is an institutionalism which steals from the worker part of the product of his labor (surplus value). In this case, the ethical criterion is "external" and "prior" to capital as such; it is the living labor, the dignity of the person of the worker *ante festum*. This is the "ethical" criterion, the realm from which interpellation emerges and in which Levinas places himself in as far as the exteriority of the Other, as the other than and of the Totality (totality as both system and current *Lebenswelt*). In other words, to explain this better:

> Political economy therefore does not recognize the unoccupied worker, the working man insofar as he is *outside* this work relationship. The swindler, the cheat, the beggar, the unemployed, the starving, the destitute and the criminal working man are *figures* which exist for *for it*, but only for other eyes—for the eyes of doctors, judges, grave-diggers, beadles, etc. Nebulous figures [*specters*] which *do not belong within the province of political economy*[31] . . . the *abstract* existence of man as a mere *workman* who therefore tumbles day after day from his fulfilled nothingness [*Nichts*] into absolute nothingness, into his social and hence real non-existence.[32]

Interpellation would be the speech act of what Marx metaphorically called "specters which remain outside the province of political economy." All this is expressed in the testimony of Tupac Amaru, a rebel Inca of Peru, in 1781, when during his trial stated:

> We are the only conspirators, Your Honor, for having burdened the country with unbearable exactions, and I for *having wanted to liberate the people* from such a tyranny.[33]

The liberators who make the interpellation of the poor their own, in the end, are declared equally guilty by the established and ruling moral order. They are "specters" of another realm.

2.2.2 Interpellation and Validity Claims

a. First, let us consider the condition of all communication: intelligibility. The speech act which I have called interpellation has a propositional content (in trying to fulfill the first condition, that of intelligibility, that is to say, in stating an interpretable meaning), which the speaker (S), being an excluded "pauper," in the exteriority, may hardly formulate a sentence correctly, due to a certain linguistic incompetence[34]—from the hearer's (H) point of view—a phonetically defective pronunciation along with the Speaker's[35] lack of knowledge of the hearer's language and, essentially, the meaning in its full pragmatic[36] sense (and not reductively from a pre-communicative "semanticism"[37]) which S grants to 1 in 2. (see list of sentences above) and to both in 4. Therefore, at the beginning at least, only "quasi-intelligibility" is obtained, a quasi-communication, a quasi-interpretation of meaning, which puts us on guard regarding the real difficulty of all communication and of its necessary pathologies.[38] Full intelligibility becomes possible in a path of solidarity (in the praxis of liberation, represented by arrows *e* and *f* in Schema 2, as a diachronical process). Here we have at least to note the critical intention of the postmoderns—or Richard Rorty, for example—in the sense that communication can be frequently no more than an act of "conversation," who acknowledge the difficulty and maybe even impossibility of achieving full communication. Without agreeing with the postmoderns, we wish, however, to listen to the difficulties we suffer— as persons, cultures or peripheral philosophical communities, non-hegemonic, dominated, exploited, excluded—from communication. Let us take one more step.

b. We must now consider the first validity claim: truth. Since we are dealing with a performative utterance and not a *constatif* (assertive) one, it does not originally claim to be a true speech act. However, the propositional and full pragmatic content of the interpellative speech act allows us to develop it as a constative speech act (which subsumes the performative in this case). Subsuming 1. (see list above, p. 22), we have:

10. *I affirm that this is an act of justice.* Or, uttered as an speech act, which subsumes 2.:

11. *I affirm that you must fulfill the act of justice for me.*

Or subsumming 4.:

12. *I affirm that I appeal to you for the act of justice you should have fulfilled for me.*

In this case there could be a validity truth-claim, insofar as *S* (an Indian, a Turk in Germany, a woman) can try to intersubjectively justify (if it were to be problematized, thanks to a possible argumentative discourse) how just is his claim to reach an "agreement" on 1. and 2., an agreement which cannot be based on the obligations and responsibilities[39] of current right, norms, or institutions, but on transcendental ethical demands regarding the dignity of a pauper as person.[40] It must be considered that the "interpellant," and this is the basis for the difference with respect to a mere demand, or the difference between intra-systemic interpellation (from the current right and as a member of the "*real* communication community") and the interpellation of the Other (as the one that demands from outside, as one excluded from current right, the without-right *[rechtsloss]*), in principle "opposes" the current consensus and the "agreement" intersubjectively obtained *in a past (communication community) that excluded him/her*. His/her argumentation will be radical and, *in fact*, difficult accept.

c. Let us now consider the second validity claim: veracity. It deals with the essential moment of the interpellative speech act. The only communicative validation of this speech act, to be "accepted" with illocutionary force by the hearer (H), is neither full intelligibility (because, at the beginning at least, it is quasi-intelligible, because the full interpretation of meaning is a complex act), nor the truth (because it is not properly a constative speech act[41]), nor even a reference to norms or rightness (because the interpellation questions the current norms of hegemonic institutionalism), but definitely full "veracity." The hearer (H) does not have another genuine possibility for "serious communication" with S, except for his rational[42] "belief" or "acceptance" of the pauper's (S) sincerity regarding his interpellation. The latter, on the other hand, must express him/herself in such a way so that his/her "intention"[43] can be clearly interpreted, so that his sincerity and veracity may be disclosed because it they are the fundamental warrant of the communicative validity claim of his/her speech act. The aforementioned is intersubjectively valid because it is a statement resulting from a sincere act; it is sincere in its intention and performance. The "appealed" (H) *believes* that 1., is convinced in 4 (see list above, p. 22). before *f2* ("You must fulfill . . ."), and decides to act before *f1* ("I *appeal to you for* . . ."), due to the veracity of the one that "appeals." The "acceptance" of such sincerity is the effect of the illocutionary force, it is the perlocutionary effect (the effect which is the practical change of H, which will be turned into a responsible subject of a "liberating praxis," arrow *e* in Schema 2, in a solidarity action with S; and, thus, arrow *f* converges in a mutual praxis addressed to the "Liberation Project"[44]). These "beliefs", "convincement", "deciding" are rational, because one has discursively reached or is willing to reach an "agreement" through argumentation (even though all this, once again, has complexities and difficulties due to the existing asymmetry between S and H).

d. Let us now consider the third validity claim: rightness. As I mentioned, the interpellant, by definition, cannot fulfill the current norms. The norms (the dominating institutionalism) are the cause of his/her misery. In any case, insofar as the dignity of the person is assumed in all rational communication as the basic norm, ethically it can not affirm the current norms, questioning them from its own basis: from the dignity denied to the pauper who "interpellates." The non-normativeness of the interpellation is inevitable, since it is founded on the originary moment of a *new* normativeness—the future institutionalism where the interpellant will have effective rights.[45]

We could follow Searle on his account of the rules for the use of the indexical device of illocutionary force,[46] regarding "reference" and "predication" (applying what he exposes regarding the "promise" for interpellation), but this would take an exceedingly long time.

2.3 The Reason of the Other, Exteriority and the Community of Communication

What has been said should only be taken as an "indication," not as a description of the interpellative speech act, but it is sufficient to stage the argumentative strategy we wish to develop.

On our part, as Latin Americans, participants in a peripheral communication community, where the experience of exclusion is an everyday starting point that is to say, an *a priori*, and not an *a posteriori*, we must find "philosophical room" from our experience of misery, poverty, difficulty to discuss (due to lack of resources), uncommunicativeness, or merely not "being part" of the hegemonic communication community.

2.3.1 Exteriority and the Ideal Community of Communication

Part A,[47] or the ethical transcendental, in Apel's terminology, the *ideal* communication community[48] (or the "ideal speech situation," which is Habermas's "communication free of domination" [*herrschaftsfreie Kommunikation*][49]), must be differentiated from the mere, real, or empirical communication community, Part B, of ethics, where one can present cases of irrationality and injustice. We will place ourselves, first, in Part A, that of transcendental pragmatics (Apel) or universal pragmatics (Habermas), to complete the minimum description required for the performance of an argumentative rationality.

In fact, the unlimited communication community, as defined by Peirce (without coercion, with equality and respect for all the possible participating persons) defines what we could call the positive moment, but this is not explicit with reference to the negative moment. There would be a certain blindness in discovering the possible negative moments or those suppositions which always permit the irruption of disagreement (the non-agreement, the "dissent" of Lyotard) as the starting point for the development of all new argumentation, if the negative moment was not to be elucidated. That is to say, in rationality, even at the transcendental or universal level, it would be necessary to include as a moment of its definition, as a critical reason, the virtual exteriority (of diverse degrees) of each person, of each participant in the community as *one other* potential, but not yet, participant. The Other, not as "other" than reason but as the "reason" of the Other is the other reason which "interpellates" and from where one may show norms to be invalid or statements to be false.

The extended description of some determinations of the ideal communication community could be stated as: 1) all argumentation always presupposes an ideal communication community, free of domination, respecting the equality of personhood of all possible participants (positively), and 2) each of the current or possible members, presupposed *a priori*, both pragmatically and transcendentally, always have the right to place themselves as the Other in the community (*negatively*).[50]

Thus, it is then a community, and only because of this is it a *human* community (which is a redundancy), in which every member has the right to place himself within a certain exteriority of the community. Evidently there are degrees of exteriority, which range from those of the absolute situation (such as death and madness) to those of the right to dissent, which still does not yet find *sufficient* reasons to prove the validity of the *new* discovery—and probably will never find them—but which nevertheless had the right to reasonable dissent. There is virtual exteriority, which does not deny the community but always discovers it as a "re-union" or a "con-vergence" of *free* persons.[51] No "agreement" may be granted the claim of denying the possibility for each current or possible member to place him/herself before a community as an Other (this would amount to the "*absolute* agreement" in Hegel's account of "*absolute* knowledge [*Wissen*]." It would be the end of all possible argumentation). Reason, which bears that name, is always open to the "reason *of the Other*," to *another* reason and only this is a *critical* and *historical* reason; more than that, it is an *ethical* reason.

If this explicit determination is admitted in the description of "ideal" communication community, explaining the *negative* moment, we thus have a sort of path on which we will now be able to move to less abstract levels, having thereby also warranted the grounds for the "application" (*Anwendung*) of discourse ethics (in Part B).

2.3.2 Exteriority and the Scientific Community

In general, and with reason, more importance has been given in epistemology to scientific reason, referred to in the debate concerning explanation (*Erklären*). Apel showed that this always presupposes transcendentally a hermeneutic-comprehensive reason (*Verstehen*), which from an unlimited communication community intersubjectively opens itself to an every day life-world (*Lebenswelt*), in which all pragmatic statements[52] are uttered.

All this presupposes, evidently, "being-part" of the community, participating in a "linguistic game," in the "agreement." Our problem begins when one tries to explicitly problematicize the "non-agreement," the "dis-agreement" of that participant (or if not an actual participant, when he/she is excluded or simply ignored), which is no longer "in agreement" because of a "discovery" which is presented by him/her with the evidence of something with a truth-claim, not yet valid for the community, because the current agreement has not been falsified to that moment. Here I am interested in the "inventing" or the "discovering" moment (and the logic of the discovery, which may seem chaotic, as Paul Feyerabend's saw it[53]) more than in the "comprehension-explication" moment (of the logic of explanation).

From the moment a member of a community no longer agrees with the current agreement, because of a discovery given to him/her "as certain" (certainty not yet validated; that is to say, not publicly discussed and accepted as justified and, thus, as true or valid), the subjectivity of the discoverer is located with reference to the scientific communication community as Other.[54] It is not someone absolutely other, because it frequently starts from the same linguistic game, but it begins to be "alienated," distanced, made into an otherness. And there are even cases where the community expels them, excludes them (as in the case of Galileo, condemned by the Inquisition, under the power of Bellarmino); they are pursued and even killed—the "victims." The community, negatively and irrationally, based on an institutional inertia principle, defends itself against novelties, reaffirms the current agreement. Even though the community proposes it as falsiable, it impedes, fears and intends its agreement to be non-falsifiable. To start, the Philosophy of Liberation is interested in the novel and in scientific discoveries,[55] not as an end but as a moment in the realization process of a person's dignity.

In the same manner, the interpellation of the pauper is played at the scientific community's level by a speech act which could be called the proposal of the scientist (like arrow d of Schema 2):[56]

13. *I "propose"[57] this new explanation (or comprehension) x for the state of affairs z, not yet explained (or comprehended or not yet observed).*

If the proposal supposes a new paradigm (to speak like Kuhn), or a degree of greater than standard novelty, the discoverer is frequently, or for a certain period of time, not comprehended, excluded, not taken into consideration. It is the moment of experiencing a certain exteriority of being-Other from the scientific community, which begins to appear to him/her as outdated, overcame, closed—defending its interests with growing egotism.[58] What has to be remembered is that all new argumentation (and novelty bears, in the long run, the realization of an unlimited rationality in time) supposes placing oneself as the Other before those who continue sustaining that which is valid up to that moment. The scientists included in the annals of the history of science are the innovators who were to be honored, and their biographies relate their suffering, isolation, silence, and even obscure deaths.

These comprehensive lines of argumentation serve as an indication of the problematic.

2.3.3 Concrete Types of Interpellation. From those Excluded from their Respective Hegemonic Communities of Communication

Continuing with Part B, we can now return to the interpellation in the real, everyday communication community (in the life-world [*Lebenswelt*]), of every person who can argue because he/she is rational (and not because he/she has or does not have the ability or control of a science). Once again it is a question of exteriority, but now at various possible levels.

For example, Apel in *Diskurs und Verantwortung* discusses "social class conflicts"[59] or "North-South conflicts."[60] In reality the euphemism "conflict" does not clearly describe the structures of domination, exploitation, and alienation of the Other. In the subject we are discussing it is stated as "exclusion" of the Other from the corresponding communication community.

To start, it is worthwhile to underscore a point already mentioned. Habermas has proposed a distinction between life-world (*Lebenswelt*)[61] and system.[62] In an economic system, such as the capitalist, or political system, or the liberal democratic system (in the North American and West European societies), the life-world sustains a double relationship: on the one hand, it maintains a certain measure of exteriority, where subjectivity may insure for itself a genuine everyday room; and on the other, it is kept as a realm for colonization. However, the life-world (European-North American) of the North can locate the "world of life" of the South, the peripheral, for example, as the excluded, that which is "disconnected" (as Samir Amin wold say), the underdeveloped, the barbarian. That is to say, a life-world that is the hegemonic, dominating one that, with respect to the other worlds, exercises a function very similar to that of the colonizing systems.

a. We can begin, thus, with the interpellation which starts from the exclusion of persons of other races, by the racism of Apartheid in South Africa, Black discrimination in the United States, or discrimination of Turks in Germany, of Palestinians in Israel, of Afro-Americans[63] and Indians in Latin America in general. For example, the racially excluded launches an interpellation to the real communication community of the "whites." It holds them accountable for the legitimate rights which have not been granted or fulfilled. All that was discussed in paragraph 2.2, above, should now be specified in the case of the anti-racist interpellation. The struggle for the defense of equal racial rights is a central thematic of the Philosophy of Liberation.

b. In the same manner, in the *machistic* life-world, women, who with greater or smaller differences for all humanity, classes, and cultures, are dominated, alienated, and used as sexual objects (as indicated by Freud)[64] "appeal." Feminist liberation is also one of the central subjects of the Philosophy of Liberation.

c. In the same way, in a capitalist society, the domination of the salaried laborer, who must sell his living labor for money[65] to the owner of capital, appears as a new type of excluded from the communication community of businessmen, capitalists, the hegemonic members in the life world of the society colonized by the system they control. This is what the struggle of the classes consists in (always virtual for the anti-ethical essence of capital,[66] and frequently effective), a matter which Habermas and Apel no longer take into consideration, because they do not find it pertinent.

d. No less essential is the ecological problem, which Apel frequently contemplates, because it virtually excludes future generations from the benefits we are currently destroying. In this case, the responsible interpellation is launched by ecologists, with an acute and just ethical conscience. Even here, once again, they do not sufficiently take into consideration that the ecological destruction is to a great extent induced by industrial powers (North America, Europe, and Japan), while all humanity is held responsible. There is consciousness of the destruction of the Amazonian jungles, but not for the death of its Indians, nor for the fifty million northeasterners whom the Brazilian peripheral capitalism has impoverished to extreme and inhuman misery, who in order to eat have to destroy the jungle.

e. We must also remember the cultural eurocentrism (including the Anglo-North American culture), which plays the civilized life-world role for all human culture, and presents itself as the paradigm for all other cultures. Here, once again, the position of Richard Rorty regarding the "incommensurability" of an intercultural dialogue always remains healthy if we consider the irresponsibility of those who do not believe that the chore of dialogue also demands a theory that implies *the difficulties*. The members of another culture, the cultural Other, "interpellate" for their own cultural popular rights (Africans, Asians, Indians, Latin Americans, North American Blacks, et al.). It is a life-or-death struggle.

f. Last, maybe the most serious problem at the end of the 20th century, which began in 1492 (when Latin America was incorporated as the first European periphery,[67] because Africa and Asia up to the 19th century were only an exterior forum) is the ever increasing distance between the richness of Northern Central capitalism and the ever growing misery of Southern peripheral capitalism. Be it clearly understood: Africa, Asia, and Latin America (with the exception of China, Vietnam, Cuba, and some other countries) are "capitalist dependent" regions.[68] This is the subject that should be the focus of our dialogue: the interpellation which the majority of the population of the planet, located in the South, raises, demanding their right to live, their right to develop their own culture, economy, politics, etc.

This subject (because hunger, misery, poverty are effects of a capitalism which is exhibited as triumphant before Eastern European socialism, but which, in fact, impoverishes and peremptorily fails the South) demands from the Philosophy of Liberation that it overcome (and adequately integrate) mere pragmatic rationality to other types of rationality, which the Northern philosophy of developed capitalism pretends to abandon: the rationality of a practical, ethical economics; of an interpersonal communitarian relationship, and not only as a system, the way Habermas considers it and Apel accepts.

In any case, we agree with Apel that all interpellation in Part B must always proceed rationally, starting from a basic ethical norm which is presupposed in all argumentative discourse[69] (procedurally democratic), but which in our case, and because of the reality in which we live, gives more attention to the negative aspects of domination and to the demands for a liberation struggle at each of these levels: racial, erotic, social, cultural, economic, North-South, etc.

It would be too exhaustive to try to show, at this point, the different ways one may think these problems, such as the *a priori* responsibility for all life—and not *a posteriori* as is done by Apel and Hans Jonas—or that of an "ethical" consciousness, which does not apply principles as is done by the "moral" conscience. These are possible subjects for future dialogues.

2.4   From Pragmatics to Economics

The originary interpellation is, above all, a communicative act; that is to say, it explicitly puts in contact persons as persons (what we have called face-to-face). It is an encounter resulting from the illocutionary component of the speech act as such. In uttering the performative statement (from 2, see list above), in the first moment, S enters into a relationship, a communicative contact; she encounters H. The a in H effect may or may not be performed, even though it must be noted that the said encounter may not be performed, if H does not allow S to express herself or, simply, does not pay any attention to her utterance. Thus, it is necessary to analyze this same practical relationship ("ethical," according to Levinas) among persons, which cannot be identified as the "communicative action" of Habermas.

All relations among persons, as such, can be called *praxis* and not *poiesis*.[70] But a practical relationship is more than a mere communicative action. On the contrary, all communicative action is always a practical relationship. With this we want to point out that in practical relations there are other dimensions which are not exclusively communicative, even though every practical relationship (virtual or potential) must always be able to become a relationship when the linguistic or pragmatic communicative action is performed—on the "principle of expressiability" of Searle. That is to say, the communicative, linguistic, pragmatic, argumentative action can always be explained in all interpersonal practical relations. When someone shakes hands with another person, he/she may say nothing, or a practical relation may develop with a linguistic expression, such as:

14. *Good morning!*

But there are dimensions of the practical relation which are not only communicative, as for example, the erotic relationship—which Levinas considered to overcome the eidetic, intellectual, or wordly moment of the phenomenology. Consider the following expressions of Levinas of a trans- or pre-communicative erotics:

> In the caress, a relation yet, in one aspect, sensible, the body already denudes itself of its very form, offering itself as erotic nudity. In the carnal given to tenderness, the body quits the status of being [*étant*]".[71]
>
> Voluptuosity profanes; it does not see. *An intentionality without vision*, discovery does not shed light: what it discovers does not present itself as *signification* and illuminates no horizon.... Profanation, the revelation of the hidden as hidden, constitutes a model of being irreducible to intentionality.... It graps nothing, issues in no concept, does not *issue*, has neither the subject-object structure nor the I-thou structures.... Being-for-the-Other must not suggest any finality and not imply the antecedent positing or valorization of any value.[72] To be for the Other is to be good. The concept of the Other has, to be sure, no new content with respect to the concept of the I ... [t]he fact that in existing for another I exist otherwise than in existing for me is morality itself.[73]
>
> The relationship established between lovers in voluptuosity, fundamentally refractory to universalization, is the very contrary of the social relation. It excludes the third party, it remains intimacy, dual solitude, closed society, the supremely non-public.... The feminine is the other refractory to society, member of a dual society, an intimate society, *a society without language*.[74]
>
> Speech refuses vision, because the speaker does not deliver images of himself only, but is personally present in his speech, absolutely exterior to every image he would leave. In language exteriority is exercised, deployed, brought about.... Language is the incessant surpassing of the *Sinngebung* by the signification.[75]
>
> The ethical, beyond vision and certitude, delineates the structure of exteriority as such. Ethics is not a branch of philosophy, but *first philosophy*.[76]

We suggest that the effect of the illocutionary component, the practical-communicative relationship itself with the Other (face-to-face) in proximity, cannot be reduced to a communicative-linguistic act. The *Linguistic*, like the *erotic* or *economic* aspects of the practical relation, is a moment of the relationship.[77] And, as the performative moment could constitute a relationship under the ruling of instrumental reason (uttering a speech act to reach an effect *A*, but not to establish a face-to-face relation regarding the Other), in the same manner all the remaining dimensions (the erotic, the economic, etc.), may equally constitute themselves as the finality of an instrumental reason;[78] but not necessarily.

Gadamer demonstrated how the Heideggerian "finding oneself in the world" (*Befindlichkeit*) was always to "find oneself linguistically."[79] In the same way,[80] as living beings in a culture (as a material-symbolic instrumental totality), we can say that we always *a priori* live in a community and world where we find ourselves being instrumentally. The material instrument (Heidegger's hammer, Plato or Aristotle's shoe), product of human manual labor, analogously plays in economics the role of the sign in pragmatics. Let us observe the various

degrees of interpersonal and instrumental relationships in these three statements:
15. *I ask you to accept this flower as a gift.*
16. *I need you to trade this flower for this fruit.*
17. *I need you to buy this flower for x money.*

In the first case, 15, we are dealing with a gift. The flower (product of the labor-act of the gardener) is a mere free mediation of the interpersonal, face-to-face practical relation (which plays the role of the illocutionary moment performance). In the second case, 16, we find ourselves in a pre-monetary society of trade. In the third, 17, we are in a monetary interchange relationship (purchase-sale). In 17, the essential is not to forget that the interpersonal practical relation is always present, as an ethical, constitutive and genuine situation (regarding the medieval *Justitiam ad alterum est*). Let us see these aspects in a comparative scheme.

Schema 3. Pragmatic and Economic Moments

Efficient subject	Material effect	Practical relation		Receptor subject
		Genuine relationship	Instrumental reason	
Utters the speech act	Sign	Practical reason Communication	Instrumental effect[81]	Interpreter
Performs the labor act	Product or object (flower)	Economic community[83] relationship	Capitalist social relationship[84]	Consumer

As the speech act always presupposes *a priori* a communication community (ideal and factually real), in the same manner all labor acts (which, for example, produce something: a flower, bread, or wine) always presupposes *a priori* a community of producers, in order to fulfill "*human* life needs."[85] If Apel speaks of a "transcendental *pragmatics*" (at the linguistic-communication level), with the same right one could speak of a "transcendental *economics*" (at the productive-practical relationship level). That which is for a speech act the illocutionary moment, for the labor act is the practical relation with the Other, as clearly shown in the case of the gift (example 15.), which intentionally *a priori* determines all the productive process (I produce the flower "for" him/her). The moment of the interpersonal relationship (denied in the "social" capital relationship) is what Marx indicated when speaking of the community, of the "Realm of Freedom" or of "communism" (where each one would have to work "according to his/her capacity" and consume "according to his/her needs"[86]), the presupposed community always ideally *a priori* and factually denied in "capital" (as a "*social* relationship"[87]).

Here we are now able to consider the second example, specifying economically the abstract interpellation formulated in item 4 at the beginning of this paper:

18. *I "appeal" to you for the food[88] you should have given me.*

Giving something supposes a previous production, supposes the labor act of the material transformation of nature. It is not a sign, a material word as in the speech act. It is a product, a material object: flower, bread, wine, oil, food (products), as cultural symbol or food to eat, or an instrument (machinery, computer). But in this realm, economics is not merely a system (in the Habermasian sense[89]) which colonizes the everyday life-world (which can also be colonized by advertising and manipulative communication of instrumental reason by the media), but it is equally the *a priori* always presupposed in all labor acts or consumption acts: the community of producers/consumers (ideal or real; in the latter case colonized today by capitalism as a defective form of the domination of instrumental reason). But the community of producers/consumers, *transcendentally presupposed in all economic labor-act/consumption*, has as constitutive moment the establishment of an interpersonal practical relation (as much as, even though in another dimension, the illocutionary moment of a speech act). Communicative action or economic action are two dimmensions of the practical relation among persons.

The one who "appeals" from outside the real community of producers/consumers (whose material objects are also always cultural and symbolic), the "pauper," places as the content, referent, and meaning of his speech act (in statements 4. or 18.) his/her *suffering corporality* (what was implicit, presupposed in the interpellation launched before the one who had not assumed his responsibility before the Other). In modern history, the hearer (H) never heard the speech act, which at the end of our 20th century becomes an imperative:

19. *I am hungry, thus, 4 and 18!*

This suffering corporality is the subject of an economics in the critical (and even transcendental) sense of Marx. The "misery" (*Elend*) of the worker is the subject, but it has "noroom" in the bourgeois "moral system" (because it is only an intra-institutional moment, in Rawls' sense[90]). It is from that "noroom" (*ouk-topos*; Utopia) that interpellation emerged.

In all acts of work (economic, and not only technologically) one always presupposes *a priori* a community of producers, to reproduce life, which equally and radically presupposes an ethic,[91] in the same way that all speech act presupposes a communication community. But in both communities (which are truly two aspects of the same human community), insofar as they are real (not ideal), there are equally the excluded ones, the Others (but in a different way: some as speakers, others as producers-consumers). These Others, however, are not the others "of reason," but they are the Others who have their "reasons" to propose, to "interpellate" against exclusion and in favor of their inclusion in a community-of-justice.

The Other, excluded from the communities of communication and producers, is the pauper (as Marx used to say). The interpellation is an originary speech act, with which the pauper erupts into the real community of communication and producers (in the name of the ideal), and makes them accountable, demands a universal right, as a human being-part of the community; and, in addition, expects to transform it by means of a liberation praxis (which is also frequently a struggle), into a future, possibly more just society. It is the excluded one who appears from a certain *nothing* to create a *new* moment in the history of the community. He/she erupts, then, not only as excluded from the argumentation, affected without being-part, but as the excluded from life, from production and consumption, in misery, poverty, hunger, and imminent death. This is a painful problematic that produces a wound caused by the daily anguish of the premature death of the majority of people in Latin America, Africa, Asia, and the excluded so-called minorities in the metropolitan centers of the "North." This is the philosophical subject of the peripheral world, the South; this is the subject of the Philosophy of Liberation, a liberation from exclusion, from misery, from oppression. This is the foundation, reason (*Grund*), "reason (*Vernunft*) of the Other, a philosophy which has the right to give its reasons. There is no liberation without rationality; but there is no *critical* rationality without accepting the interpellation of the excluded, or this would inadvertently be only the rationality *of domination*.

To end, I would like to recall the ethical reflections of the Bedouins:

The wealthy speaks and many approve and consider eloquent the senseless speech. . . . *the pauper speaks with sense and the words are not regarded.*

The wealthy speaks and is heard in silence and the talent highly praised; *the pauper speaks and they say, "Who is he?" and if he falls over he is shoved.* (Ben Sira 13: 22–23).

Notes

1. See Apel's "Habilitation" in *Die Idee der Sprache in der Tradition des Humanismus von Dante bis Vico* (Bonn: Bouvier, 1963). Apel, beginning with Dante's discovery of the question of the "mother tongue," and going up through Vico's "institution of institutions" (language), treats the theme of intersubjective validity through language. He began on this path, in his doctoral dissertation, *Dasein und Erkennen. Eine erkenntnistheoretische Interpretation der Philosophie Martin Heideggers* (Doctoral Dissertation, Rheinischen-Friedrich-Wilhelm Universität, Bonn, 1950).
2. In German, *Transformation der Philosophie*. A partial translation has appeared in English: *Towards a Transformation of Philosophy* (London: Routledge, Kegan and Paul, 1980).

3. Apel, *Transformation der Philosophie* 1973, 1, p. 223; pp. 217ff.
4. Apel, 1973, 2, pp. 157ff. English, Apel, *Towards a Transformation of Philosophy*, trans. Glyn Adey and David Frisby. (London: Routledge Kegan & Paul, 1980), pp. 77ff.
5. This especially since his work "Das Apriori der Kommunikationsgemeinschaft und die Grundlage der Ethik" (translated as "The *a priori* of the Communication Community and the Foundations Ethics: The Problem of a Rational Foundation of Ethics in the Scientific Age," *Towards a Transformation of Philosophy*, pp. 225ff). This last article was elaborated between 1967 and 1972.
6. Apel immediately abandons the project of a "philosophical anthropology" and discovers the "already always presupposed ethics" in the communication community itself, still scientific. This question has formulated in the previously mentioned article.
7. This question absorbs the Apelian reflection up to the present. See, for example, Apel's "Notwendigkeit, Schwierigkeit und Möglichkeit einer philosophischen Begründung der Ethik im Zeitalter der Wissenschaft," in P. Kanellopoulos, ed. *Festschrift für K. Tsatsos* (Athens; Nomikai Ekoloseis Ant., 1980); up to the recent article; "Normatively Grounding "Critical Theory" through Recourse to the Lifeworld? A Transcendental-Pragmatic Attempt to Think with Habermas against Habermas" in Honneth, Axel, McCarthy, Thomas, et al., ed., *Philosophical Interventions in the Unfinished Project of Enlightenment* (Cambridge: The MIT Press, 1992).
8. I am thinking of Jürgen Habermas's work "What Is Universal Pragmatics?" in Jürgen Habermas, *Communication and the Evolution of Society*; and later *The Theory of Communicative Action*, 2 vols. These works gave Apel much material for reflection. In any event, the work of John Austin, *How to Do Things with Words* (Cambridge: Harvard University Press, 1962), and that of John Searle, *Speech Acts. An Essay in the Philosophy of Language* (Cambridge: Cambridge University Press, 1969), will be determinant in Apel's work.
9. In fact, J. Searle, in his *Intentionality. An Essay in the Philosophy of Mind* (Cambridge: Cambridge University Press, 1983), writes: "Language is derived from Intentionality and not conversely" (p. 5); or "We define speakers' meaning in terms of forms of Intentionaliy that are not intrinsically linguistic" (p.160). This leads Apel to critique Searle II from the perspective of Searle I of *Speech Acts*, in Apel's works "Linguistic Meaning und Intentionality: The Compatibility of the *Linguistic Turn* and the *Pragmatic Turn* of Meaning-Theory within the Framework of a Transcendental Semiotics" in A. Eschbach, ed., *Foundations of Semiotics* (Amsterdam: John Benjamin Pub. Co., 1989); with different versions in German: "Ist Intentionalität fundamentaler als sprachliche Bedeutung? Transzendental-pragmatische Argumente gegen die Rückkehr zum semantischen Intentionalismus der Bewusstseinsphilosophie" in *Intentionalität und Verstehen* (Frankfurt: Suhrkamp, 1990), pp. 13–54. For a slightly altered version in English see "Is Intentionality More Basic than Linguistic Meaning?" in E. Lepore and R. Van Gulick, eds. *John Searle and His Critics* (Cambridge: Basil Blackwell, 1991), pp. 31–55. The small work by Habermas "Intentionalistische Semantik" (1975–76), in *Vorstudien und Ergänzungen* (Frankfurt: Suhrkamp Verlag, 1984), pp. 332–351, is an anticipation of this problematic.
10. In Karl-Otto Apel *Diskurs und Verantwortung*, this intention can be observed, which departs from the challenge of Max Weber, and especially of Hans Jonas's *The Imperative of Responsibility: In Search of an Ethics for the Technological Age* (Chicago: The University of Chicago Press, 1984).

11. See his presentation in Hawaii of July 1989: "A Planetary Macro-Ethics for Humanity: The Need, the Apparent Difficulty, and the Eventual Possibility" in Karl-Otto Apel, *Ethics and the Theory of Rationality: Selected Essays*, Vol. 2 (Atlantic Highlands: Humanities Press, 1996).
12. Hence the need for a "philosophy of misery." Marx criticized Proudhon in *The Misery of Philosophy*, but, in reality, the important theme was already pointed to by Proudhon himself: misery. If in the Parisian marginality of the 19*th* century there were poor, this cannot be compared, in either relative or absolute numbers, with the poverty of the 20*th* century; that is, with the peripheral capitalism of India, Nigeria, or Brazil. Today there are a thousand times more poor people than there in 1847.
13. On the theory of dependence as re-thought in the present, see my work, "Marx's Economic Manuscripts of 1861–63 and the *Concept* of Dependency" in *Latin American Perspectives*, 17, 2, 1990, pp. 61–101.
14. Especially in the work of Augusto Salazar Bondy, *¿Es posible una filosofía en nuestra América?* (México: Siglo XXI, 1968).
15. We therefore should not only concern ourselves with a political-economic liberation, but also with an erotic liberation (see my work *Filosofía ética de la liberación*, vol. III (México: Edicol, 1977), whose Chap. is entitled "La erótica latinoamericana," pp. 50–122. In the same work I deal with "La pedagógica latinoamericana," pp. 123–226, which concerns the pedagogic liberation of the child, the youth, and thought through the experiences of the "Reforma de Córdoba en 1918" and 1968. Vol. 4 deals with political liberation: "La política latinoamericana" (Bogota: USTA, 1979), pp. 15–124. The fifth volume deals with the "Latin American Archeology: A Philosophy of Antifetischist Religion" (Bogotá: USTA, 1980). This work will be continued in 1993 with *Las metáforas teológicas de Marx*. We have thus traversed several "regions" of oppression-liberation, from the perspective of a Latin American poietics.
16. This hypothesis, when applied to a re-reading of Marx since 1976, can result in a new transcendental interpretation of the ethical *critique* of political economy as it was practiced by this great philosopher economist. See my recent *El último Marx (1863–1882)*, especially Chaps. 8 and 10, pp. 295–450.
17. As we will see later, this totality can also be the Habermasian *Lebenswelt* and also the "systems" (economic or political). The life-world can also functions as a ruling and dominating totality (in Levinas's thought). See Schema 2.
18. In *Philosophy of Liberation* I wrote in the prologue: "Philosophy of liberation, postmodern philosophy, popular, feminist, of the youth, of the oppressed, of the wretched of the earth, of the condemned of the world and history" (p. viii).
19. See Vol. 1 of my *Para una ética de la liberación latinoamericana*, Chap. 3, pp. 108ff, where I criticized the solipsistic totalization of modern thinking up to Husserl ("*Lo otro* como di-ferencia interna de la mismidad moderna," where I show that in the *Cartesian Meditation* of Husserl solipsism is not superseded), Heidegger himself, and the Frankfurt school. During those times, I criticized Adorno, Marcuse, et al. for remaining totalized in a "purely *negative*" dialectic, one without exteriority (See my *Método para una filosofía de la liberación. Superación analectica de la dialectica hegeliana* (Salamanca: Sigueme, 1974) where I attempted from Schelling up through Levinas to discover a "point of support" *external* to the totalizing solipsism of European thinking, which includes, as we have already indicated, the Frankfurt school itself. The confrontation with the later Heidegger, however, was carried out in Vol. 2, paragraphs 34 and 35: "La hermenéutica existenciaria" (pp. 141ff),

and "¿Es la tematización dialéctica el límite del pensar?" (pp. 146ff).
20. See J. Habermas, 11th lecture "An Alternative Way out of the Philosophy of the Subject: Communicative versus Subject-Centered Reason" in J. Habermas, *The Philosophical Discourse of Modernity: twelve lectures*, trans. Frederick G. Lawrence (Cambridge: The MIT Press, 1987), pp. 294ff, where Habermas refers to the expression *das Andere der Vernunft*, taken from the Böhme brothers' work *Das Andere der Vernunft*—a position which I do not share. Habermas has not considered seriously Levinas's work. I must also clarify that Levinas was determinant in the late sixties in my development of a Philosophy of Liberation, just as Feuerbach was able to help Marx (between 1842 and 1844): Levinas awakened us from the "closed" ontological dream. But we had to go beyond him rapidly because of his inability to develop a politics of liberation (see the doctoral thesis of Enrique Guillot, *La política de Emmanuel Levinas* [Universidad Nacional de Cuyo, Mendoza, 1975, 410 pages]).—Guillot is the translator of *Totality and Infinity* into Spanish. See my work *Emmanuel Levinas y la Filosofía de la Liberación* (Buenos Aires: Bonum, 1974), where I showed the points on which we needed to transcend Levinasean philosophy. In any event, for Levinas the Other is anthropologically the poor. Evidently, a Philosophy of Liberation took exteriority as the poor, and only years later could we develop this "analectic category" (of a critical political economy) through Marx (this is the fundamental intention of the four volumes which I have written on the four redaction of *Capital* and fetishism).
21. Through Schelling (see Dussel, *Método para filosofía de la liberación*. . . . pp. 116ff) we were able to point the theme. See the doctoral dissertation of Hans Schelkshorn, *Diskursethik und Befreiungsethik* (University of Vienna, March 1994, 450 pages). On the theme of the Other consult the work of Michael Theunissen, *The Other: Studies in the Social Ontology of Husserl, Heidegger, Sartre, and Buber*, trans. Christopher Macann (Cambridge: The MIT Press, 1984), which nevertheless does not deal with Levinas; and Berhard Waldenfels, *Das Zwischenreich des Dialogs* (The Hague: Nijhoff, 1971).
22. See my *Philosophy of Liberation*, 2.4.4.; *Para una ética de la liberación latinoamericana*, Vol. 1, paragraphs 16ff, pp. 118ff.
23. "You must fulfill" is the performative moment F. The formulation would be, just as we indicated above: $F \vdash p$
24. The formulation would then be: $F1 \vdash (F2 \vdash p)$. Incidentally, in the recrimination the responsible person is only made culpable for an improper act, but both subjects (the one who speaks, S, and the hearer, H) are passive.
25. From the latin *interappellare*, which does not exist in English. "Appeal," however, comes from the same root. We write the Spanish, *interpelar* (to confront someone asking them to give account of a responsibility or a contracted duty) between quotation marks in order to indicate that it has a meaning different from the usual one. In Latin *interpellare* is to "call" (*apellare*) or to "confront" someone, with whom a relationship is established (*inter-*); one interpellates before a judge in a tribunal (the responsible). In contrast to recrimination, *interpelar* is active, it demands a reparation, a change.
26. In *Philosophy of Liberation* I distinguished between *proxemia* (relation between "things" or with things) and *proximity*: the practical relation between persons (paragraph 2.1).
27. *Speech Acts*, 1,5 (pp. 19ff). That one may be able to "express" a speech-act does not imply that "the thing said" (*le dit*) is the same thing as "the saying" (*le Dire*) of the "face-to-face" that is always already presupposed. The "illocutionary moment"

(and even the "illocutionary act" as a "communicative act") is precisely what Levinas calls the "face-à-face": "The fact that the face maintains a relation with me by *discourse* does not range him in the same; he remains absolute within the relation.... For the ethical relationship which subtends discourse is not a species of consciousness whose ray emanates from the I; it puts the I in question. This putting in question emanates from the other." (Emmanuel Levinas, *Totality and Infinity*, p. 195). "It is not the mediation of the sign that forms signification, but signification (whose primordial event is the face to face) that makes the sign function possible" (ibid., p. 206). "If, on the contrary, reason lives in language, if the first rationality gleams forth in the opposition of the face to face, if the first intelligible, the first signification, is the infinity of the intelligence that presents itself (that is, speaks to me) in the face..." (ibid., p. 208). "The thing becomes a theme. To thematize is to offer the world to the Other in speech" (ibid., p. 209). My entire work, *Philosophy of Liberation* is based on this fundamental category of "proximity"(which Habermas would call the "illocutionary moment" of the performative speech act).
28. See Martin Jay, *Marxism and Totality* (Berkeley: University of California Press, 1984).
29. Ibid., p. 186. In paragraph 59 of John Rawls's *Theory of Justice*, pp. 382ff, which deals with "The Role of Civil Disobedience," the author contemplates the "illegal device" of a just act which has its support in the constitution: "The parties would adopt the conditions defining justified civil disobedience as a way of setting up, within the limits of fidelity to law, a final device to maintain the stability of a just constitution," (ibid, p. 384). But, what if the constitution were unjust or no longer valid (as English law was no longer valid for Washington, the liberator)? Rawls situates "civil disobedience" *between the constitution and the proclaimed law*. How can civil disobedience be located *between the basic ethical norm and the constitution*? This is the case that we would like to define as "trans-institutional," namely, as "outside" the institution. That is where the *Philosophy of Liberation*, Levinas, or Marx locate themselves, and certainly not Rawls or Habermas.
30. Karl Marx, *Capital*, Vol. 3, p. 339–40; German: *MEW* 25, pp. 351–52.
31. Karl Marx, *Economic and Philosophic Manuscripts of 1844*, in Karl Marx *Early Writing*, p. 335; German: *MEW*, EB 1, p. 523.
32. Ibid., p. 336. For the sense of this term, see my works *La producción teórica de Marx* (Mexico: Siglo XXI, 1985), pp. 140ff; *Hacia un Marx desconocido* (Mexico: Siglo XXI, 1988), pp. 61ff; and Chap. 10 of *El último Marx (1863–1882)* (Mexico: Siglo XXI, 1990).
33. B. Lewis, *La rebelión de Túpac Amaru* (Buenos Aires: Paidos, 1967), p. 392.
34. "Incompetence" not because of irrationality, but because the institutional world of H is unknown, it is not the same as that of S.
35. Here I refer to, for example, an Indian who would make a pronouncement to a Hispanic *conquistador* of the 16th century in Mexico or Peru; or a Turk who may express him/herself in incorrect German to an employer in Germany.
36. "Full pragmatic meaning" supposes not only the "conceptual content" of the "propositional content" of a sentence (p), but the "mental intention" (with its "intentional content") which has its "meaning intention." This entire level of "intentionality" is simultaneously given at the same level of the "sign", name, or term, which directs itself to a "designatum" that cannot be identified with the *real* "denotatum" (the object of the "reference dimension). The "meaning," in a pragmatic sense, ought to, in addition, take in to account that the "denotatum" (the

referent) is situated within the inter-subjective sphere of "public validity," or within the "agreement" of an "unlimited communication community" (always presupposed by any "meaning intention" or "meaning content.") Therefore, as in the case of the "poor" who "interpellates," the search for a *publicly sharable meaning-claim* (Apel, "Linguistic Meaning and Intentionality" p. 56) turns into an impossible task since the "public intersubjectivity" is that of a *real* communication community, of a "life world" hegemonized by another culture, another language, etc., where the "poor-excluded" cannot reach to *signify* what his/her "communicative intention" pretends.

37. Apel's article, mentioned in the prior note, give us an opportunity to clarify several things. The "poor" certainly have "meaning intentions," as much in "interpelar" (*F1*), as in demanding the fulfillment of a duty by the hearer (*H*), out of their right as a transcendental person with respect (this is the entire question of *reference*) to the established order (institutionality 1, of Schema 2) (*F2*), as well as item 1. ("an act of justice," *p*). The poor's "referential intentionality" directs itself to a historically possible "denotatum." (See my article, based on my Freiburg dialogue with Apel: "Die *Lebensgemeinschaft* un die *Interpellation des Armen*. Die Praxis des Volkes," 2; in Fornet-Betancourt, ed., *Ethik und Bekreiung* (Aachen: Augustinus Buchhandlung, 1990), pp. 74–77. It is obvious that the "public validity" of the "denotatum" (a "pro-ject of liberation" which delineates itself as an intended finality in "hope"—in E. Bloch's sense of the *Hoffnungsprinzip*) cannot be "understood" or "correctly interpreted" by *H* (who finds himself in a ruling and hegemonic "institutional totality 1").

38. J. Habermas, in "Considerations on the Pathologies of Communication" in *Vorstudien und Ergänzungen*, pp. 226–71, deals with the questions of pathologies, what we could call *intra-systemic* pathologies. I am referring to the quasi-pathology (or what appears as a pathology to *H*), in the case in which *S* finds itself outside the normativity and life world of *H*. Thereof the difficulty of the four validity pretentions required for communication: "to *express* oneself intelligibly, to make understandable *something*, and thus to make *oneself* intelligible, and to be understood *by others*." Habermas, *Vorstudien und Ergänzungen*, p. 233.

39. In its daily sense, responsibility is to assume charge for someone (Latin *spondere*: to take charge of someone). In a Levinasean sense, "res-ponsibility" is to take charge of the Other, the poor, she who finds herself without the protection or security of the ruling institutionality. See my *Philosophy of Liberation*, 2.1.2.2 and 2.6.3; and especially my work *Religión* (Mexico: Edicol, 1980).

40. It is here where the question of an "ultimate foundation of ethics" receives its entire meaning, since the life world, or *Sittlichkeit*, of a *conquistador* cannot be the last point of reference of an argumentation or "discourse" (although in fact it has always been, and there never was or has been in reality an argumentative communication community in which the Indian could give his reasons). The violence of the Conquest was the way in which modernity opened its way from 1492 up to today. It was not thanks to "argumentation," as Bartolomé de las Casas intended in his work *The Only Way*. The United States occupies Panama by force, and the moral consciences of the West applaud. Hussein occupies Kuwait, and everyone, scandalized, protests. The "dictator" Hussein should not be compared to Bush? We need a "planetary ethics" where the South is considered human, persons with equal rights.

41. In addition, it would be extremely difficult—because of their own culture, etc—*to justify* the validity of the truth of his pronouncement, which opposes itself to

everything which is held as true or "justified" within the normativity of the life world of a hegemonic system.

42. This has been the source of the misunderstanding in which Liberation Philosophy is accussed of fideism. The rational "faith" act has to do precisely with the rational evaluation which precedes the "acceptance" of the veracity of the Other (*Philosophy of Liberation*, 2.4.7, pp. 45–47).

43. Here the "intention" is complex. There is intention to meaning (thus it is expressed) a "propositional content" (p); furthermore, an intention to manifest a "right" ($F1$), and another intention of demanding rights through interpellation to H as responsible for the fate of S ($F2$). The complete analysis of this pragmatic-linguistic intention would take us again to Apel's article ("Linguistic Meaning and Intentionality"). The important thing is not to separate, although knowing how to distinguish them, between the intentional and linguistic moments within the frame of reference of a pragmatic community always already presupposed. But, again, in the case of S all of this turns problematic because of her actual, empirical *exteriority*.

44. On this theme I have written a paragraph in *Para una ética de la liberación latinoamericana*, Chap. 2: "El Otro, el bien común y el Infinito", pp. 59ff. In 1971, when writing these lines, I was distancing from myself Levinas when discovering the necessity of "a *new* political Totality" (p. 62), or, in other words, the future historically possible order, which is neither the actual "*real* community" nor the ideal (it is a *tertium quid* that Apel does not consider, because for him there is only an "open society" and "ideal"; for us there are: 1) "closed society," 2) "historically possible society of liberation," and 3) "ideal community." This is the difference between being in the rich North or in the poor South. The North does not need to change radically the society in which it finds itself; the South, instead, needs this change, and urgently.

45. Rawls's *A Theory of Justice* departs always from a given institutionalization (in fact the North American). See for instance the following text: "By major institutions I understand the political constitution and the principal economic and social arrangements. Thus the legal protection of freedom of thought and liberty of conscience, competitive markets, private property in the means of production, and the monogamous family are examples of major social institutions" (ibid., paragraph 2, p. 7). Rawls always speaks of the "least advantaged" (see paragraph 13, p. 75), but he never asks: "From where have these historical differences emerged?" The structures of domination have been dehistoricized (or they have been naturalized). Better said, perhaps, is that there is no consciousness of domination in Rawls. Our interpellation locates itself, then, underneath and before Rawls's "original position."

46. *Speech Acts*, III, 3.3 (p. 62ff). It would be worthwhile to go step-by-step through Searle in order to clarify conclusively this interpellative speech act.

47. On Part A of discourse ethics see "Diskursethik als Verantwortungsethik—eine postmetaphysische Transformation der Ethik Kants," Fornet-Betancourt, ed., *Ethik und Befreiung*, pp. 21ff.

48. In 1969 Apel spoke of an "unlimited communication of critics," or the "critical communication community" ("Wissenschaft als Emanzipation?" in *Transformation der Philosophie*, Vol. 2, pp. 153–54). From then on the texts become frequent. Apel recognizes that for this community there exist some essential determinations: namely an "unlimited communication community of *persons* who recognize each other as equals" ("Notwendigkeit, Schwierigkeit und Möglichkeit einer philosophischen

Begründung der Ethik im Zeitalter der Wissenschaft" in P. Kanellopoulos, ed. *Festschrift für K. Tsatsos* (Athens: Nomikai Ekdoseis Ant. 1980), p. 264).

49. The theme of Apel's ideal communication community receives a different treatment by Habermas. Thus, for instance, in "Warheitstheorien" (*Vorstudien und Ergänzungen*), Habermas writes: "I call ideal a speech situation in which communication is neither hindered only by contingent external factors, nor by the co-actions which follow from the very structure of communication" p. 177.

50. Someone may object that this possibility cannot obtain because another person that is "other" stops being a person. It then becomes the question of defining the *degrees* of "exteriority" that reason knows how to deal with practically and daily. The question rides on considering explicitly the "rights of the *other* reason": "the reason of the Other." This has not been negated by Apel. It simply has not been made explicit, and this is required in order to continue our argumentation.

51. And "free" of "domination" (*herrschaftsfrei*) means, exactly, to be able to situate oneself in the exteriority of the community itself; for it is the free subjects which can, through their "alterity," constitute a community (the "thou" as *alien*). A community without virtual exteriority would be that of a hegemonic, dominating, *one dimensional* reason (which Marcuse criticized in his famous book).

52. See Karl-Otto Apel, *Understanding and Explanation: A Transcendental-Pragmatic Perspective*, trans. Georgia Warnke (Cambridge: The MIT Press, 1984), which contains an exceptionally profound account of the thematic that in the decade of the eighties was still central, but which is in crisis today because of the abandonment of the Hempelian position.

53. Apel criticized Feyerabend's irrationalism and Lyotard's position (see *Diskurs und Verantwortung*, pp. 156ff). Apel states: "Und Erfindung (*invention*) entsteht immer aus dem Dissens. Postmodernes Wissen ist nicht einfach ein Werkzeug der Autoritäten, es verfeinert unsere Sensibilität für Differenzen un verstärk unsere Fähigkeit, das Inkommensurable zu tolerieren. Sein Prinzip ist nicht die Homologie der Experten, sondern die Paralogie der Erfinder" (p. 158). Paul Feyerabend appears as the irrational, the anti-methodical. But what if he precisely indicates the difficulty with a *logic of discovery*? Is not a "discovery" the creative moment par excellence of every science? Are not the great "discoverers" of science (Newton, Einstein) whom science remembers as its founders? What is essential to science is "explanation," but every explanation was "discovery" in its origin.

54. Luis Villoro in *Creer, saber, conocer* (México: Siglo XXI, 1982), pp.145ff, has formulated this problem ("epistemic communities"): "If in the epoch of scientific normality the consensus of the scientific communities approach intersubjectivity, this situation is *ruptured when the problems that normal science can not solve are formulated*. When *new* reasons appear ... the progress of knowledge is not possible if this discrepancy is not admitted. ... A *person* may be justified in affirming that they know although the general consensus denies it" (pp. 151–52). This work, of great importance for the Latin American philosophy of language, however, still situates itself in a pre-pragmatic or pre-communicative moment; that is, what is there affirmed would have to be unfolded within a communicative or pragmatic horizon in order to be able to reach new possibilities of description. Thomas Kuhn himself calls this the "emergence of a discovery or a new theory" (*The Structure of Scientific Revolutions* [Chicago: University of Chicago Press, 1962]). For Kuhn, the appearance of new paradigms is not a question of the accretion of new discoveries, but complete changes in perspective (ibid., pp 144ff). This is the whole question of alterity, the new, and that which cannot be anticipated from within a

given interpretative horizon. Richard Rorty explores this question also when he writes: "So bad arguments for brilliant hunches must *necessarily precede* the normalization of a new vocabulary which incorporates the hunch. Given that new vocabulary, better arguments become possible, although these will always be found question-begging by the revolution's *victims*" (*Philosophy and the Mirror of Nature* [Princeton: Princeton University Press, 1979], p. 58; n. 28). Latin American Philosophy of Liberation finds itself in this situation.

55. See my work "Histoire et praxis (orthopraxie et objectivité)" in *A la recherche du sens/In search of meaning*, Revue de l'Université d'Ottawa (Ottawa) 4, Vol. 55 (Oct.–Dec. 1985), pp. 147–61, a *Festschrift* in honor of Paul Ricoeur, as a reaction to a presentation by Carlos Pereyra (Oaxtepec, 1984).
56. The "institutional totality 1" is the community of scientists as an already superseded paradigm by the subjectivity of the discoverer (*S*). The praxis of liberation is now the constructive action of a new scientific community ("*new* institutional totality 2"), which departs from another paradigm, theory, explication, or agreement.
57. I "propose" (put forward, place before) or "to consider" (*pro-poner*) are placed in quotation marks in order to indicate this stronger sense.
58. Richard Rorty refers to another type of egotism when he writes, not without a certain sadness: "My story has been one of struggles between different kinds of professors, professors with different aptitudes and consequently with different paradigms and interests. It is a story of academic politics—not much more, in the long run, than a matter of what sort of professors come under which departmental budget" (Rorty *The Consequences of Pragmatism* (Minneapolis: Minnesota University Press, 1982), p. 228). It is at this level of the "*real* scientific community" that the theme of exteriority plays all of its role: the tolerance of which Rorty speaks can only be founded on the equal dignity of the reason of the other. This does not negate that there is reason; rather it suggests that there is a reason that is critical, historical, open to *other* reason (in its double sense, namely, open to other arguments and other persons with *their* other reason).
59. Karl-Otto Apel, *Diskurs und Verantwortung*, pp. 20ff.
60. Ibid. In his presentation from Hawaii (1989), "A Planetary Macro-Ethics for Humanity: The Need, the Apparent Difficulty, and the eventual Possibility" *Ethics and the Theory of Rationality, Selected Essays*, Vol. 2 (Atlantic Highlands: Humanities Press, 1996) Apel proposed a "universally valid principle of co-responsibility." But, with Rawls in mind, what type of global legality can there be in the organization of the United Nations when the great powers have veto power (an anti-rational, anti-democratic principle, and, in reality, non-*herrschaftsfrei*)? In reality, at the level of North-South relations imposed by the United States, there exists the irrationality of violence. How can one, from this juridical fact, think of co-responsibility?
61. This "Lifeworld" is of Heideggerian origin, inasmuch as the facticity of being-in-the-world, from which (the later) Husserl developed his own notion of *Lebenswelt*, and from where later social scientists are inspired to develop a social phenomenology, such as Alfred Schütz's. See Alfred Schutz and Thomas Luckmann, *The Structures of the Life-World*, trans. Richard M. Zaner and H. Tristan Engelhardt (Evanston: Northwestern University Press, 1973).
62. See Habermas, *The Theory of Communicative Action*, 2 volumes, (Boston: Beacon Press, 1983–87).
63. See my article "Racismo y América latina negra" in *Servir* (México) 86, 1980, pp. 163–210.

64. See my *Filosofía ética de la liberación*, vol. III, "La erótica latinoamericana."
65. This is the theme of "economics"—still in a universal or transcendental sense, virtually—just as Marx formulated it. It concerns a "critique" (from the exteriority of living labor) of the capitalist system as an anti-ethical perversion of the communitarian "practical relationship." We will deal with this in section 2.4, below.
66. See my *El último Marx (1863–1882) y la liberación latinoamericana*; Chap. 10.4: "El capital es una ética" (pp. 429ff).
67. This is the correct thesis by Emmanuel Wallerstein in his work *The modern World System. Capitalist Agriculture and the Origins of the European World Economy in the Sixteenth Century* (New York: Academic Press, 1974).
68. See my article on the concept of dependency cited in note 13, where I deal with the issue of the transfer of value from the South to the North.
69. Apel describes this problem in the following manner: "Who argues—and this means, one who, for example, seriously formulates the question of the basic ethical norm in a dialogue or also in a solitary self-understanding qua internalized dialogue—can be led to recognize or to be convinced through self-reflection that, necessarily, inasmuch *as arguer*, he or she has already recognized a *basic ethical norm*. The arguer has already given evidence *in actu*, and with that has recognized that *practical reason* is *responsible for human action*. That is to say, that the *truth pretensions* can and ought to be satisfied through *arguments*. This means that the *ideal rules of argumentation* in an, in principle unlimited, communication community of persons who recognize each other reciprocally as equals, represent *normative conditions of possibility of the decision on ethical validity claims [ethischen Geltungsansprüchen] through the formation of consensus*, and that therefore, *with respect to all the ethically relevant questions of practical life, it is possible, in a discourse* which respects the rules of argumentation of a an ideal communication community, to *arrive*, in principle, at a *consensus*, and, therefore, that one *ought to aspire* to bring about this consensus in practice" Karl-Otto Apel, "Notwendigkeit, Schwierigkeit und Möglichkeit einer philosophischen Begründung der Ethik im Zeitalter der Wissenschaft", in P. Kanellopoulos, ed., *Festschrift für K. Tsatsos* (Athens: Nomikai Ekdoseis Ant., 1980), pp. 264–265.
70. See my work *Filosofía de la producción*. The *praxis* relation is practical (in a last instance, ethical); the *poiesis* relation is technological. The economic relation is ethical-technological (practical-poietical) and not only productive (as is reductively interpreted by Habermas in his "Excursus on the Obsolescence of the Production Paradigm," against Marx, in his *The Philosophical Discourse of Modernity*, (Cambridge: The MIT Press, 1987) pp. 75–82). Habermas does not arrive at the discovery of the moment of the "practical relation" (ethical or interpersonal) that is included in economics.
71. Emmanuel Levinas, *Totality and Infinity*, p. 258.
72. Note the concepts of "instrumental" or "strategic" reason.
73. Ibid., pp. 260–61.
74. Ibid., pp. 264–65. This could be understood along the lines of the second Searle, and even still more radically. However, by the "principle of expressibility" we could say that it is "a society without language," *still*, in the "origin" of language and qua language "already presupposed but not expressed." The following text expresses this sense.
75. Ibid., pp. 296, 273. Now language is made "explicit." It is "expressed."
76. Ibid., pp. 304, 281. "La morale n'est pas une branche de la philosophie, mais la philosophie première." What Levinas calls "La morale" is here translated as "ethics,"

and has parallels with Habermas's "communicative action," but is even more radical.
77. Once again we agree with Apel, as with the theme of "intention" in the second Searle, namely, that intention, linguisticality or significance (as much the sign as the meaning) are given organically, co-implicated, simultaneously. To have an intention is to constitute it linguistically. In other words, the "economicidad" (the *economic* relation between persons by means of *instrumentalized* culture, even if it is the hand itself, as Aristotle put it: "the tool of all tools"; that is, as corporality) is also simultaneously co-implicated and organically related to intentionality, linguisticality, etc.
78. And this case would be, for example, an economic colonizing system of the life world.
79. See Hans-Georg Gadamer, *Truth and Method* trans. Joel Weinsheimer and Donald G. Marschal (New York: Continuum, 1993) part III, pp. 381ff.
80. It is interesting that in *Sein und Zeit*, paragraph 15, the analysis begins with the *Werkzeug* (tools), which is precisely to "find oneself instrumentally" (in a cultural, technical, material, and symbolic sense) always already.
81. If the performative act transforms itself into the fundamental intention of the speech act, then it is a matter of an act of instrumental reason and not of communicative reason.
82. The Consumer is the Receiver of the gift, the other party of the exchange or the buyer. In the end, these are moments which are accomplished *in actu*, in the use or consumption.
83. We will see the meaning of this *communitarian* relationship (*gemeinschaftliche Verhältnis*) in Marx.
84. For Marx the "social [*gesellschaftliche*] relation" has an instrumental sense, as we will see. The capitalist constitutes the person, the living labor, as a means (an instrument for the valorization of value: thing) and not as an end in itself (the person). The commodity (or the increase in the rate of profit) is the goal of the productive act of capital, and as much is an act of instrumental rationality. It is strange that Habermas (or Apel) has not been able to reason in this clear and evident manner. Can it be that because "they find themselves trapped within the bourgeois horizon" (as Marx loved to write) they cannot account for their own life world as it falsely projects itself as the actual-universal-human world (*Spätkapitalismus*)? In the example given, the flower is a product of the labor from which surplus value was obtained (that is, ethically, from the trans-institutional right of the person of the worker, and not "morally" from the capitalist system, as robbery), and which is sold in an *instrumental* "practical relation" (in the speech act it is the performative).
85. Apel writes: "Furthermore, I believe that the members of the communication community (and this implies all thinking beings) are also committed to considering all the potential claims of all the potential members—and this means all human 'needs' inasmuch as they could be affected by norms and consequently make *claims* on their fellow human beings. As potential 'claims' that can be communicated interpersonally, all human 'needs' are ethically relevant" (Apel, "The a Priori of the Communication Community and the Foundations of Ethics: The Problem of a Rational Foundation of Ethics in the Scientific Age," Karl-Otto Apel, *Towards A Transformation of Philosophy*, paragraph 2.3.5, p. 277. To speak of "needs," evidently, means to refer to the needing-productive-consuming corporality. It is to go over to the level of economics.
86. It concerns, precisely, an "ideal" (transcendental?) which is *a priori* to every act of

production or consumption. The community (*Gemeinschaft*) is the ultimate horizon of the constitution of all philosophical-economic categories of Marx (See my work *La producción teórica de Marx* pp. 87ff, 265ff, 291ff, 355ff. This is the horizon where the question of fetishism is formulated; see my work *Hacia un Marx desconocido*, pp. 226ff; it is the transcendental formulation of the "kingdom of freedom" (this theme is elaborated in my work *The metáforas teológicas de Marx*). In fact, according to Apel, "*The realm of freedom [Reich der Freiheit]* really begins only where labour determined by necessity and external expediency ends; it lies by its very nature beyond [*jenseits*] the sphere of material production proper. Freedom, in this sphere, can consist only in this, that socialized man, the *associated producers*, govern the human metabolism with nature in a rational way, bringing it under their collective [*gemeinschaftliche*] control instead of being dominated by it as a blind power" (This refers to Part A of Apel) (Karl Marx, *Capital*, Vol. 3, pp. 958–59; German: *MEW*, 25, p. 828). That which for Marx was "beyond" as a transcendental "after" is, for Apel, a "beyond" as presupposed (*Vor-aus-setzung*) transcendental. It is not difficult to see the Kantian-Hegelian presence. In the *Critique of the Gotha Program*, Marx proposes an ethical norm *that is not possible to institutionalize*: "from each according to his capacity; to each according to his needs!" (*MEW*, 19, p. 21). It is my opinion that Marx touches on the transcendental problem or the "regulative idea" of an *utopian-transcendental* "community of producers." This would be the "economics" in his Part A.

87. This is dealt with in my three volumes of commentary on the four redactions of *Capital*, already cited. I think that, as with all peripheral production (and in the Spanish language) this work, in fact and until now, remains "excluded" from the European-North American philosophical communication community. It is a question, then, of a "manuscript" published for the "critique of rodents." On the difference between the "social" (defective) and "communitarian" (genuine) relationship see my work *El último Marx (1863–1882) y la liberación latinoamericana*, Chap. 10.4, notes 131 to 148.
88. Food, clothing, housing are the three fundamental *human*-material needs (see F. Engels, *The Origin of the Family*, prologue; *MEW* 21, pp. 27–28: "Nahrung, Kleidung, Wohnung"), where there is a coincidence with the founder of Christianity, whose absolute ethical criterion is formulated as: "For when I was hungry, you gave me food; when thirsty, you gave me drink; when I was a stranger, you took me in your home; when naked, you clothed me" (Matthew, 25: 42–44. In item 18, the South "appeals" to the North, for "food" symbolically; objectively, for the economic and political system that the South has a right to constitute, and that has been blocked by the colonial powers since the 15th century: neocolonialism under mercantilism, imperialism in the 19th century, and financial-transnational in the 20th century.
89. Apel refers to the science of economics (see *Diskurs und Vertantwortung*, pp. 270ff: "Diskursethik als Vertantwortungsethik und das Problem der ökonomischen Rationalität"), but he deals with economics as an empirical science and not in the transcendental sense which we have given it in our re-reading of Marx.
90. We have already made reference to *A Theory of Justice*, to the whole second section: "Institutions." Marx refers to how, theoretically, the intra-institutionality disallows arriving at a critical interpretation (which is what takes place in Rawls, and perhaps also with Habermas): "from the bourgeoise point of view, within the *limits of capitalist understanding*" (*El capital* III, cap. 15, III; *MEW* 25, p. 270). Here we could copy, applying it analogically, Apel's text from note 69: "Who *works* . . .

has already recognized a basic norm.... One who *works* has already given testimony *in actu* that practical reason, which regulates the act-of-work, is responsible for the pretension of *justice* in the community and with respect to the Other (and not merely of the validity, because we are at the level of *economics* and not that of *pragmatics*), and said pretention ought to be satisfied through the technically adequate acts-of-work (analogically to linguistic competence) and ethically just." All of this will have to be developed in the future.

91. In the previously cited paragraph "*Capital* is an Ethics," Chap. 10.4, of my work *El último Marx*, pp. 429–49, I justified this affirmation. I ought to indicate that presupposed "ethics" is the same for a "community of producers" as it is for a "communication community"; although it may specify some different principles.

3

Toward a North-South Dialogue[1]

I have noted elsewhere that the thought of Karl-Otto Apel is extremely healthy for Latin American philosophy, especially as it concerns his critical stance toward the linguistic turn,[2] which he does not negate but instead subsumes under his pragmatics. In this manner, the "communication community" is situated as the always already presupposed *a priori* moment, which, more radically put, is transformed into an ethics. This is where it coincides with Liberation Philosophy, which also considers the importance of overcoming solipsism, and views ethics as *prima philosophia*.

3.1 State of the Question

In November of 1989, I presented the fourth part of a much larger work entitled "Introduction to the *Transformation of Philosophy* of Karl-Otto Apel and Liberation Philosophy: Reflections from a Latin American perspective."[3] Apel clarified his position in a conference, an oral presentation given on 1 March 1991, in Mexico, with the title "Transcendental Pragmatics and North-South Ethical Problems." There, in the first place, Apel showed (from a "standard" interpretation of Marxism) that the crisis of 1989 in Eastern Europe was a determinant for the overcoming of Marxism. A great part of his conference referred especially to this theme—thinking to critique the position I had presented in a lecture in Freiburg—and to the possible error of confusing utopia (in Marxism) with the transcendental plane itself, as is seen in the Apelian sense. In the same sense he insisted that the "life community" (*Lebensgemeinschaft*) that I had proposed in Freiburg cannot be transcendental; that the co-responsibility of all possible members of a community of argumentation is *a priori* and not, as is the case with Hans Jonas, *a posteriori*. He concluded by indicating that the standard of living of the North is neither convenient nor is it possible to be imitated by the South. The South cannot renounce its standard of living, because of an ambiguous anti-ecological development, proposed Apel.

As for me, in the seminar organized in Mexico in 1991, I presented the already mentioned lecture on the "Reason of the Other: *Interpellation* as a

Speech Act." There I developed, working from the very same discourse of Apel and Habermas, the theme from the perspective of Liberation Philosophy.

As for Apel, he continues to discover new arguments in the line of the performative self-contradiction,[4] in order to attain what could be called an *apologia rationis* against the skeptics and irrationalists. But if one were to ask, outside the consequences in the realm of theoretical reason, Why reason? Apel demonstrates the practical "danger" of irrationalism, and among those dangers he always takes as an example German nazism. Reason is defended in order not to fall again into the traumatic experience of National Socialism. But what was nazism, if not a concrete expression of the "irrational face" of modernity? Like Janus, modernity has two faces. One face is the rational emancipatory nucleus that, in the last instance, Apel defines as the ethical position that respects every person as person, as equal (to which I would add: as Other), and as possible participant of an ideal communication community. The other face of Janus is exactly the negation of this principle, which could be enunciated as: some persons are superior as persons over other persons. In this conviction or belief is grounded a type of irrationalism.[5] Indeed, modernity inaugurates the first irrationalism in a global scale:[6] Racism and ethnocentrism as expressions of the superiority of Europe over the other races and peripheral cultures (eurocentrism), *ad extra*, with two holocausts: the holocaust of the conquest of America with more than 15 million exterminated Indians; and the holocaust of slavery with 13 million Africans (more than 30 percent would die in the Middle Passage—the transatlantic transport). The second irrationalism is nazism as the corollary *ad intra* of racist eurocentrism: the superiority of the supposed Aryan race over the Jewish race, with the third modern holocaust of the systematic assassination of 6 million Jews (with the complicity of the nationalist capitalism of the German bourgeoisie through firms like Siemens, Thiessen, Krupp, Volkswagen, etc., who saw the disappearance of a competitor: transnational Jewish capital with a presence in France, England, and the United States). Indeed, little has this second face of Janus been developed in discourse ethics, that is, the tradition of the irrationalism of modernity, which is the *negation of the Other*, negation of Alterity, by the "evident" affirmation of the superiority of European culture over other cultures.

To negate the Other is to exclude the majority of humanity. The more than 75 percent of humanity that is found in the South faces a structural crisis which increases with the fall of socialism in Eastern Europe and that precipitates millions of women and men in the periphery into a growing misery. "Peripheral" capitalism (not the *Spätkapitalismus* of the North, *the minority* of the ones who suffer the "colonization" of the capitalist system in the world) has been in crisis since its origin because of a structural transference of value.[7] A philosophy that departs from this reality cannot simply imitate the philosophical discourse of Europe or the United States. A certain creativity is required in the discovery of the very point of departure, of the method to be used, of the categories to be developed, etc. Neither science nor philosophical skepticism is the interlocutor in this case of philosophical discourse, but instead the misery, the person of the "poor" (*pauper ante festum* as Marx called them[8]), as exteriority.

3.2 Toward the Origin of "The Myth of Modernity"

On a historical plane, which in any case is empirically already presupposed (not transcendentally, but concretely), the modern philosopher departs from a belief in European common sense that situates itself in the "life world" and that manifests itself in descriptions such as those of Kant with respect to the Enlightenment:

> Enlightenment is man's emergence from his self-incurred immaturity [*Unmündigkeit*].... Laziness and cowardice are the reasons why such a large proportion of men ... nevertheless gladly remain immature for life.[9]

This "immaturity" (*Unmündigkeit*), which is culpable (i.e., self-incurred), will also be posteriorly applied by Hegel in a global historical vision to Africa, Latin America, and even Asia, finalizing his judgment with the well-known eurocentric conclusion:

> World history travels from east to west; for Europe is the absolute end of history, just as Asia is the beginning....[10] just as Europe is the centre and end of the Old World—i.e. absolutely the west—so also is Asia absolutely the east....[11] the western part, which includes Germany, France, Denmark, and Scandinavia, is the *heart of Europe*....[12]

From this narrow, ethnocentric point of view, modernity inherits an eurocentric point of departure. Commenting on the Hegelian position, Habermas writes:

> The key historical events in establishing the principle of subjectivity[13] are the *Reformation*, the *Enlightenment*, and the *French Revolution*.[14]

For Hegel the south of Europe is only valid as the Italian Renaissance (Spain is outside history, and with it, Latin America, which is not even periphery). The culmination of modernity is found in Germany and France, or in England:

> And the English have undertaken the weighty responsibility of being the missionaries of *civilization* [*Zivilisation*] to the whole world.[15]

Modernity, in its *emancipatory rational nucleus*, is a departure or exit (*Ausgang*) of reason (*Vernunft*) out of a state of "self-incurred immaturity" in order to reach the universality of the equality of all persons as such. Against, in contrast, the background of a global horizon, this modernity is born. This is my hypothesis.[16] Modernity is born when Europe (the peripheral Europe of the Muslim and Ottoman world[17]), begins its expansion beyond its historical limits. Europe arrives in Africa; in India and Japan, thanks to Portugal; in Latin America,[18] and from there to the Philippines, thanks to the Spanish conquest. That is to say, Europe has become itself "center."[19] The other races and cultures now appear as "immature," barbarous, underdeveloped. It is thus that the second moment of modernity is inaugurated,[20] no longer as an *emancipatory rational nucleus* but as a *irrational sacrificial myth*.[21] The argument was clearly developed by Ginés de Sepúlveda, in the Valladolid dispute of 1550 with Bartolomé de las Casas. This argument can be summarize in the following way:

1) European culture is the most developed,[22] superior to all other cultures (eurocentric).

2) That other cultures abandon (the Kantian *Ausgang*) or exit from their own barbarity by means of the modern civilizing process constitutes their progress.[23]

3) But the underdeveloped are opposed to the civilizing process, and therefore it is just and necessary to utilize violence in order to destroy such opposition.[24]

4) On the other hand, the modern violent warrior (who exterminates Amerindians, enslaves Africans, etc) thinks that he is innocent because he exercises violence as a duty and virtue.[25]

5) And lastly, the victims of modernity in the periphery (the extermination of the indians, the enslavement of the Africans, the colonization of the Asians) and in the center (the genocide of Jews, the third holocaust) are the "responsible" ones[26] for their own victimization.

This irrational myth of modernity will be applied from the conquest of America (genocide of the Amerindian), to the enslavement of the African, to the Chinese Opium War, to the invasion of Panama (1990) or the Gulf War (1991).[27] We read in Torquemada's *Monarquia Indiana*, on the conquest of the Aztec empire:

> Less than one hundred castellians died, a few horses... Of the Mexicans one hundred thousand died, without counting the ones who died of hunger and plague.[28]

It is irrational to argue in favor of the inferiority of other persons as such, or to attempt to treat them in practice as inferior. Ginés de Sepúlveda held the opinion that a "just war" could be undertaken in order to destroy the opposition to the civilizing process, and, posteriorly, these barbarians would be educated with rational arguments. Bartolomé de las Cases, on the contrary, was of the opinion that every war or use of violence was irrational. Rational argumentation and the testimony of an exemplary moral life ought to be used from the beginning:

> The rational creature (the Indians) have a natural aptitude so that they may be led.... so that they may voluntarily listen, voluntarily obey, and voluntarily lend their respect.... In such a way that out of their own motive, with free deliberation and with natural faculties and disposition, they may hear everything that is proposed to them.[29]

In analogy to Bartolomé de las Casas, Liberation Philosophy criticizes the "the sacrificial myth" of modernity as irrational, albeit presupposing its "rational emancipatory nucleus," thereby also transcending modernity itself. Our project of liberation can be neither anti- nor pre- nor post-modern, but instead trans-modern. As rational critique from the Exteriority of modernity, the "other face" of modernity, trans-modernity (Amerindians, Africans, Asians, etc.) criticizes the irrational myth of violence against the colonies, peripheral capitalism, against the South.

To take into account this question is the condition of all possible philosophical dialogue between the North and the South, because we are situated in an asymmetrical situation.

3.3 Exteriority-Totality, "Lebenswelt"-System

A second theme of dialogue, which is related to the prior one and which deserves to be treated anew, is that of exteriority. When I say that in every real communication community there is an irrationally excluded one, the Other, in the exteriority, I am referring to a Levinasean category, but all the same to one also elaborated by Liberation Philosophy.

When, for instance, Habermas speaks of the life world as suffering a colonization by the economic or political systems, such a *Lebenswelt* retains a certain exteriority and priority with respect to the system. It would be the case of a *concrete* exteriority (the life-world) with respect to a Totality (the economic or political system as self-referential or autopoetic).[30]

Emmanuel Levinas, in his work *Totality and Infinity*,[31] locates exteriority in a trans-ontological realm from which the Other (*Autrui*) irrupts as the origin of the ethical interpellation, as "poor." But, in this case, the contradiction Exteriority-Totality is absolutely *abstract* with respect to every possible system, including the "world" (in the Hegelian phenomenological or existential Heideggerian sense). From a "beyond" of the horizon of the world, the Other irrupts "into the world," demanding justice. This is the ethical stance par excellence, the face-to-face stance.[32]

At a more concrete level than that of Levinas (but much more abstract than that of Habermas's *Lebenswelt*-system), Marx situated "living labor" as

Nicht-Kapital,³³ as the Nothing (*Nichts*) outside capital, prior to any contract. We read in the *Manuscripts of 44* of

> the *abstract* existence of man as a mere *workman* who therefore tumbles day after day from his fulfilled nothingness [*Nichts*] into absolute nothingness, into his social and hence real non-existence.³⁴

This radical Other with respect to capital is living labor as absolute poverty (*absolute Armut*);³⁵ the person, subjectivity as capacity (*Tätigkeit*), as the corporeality (*Leiblichkeit*) of the worker. In this sense, extremely abstract in its essence, capital is a system *apparently* self-referential and autopoetic, because in fact it "subsumes" (the "substitution" is the act by which Exteriority is incorporated into the Totality or the system of capital in the abstract), formally or actually,³⁶ living labor as the "creative³⁷ source³⁸ of value out nothing"³⁹ of capital itself (hetero-referential and hetero-poetic moment). This was done in such a way that, against Lukács, Marcuse, and others, Totality was not the generative and primordial category for Marx, but instead living labor (which is not the labor force [*Arbeitskraft*]⁴⁰).

The "transcendentality" of Exteriority with respect to Totality, evidently, does not have a Kantian or Apelian sense. It is the trans-ontologocity of that located "beyond" the horizon of the world, the system: the Other as free, unconditioned.⁴¹ The "transcendentality" of Alterity or Exteriority can also be applied at the empirical level.⁴² This meta-category aids Liberation Philosophy as a radical negativity with respect to every transcendental (in the Kantian or Apelian sense) or empirical system: from this position (inasmuch as they are social, the totalization of systems as self-referential "fetishization"), domination, exclusion, and the negation of the Other can be discovered. From this negated Other departs the praxis of liberation as "affirmation" of the Exteriority and as origin of the movement of negation of the negation.⁴³

Exteriority can likewise be situated at the erotic level—and in this case with appeal not to Marx but to Freud⁴⁴—at a pedagogical level (in this case we would appeal to Paulo Freire⁴⁵), or in other practical dimensions of human existence, from which Liberation Philosophy departs.

3.4 Communication Community and Life Community

I would like now to deal with a third question. Accepting the Apelian denomination of a communication community at a linguistic level, I ask, How could we now denominate that community which is presupposed in every just "labor act," when a useful product is made? I have called this the life community (*Lebensgemeinschaft*) or community of producers. It is this community which is always already presupposed *a priori* by every labor act,⁴⁶ for which and through which something is produced or is made as a product. Every product is "for another" in a community. Like the originary linguisticality (*Sprachlichkeit*; Gadamer), the instrumentality (*Werkzeuglichkeit*) is also an originary, equiprimordial ontological moment, because both are the fundamental existentialle of being-in-the-world, to use Heidegger's terminology. The community of producers or of life does not make reference to communication, but instead is the community that serves as support for the labor-act as this is directed to the reproduction of human life. Marx speaks of it explicitly; as if anticipating our suspicions he writes:

> Production by an isolated individual outside society . . . is as much of an absurdity as is the development of language without individuals living together and talking to each other.[47]

If language presupposes a community, then no less does production. At the level of production, in the economic dimension, Marx accomplished a critique from the Exteriority of the capital-system in the abstract, from the standpoint of living labor, an exteriority presupposed *a priori* before every possible economic system (the Levinasian Totality).[48] The community, instead, is a horizon or ideal moment—the "third stage" of the *Grundrisse*:

> Relations of personal dependence . . . are the first social forms, in which human productive capacity develops only to a slight extent and at isolated points. Personal independence founded on *objective* [*sachlicher*] dependence is the second great form, in which a system of general social metabolism, of universal relations, of all-round needs and universal capacities is formed for the first time. Free individuality, based on the universal development of individuals and on their subordination of their communal [*gemeinschaftlichen*], social productivity as their social wealth, is the third stage.[49]

The second stage is the colonized form of the *Lebenswelt*, which determines between individuals an abstract individual relation, a non-communitarian "social relationship."[50] For Marx, the communitarian, or pertaining-to-the-community[51] horizon, is the necessary reference "from which" the defective status of society can be understood. The "social," as determining interpersonal relation, is comprehended from the communitarian relation. This is Marx's definitive position, simply repeated in the future. Let us look at some examples. In the *Manuscripts of 61–63*, there are frequent references. In one of them, speaking of the "worshipper of fetishes," Samuel Bailey, Marx writes:

> The labour embodied in them [commodities] must be represented as *social* labour, as alienated labour. . . .This transformation of the labour of private individuals contained in the commodities into *uniform social labour*. . . .[52]

The references are even more frequent in the *Manuscripts of 63–65*, especially in the *Unpublished Chapter 6*, where there are continuous reflections on fetishism (but not necessarily on the distinction between "social" and "communitarian"), and in Chapter 7 of the *Main Manuscript* of Book III of *Capital*. In fact, Marx writes:

> The command that the products of past labour exercise over living surplus labour [*lebendige Mehrarbeit*] lasts only as long as the capital relation, the specific social relation in which past labour confronts living labour as independent and superior.[53]

The "ideal community of producers" or of "life" is found in the *Main Manuscript* of Volume III, of 1865, in a central text on the theme with which we are here dealing, namely, when Marx submits the following formulations concerning the "realm of freedom"—so much belonging to Schiller—"*The realm of freedom [Reich der Freiheit]* really begins[54] . . . beyond [*jenseits*] the sphere of material production proper.[55]

Here we ought to ask what constitutes this "beyond" (a transcendentality to be defined) of the "realm of necessity" and of material production. Whether it is located *beyond* history or in it as future, or whether it is located as a transcendental "horizon" of understanding, as a regulative idea, as an "always already presupposed *a priori*." The text continues with reference to the theme that, from the savage to the civilized man (this is the "developmentalism" of Marx before the great "turn" of the late Marx[56]), although necessities continue to be fullfilled, continue to grow at the same time, therefore, they are never able to be met fully:

> Freedom, in this sphere, can consist only in this, that socialized man, the *associated producers*, govern the human metabolism with nature in a rational way, bringing it under their communal [*gemeinschaftliche*] control instead of being dominated by it as a blind power.[57]

The communitarian level appears again, but now it receives a concrete content, which will be postulated as an "economics," as an *ideal* community of producers,

> under communal control . . . accomplishing it with the least expenditure of energy and in conditions most worthy [*würdigsten*] and appropriate for their human nature.

It concerns, exactly, the definition of an *ideal* community of producers: minimal effort, maximum adequacy to human dignity and worth. Already in the *Manuscripts of 44*, the third notebook, in the paragraph on "Private property and communism," the young Marx had written:

> Social activity and social enjoyment exist by no means *only* in the form of some *directly* communal activity and directly *communal* enjoyment, although *communal* activity and communal enjoyment—i.e. activity and enjoyment which are manifested and affirmed in *actual* direct *association* with other

men—will occur wherever such a *direct* expression of sociality stems from the true character of the activity's content and is appropriate to the nature of enjoyment.[58]

What catches the attention in this formulation, "will occur wherever such . . .," is that it makes us think of how the *"ideal* community" is actualized in the empirical *"real* community."

Only now can we confront the definitive text on fetishism published by Marx in 1873, in section 4 of Chapter 1 of *Capital*.[59] We will not repeat everything there said. We will only cite some texts:

> As the foregoing analysis has already demonstrated, this fetishism of the *world of commodities* [this is the question of a phenomenology] arises from the *peculiar social character* of the labour which produces them.[60]

As in the *Grundrisse* and the *Contributions*, Marx always begins by criticizing the solipsism of Robinson Crusoe utopias;[61] later he refers, in order to elucidate the theme of fetishism, to pre-capitalist communities.[62] In the third place, Marx refers to an *"ideal* community," and this is perfectly coherent with our interpretative hypothesis:

> Let us finally imagine, for a change, an *association of free men* [*Freier Menschen*], working with he means of production *held in common* [*gemeinschaftlichen*], and expending their many different forms of labour-power in full self-awareness as one single social labour force.[63]

It is clear that this example, this regulative idea, serves analogically (as a parallel or metaphorically) to clarify the case of an *empirical* society which he intends to analyze: the capitalist ("For a society of producers, whose general *social* relation of production consists in the fact . . ."[64]).

I believe we have indicated sufficiently how Marx uses the ideal *"communitarian* relation" as a point of reference to critically clarify the *empirical "social* relation" (capitalist).

We have seen, then, that in the nucleus of Marx's thought itself there lies the theme of community (*Gemeinschaft*).[65] This community of producers is the "transcendental condition of possibility" that is always already *a priori* presupposed when simply working "honestly," "earnestly" (as in the case of the speakers or arguers in Apel or Habermas). In fact, all persons who *honestly* engage in an act of work do so, evidently, as a means to reproduce communitarian human life. If one intends to reproduce only one's *own* life, as a solipsistic experience, this means we are already determined by a system which has colonized him/her: the "mode of capitalist *production*." Thus, the mere *honest* act of work presupposes a community of producers of human life. This warrants our copying a text of Apel, applying it to our problem (when Apel speaks of "arguing," we write "work," etc.):

> Who *works* can be led to recognize or be convinced through self-reflection that, inasmuch as *producer*, he or she has necessarily already recognized an *ethical norm*. This ethical norm can be made explicit in the following manner: who *works* has already attested *in actu*, and with that has recognized, that practical reason is responsible for human action; that is, that the claims to *justice* can be and ought to be satisfied through *acts-of-work*, which are not only technically adequate, but also practically *just*.[66]

The basic ethical norm can be formulated approximately. Taking into account the dignity of persons, I respect them when engaging in act x. This x can be an act of arguing (or a discursive speech act) or an act of work. Why do I say that in working honestly it is always already presupposed as an *a priori* ethical norm? Because just as the arguer does not "impose" his reason by means of force, but instead intends to convince with arguments, in the same way, one who works does not intend to attain the necessary product through force or robbery, but instead through labor. That is, one respects and considers the other person as one's equal, in such a way that one applies oneself to work just as the Other works in what is ours. One works honestly (and not in a solipsistically distorted system like capitalism) in the production of a product which is "ours," which will be "distributed" by "us," in order to be consumed by each one of the members of the community (the best example is the feast):[67]

> This ethical norm can be made explicit in the following manner: who *works* has already attested *in actu*, and with that has recognized, that practical reason is responsible for human actions, that is, that the claims to *justice*, can and ought to be satisfied through *acts-of-work*, not only technically adequate, but instead practically just.

We have simply changed "argue" for "work," and the "claim to truth" for "claim to justice." What does this mean? Simply that when someone works, considering that they do so always within a community always already presupposed *a priori*, they also presuppose that all the other members of the community work in just proportions ("according to their capabilities"; and therefore, ethically according to the ethical norm, each one should consume "according to their needs"). If this were not presupposed, they would stop working honestly and seriously (that is, they would begin to work intentionally, against the community, in lesser degree than they can or to consume in greater degree than they ought). On this depends not "truth" (because it is not a theoretical argument), but "justice" (which is an act of "equality" about the products of work: to each according to what corresponds to them according to their capacities and their necessities in a *community*).

A Liberation Philosophy must know how to unfold a discourse from the misery and oppression of the periphery of global capitalism, from the oppression of woman under machist rule, of the child, the youth, and the popular culture that struggles in order to supersede the control of the hegemonic culture (post-conventional in Kohlberg's position, against which we will defend a post-contractualist moment, since his position inscribes itself within a liberal tradition).

To summarize, Liberation Philosophy thinks that the "absolute *pragmatic* condition of all argumentation" (therefore of all communication communities) is the *factum* of reason that the "subject be *alive*" (a *dead* subject can hardly argue). With respect to real "life" (and therefore just the same transcendentally for the possible subject), economics[68] (*Oekonomik* and not the economy, or *Wirtschaftwissenchaft*) is an equally transcendental pragmatic condition. That economics (*ordo rationis*) is argued about in the communication community does not mean that it could be its *a priori* (*ordo realitatis*). We will return to this theme in later essays.

Notes

1. Lecture presented at the Forum für Philosophie Bad-Homburg, 13 March 1992, on the occasion of Karl-Otto Apel's seventieth birthday.
2. See Chapter 2: "The Reason of the Other: 'Interpellation' as Speech Act," pp. 19ff.
3. The fourth part was published in Fornet-Betancourt, ed., *Ethik und Befreiung* (Aachen: Augustinus Buchhandlung, 1990). The complete text has appeared in Spanish in Karl-Otto Apel, Enrique Dussel, Raúl Fornet-Betancourt, eds. *Fundamentación de la ética y filosofía de la liberación* (Mexico: Siglo XXI, 1992).
4. See Apel's "Fallibilismus. Konsenstheorie der Wahrheit und Letztbegründung," in Forum für Philosophie Bad Homburg, ed., *Philosophie und Begründung* (Frankfurt: Suhrkamp, 1987).
5. It is thus announced: "Argue that some persons are as such, as possible participants of a communication community, *superior* to other persons." This argument falls into performative self-contradiction because it negates the equality which it presupposes in the very act of arguing. It is clear, as we will see, that it will pretend to make do without negating a potential equality, but a real; that is, here and now are inferior, which will allow us to "negate their alterity" and with that the dignity of person *as other*. Because of that, the equality of the other is not sufficient. Instead, what is needed is the affirmation of the dignity of the alterity of the Other.
6. Simply because before 1492 there was no empirical "global" history.
7. On this theme see my article "Marx's Economic Manuscripts of 1861–1863 and the 'Concept' of Dependency," in *Latin American Perspectives* 17, 2 (1990), pp. 61–101. This article contains a substantive bibliography. The "transference of value" began with the extraction and robbery of the precious metals (gold, silver, first global currency) at the expense of the lives of the Indians during the 16th and 17th centuries; it continued with the slavery of the tropical plantations, with unequal exchange, the price monopoly of raw materials (undervalued), the manufactures of the center (overvalued) controlled by the colonial metropolis, and with the payment of international interest arbitrarily raised, etc.

8. See my works *La producción teórica de Marx* (Mexico: Siglo XXI, 1985) pp. 138ff; *Hacia un Marx desconocido*, (Mexico: Siglo XXI, 1988) pp. 61ff; *El último Marx (1863–1882)*, (Mexico: Siglo XXI, 1990) pp. 334ff.
9. Immanuel Kant, "An Answer to the Quetion: 'What is Enlightenment?'" *Political Writings* (Cambridge: Cambridge University Press, 1990), p. 54.
10. Georg Wilhelm Friedrich Hegel, *Lectures on the Philosophy of World History. Introduction: Reason in History*, trans. H.B. Nisbet (Cambridge: Cambridge University Press, 1975), p. 197.
11. Ibid., p. 191.
12. Ibid., p. 195.
13. In my *The Invention of the Americas: Eclipse of "the Other" and the Myth of Modernity* (New York: Continuum, 1995) I show that 1492 begins the constitution of this "subjectivity," as an *ego conquiro* (I conquer), a century before its ontological expression as an *ego cogito* (in 1636).
14. Jürgen Habermas, *The Philosophical Discourse of Modernity: Twelve Lecture* (Cambridge: The MIT Press, 1987) p. 17 (emphasis added).
15. G. W. F. Hegel, *The Philosophy of History*, trans. J. Sibree (New York: The Colonial Press, 1900), p. 455; German: *Vorlesungen über die Philosophie der Geschichte*, in *Werke*, Vol. 12 (Frankfurt: Suhrkamp, 1970), p. 538. Emphasis added, and translation slightly altered. See my *The Invention of the Americas. . . .*, Chap. 1, "El eurocentrismo."
16. I want to distinguish between "origin," in the free medieval cities, and "birth," in 1492.
17. See Chap. 6 of *The Invention of the Americas*.
18. Latin America, and not New England, was the first periphery, in the strict sense, of modern Europe. See Immanuel Wallerstein, *The Modern World-System* (New York: Academic Press, 1974).
19. Before 1492, Europe could not have any effective self-consciousness of superiority, because it knew well the wealth, wisdom, and power of the Muslim and Ottoman worlds. It is in Mexico, with Cortés, that Europe first exercises its triumphant "will-to-power" (see my *The Invention of the Americas*, Chap. 3).
20. This second moment has disappeared in Apel and Habermas.
21. "Myth" in the totally different sense meant by M. Horkheimer and T. Adorno in *Dialektik der Aufklärung* (Frankfurt: Fischer, 1971), and to which Habermas refers in *The Philosophical Discourse of Modernity*, Chap. 5, pp. 106ff. On sacrificial irrationality, one would have to think of a René Girard, *Le sacré et le profane* (Paris: Gallimard, 1965); and his *Le Bouc émissaire* (Paris: Grasset, 1982). See also Franz Hinkelammert, *Sacrificios humanos y Sociedad occidental* (San José, Costa Rica: DEI, 1991).
22. Departing from the arguments for slavery of Aristotle's *Politics*, Ginés de Sepúlveda thinks that "the perfect ought to dominate and reign the imperfect, the excellent over its contrary" (*De la justa causa de la guerra contra los indios* [Mexico: FCE, 1987], p. 83). Or: "Being by nature slaves, the barbarians, uncultured and inhuman men, . . . being furthermore a just matter by natural right that matter obey form, the body the soul, the appetites reason, the brutes men, women men, the imperfect the perfect, the worse the better, for the good of all" (ibid., p. 153). In this major argument there resides the racism of eurocentrism, of ethnocentrism, of extreme nationalism, etc. It is an *argument* that falls into a performative self-contradiction.
23. "What other better or more healthy thing can occur to these barbarians, but that

they be governed by the empire of those whose prudence, virtue and religion will convert the barbarian... into civilized men" (ibid., 133).

24. "And if they refuse our empire [*imperium*], they can be compelled by arms to accept it, and this will be just war by natural law" (ibid, p. 135).
25. "Were we not to do it, we would fulfill neither the natural law nor the commandment of Christ" (ibid., 137).
26. Is this not the "global" sense of the "culpable immaturity" of which Kant speaks? It is clear that Kant finds "culpability" in the "laziness" and "cowardice," but already a natural ineptitude had been projected on the Indian as a cultural culpability. See my work *1492: el encubrimiento del Otro*. Furthermore, Kant associates cool weather with the white race as being superior, over those that inhabit the regions of tropical climates, etc. The culpability of the barbarians resides in their "opposition" to modernization and Christianization. Never could modernity understand such an opposition as a desperate act of affirming their "identity" as alterity.
27. In Panama there was no culpability in the invasion of a sovereign country (personally, I cannot defend Noriega, but with less ethical reasons I can also not defend an "invasion").
28. Juan de Torquemada, *Monarquia India* (Mexico: UNAM, 1975), Vol. II, p. 312. This was in 1521. In 1991 we read in the newspapers that 125 "boys" died and something more than one hundred thousand Iraqi soldiers died in the Gulf War. The same proportion, almost 500 years later, out of the same logic of modernity. The horses in 1521 are the airplanes of today.
29. *De unico modo*, in 1536, a century before Descartes' *Discourse on Method*: Bartolomé de las Casas, *De Unico Modo* (Mexico: FCE, 1975), p. 71.
30. See Niklas Luhmann, *Soziale System* (Frankfurt: Suhrkamp Verlag, 1988). In Spanish see the excellent introduction by Ignacio Izuzquia, *La sociedad sin hombres. Niklas Luhmann o la Teoria del escándalo* (Barcelona: Anthropos, 1990).
31. Emmanuel Levinas, *Totality and Infinity* (Pittsburgh: Duquesne University Press, 1969).
32. See my *Philosophy of Liberation* (Maryknoll: Orbis Books, 1985), 2.1 and 2.4; and *Para una ética de la liberación latinoamericana* (Buenos Aires: Siglo XXI, 1973) Vols. I and II; and *Método para una Filosofía de la Liberación* (Salamanca: Sigueme, 1974).
33. Karl Marx, *Grundrisse*, p. 295; German (Berlin: Dietz, 1974), p. 203, lines 8–45.
34. Karl Marx, *Economic and Philosophic Manuscripts of 1844* in Marx, *Early Writings*, (New York: Penguin Books, 1992) p. 336; German (*MEW*, EB 1), pp. 524–25.
35. See *Grundrisse*, p. 295–96.
36. On real or formal "sublation," see my *El último Marx (1863–1882)* (Mexico: Siglo XXI, 1990), on the "Capítulo VI inédito" (pp. 33–49).
37. Marx distinguishes between "producing" (*produktion*) and "foundation" (*Grund*) as well as between "to create" (*schaffen*) and "creation" (*Schöpfung*).
38. As *Quelle* (source, in a Schellingian sense) and not as *Grund* (in the Hegelian sense).
39. On the "creation out of nothing" (*aus Nichts*), see my work *El último Marx (1863–1882)*, Chap. 9.3: "El trabajo vivo como fuente creadora del valor" (pp. 368ff). This means the "creation of surplus out of the nothing of capital"; or put another way: from beyond the grounding, it indicates that for Marx capital is not self-referential nor autopoetic (this is fetishism, the pretension of self-reference and autopoesis of capital as system).

40. See my *El último Marx (1863–1882)*, pp. 162ff.
41. In "Exteriority and the Ideal Communication Community," Chap. 2.3.1, above I situate the exteriority of the Other at the transcendental level of the ideal communication community, when I indicated that equal persons, participants in said community, ought, in addition, always respect every member as an Other (as potential origin of a *new* discourse). Levinas's exteriority is abstract, and therefore it needs to be located at the transcendental or empirical level of Apel, or in both. In the transcendental, as respect and recognition of the unconditional dignity and liberty of the Other; at the empirical level, as "excluded," as the "dominated," the "poor."
42. See above, Chap. 2.3.2, "Exteriority and the Community of Scientists," 2.3.3, "Concrete Types of *Interpellation*, from the Excluded Ones of Such Respective Hegemonic Communication Communities."
43. See my *Método para una filosofía de la liberación*.
44. See "La erótica latinoamericana," in my *Filosofía ética latinoamericana*, Vol. III, pp. 49ff.
45. See "La pedagógica latinoamericana" in Ibid., pp.123ff.
46. In the speech act there is a propositional content; in the labor act there is a functional content. In this way one may proceed to analyze the analogies.
47. Karl Marx, *Grundrisse*, p. 84.
48. This is the question I have dealt with in *El último Marx (1863–1882)*, Chaps. 9 and 10, pp. 334–450, under the title "Generative Matrix" of every possible economics (as concrete economic moment of the still more abstract philosophical-ethical "rational matrix": the non-being as creative source of Being).
49. *Grundrisse*, p. 158; German, p. 75, lines 34–45.
50. "The conditions of labour from which exchange value emerge . . . are *social determinations* [*geselschaftliche*] of labour or determinations of *social labour* [*geselschaftlicher*], but not social [*geselschaflich*] in any form [!], but instead in a particular manner . . . of the *single [einzelnen] individual*." (*Zur Kritik* [1859], Chap. 1; *MEW*, 13, p. 19). "Something which characterizes labour that originates exchange value is that the *social relation of persons [gesellschaftliche Beziehung der Personen]* presents itself, so to say, *inverted [verkehrt]*. It could be said as a social relation of things" (ibid, p. 21). For Marx, in this case, "social relation" is a defective relation, negative, non-communitarian.
51. Marx, writing on Ricardo, says that he was imprisioned within the "bourgeois horizon" (*Zur Kritik*, p. 46). It is properly a phenomenological category of great importance in our theme.
52. Karl Marx, *Theories of Surplus Value*, Part III, trans. Jack Cohen (London: Lawrence & Wishart, 1973), p. 131; German (*MEGA* II, 3), p. 1318. Each time we use "social" we are translating from the German *gesellschaftliche*.
53. Karl Marx, *Capital*, Vol. 3, trans. by David Fernbach (New York: Penguin, 1981), p. 524; German (*MEGA* III/7), p. 509; (*MEW* 25), p. 412.
54. Which would be the realm of "instrumental rationality" inasmuch as it concerns goals (*Zweckmässigkeit*).
55. Marx, *Capital*, Vol. 3, pp. 958–59. The entire text is found in Chap. 7 of the *Main Manuscript*, posteriorly Chap. 48 of Engels's edition ("The Trinity Formula") of Engels (German [*MEGA*, III/8], p. 1044; [*MEW* 25], p. 828).
56. See my *El último Marx*, Chap. 7, pp. 243ff.
57. Marx, *Capital*, Vol. 3, p. 959; German (*MEW* 25), p. 828.
58. Marx and Engels, *Collected Works*, Vol. 3, p. 298; German (*MEW*, EB 1), p. 538.

59. See *El último Marx*, Chap. 5.7.c, especially pp. 192–93. On the history of fetishism in commodities see Thomas Marxhausen, "Die Entwicklung der Theorie des Waren fetichismus in Marx oekonomischen Schiften zwischen 1850 und 1863" in *Arbeitsblätter zur Marx-Engels Forschung*, 1, 1976, pp. 75–95.
60. *Capital*, Vol. 1, p. 165. Emphasis added.
61. Ibid., pp. 169–70.
62. Ibid., p. 170.
63. Ibid., p. 171. Emphasis added.
64. Ibid., p. 172.
65. See my work *La producción teórica de Marx*, Chap. 4.2 (pp. 87ff); 14.4 (pp. 291ff); 17.4 (pp. 355ff). In the present work see Chap. 1.1 and 3.2.a. Also the "Introduction to the *Transformation der Philosophie* of K-O. Apel and the Philosophy of Liberation" cited in Apel, ed., *Fundamentación de la ética y filosifía de la liberación* pp. 39ff, and pp. 73ff; also published in Fornet-Betancourt, ed., *Ethik und Befreiung* (Aachen: Augustinus Buchhandlung, 1990). The expression "ideal community of producers" was then criticized by Apel. In part, this is my response to that criticism. This community has to do with the "ethical community" of Kant, with the "Invisible Church" of Hegel, and with the "Kingdom of God" on earth of Württemberg pietism.
66. See Karl-Otto Apel, "Notwendigkeit, Schwierigkeit und Möglichkeit einer Philosophischen Begründung der Ethik im Zeitalter der Wissenschaft" in P. Kanellopoulos, ed., *Festschrift für K. Tsatsos* (Athens: Nomikaí Ekdoseis Ant., 1980), pp. 264–65.
67. See my *Philosophy of Liberation*, 4.3.9.6 and 4.4.9.2–4.4.9.3.
68. We understand by it the ideally presupposed belonging of every human being to a "community of producers/consumers" where life is reproduced as condition of the "living" character of the rational subject.

4

From the Skeptic to the Cynic

I would like to elaborate in depth the theme that I suggested in 1982 when I wrote, referring to Wittgenstein, "that *skepticism* turns ethically *cynical*...."[1] At the same time, I am interested in continuing the North-South dialogue initiated in Freiburg (November of 1989)[2] and continued in Mexico (February and March of 1991).[3] Now, however, I will attempt to show that the point of departure of discourse ethics is perhaps a moment within Liberation Philosophy, philosophy which philosophizes from the periphery of a capitalism that presents itself today cynically without alternatives.[4]

Our argumentative strategy in this chapter will be extremely simple: Apel's discourse ethics attempts an "ultimate grounding" (*Letztebegründung*) before an opponent, the *skeptic*, to whom it can be shown that if they want to be radically skeptical, they will inevitably fall into a "performative self-contradiction." The Philosophy of Liberation, instead, departs from its confrontation with another opponent. Its original position is constituted in its confrontation with the *cynic*, who grounds the "moral system" of the established structure on the irrational force of power (of the Will to Power we would say with Nietzsche), and which commands the Totality with strategic rationality. Both philosophical discourses, as much in their strategies as in their architectonic structure, are, because of this, different. Not without reason Levinas wrote:

> Does not lucidity, the mind's openness upon the true, consist in catching sight of the permanent possibility of war? *The state of war suspends morality*; it divests the eternal institutions and obligations of their eternity and rescinds ad interim the unconditional imperatives.[5]

In *Philosophy of Liberation*, I have written,

> From Heraclitus to Karl von Clausewitz and Henry Kissinger, "war is the origin of everything," if by "everything" one understands the order or system that world dominators control by their power and armies. We are at war.[6]

Both texts deal with the Totality, the system, already dominated or controlled by "strategic rationality," but which now we will denominate, with greater precision, *cynical reason*.

4.1 The Skeptic and the Ultimate Grounding of Discourse Ethics

The architectonic[7] of discourse ethics culminates (and this is the point of departure for its *Anwendung* [application]) with the "ultimate grounding," thanks to its taking recourse to the "performative contradiction," in which the skeptic inevitably falls if he/she is to be radically skeptical, as it was mentioned. It would appear that, outside the skeptic,[8] in its most varied forms (which Apel attacks in each case), no one can any longer be in opposition to the rational acceptance of the always already, *a priori* presupposed moments of any argumentation. In this manner, by destroying all the pseudo arguments of the skeptic, discourse ethics has attained an ultimate grounding, which is what Aristotle called a dialectical refutation.

Apel, ever since his earliest works on the theme,[9] confronts positions like that of Hans Albert,[10] or those of the decisionist Karl Popper. For the latter, no reason can be given in favor of "opting for reason": critical rationalism falls into irrationalism, since the original decision in favor of reason is only a moral but not a rational decision.[11] Apel begins his rebuttal by demonstrating that grounding (*begründung*) cannot and ought not to be thought of in logical terms, and thus takes seriously what Aristotle wrote:

> For it is impossible that there should be demonstration of absolutely everything; there would an infinite regress, so that there would still be no demonstration.[12]

The point of departure for Apelian argumentation is the following:

> Anyone who takes part in an argument implicitly acknowledges all the *potential claims* of all the members of the communication community that *can* be justified by rational arguments.[13]

These "validity claims" (*geltung Ansprüchen*) of every communication can be neither negated without *contradiction* nor demonstrated without *begging the question*. This is, however, not simply a traditional logical contradiction; instead, departing from the speech-act theory of Searle and Austin, the "performative self-contradiction" (*performative Selbstwiderspruch*) is defined as the new form of the dialectical contradiction. The "Münchausen trilemma" (the regress ad infinitum, the vicious logical circle, the dogmatic interruption in an arbitrary point) only demonstrates the impossibility of deducing a proposition from other propositions. On the contrary, in *pragmatics* there enters in play, in addition, the validity claims which all communication always presupposes *a priori*, in such a way that a new realm of argumentative grounding is reached.[14]

The entire transcendental, pragmatic, argumentative strategy always confronts a *skeptic*. If the skeptic "enters" into the argumentation (that is to say, participates in the communication community, thus preparing himself to effectively argue), he will fall inevitably in a performative self-contradiction when attempting, for example, to claim that "every principle is falsifiable" or "I always lie." The skeptic will never be able to put in question or negate the validity claim presupposed in the very act of argumentation itself (even when pretending to argue against all possible argumentation).

Jürgen Habermas, on the other hand, searches for arguments against Apel's position.[15] Habermas points out that the entire Apelian argumentation depends on the position of the skeptic, and has some effect on the opponent if the opponent "enters" into argumentation. But if the opponent decides not to enter into discussion, the possible effect of the Apelian argumentation would be annulled. However, under the *definition itself of the skeptic*, and Habermas does not seem to take note of this, he cannot abandon the discussion, lest he stops being a skeptic.

In fact, the skeptic is the *rhetorical figure* of an opponent *in the discussion* who has a "rational position" of negation or doubt concerning some moment of the exercise of the rational act itself, but that *includes in its definition the Other* of the discussion, as affirmation (of the *person* of the naive dogmatist or rationalist, for the skeptic) of what is negated (some moment of the rational act). That is, the skeptic *supposes* the "encounter" with the argumentative Other, but negates the validity of some of the rational moments. Thus, the pretense of assuming a radical position is contradicted "by its very definition": the skeptic uses before the Other (pragmatic position) a reason that attempts to be negated. In addition to that already mentioned, the case of the postmoderns, and especially that of Richard Rorty, operates under the definition of the skeptic. Rorty "enters" into the discussion, in the "encounter" with the Other, but negates that it is an argumentative, *rational* encounter; Rorty "enters" only in order to establish a "conversation."[16] He cannot but fall into a performative self-contradiction, in Apelian terminology. If he does not enter, just the same he contradicts himself if he attempts any other action (rational or practical), because in order to carry it out he ought to have some reason, and, by definition, affirms not to want to argue or give any reason (*Grund, ratio*).

But, is this not entering into the discussion always a contradiction? Is there no other rhetorical figure that allows perfectly *not to enter* into the discussion, and, nevertheless, not to fall into any contradiction (whether logical or pragmatic)? I believe that this figure exists, and it would clarify the intention (not achieved if the figure of the skeptic is the only one taken) of the path undertaken by Habermas when he points out that the opponent can decide "not to enter" or would like to dispense with participating in the community, in the discussion or in argument. If there was a virtual or real opponent who could *not enter* into discussion, and, however, would not bring about with that a *contradiction*, the Apelian argument for the ultimate grounding would lose its logical efficacy, as well as its social and historical applicability—a loss that many judge to be precisely the practical problem of Apel's ultimate grounding, namely, that it has no real effectiveness.[17]

4.2 The Cynic and the Power of Strategic Rationality as Criticized by Liberation Philosophy

The skeptic affirms the Other, enters into argument (and by not entering, stops being a skeptic, because then the skeptic simply stops being an arguer), and by entering contradicts herself (because she cannot radically use reason pragmatically against itself). The cynic,[18] on the contrary, *negates the other* from the beginning. It is a *practical* position that has decided (implicitly or explicitly) to negate the Other, thus negating all priority of discursive rationality: that is to say, it supposes the *negation* of any argumentative "encounter." The face-to-face is the ethical position of the illocutory moment of the speech act, the primary moment of the communication community as the "encounter" between persons, since it is the "entering" itself (face-to-face) into argumentation. This face-to-face is negated by the cynic; given that the Other, for the cynic, is a mediation of his project (a means for "systematic," i.e., political, economic, educational, military, interests), an "object" as *mediation* with respect to *goals* that are managed by strategic rationality. Strategic rationality, on the other hand, is also a mediation (as in the attitude of "disenchantment" of Max Weber, or in Karl Popper's anti-utopian "Open Society") of Power. Power here is not the affirmation of the dignity of persons in community, as is the case with discursive rationality; instead, it is the autopoietic, totalitarian totalization of the Totality, the mere self-referential Will.[19] *Power* (read Nietzsche, Foucault, but now interpreted in its naked cynicism, and not as simple actuality, but as the reality of a "closed Totality," as Levinas would say) is the ground of *cynical* reason (and not vice versa), a reason of terror—against which the postmoderns rebel, without noticing that it is only a modality of reason and not reason itself.

In the face of cynicism, discourse ethics cannot argue for its claim to ultimate grounding, because, the cynic *will not enter*, without contradiction (neither logical nor pragmatic), ever, into any ethical argumentation. The cynic's strategic rationality is only interested in entering into an argument of negotiation, of Power to Power, of force, of efficacy. It is a *poietic* (autopoietic) rationality. Through power, through the use of strategical rationality as an instrument, is established the "morality" of the system (self-referential, autopoietic, without subject),[20] in its one-dimensionality, as articulated by Herbert Marcuse.[21]

Liberation Philosophy confronts, from the outset, "within" a Totality (system or world), and opposes the domination of cynical reason: for example, that of the transnational businessman who leaves workers unemployed in order to receive greater profits from cheaper labor in "underdeveloped countries"; or that of the military general who must win the war; or that of the director of the intelligence service who must plan an assassination attempt against an enemy; or that of the torturer before the tortured. Liberation philosophy confronts the cunning of such a *strategic rationality grounded in Power*.[22]

This determines the architectonic of Liberation Philosophy. In the first place, it needs to describe what cynical reason negates above all: the Other (the question of "proximity").[23] In the second place, it describes the necessary categories[24] in order to be able to locate the process of totalization, which we described under the rubric of the domination of cynical reason[25] (See Chap. 2.5.2, "The Other as Enemy"; 2.5.3, "The Negation of Difference"; 2.5.4, "The Totalization of Exteriority"; 2.5.5, "Alienation"[26]). This architectonic of the discourse is radically necessary as an *a priori* of all *a posteriori* philosophical reflection. Not even the discourse on ultimate grounding in the face of the skeptic is prior, because—and this is unnoticed by Apel—the transcendental-pragmatic philosopher who argues in the face of the skeptic finds him/herself already within a system where cynical reason reigns. The argumentative action of discourse ethics accomplishes an "internal" function to that system, since it only confronts the skeptic, the academic, the scientist (who may be a "functionary" of cynical reason), but does not discover its most deep and real opponent: the "cynical reason" that dominates and controls the system as Totality. Emmanuel Levinas begins all discourse having as the opponent this Totality. Marx was aware that capital (as a self-referential and autopoietic system) negates the personhood of the Other (the *lebendige Arbeit*) when this is transformed into a "mediation of the valorization of value" (the Being of Capital, *Sein des Kapitals*);[27] it is the inversion which consists in fetishism: for cynical reason the person becomes a thing (*Ding*), and the thing (the system as totality) becomes an autonomous subjectivity, like the person (the power out of which strategic rationality deploys itself).

Schema 1. Opponents of the Different Philosophical Discourses

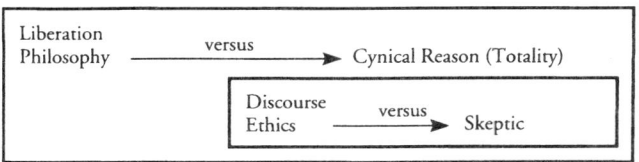

It is because of this that the process of liberation[28] only begins when, in the interior of the system, dominated by cynical reason, the Other manifests him/herself, the face of the other as someone. We call "ethical consciousness"[29] the

"practical action" which re-establishes a relation of communication (it is an authentic *kommunikativen Handeln*) with the Other. Only from the manifestation, as revelation (*Offenbarung*, in the Schellingian sense) of the Other, is received, without a prior decision, responsibility (*Verantwortung*) for the destiny of the oppressed who is negated by the movement of totalization of cynical reason as domination (as non-ethics par excellence). This constitutes *a priori* responsibility, prior to any discursive argumentation, prior to any ultimate grounding, prior to any possible *Anwendung* (application), which, in fact, initiates the path of a Weberian (or also, in the sense of Hans Jonas) *a posteriori* responsibility, as political or practical responsibility in order to act empirically in the organization of institutions and carry out actions, public works, etc.

In this case, in order to act institutionally and rationally, the liberation philosopher can now, and only now, have recourse to universal or transcendental pragmatics and attempt an ultimate grounding against the skeptic (of the system), and as a function of an indirect critique of cynical reason. This cannot be accomplished before, because in the confrontation with cynical reason liberation philosophy does not begin with arguments (by definition, the cynic does not "enter" or is not interested in any argumentation, since he already has Power, and this is deployed by means of a strategic rationality, which is not interested in the results of an ethical discursive rationality). Liberation Philosophy, in contrast to discourse ethics, ought to be articulated in action, or praxis, in order to challenge Power. In this case, philosophy is a moment in the "assumption of consciousness" (the *concientização* of Paulo Freire) of the oppressed, of and in their praxis, which describes, and with that criticizes, the mechanisms of cynical rationality.[30] It is only now that the ultimate grounding can *assure* the use of discursive rationality, the validity of ethical norms (necessary in the struggle of the liberation praxis) and their posterior application (*Anwendung*) in the process of liberation itself.

However, at this moment of application, we can now have a fundamental *criterion* of difference: between 1) the application of actions directed to the accomplishment of the goals of strategic rationality, as a moment which is grounded in the cynical reason of the system (which is a contradiction);[31] and 2) the application of normativity to actions directed at accomplishing a liberation project (partially reformist, or more radical, as the case may be) of an ethically justified strategic rationality. This is the problematic which, in *Philosophy of Liberation*, I have schamatized under the heading "Liberation."[32] But it is precisely because of the prudential and consensual complexity of the innovative or creative action of liberation that the reformer, innovator, or liberator has difficulty in justifying as ethically valid what is being realized in praxis. Hence the need for a philosophy that attempts to prove the justice of the apparent "Illegitimacy of the Good."[33] It is necessary to prove that the *praxis* of liberation of the oppressed, against cynicism, is legitimate because of the grounding of the supreme ethical norm. It is no little task for Liberation Philosophy, then, to attempt to prove the ethical validity of the action of heroes (from Joan of Arc to Washington, to Martin Luther King, Jr., to Carlos Fonseca, or to Jean Bertrand Aristide), who rise up against the reigning legality (and even the accepted morality).

4.3 The Skeptic as a Functionary of Cynical Reason

I have repeatedly said that Apel's proposal is extremely "healthy" for Latin America (as well as for Asia and Africa), because it demonstrates the contradiction of the academic skeptic, of Popperian critical rationalism, of the linguistic-turn philosopher who uses sophistical cunning in order to confuse the uninitiated. These skeptics pretend to destroy the reason of an ethics of liberation and allow cynical decisionism to reign without scruples. Just as Apel fears the return of nazism and discovers certain affinities of it with some skeptics, in the same way we, in Latin America, have lived the functionality of many skeptics within the military regimes of "national security." There is in skepticism, then, a degree of functionality[34] with respect to a system under the control of cynical reason. Max Weber can be used in this sense, just as John Rawls or Richard Rorty.[35]

For Apel's discourse ethics, Liberation Philosophy may perhaps be seen as a complementary horizon to the empirical order (level B in Apel's philosophy). Liberation philosophy cannot accept this "classification" without challenging it. What if it were the reverse? Could not discourse ethics be a moment within Liberation Philosophy, given that it occupies a very precise location within the order of discourses, under the exigency of the imperative of ethical-emancipatory rationality, which takes a different real and historical point of departure for discourse? Discourse ethics will say that nothing can be prior to the ultimate foundation or justification. What if said foundation or justification is carried out in the face of a skeptic who is already determined by prior moments, such as being an accomplice to a Totality under the reign of cynical reason, who does not enter, and will never enter into discussion with the pragmatic philosopher? Or put differently: What if the discussion itself against the skeptic is allowed and serves the interests of the strategic rationality of the cynic? In this case discourse ethics would attack a secondary moment and with disproportionate means: first, it would attack the skeptic, and not the cynic (hiding it, occluding it in its forgetfulness); second, it would argue in the face of a Power that does not give any importance, space, or efficacy to theoretical action (it would be, then, a naive activity, without public effectiveness). And what if, on the contrary, Liberation Philosophy attacks the principal opponent (cynical reason in power), and with appropriate means? When we refer to the appropriate means we want to *indicate the exercise of another type of philosophy*; a philosophy as a service of *solidaristic theoretical action* (of Gramsci's "organic intellectual"), of critical-discursive reason as a function of the organization of an actual or future counter-power, as a fruit of the praxis of the oppressed (women in machist systems, discriminated races, miserable urban dwellers, exploited wage earners, indigenous ethnicities, national interests, peripheral capitalist or poor socialist countries, popular cultures, future generations immolated beforehand by ecological destruction, etc.), in view of one day coming to exercise the power of justice, in the new institutional order that will have to be established through reform or founded by the legitimate (by liberation philosophy validly proved) praxis of liberation.

Notes

1. In my article "Etica de la liberación," *Iglesia viva*, 102, 1982, p. 599.
2. Karl-Otto Apel, et al., eds., *Fundamentación de la ética y filosofía de la liberación* (Mexico: Siglo XXI, 1992); Raúl Fornert-Betancourt, ed., *Ethik und Befreiung* (Aachen: Augustinus Buchhandlung, 1990).
3. Raúl Fornet-Betancourt, ed., *Diskursethik oder Befreieungsethik?* (Aachen: Augustinus Buchhandlung, 1992) and Apel, *Fundamentación de la ética y filosofía de la liberación*.
4. See Francis Fukayama, *The End of History and the Last Man* (New York: Free Press, 1992).
5. Emmanuel Levinas, *Totality and Infinity* (Pittsburgh: Duquesne University Press, 1969), p. 21 (emphasis added).
6. Enrique Dussel *Philosophy of Liberation* (Maryknoll: Orbis Books, 1985), p. 1.
7. On the "architectonic" of the ethics of liberation see the work by Hans Schelkshorn, *Ethik der Befreiung. Eine Einführung in der Philosophie Enrique Dussels* (Freiburg: Herder, 1992).
8. Concerning this, we would have to be aware of the evolution of this philosophical position, since it was born with the Greeks, and it suffers an important transformation with modernity (with Descartes and Montaigne) and later with Hegel, for instance. See my work *Método para una filosofía de la liberación*, where I indicate how Aristotle, Descartes, or Kant knew how to confront the skeptic.
9. See "The a Priori of the Communication Community and the Foundations of Ethics: The Problem of a Rational Foundation of Ethics in the Scientific Age" in Apel, *Towards a Transformation of Philosophy*, also Apel's *Ethics and the Theory of Rationality. Selected Essays*, Vol. 2 (Atlantic Highlands: Humanities Press, 1996).
10. Karl-Otto Apel, *Towards a Transformation of Philosophy*, p. 262ff. See also by Hans Albert, "Ethik und Metaethik," *Archiv für Philosophie*, II, 1961, pp. 28–63, and later *Traktak über kritische Vernunft* (Tübingen: Mohr 1968).
11. And in the same way Paul Lorenzen ends up in decisionism, see his *Normative Logic and Ethics* (Mannheim-Zürich: Hoch schultaschenbücher verlag, 1969).
12. Aristotle, *Metaphysics*, IV, 1006a; see Jonathan Barnes, ed. *The Complete Works of Aristotle*, 2 vols. (Princeton: Princeton University Press, 1984), p. 1588.
13. Karl-Otto Apel "The a priori of the communication community...", p. 277.
14. See Karl-Otto Apel "Das Problem der philosophischen Letztbegründung im Lichte einer transzendentalen Sprachpragmatik" in Bernulf Kanitschelder, ed., *Sprache und Erkenntnis, Festschrift* for G. Frey (Innsbruck: Inst. F. Sprachwissenschaft d. Univ. Innsbruch, 1976), pp. 55ff; and "Fallibilismus, Konsenstheorie der Wahrheit und

Letztbegründung" in *Philosophie und Begründung* (Frankfurt: Suhrkamp Verlag, 1987), sections V and VI.
15. Jürgen Habermas, *Moral Consciousness and Communicative Action* (Cambridge: The MIT Press, 1990), Chap. 3, section 7, pp. 82ff.
16. See K-O. Apel, "Zurück zur Normalität? Oder könnten wir aus der nationalen Katastrophe etwas Besonderes gelernt haben?" in *Diskurs und Verantwortung* (Frankfurt: Suhrkamp Verlag, 1988).
17. It is like the medieval proof of the existence of God, which never effectively moved anyone to a subjective acceptance of said existence. No atheist stopped being one because of such proofs, but their atheism was fruit of a practical position that denied "entering" into the discussion of such proofs.
18. We will give the concept "cynic" a radical meaning. Peter Sloterdijk, *Kritik der zynischen Vernuft*, 2 vols. (Frankfurt: Suhrkamp Verlag, 1983), gives it an individualistic, ontic sense when he defines it as: "Cynicism—analysis, on the other hand, describes the interaction between relentless subjectivism, supra-elevated center of private reason, gunslinger power conglomerations, and science-supported systems of hyper-production. They all do not think on the reverie of how to submit themselves to a communicative reason ..." (II, p. 947). In contradistinction, I define cynicism as the *affirmation of the power of the system as the grounding* of a reason which controls or governs strategic rationality as mediation of its own realization (as absolute power). It has an ontological sense (Being as a Will-to-Power). The soldier who discovers an argument in order to avoid death in a cowardly moment in war is not cynical (ibid., II, pp. 403ff), but he who, *inasmuch as a soldier with courage*, defines the enemy "as the defeated thing," before whom there is no place for the exercise of any ethical-discursive rationality. Sloterdeijk still moves within the "innocent" meaning of cynicism, and thus does not discover the meaning of "cynical reason" as Terror, as the self-affirmation of the system (which meaning, for Levinas, is the "Truth" of the Totality as negation of the Other).
19. In my *Para una ética de la liberación latinoamericana*, Vol. II, I entitled Paragraph 21: "Ethical-Ontological Evil as Totalitarian Totalization of the Totality" (pp. 13ff). I wrote there twenty years ago: "We have thus quickly traversed the ontological tradition of Totality, within which is possible the "closed society" [without alterity], where men live next to one another indifferent to the rest of humanity, always alert in order to attack or to defend themselves, reduced to the attitude of combat (Henri Bergson, *Les deux sources de la morale et de la religion*, [Paris: PUF, 1969, p. 283]; just as in the "open society" [read *closed*] of Popper). The triumphant hero is practically in charge of fighting for Everything against the other who is different and who attempts to be different; the sage (wise man) is he who has theoretically discovered the Other as the natural evil of the different as plurality. Perfection is attained through the honor of killing whoever opposes, thus annihilating plurality, alterity, and knowing the Totality (the same) as the self-identical origin of the difference. The whole (the totality), as grounding, is not ethical: it is simply true" (pp. 21–22). The affirmation of the whole, without alterity, is the first moment within cynical reason.
20. The definition of system in Niklas Luhmann, *Soziale Systeme*, corresponds exactly to a "cynical totality": "Das selbstreferentielle Subjekt und das selbstreferentialle Objekt, werden isomorph gedacht" (p. 595).
21. See Douglass Kellner, *Herbert Marcuse and the Crisis of Marxism* (London: Macmillan, 1984), Chap. 8, "Marcuse's Theory of Advanced Industrial Society: *One Dimensional Man*" (pp. 229ff). Marcuse has a clear consciousness that the "open society"

of "late capitalism" is a cynical system, although he does not use this word.
22. In fact, strategic rationality acts as a means toward ends. Cynical reason grounds strategic rationality in the power of the system that negates the Other: it is self-referential, autopoietic, and strategic rationality. The Will-to-Power, which for Nietzsche was modern subjectivity's grounding, could now be understood only and reductively as the "grounding" of the exercise of a cynical rationality. The definition is tripolar: 1) Power as grounding, 2) Cynical reason grounded in power (and as such, a specific "type" of rationality, neither strategic, nor instrumental, nor discursive, but the reason of a dominant system as morally dominating and controlling or governing strategic and instrumental rationality in turn), 3) Strategic rationality governed by cynical reason.
23. See my *Philosophy of Liberation*, 2.1, "Proximity" (pp. 16ff). Furthermore the face-to-face is located *underneath* every argument as argument that "proposes" something to an Other by definition.
24. Enrique Dussel, *Philosophy of Liberation*, "Totality, Mediation, Exteriority," 2.2–2.4, pp. 21ff.
25. All of these categories have been extensively elaborated in the five volumes of my work *Para una ética de la liberación latinoamericana*.
26. Enrique Dussel, *Philosophy of Liberation*, pp. 49ff.
27. See my work *El último Marx (1863–1882)*, Chaps. 8–10. I argue, departing from Schelling, that Marx affirms "living labor" as the "creative source" (*schöpferische Quelle*) of value (being), from "the nothingness" of capital: this is surplus. Marx's categories resist contemporary criticism, and he show himself to be the only fundamental critic of capital, which today has pretensions of being triumphant.
28. Enrique Dussel, *Philosophy of Liberation*, 2.6, "Liberation," pp. 58ff.
29. Enrique Dussel, *Philosophy of Liberation* "Ethical Conscience," 2.6.2, pp. 59ff).
30. Everything that has been indicated in the categories such as Proximity (positivity later negated), Totality (and its meditations), and negated Exteriority (as alienation, as subsumption in the system of domination) allows this critical description.
31. The *Anwendung* of an ethical norm (of level A) in a totality under the reign of cynical reason (level B) is ethically contradictory, but discourse ethics does not have any means in order to observe such contradiction because it adopts the Popperian Open Society or Habermas's Late Capitalism as society as such [*sin más*], ambiguous but not intrinsically cynical.
32. Dussel, *Philosophy of Liberation*, 2.6, pp. 58ff. With the following possible moments: 2.6.3, "Responsibility for the Other"; 2.6.4, "The Destruction of the Order" (proportional to concrete, practical needs, from an insignificant institutional reform to a process of radical change; *a priori* it can not be judged on the viability of each case); 2.6.5, "Liberation or *Anarchy*" (proportional novelty to the degree of undertaken action, be it of a small reform or of profound change).
33. Dussel, *Philosophy of Liberation*, 2.6.9, pp. 66ff. Illegitimacy before the established law, of the "good" act which innovates and demands "new" laws.
34. This is what Noam Chomsky has clearly demonstrated with respect to the United States, where the greatest researchers of the most famous universities collaborated with the CIA and other organizations of power, see *American Power and the New Mandarins* (New York: Pantheon Books, 1969), especially the chapter "The Responsibility of The Intellectuals," pp. 323ff.
35. In this case because in the "Principle of Difference" he raises as "natural" the liberal position of North American liberal individualism, especially the economic inequality (between rich and poor).

5

Hermeneutics and Liberation[1]

My argumentative strategy will consist in following step by step the thought of Paul Ricoeur (who was born in Valence in 1913), whom we know through being his avid reader, and whose student I was in the Sorbonne during the early sixties, in order to slowly detect the differences and constructive possibilities for a mutually creative dialogue.

5.1 Following Ricoeur's Philosophical Project Step by Step

There is nothing better, in order to follow the steps of the development of Ricouer's thought, than his own testimony:

> What are the presuppositions that characterize the philosophical tradition to which I recognize myself as belonging? . . . I should like to characterize this philosophical tradition by three features: it stands in the line of a *reflexive* philosophy; it remains within the sphere of Husserlian *phenomenology*; it strives to be a *hermeneutical* variation of this phenomenology.[2]

We have, then, three levels, as much of depth as of a certain initial biographic development of the author. From the French philosopher Jean Nabert,[3] Ricoeur takes his "reflexive" philosophy[4]—first level. From Husserl,[5] obviously, Ricoeur inherits phenomenology, which he practices in a uniquely creative manner—second level. Lastly, and this is essential in the philosophical biography of our philosopher, he subsumes phenomenology within a hermeneutical position, which we could call definitive in Ricoeur. This "turn" was made between the first and the second volumes of his *Philosophy of the Will*.

In fact, in the first volume of this work, *Le volontaire et l'involontaire*,[6] it can be seen that we still find ourselves within the reflexive-phenomenological moment of an eidetic description-comprehension of emotional experience, of desiring, of loving, of the living I, of the existing body, of the "vicissitudes of freedom." In the second volume, *Finitude et culpabilité*, part 1, the human, the incommensurability and contradiction between the infinitude of the will and the finitude of intelligence, demands from philosophy that it describe the "pitifulness of misery." But it is only in the second part, *La symbolique du Mal* (1960), under the inflence of Mircea Eliade, among others, that the phenomenological hermeneutics of the definitive Ricoeur irrupts—third level. "Le symbole donne à penser"[7] will be the motto. Hermeneutics ought to have lead to an ethics, a politics, which were promised, but perhaps never accomplished. In this sense, the shorter work, parallel to his larger works, but of a greater resonance at the concrete level, was *Histoire et vérité*,[8] which helped the militant to comprehend history—especially those linked to the magazine *Esprit*, as was my case.

The next systematic step is clearly indicated by Ricoeur, being

> the circuitous route [*long détour*] by which I take up the problem left unresolved at the end of my *Symbolism of Evil*, namely the relationship between a hermeneutic of symbols and a philosophy of concrete reflection.[9]

The "circuitous route" of the hermeneutics of "desire," of symbols, of culture, had commenced—against Heidegger's ontological "short route."[10] For this task, Freud was an irreplaceable critical author, whom Ricoeur knows how to use splendidly. It is Ricoeur's *linguistic turn*, "the search of a comprehensive philosophy of language...."[11] In the end, what is of interest is not "the dream ... but *the text* of the dream account."[12]

In 1969 appeared the set of shorter works, such as the "goodbye" to France, *Le conflit des interprétations. Essais d'herméneutique.*[13] Having structuralism as his interlocutor, and always affirming the importance of reflexive philosophy, as well as the importance of the understanding of the historical context, Ricoeur takes the hermeneutics of language as the hermeneutics of history: hermeneutical phenomenology, phenomenological hermeneutics. The "linguistic model" must be referred to "structural anthropology," through the "semantic problem" of "double sense." Now it is not only Husserl, but also Heidegger, who makes himself present (hermeneutics is also ontological).[14]

When *La métaphore vive*[15] appears in 1975—the same year when my exile in Mexico begins—we can see the richness that Ricouer's own "exile" has allowed him to accumulate: Louvain, Paris, Chicago. The philosopher himself gives us his background intention:

> Three major preocuppations are apparent here. The irreducibility of the various *uses* of language.[16] ... [2] The *gathering together* the diverse forms and modes of the game of storytelling. ... [3] the text is the linguistic unit we are looking for.[17]

The "metaphor"—as well as narrative [18]—beyond the *word* and the *phrase*, and in poetic *discourse*, finds itself at ""au service de la fonction poétique, cette stratégie de discours par laquelle le langage se dépouille de sa fonction de description directe pour accéder au niveau mythique où sa fonction de découverte est libérée."[19] By reference to a "double sense," the metaphor thus opens up a *new world* of meaning.[20] Ricoeur now incorporates the British-North American and analytical philosophers in general (Strawson, Austin, Searle, Grice, Greimas, Propp, Black, Jakobson, Richards) but without losing sight of his own philosophical horizon of the phenomenological question.[21]

The impressive trilogy *Time and Narrative*[22] shows us the mature Ricoeur. In the first volume, from Aristotle to Augustine, following some hypotheses from *History and Truth*, Ricoeur describes, out of temporality, the circle of narrative and temporality, including even quasi-narrative in explicative scientific history. "Time becomes human time to the extent that it is organized after the manner of a narrative; a narrative, in turn, is meaningful to the extent that it portrays the features of temporal experience."[23] The second volume extends itself over the theme of *The Configuration of Time in Fictional Narrative*;[24] that is, over the rubrics of the popular story, the epic poem, the tragedy, the comedy, and the modern novel, all of which are different modes of the *mise en intrigue*. It is a complete *poétique du récit* which allows understanding of the productive moment in the ficticious narrative. Lastly, in volume three[25] Ricoeur articulates both *récits*, namely, the historical and the ficticious, in order to conclude with a phenomenological-hermeneutical result:

> Temporality cannot be spoken of in the direct discourse of phenomenology, but rather requires the mediation of the indirect discourse of narration.[26]

If *mimesis I* is what is given in daily human action, the *Lebenswelt* which always already presupposes a pre-understanding,[27] *mimesis II* is the poetics of discourse as an "operation of configuration,"[28] which always departs from *mimesis I*. *Mimesis III*, in turn, is now the return of the work and the produced text toward the hearer or reader,[29] who must interpret meaning hermeneutically (as Gadamer showed in *Truth and Method*). This is the theme of *From Text to Action* (1986).

As a matter of fact, this last work closes the cycle opened by *Time and Narrative, I*. It explains the meaning of a hermeneutical-phenomenology,[30] that is, how it is phenomenlogy and how it is hermeneutics. It analyzes the transition of language as "discourse," as "work," and as "text,"[31] in order to attempt a "return" to or "application" of phenomenological hermeneutics to action.[32] And just as the discourse of the metaphor was the realm of "semantic innovation," "imagination" plays a fundamental role in creative action (in social imagination, this is the whole question of utopia, of incipiency", etc.).[33] The work concludes with an opening up toward ideological, utopian, and political questions.[34]

To conclude his work, but now from out of the origin itself of his philosophical project as a "philosophy of reflection," Ricoeur wrote *Oneself as Another*,[35] which, on the one hand, still remembers Nabert and, on the other hand, appears as though it were a polemic with Levinas. Without having to reconstruct the entire discourse of Ricoeur, I would like to take up one question so as to be able to come to a conclusion, a question which is suggested by the title of the work:

> I should like to show essentially that it is impossible to construct this dialectic in a unilateral manner, whether one attempts, with Husserl, to derive the alter ego from the ego, or whether, with Levinas, one reserves for the Other the exclusive initiative for assigning responsibility to the self. A two-pronged conception of otherness remains to be constructed here, one that does justice in turn to the primacy of self-esteem and also to the primacy of the convocation to justice coming from the other.[36] Now the theme of exteriority does not reach the end of its trajectory, namely awakening a responsible response to the other's call, except by presupposing a capacity of reception, of discrimination, and of recognition that, in my opinion, belongs to another philosophy of the Same than that to which the philosophy of the Other replies.[37]

In any event, at the end, the ethics (of conviction) and the politics (of responsibility), always promised and suggested, are never developed, much less an economics, which was not even attempted. The subject (the *soi même*) of a narrative never arrives at its clarification as a subject of a transforming political action, ethically liberating, but instead provides us with immense hermeneutical material for the description of the *identity of cultures*, still at the popular level, for intercultural dialogue, out of a daily narrativity and metaphorical and ficticious poetics.

5.2 Toward a Latin American Symbolics (up to 1969)

Since 1952 at the National University of Cuyo (Mendoza, Argentina), I traversed, in seven opportunities, a variety of ethical programs (Aristotelian, Thomist, phenomenological, in the tradition of Scheler or von Hildebrand). I read Aristotle in Greek, Augustine and Thomas in Latin, Descartes or Leibniz in French, Scheler or Heidegger in German. Democratic followers of Jacques Maritain—against the fascism of our professors—we soon met Emmanuel Mounier. My doctorate in Madrid (1957–59) on the Common Good (from the pre-Socratics to Kelsen), with Maritain against Charles de Konnick, opened me to political philosophy. The discovery of the misery of my own people, which I had noticed since my childhood in the almost desert-like farm lands, took me to Europe and Israel. I discovered then, as the Mexican philosopher Leopoldo Zea indicated in his work *The Role of the Americas in History* (1957), that Latin America lies outside history. It is necessary, out of this misery, to find its place in world history, to discover its hidden being.

In 1961, returning after two years of manual labor experience in Nazareth

(Israel), where I spoke in Hebrew with the Palestinian Arabs, I began my studies in France. *The Symbolism of Evil* was Ricoeur's first book that I worked on in depth. My project of Latin American philosophizing was transformed to its foundations.

Following Ricoeur's courses at the Sorbonne, I undertook the path of the "circuitous route." I reviewed my doctoral dissertation and wrote, as a hermeneutics of symbols—in view of a hermeneutical phenomenlogy of Latin American "culture"—*Hellenistic Humanism*.[38] This work was an Indo-European anthropology, ontology, and ethics, where the body-soul dualism, the solitude of contemplation, and the ethics of asceticism (the tragic "Promethean myth" without history), and the monism of being were illustrated and studied. It was an anti-Hellenistic philosophical-hermeneutical critique. In 1964, I wrote my second work, also begun in Israel, *Semitic Humanism*,[39] where, within the same hermeneutical-philosophical tradition, I placed myself within the tradition of Rosenzweig and Buber,[40] following the analysis of a unifying "carnal" (in the sense of flesh, from the Hebrew word *basar*) anthropology, a creationist metaphysics, and a political ethics of engagement for justice. The Semitic "ethical-mythical nucleus"[41] constituted itself thus (from the dramatic Adamic myth which initiates history) in the posterior point of departure for Latin American culture.

In 1964 we organized, with Latin American students who lived in Europe, a Latin American Seminar,—whose proceedings were later published in *Esprit*.[42] Personally, I asked Ricoeur to talk about "Tâches de l'educateur politique." Among other things he said:

> Il me semble d'abord que la tâche majeure des éducateurs est d'intégrer la civilisation technique universelle à la personalité culturelle, telle que je l'ai définie plus haut, à la singularité historique de chaque groupe humain.[43]

These proposals were taken very seriously by us. This was a generational political-philosophical project.

In 1965, in Münster, I wrote a book on Latin American history (I had already written a thesis on the theme at the Sorbonne with Robert Ricard), which was published in 1967, the moment of my return to Latin America (after almost ten years in Europe). In this book I wrote:

> Every civilization has a *meaning*, though said meaning is diffused, inconsistent and it may be difficult to make out. This entire system organizes itself around an *ethical-mythical nucleus* which structures the ultimate intentional contents of a group, and which may be discovered by the hermeneutics of fundamental myths of community.[44]

As a professor of philosophy and culture (1967) at the Universidad Nacional de Resistencia (Argentina), I wrote an entire course, still unpublished, on "Latin

America in World History" where I developed integrally a hermeneutical vision of Latin America from the perspective of Asia, in its pre-Columbian history, and from Europe since 1492. My lecture of 1966, which was delivered during a preliminary visit to Argentina, entitled "Hypotheses toward the Study of Latin America in Universal History," was truly a declaration of hermeneutical principles.[45] I carried out, with numerous positive materials, an analysis of universal "civilization," from the perspective of Latin American culture as a whole, and within this, out of national histories.

From accumulated materials, collected during the preceding years, I wrote, in Mendoza in 1968, *Dualism in the Anthropology of Christendom*,[46] subtitled "From the Origin of Christianity to before the Conquest of America." Thus, I closed the trilogy: the anthropological-ethical hermeneutics of the Greeks, Semites, and Christians. Christianity passed thus from the reconquest of Spain to the conquest of America. It concerned the "clash" of world views (of the Semites in the Hellenistic world at the beginning of Christianity, as a propaedeutic of the clash that Christians will have in the colonial world).

It was precisely this clash between the "European" and the "Indian" (Caribbean, Aztec, Chibcha, Inca) worlds that deeply concerned me, and with which I dealt in depth. It was the confrontation between two worlds; the domination of one over the other; the destruction of the Amerindian world by conquest in the name of Christianity. All of these will put in crisis the Ricoeurian world, appropriate for the hermeneutics *of a culture*, but not enough for the *asymmetrical* confrontation between several cultures (one dominating, the others dominated).

5.3 Origins of Liberation Philosophy (1969–76)

After my return to Latin America, from Europe, the political situation worsened. Students asked greater political clarity from their teacher. The dictatorship of Ongania in Argentina faced growing popular opposition. In 1969 occurred the "Cordobazo" (the city of Cordoba was taken by students and workers, thus repeating what had already taken place in Mexico, Paris, and Frankfurt the year before). The "theory of dependence" began to make its inroads, showing the North-periphery economic asymmetry, as caused by the underdevelopment of the South. Fals Borda published *Sociology of Liberation* in Colombia; Augusto Salazar Bondy published *Does a Philosophy Exist in Latin America?* where he linked the impossibility of an authentic philosophy to the structural situation of dominated neocolonies. At the time I was lecturing on Ontological Ethics,[47] in the Heideggerian line, at the Universidad Nacional de Cuyo (Mendoza), when, as a member of a group of philosophers, I discovered the work of Emmanuel Levinas, *Totality and Infinity: An Essay on Exteriority*. My ontological ethics became *Towards an Ethics of Latin American Liberation*.[48]

The transition happened between the second and third chapters. In the first two chapters I argued the position of an ontological ethics (inspired by the late Heidegger, Aristotle, and others), the "circuitous route" of Ricoeur. Chapter 3 is entitled: "The Metaphysical Exteriority of the Other."[49] Why Levinas?

Because the *originary experience* of Liberation Philosophy consists in discovering the massive "fact" of domination, of the constitution of a subjectivity as "lord" of another subjectivity at the world level (from the begining of European expansion in 1492, the originary constitutive event of "modernity"), center-periphery; at the national level (elites-masses, national bourgeoise-working class and people); at the erotic level (male-female); at the pedagogical level (imperial culture, elitist, versus peripheral culture, popular, etc.); at the religious level (the fetishism of all the different levels, as idolotry). This originary "experience" —lived by all Latin Americans even in the halls of European universities, is best indicated by the category "Autrui" (another person as Other), as *pauper*.[50] The poor, the dominated, the massacred Amerindian, the Black slave, the Asiatic of the opium wars, the Jew of the concentration camps, the woman as sexual object, the child under ideological manipulation (or the youth, popular culture, or the market under the imperatives of publicity and advertisement), can never simply depart from the *l'estime de soi* (self-esteem).[51] The oppressed, tortured, destroyed, in her suffering corporeality, simply cries out, clamoring for justice:

I am hungry! Don't kill me! Have compassion for me!—cries out the miserable.

The *radical origin* is not the affirmation of one's self (the *soi-même*), for that one must be able to first reflect, assume oneself as possesing value, that is, discover onself as a person. We are before all of that. We are before the slave who was born slave and who therefore does not know he is a person. He simply cries out. The cry, as noise, as clamor, as exclamation, proto-word still not articulated, which is interpreted in its sense and meaning by those "who have ears to hear," indicates simply that someone suffers, and that from out of their suffering they emit a wail, a howl, a supplication. This is the originary "interpellation."[52] It is evident that someone ought to have "a responsible response to the other's call"[53]—this is still the question of "*ethical* conscience,"[54] and for that it must affirm itself. But, it seems to me, the *soi-même* of the responsible-hearer affirms itself as valuable in the measure to which it has previously been affected by the supplication of the other; priority which is anterior to all possible reflection, responsibility for the "taking-charge-of-the-other" is *a priori* to all reflective consciousness. We respond, responsibly before the miserable, when she has already "touched" us. The "self" reflexively comprehends itself as valuable in the "act of justice" toward the Other as an answer, and in the carrying out of the act of justice demanded by the Other. Ricoeur remains modern under the empire of the *soi-même* as origin; Levinas allows us to localize the *Autrui* as radical origin of the affirmation of the *soi-même*. Liberation Philosophy was, around the end of the sixties, that which Ricoeur required when he wrote: "A two-pronged conception of otherness remains to be constructed here, one that does justice in turn to the primacy of self-esteem and also to the primacy of the convocation to justice coming from the other."[55] The priority of the Other who interpellates constitutes the possibility of the *soi-même* as reflexively valuable, who becomes the foundation of the act of justice toward the Other. It is a circle, but one which is begun by the Other—at least on this point Liberation Philosophy agrees with Levinas.

But it was not only Levinas, it was also Marcuse and the Frankfurt school, when they "politicized" Heideggerian ontology:

> The state of capitalist well-being is a state of war. It must have an enemy, with capital E, a total enemy; because the perpetuation of servitude, the perpetuation of the struggle for existence before the new possibilities of active freedom intensify in that society a primary aggression to an extreme that history, I believe, has never known until now.[56]

But, at this moment, and because of a critique of Hegel—which was studied very much during those years since it was the second centenary of his birth, 1770–1970—we discovered the importance of the late Schelling, the Schelling of the *Philosophy of Revelation*, of the lectures from 1841 in Berlin (which were attended by Engels, Bakunin, Feuerbach, Kierkegaard). The post-Hegelians had a sense of reality (*Wirklichkeit, realitas*) which transcended the horizon of Hegel's Being.[57] The Other is beyond-Being, and in this coincided with Levinas, Sartre (of the *Critique of Dialectical Reason*), Xavier Zubiri (*On Essence*), and, as we discovered later, Marx himself. Schelling, against Hegel, speaks of the Lord of Being (*Herr des Seins*),[58] the one who creates from and out of Nothingness, metaphysical position which is also found in Marx, for example.[59]

Years later, in a retraction, under the title of "Beyond Culturalism,"[60] I criticized my position prior to 1969 (and thus Ricoeur as well), indicating by "culturalism" a certain blindness to the "asymmetries" of the subjects (a culture dominated by another, a class by another, a country by another, a sex by another), allowing thus a "naive, conservative, and apologetic" view of Latin American culture. In the background, hermeneutical phenomenology places the subject as a "reader" before a "text." Now, Liberation Philosophy discovers a "person in hunger" before a "no-bread" (that is to say, without a product for consumption, because of poverty or because of the robbery of the fruits of labor), or an "illiterate" before a "non-text" (which she cannot buy, or a culture which cannot express itself).

Soon enough, however, I realized that Levinas himself could not address our hopes.[61] Levinas showed us how to formulate the question of the irruption of the Other, but we could still not develop a politics (erotics, pedagogics, etc.)

which placed in question the ruling Totality (which dominates and excludes the Other) and could develop a *new Totality*. This critical-practical questioning of a new Totality was exactly the question of "liberation." With this Levinas could not help us.

The second volume of *Towards an Ethics of Latin American Liberation*[62] focuses on this problematic. It furnished us with many new novelties, that is, the demand to develop "new" categories for the history of political philosophy,[63] and, above all, the necessity to develop a new architectonics. The first of the categories on which we ought to focus our attention is "totality" in an oppressed world. Ontology is to think the foundation, the ground, of the Being of a *ruling Totality*. The project (the Heideggerian ontological *Entwurf*) of the ruling system justifes the oppression of the oppressed and the exclusion of the Other. Little by little, light is put on utopia (*ouk-tópos*: "without place" in the Totality); the project of the liberation of the Other. It is a question of the production of another analogical Totality, constituted with the best of the old one and the exteriority of the Other. From the interpellation of the Other, and as a response to the other, the affirmation of the Other *as other*[64] is the origin of the possibility of the negation of the dialectical negation (this is what I called the analectic method or the originary affirmation of the Other).[65]

Later, we assumed the task of delving deeper into more concrete levels: Chapter 7: "Latin American erotics"[66]; Chapter 8, "Latin American pedagogics"[67]; Chapter 9, "Latin American Politics"[68]; and Chapter 10, "Latin American Archeologics."[69] Each of these "treatises" begins—in a Ricoeurian fashion—with a "symbolics": "A symbolic erotics" (paragraph 42); "symbolic pedagogics" (paragraph 48); "symbolic politics" (paragraph 61); "symbolic archeology" (paragraph 67). In each we began with a hermeneutics of the ruling symbols in the history of Latin American culture (from Amerindian cultures through colonial and contemporary cultures). We used myths, epic narratives, oral traditions, and contemporary novels. At a second level, it was necessary to place the question ontologically, in order to allow for 1) the irruption of Other in the ruling totality (oppressed women in machist erotics; son/daughter-youth/people in the pedagogics of domination; the poor in the political economy of capitalist exploitation in the double dialectic capital/work and North/South; the fetishization of the Totality, atheistically negated in the affirmation of the Other, etc.), 2) the negation of the Totality, and 3) the process of liberation in view of the project of liberation (describing the levels of praxis and the ethos of liberation). This constituted an entire thematics *never dealt with in the European ethics* with which I am familiar. These allowed us to reflect on new problems, both categorically and architectonically.[70]

When repression grew more accute—I suffered a bomb attempt at my home—I was expulled from the university (1975). I was condemned to death by the paramilitary squadrons. I left Argentina and began my exile in a new *patria*:

Mexico. There, during two months, without my library, since this had been left in Argentina, I wrote my *Philosophy of Liberation*.[71] An epoch had ended for me. A new one began.

5.4 From Hermeneutical Pragmatics to Economics

Immediately, in Mexico, it became necessary to clarify the philosophical ambiguities that Liberation Philosophy still contained in its first stage. Among the philosophers of liberation (all of them, more than 30 university professors, were persecuted in the Argentinian universities by pro-North American, neoliberal, "modernizing" militarism since 1976, which to a certain extent is evidence of the degree to which the movement has become historically engaged), there were some who supported the Peronist right, arriving thus at extreme nationalist positions; others returned to the hermeneutics of popular symbolics, thus falling into a naive political populism; the majority had to maintain silence (because of either internal or external censure). The "populist" question became central. It became necessary to clarify the categories *pueblo* (people) and *nación* (nation) (as well as "popular" and "nationalism"), in order to prevent fascism, as well as the abstract fallacy of either classist Althusserian Marxism or Anglo-Saxon analytic thinking, both of which were in fashion at the time. It was thus that I came to delve deeper into Marx. This would distance me for some years from the hermeneutic enterprise (to which I will return later, but with clear differentiations concerning the existing *asymmetries*).[72]

A note of warning is in order. The systematic return to Marx which I undertook at the end of the decade of the seventies was due to three facts. In first place, the growing misery of the Latin American continent (which has not ceased to became poorer, to the point that it now suffers from a cholera epidemic due to the accelerated malnutrition of the majority of the people). In second place, in order to be able to carry out a critique of capitalism, which apparently was triumphant in the North (a view reinforced since 1989), but which failed unquestionably for 75 percent of humanity, in the South (Africa, Asia, Latin America). In the third place, because liberation philosophy had to construct a firm economics and politics, in order to posteriorly also secure a pragmatics, as a subsumption of analytics (in the sense already indicated). Instead of studying the European commentators of Marx, I imposed on myself the task of an integral re-reading, in university seminars. My first point of verification was to discover the abandonment of the serious, integral, creative study that the investigations on Marx had suffered at the hands of the "great" European-North American philosophers (in recent years Marx has not been read *seriously*[73]). Some "marxiologists" edited too slowly some of his works—at the Marxist-Leninist Institute, in Berlin as well as in Moscow. Marx was agreeable to neither Capitalism nor to Stalinism.

Through the hermeneutical-philosophical and chronological re-reading of Marx's work, we arrived at a moment in which *inverting the hypothesis of traditional readings* imposed itself on us as a necessity. The more anthropological, ethical, and anti-materialist (in the naive sense) Marx was not the young one (1835–48) but the definitive Marx, the Marx of the "four redactions" of *Capital* (1857–82). A great *philosopher*-economist slowly profiled himself before our eyes. Neither Lukács, Korsch, Kosík, Marcuse, Althusser, Coletti, nor Habermas fulfilled our aspirations.[74]

It was necessary to undertake the "circuitous route" of a *philosophy of economics* (just as Ricoeur had transvered the circuitous route of the hermeneutics of discourse, of the text). It was necessary to "reconstruct" the totality of Marx's central work, thus liberating him not only from dogmatic Stalinism, but also from the layers of western Marxism which had began to bury his own thought from Engels to Kautsky, and afterwards. Our Latin American philosophical goal was to consolidate economics through a "poietics" or "technology," just as Liberation Philosophy hopes to do.[75] But at the same time, we had to reformulate the concept of dependence in order to discover the cause of the North/South difference (the "transfer of value" by the different organic compositions of capital of developed and underdeveloped nations in the process of the competition of capital in the world market).[76] This led us to discover that Marx had written *Capital* four times. We took the German published texts[77] and began a close, paragraph by paragraph commentary, with the philosophical-hermeneutical intention of reconstructing the process of the theoretical production of categories and their corresponding "system."[78] In the case of the third (1863–65) and fourth (1866–82) redactions of *Capital*, we had recourse to the unpublished manuscripts, in Amsterdam (with reproductions in Berlin and Moscow).[79] We had obtained, perhaps for the first time in the history of philosophy, a global view of Marx. Now the hermeneutical reinterpretation of his work can begin. This determined a change in the architectonic of the categories of our philosophy of liberation.

In *Philosophy of Liberation* we privileged the interpersonal practical relation; that which in Austin's theory of speech acts is called the illocutionary moment, or, in Habermas, communicative action. However, from Levinas, the *face-à-face* establishes itself even in silence (before developed language, in accordance with Searle's principle of expressibility). The illocutionary is the face-to-face of two persons, or many, or of a community. It is what we call proximity (*proximité*). In fact, in *Philosophy of Liberation*, we dedicate the first section (2.1) to the description of this "original ethical situation." In second place we show the four possible levels of proximity (or the illocutionary moment of every possible speech act): the political practical relation (3.1), erotics (3.2), pedagogics (3.3), or the religious (3.4). At this level, proximity is properly *ethical*. Levinas has described with masterful hand this "ethical moment." We, on the other hand, thought that it was on this level that we and see the originality of Marx's economics (against the entire Marxist and anti-Marxist criticism tradition).[80]

At a second level, the ethical community or practical community (to speak with the Kant of *Religion within the Limits of Reason Alone*) has in its "finding-oneself-in-the-world" (Heidegger's *Befindlichkeit*) two first, *a priori* moments, always already presupposed: "linguisticality" (Gadamer's *Sprachlichkeit*) and what we could call instrumentality. That is to say, we always presuppose a world where we *speak* (we are educated in culture, by the Other, in and through a particular language), and where *tools are used* (we live in a cultural world as a system of instruments, tools). "Pragmatics" subsumes mere linguisticality in a communicative relation with the Other, in the communication community (the overcoming of solipsism by Apel and Habermas). "Signs" (as Peirce or Charles Morris would say) have a syntactic, semantic, and *pragmatic* dimension. As such, the sign is a material reality produced by human, cultural, signifying (producing) work (*le travail du texte*, we could say with Ricoeur).

In the same fashion, economics (in the *new* sense we want to give it) subsumes mere instrumentality in a practical relationship with the Other, in the "community of producers/consumers." Products (bread, for example) have a systematic (syntax) relationship among themselves, a cultural or symbolic (semantic, with reference to a need), or *economic* character (with respect to the Other and the community). As such, the product is a material-reality product of labor referred to a human, carnal need in the community. In this fashion we have indicated the parallelism between pragmatics and economics, as the two dimensions of the interpersonal practical relation which is mediated by material-cultural objects: the *communicative* relationship is mediated by signifying (interpretable) signs[81] and the *economic* relation is mediated by instrumental products of use (utility) or consumption (consumptionablity). The *production of the text* (to go directly to a final moment of Ricoeurian hermeneutics) is analogous (non-identical) to the *production of the product/commodity*. The "text" and the "product/commodity" retain independence or autonomy vis-à-vis the producer (and no one showed better than Marx how autonomy could constitute the product into a *Macht* (power) which turns against the producer as a fetish). The interpretation of the reader of a text (Ricoeur) is *analogous* to the use/comsumption of the user/consumer of the product/commodity (Marx).

Alienation before a text would consist in that, in "the self-understanding before a text," understanding would be alienating, strange, against the ethical interests of the reader. The text would constitute the reader as a mediation of the "thing of the text"; it would be manipulation, propaganda. The reader would only be "public," a market, a "follower" of the content of the text: instrumental mediation of the text. In the same fashion the product/capital can constitute the producer/worker ("living labor" for Marx) as a mediation of its own product (a thing): "the valorization of value" (the essence of capital). In this way the creator of the text can be transformed into a mediation of the social realization of the text; just as the creator of the value of capital (through accumulated surplus) can be transformed into a mediation of the realization or accumulation of capital. In both cases a "fetishist inversion" has taken place: the person has become a thing (mediation) and the thing (the text or capital) has become as if it were a person.

Liberation Philosophy presents an even more concrete and complex situation, from which there emerges a demand for a new development of hermeneutics and a transition to economics. Take, for example, a real, historical case from the 16th century, from the so-called conquest of America. Alvarado, the white, blond, European conqueror (he was thus called *Tonatiuh*, the sun, because of the shine of his hair), conquered the Mayan world of Guatemala. The Mayas were "readers" of many "texts," one of which was transcribed in the 17th century in Chichicastenango, Guatemala, and is called the *Popol-Vuh*, their sacred book.

Schema 1. Domination of "Readers" and Their "Texts"

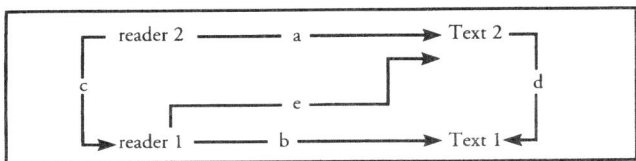

The *conquistador* (reader 2), who interprets (arrow a) his/her text (Text 2, the Hebrew-Christian Bible, for example), imposed his/her text on the Maya (reader 1), who interpreted (arrow b) his/her text (Text 1, the *Popol-Vuh*). The process which goes by the name of evangelization, for example, was precisely the process of "substitution," through domination, of Text 1 for Text 2 (arrow d), through a military, political, and economic conquest (arrow c). The Maya found herself obliged to interpret (arrow e) a strange text, from another world. In this case the hermeneutic process is complicated by the determination of a situation of "domination" of the *praxis* of a "reader" by another. These types of situations are not considered with *care* by Ricoeur. For a liberation philosophy this is the *point of departure itself* of the hermeneutical question in Latin America. That is, when Ricoeurian philosophy would seem to conclude its labor, only there begins that of a philosophy of liberation. Its questions are: Can the dominated "interpret" the "text" produced and interpreted "in-the-world" of the dominator? Under what subjective, objective, hermeneutic, textual circumstances can such interpretation be "adequately" undertaken? For someone like Salazar Bondy, in his work *Does a Philosophy Exist in Latin America?* the answer is negative. It is not possible to philosophize in such a situation! For us, from the perspective of a liberation philosophy, it is possible, but only

Hermeneutics and Liberation

it the reader, interpreter, or philosopher, engages himself in a *practical process of liberation*—all of this is precisely the theme of a philosophy and ethics of liberation.

In reality, the situation exemplified in Schema 1 can be related, as mutually conditioned, with the example of Schema 2.

Schema 2. Domination of "Producers" by "Products" in Capital

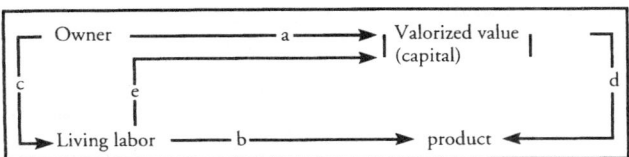

By analogy to pragmatics, in economics (in the way it was practiced by Marx, that is, philosophically and not merely as an empirical science, and thus already as "critique"[82]) the producer (as well as reader 1, and in this case "living labor") produces a product which is already "dominated" (arrow d), out of a "social relation" (arrow c) of domination (the relation capital-labor, which is unknown in Rawls's *A Theory of Justice*). The capitalist possesses (arrow a) the value, the product of the work of living labor. In reality, living labor *creates out of nothing* the surplus value (arrow e) which, through successive rotations, will finally constitute the *whole* of capital. The relation reader-text is analogous to producer-product. An alienated reader can understand himself "inauthentically" in the text; the alienated producer does not recover herself at the end of the process of labor, but instead encounters herself as negation: labor "posits itself objectively [in the product], but it posits its objectivity as *its own non-Being* [*Nichtsein*], or as the Being of its non-Being [*das Sein ihres Nichtseins*]: of capital."[83]

What we want to suggest is that it is possible to treat economics in a similar way to how we treat pragmatics or hermeneutics. The possible relations and similarites between both ought to be studied, within the Habermasian and Apelian categorizations.

For Marx, the ideal situation of every labor act is the community of producers. In the empirical situation of capitalism, relationships are solely "social"—each worker remains isolated, without community. The genuine practical and ethical relation (which Levinas calls the face-to-face) is negated by a relation which stands under the domination of instrumental reason (the capitalist "social" relation). For Marx's economics it is a question of a "critique" of capitalism from the standpoint of an *ideal community of producers* (in the Apelian sense), which is universal (for Habermas) or is simply an economic "regulative idea" from which the relation capital-labor is criticized as defective, non-ethical, and exploitative.

Without an economics, hermeneutics (or pragmatics) remains without carnal (material) content: it is a mere communication community or community of interpretation, without carnality or corporality, without subsuming in its reflection the level of "life." The human being is a "living being who has *logos*," said Aristotle. The *logos* (hermenetical or pragmatical) responds to and is the autonomous, explicit, self-reflexive, free development of the "logic" of the "living creature." Economics responds directly to the reproduction of *human life*. In this sense a communication community (*Kommunikationsgemeinschaft*) is the development of a community of life (*Lebensgemeinschaft*).

5.5 A Philosopy of "Poverty in Times of Cholera"[84]

Let us perform an exercise of "philosophical economics" such as Marx carried out. We will place ourselves at the "originary situation," where the logic of the architectonic of development of Marx's categorical system departs. It is the point of departure, today entirely pertinent and in force in every capitalist society, since the originary situation to be analyzed is so *abstract and essential* that it is also valid whenever and wherever there is capitalism, whatever its degree of development. With respect to this, the 19th and 20th centuries are different not "essentially" but "historically," contingently.

The immediate theoretical framework (which will be modified and inverted, but strictly taken into account) is the last part of the "Doctrine of Essence" of Hegel's *Science of Logic*.[85] Marx was inspired by it, and he took it as a point of reference, as a "philosophical problematic"—against what Althusser used to think some time ago. In fact, Hegel indicates that reality (*Wirklichkeit*)[86] is a moment of the phenomenon (*Erscheinung*), of the thing (*Ding*), which although already with existence (*Existenz*) has not yet developed into exteriority (*Äusserlichkeit*).[87] For Hegel, as for Marx, "being," "existence," and "reality" are three moments in the development of the "entity" (*Dasein*)[88]—for Hegel, furthermore, this is also true of the Absolute.

> Reality is the unity, become immediate, of essence with existence, or of inward with outward. The exteriorization [*Äußerung*] of the real is the real itself.[89]

The question is that of how something becomes real, that is, "posits" itself "outside" the "world of phenomena" as real. For that, it must, in first place, be "possible." Possibility (*Möglichkeit*),[90] not merely "formal,"[91] but as "identity," is what "is essential [*Wesentliche*] to reality."[92] Since that which was "possible" became real, it is said that it is contingent (*Zufällig*).[93]

> Possibility and Contingencey are the two moments of Reality—Inward and Outward, put as mere forms which constitute the *externality* of the real.[94]

So that the contingency of the "possible" can become "real," it is necessary that the condition (*Bedingungen*) be fullfilled[95]:

> If all the conditions are at hand, the thing [*Sache*] *must* be real.[96]

But a third moment is still necessary so that the "thing" can become "real." Activity (*Tätigkeit*) is still necessary:

> *a*. The Condition is (α) what is presupposed or ante-stated. . . . (ß) The Conditions are passive, are used as materials for the thing, into the content of which they must enter. *b*. The thing is also (α) something presupposed or ante-stated. . . . (ß) By using up the conditions, it receives its external existence, the realization of the determinations of its content. . . . *c*. The Activity similarly has (α) an independent existence of its own (as a man, a character), and at the same time it is possible only where the conditions are and the thing. (ß) It is the movement which translates the conditions into a thing. . . .[97]

Lastly, the "real thing," having fulfilled its conditions, is now necessary (*Notwendig*): it is substance (*Substanz*),[98] "the totality of the *Accidents*, revealing itself in them as their absolute negativity (that is to say, as absolute power) and at the same time as the wealth of all content."[99] Now we can say that "Subtance is *Cause*, insofar as substance reflects into self as against its passage into accidentality and so stands as the *primary* thing, but again no less suspends this reflection-into-self (its bare possibility), lays itself down as the negative of itself, and thus produces an *Effect*, a Reality, which, though so far only assumed as a sequence, is through the process that effectuates it at the same time."[100] We could conclude by saying that this "realm of necessity" (of cause, effect, reciprocal action, etc.) becomes in the end a "realm of freedom." "This is *the Concept*, the realm of Subjectivity or of Freedom."[101]

What does this have to do with the original situation—taking these words analogously to Rawls—described by Marx? This has a lot to do with it, because Marx, although he placed himself at an "economic" level, developed an entire metaphysics of economics (a critique of the ontology of capitalism from the Exteriority of living labor, in Levinas's sense, or better, in Schelling's sense).

The key text is always found at the begining of Marx's discourse.[102] And I say explicitly at the beginning because it is the absolute begining of economics such as it is understood by Marx. In fact, the original situation manifests itself in the contradiction between labor and money (which will later become capital). It is the first "logical" possibility of such a contradiction, in an apparent "Eden of the innate rights of man," à la Rawls.[103] For Marx this confrontation is totally asymmetrical. The possessor of money is *real*; the possesor of work is a *mere possibility*, and it is here where Marx articulated everything we have recollected of Hegel's philosophy on the "modalities" of possibility, contingency, condition, and necessity, in order to develop a philosophy of economics.

> *Separation of property from labour* appears as the necessary law of this exchange between capital and labour. Labour posited as *not-capital* as such is: (1) *not-objectified labour* [*nicht-vergegenständlichte Arbeit*], *conceived negatively* (itself still objective; the not-objective itself in objective form).[104]

Marx takes living labor (*lebendige Arbeit*) as the thing (*Sache*) which, since it has not yet exteriorized itself (in Hegel; "objectified" in Marx) is not real. In order to become real it must fulfill the "conditions." Were it not to have the possibility of fulfilling said conditions, it would simply never become real ("objective" in Marx):

> As such it is not-raw-material, not-instrument of labour, not-raw-product: labour separated from all means and objects of labour, form its entire objectivity.[105] This living labour, existing[106] as an *abstraction* from these moments of its *real Reality*[107] (also not-value[108]); this complete denudation, purely subjective existence of labour, stripped of all objectivity. Labour as *absolute poverty*: poverty not as shortage, but as total exclusion of objective wealth.[109]

Marx then takes living labor as the thing which is "pure possibility"; which has no conditions[110] in order to become real. That pure possibility is *economically determined* (this is what interests me today as a Latin American): it is poverty (*Armut*).[111] Before being a "class" (work subsumed "in" capital), living labor is poverty. The *pauper ante festum*—as Marx repeadly says—is the absolute *negative* conditon of the existence of capital. Were there no poor there would be no one who would sell their corporeality, their own person, their own *creative* subjectivity, for money (which is only "objectified labor," that is, dead in opposition to living labor). The "ethical option for the poor" is, exactly, Levinas's *a priori* res-ponsibility (and not Jonas's *a posteriori*), as well as Marx's. That existing but unreal (non-objective) thing is clearly determined in Marx's view:

> Or also as the existing *not-value*, and hence purely objective use value, existing without mediation, this objectivity can only be an objectivity not separated from the *person:* only an objectivity coinciding with his immediate *corporality* [*Leiblichkeit*].[112]

The person (Is Marx a "personalist"?) presents itself in "the world of commodities" (or of "phenomena," both expressions are frequent in Marx) through her "corporeality."[113] Marx describes, thus, the situation "prior to the contract" between capital and labor, in which the worker is not real but merely possibility, since she possesses no objective conditions for her own realization. Her own being, her personhood, her corporeality is negativity, poverty (economic subjectivity, not a question of the hermeneutic subjectivity of the reader of a text): the immediate subjectivity of a suffering corporeality, without resources, without food, without means to reproduce her life. This is the point of departure for Liberation Philosophy, as a Latin American "fact," described phenomenologically as a primary "ethical" fact by Levinas. Now Marx places it within an architectonic and categorical discourse, as a critique of the bourgeois political economy of his time.[114]

Until now living labor finds itself in the Exteriority (*ante festum*, to use Marx's expression, and just as Levinas articulates it), and negatively, as existing thing, as pure possibility, not real, without conditions—poor. It is the not-capital, the non-being, the nothing.[115] But, Marx advances, "positively," that subjectivity in extreme destitution is a "potency":[116]

> (2) *Not-objectified labour, not-value*, conceived *positively*, or as a negativity in relation to itself, is the *not-objectified*, hence non-objective, i.e. subjective existence of labour itself. Labour not as an object, but as activity [*Tätigkeit*];[117] not as itself *value*, but as the *living source [lebendige Quelle]* of value.[118] [Namely, it is] general wealth (in contrast to capital in which it exits objectively,[119] as reality) as the *general possibility*[120] of the same, which proves itself as such in action.[121]

Before which Marx concludes:

> Thus, it is not at all contradictory, or, rather, the in-every-way mutually contradictory statements that labour is *absolute poverty as object*, on one side, and is, on the other side, the *general possibility* of wealth as *subject* and as *activity*, are reciprocally determined and follow from the essence of labour, such as it is *presupposed* by capital as its contradiction and as its contradictory being,[122] and as such it, in turn, presupposes capital.[123]

Philosophically, and taking into account Hegelian ontology at its most abstract and essential moment, namely in its concept of reality, (*Wirklichkeit*), Marx develops an economics of great contemporary relevance. Today, the majority of humanity (the South, the ex-colonial and peripheral world), is sunk in poverty: it has neither the conditions for its realization, nor will it have them in the future due to ecological exigencies. It is sunk in absolute poverty, and it will descend deeper into greater degrees of poverty. Marx is the *only* European philosopher who has developed a relevant economics, albeit the *great* modern European-North American philosophers (without re-reading Marx seriously, because he is not in fashion) have declared him a "dead dog." For Liberation Philosophy it is not a question of fashion. It is a question of life or death for the majority of humanity. It is a *radical ethical* question, where the universality of reason and the meaning of all hermeneutics are at play.

Once living labor is sold, it is alienated from capital, it is subsumed in the Totality (in the Levinasian or Marcusian sense) of capital. From the ground (*Grund*) or the being of capital (the valorization of value) living labor is posited as a mediation of value: the thing becomes person (value) and the person a thing (the worker), the fetishism of capital.

In fact, "Labour is the *substance* [*Substanz*],[124] and the immanent measure of values, but it has no value itself."[125] In this is summarized the entire ethical economics of Marx. The person, subjectivity, corporeality, and human activity named living labor is the "*creative source* of value *from out of the nothing* of capital," and thus, as such it cannot have any value. "Therefore what they [the capitalist political economists] called the 'value of labour' is in fact the value of labour-power, as it exists in the personality of the worker...."[126] When this labor, which is objectified life, does not return to the worker, then its negativity is his own not-being, his own misery:

> Finally, the law [of accumulation]..... makes an *accumulation of misery* as a necessary condition, corresponding to the accumulation of wealth. *Accumulation of wealth* at one pole is, therefore, at the same time *accumulation of misery*, the torment of labour, slavery, ignorance, brutalization and moral degradation at the opposite pole, i.e. on the side of the class that produces its own product as capital.[127]

Living labor objectifies life as value, which is not recuperable. But, because of a second movement, a more developed capital can appropriate the value of others less developed, just as a more developed nation appropriates the value of a less-developed nation:

> From the possibility that profit may be *less than* surplus value.... it follows that not only individual capitalists, but also *nations* may continually exchange with one another, may even continually repeat the exchange on an ever-expanding scale.... One of the nations may continually appropriate for itself a part of the surplus labour of the other, giving back nothing for it in the exchange.[128]

It is thus that Marx allows us, as philosophers of the periphery of the world system (as Wallerstein would put it), of the South, to think a Philosophy of Liberation for the domination from the North—remaining critical of those philosophers of the North (not all, to be sure) who ignore all of these question, since they confuse economic philosophy with stalinism, thus washing their philosophical hands ("clean hands," Sartre would say) from the miserable fate of *the majority of contemporary humanity*.

It is because of this reason that liberation philosophy has as its first chapter a philosophy of misery, and Marx (today more than ever, after the fall of the Berlin Wall in 1989 and George Bush's declaration of the "American Empire," on the 29 January 1991, before the U.S. Congress) must be taken into account in order to develop the circuitous route of an economics without which hermeneutics becomes ideological, idealist, literalist. There are not only *readers* before *texts*; there are many *hungry people* before the *non-bread* (even though they have been the producers of *bread*). Someone said: "I was hungry and you gave me nothing to eat!" as the *absolute* criterion of every possible ethics. Therefore, hunger and food—as was Feuerbach's opinion—are themes of a philosophical economics, an economics which is not merely a system à la Habermas; nor a mere question of "level B" of ethics as is the case in Apel. Economics is a central moment, where hermeneutical-pragmatic is another, of a Philosophy of Liberation, of a philosophy of "poverty in times of cholera."

Notes

1. This essay was originally presented in Naples, in April of 1991, during a seminar on "Philosophy and Liberation, in Dialogue with Paul Ricoeur," published in *Filosofia e liberazione. La sfida del pensiero del Terzo-Mondo* (Lecce: Capone Editore, 1992), pp. 78–107.
2. Paul Ricoeur, *From Text to Action: Essays in Hermeneutics, II* trans. Kathleen Blamey and John B. Thompson (Evanston: Northwestern Univeristy Press, 1991), p. 12. Emphasis added.
3. See Ricoeur's preface to Nabert's work, *Elements for an Ethic*, trans. Wiliam J. Petrek (Evanston: Northwestern University Press, 1969); and the article "Nabert on Act and Sign," which appeared first in *Les études philosophiques*, 17, 1962, pp. 339–49 (reprinted in *The Conflict of Interpretations: Essays in Hermeneutics* ed. Don Ihde (Evanston: Northwestern University Press, 1979), pp. 211–22. Nabert, who stands in the tradition which stems from Maine de Biran, thinks, we are told by Ricoeur, that "the operations of active consciousness are not reducible to those which control knowledge and science, and reflective analysis applied to action must be liberated from the hegemony of epistemology (*The Conflict of Interpretations*, p. 212). Ricoeur comments: "Nabert expects the final balance of reflective philosophy from this reintegration of the objective *cogito* with and within active and productive consciousness" (ibid., p. 213).
4. Which traverses Ricoeur's entire philosophical life, from his first works to the last. Thus, in his *Oneself as Another* (which I received from his own hands in April of 1990 in Chicago), at the begining of the Introduction ("The Question of the Selfhood"), he writes: "The first intention was to indicate the primacy of reflective mediation over the immediate positing of the subject, as this is expressed in the first person singular" (p. 1).
5. Ricoeur's translation, with a long introduction, *Idées directrices pour une Phénoménologie* (Paris: Université de Paris, 1950). This work I also received from his own hands in 1964 at the Sorbonne. This work amply demonstrates his knowledge of the subject matter. Ricoeur remains faithful to phenomenology in the sense of a particular personal depth.
6. The work *La philosophie de la volonté* (Paris: Aubier, 1950–1960), is made up of two volumes, the second of these which is made up of two volumes: *Finitude et Culpabilité, 1. L'homme faillible*, and *2. La symbolique du mal*. Before these works, Ricoeur had written *Karl Jaspers* in 1947, and *Gabriel Marcel and Karl Jaspers*, in 1948. Incidentally, both authors influenced Ricoeur significantly, while, on the other hand, the influence of his friend Emmanuel Mounier is not so evident—at least in the philosophical work of this period.
7. Paul Ricoeur, *La Symbolique du Mal*, (Paris: Aubier, 1960), pp. 323ff.
8. Paul Ricoeur, *Histoire et vérité*, (Paris: Seuil, 1955). English translation, Paul

Ricoeur, *History and Truth* (Evanston: Northwestern Univeristy Press, 1965).
9. Paul Ricoeur, *Freud and Philosophy* (New Haven: Yale University press, 1970), p. xii.
10. The short article on "Universal Civilization and National Cultures," originally published in *Esprit* and later published in the second edition of *Histoire et vérité* (see *History and Truth*, pp. 271–84) had a great impact on me.
11. Paul Ricoeur *Freud*, p. 3. Only after his exit from France, posterior to 1968, will Ricoeur have the opportunity to open himself up to British-North American thinking. For the moment, "We have at our disposal a symbolic logic, an exegetical science, and anthropology, and a psychoanalysis and, perhaps for the first time, we are able to encompass in a single question the problem of the unification of *human discourse*" (ibid., pp. 3–4; emphasis added). Here Ricoeur's hermeneutical project can be seen clearly.
12. Ibid., p. 5; emphasis added. In any event the background project remains in place: "Hermeneutic Method and Reflective Philosophy" (ibid., Book 1, Chap. III, pp. 37ff). I have given an account, part by part, of the thematic of this book in the third volume of my work *Para una ética de la liberación latinoamericana* (Buenos Alves: Siglo XXI, 1973): "La erótica latinoamericana," pp. 50–122.
13. Paul Ricoeur, *Le conflit des interprétations. Essais d'nerméneutique*, (Paris: Seuil, 1969).
14. "New hermeneutical ontology" (*From Text to Action*, p. 19).
15. Paul Ricoeur, *La métaphore vive* (Paris: Seuil, 1975). This work should be considered in parallel with *Time and Narrative*, Vol. 1.
16. Ricoeur adds: "It can thus be seen that from the start I have affiliated myself with those analytical philosophers who resist the sort of reductionism according to which 'well-formed languages' are alone capable of evaluating the meaning claims and truth claims of all non-'logical' uses of language." (*From Text to Action*, p. 2).
17. *From Text to Action*, pp. 1–3.
18. "Metaphor ... narrative ... the meaning-effects produced by each of them belong to the same basic phenomenon of semantic innovation." *Time and Narrative* (Chicago: University of Chicago Press, 1984), Vol. 1, p. ix. What was of interest to me, in *Philosophy of Liberation* (Maryknoll, Orbis Book, 1985) is precisely this aspect of innovation, novelty, which frees language.
19. Ibid., p. 311. This "liberation" of novelty which the metaphor *opens up* is important for a *liberating* discourse.
20. In this strictly Ricoeurian sense I have, in my work *The Theological Metaphors of Marx* (Las Metáforas Teologicas de Marx) (Navarra, Spain: Editorial Verbo Divino, 1993), dealt not only with the religious "metaphors" in Marx's economic work, but I have also taken all of these metaphors, in their logic, and I have concluded that one can speak of an authentic "metaphorical" theology (an explicit "theology of liberation," but metaphorical in the definitive economic work of Marx of 1857 through 1882).
21. Ibid., pp. 323ff.
22. Paul Ricoeur, *Time and Narrative* Vol. 1–3 (Chicago: University of Chicago Press, 1984–88).
23. Ricoeur, *Time and Narrative*, Vol. 1, p. 3.
24. Ibid., Vol. 2.
25. Ibid., Vol. 3, *Narrated Time*.
26. Ibid., p. 241.

27. Ibid., Vol. 1, pp. 54ff.
28. Ibid., pp. 64ff.
29. "[*Mimèsis III*] marks the intersection of the world of the text and the world of the hearer or reader..." (*Time and Narrative*, Vol. 1, p. 71).
30. Paul Ricoeur, *From Text to Action* First part: "For a Hermeneutical Phenomenology," pp. 25ff.
31. Ibid., pp. 105ff. Those pages on "What is a text?" are magnificent (pp. 105ff).
32. This return begins from page 168: "Imagination in Discourse and in Action," and especially, "The Model of the Text: Meaningful Action Considered as a Text" (pp. 144ff.).
33. Ibid., pp. 213–77. I must indicate that for a philosophy of liberation these reflections are of extreme interest, if from the "initiative" we substract all reference to the "private initiative" of the market and capitalist competition.
34. Ibid., pp. 281ff. Here there are some lines on the question of the relation between ethics, politics, and economics, which depart from the works of Hannah Arendt and Eric Weil (pp. 393ff) and which place themselves in critical opposition to Marx—who neglected the political. It is interesting to note that Domenico Jervolino had anticipated this problem in his work *Il cogito e l'ermeneutica. La questione del soggetto in Ricoeur* (Napoli: Procaccini, 1984), p. 185: "Dalla *poetica della libertà* è da attendersi un'etica e forse anche una politica della liberazione (una politica come disciplina filosofica): sarebbe anche possibile cercare i precorrimenti e le prefigurazioni di tale etica e di tale politica tra gli scritti del Ricoeur."
35. Paul Ricoeur, *Oneself as Another* (Chicago: The University of Chicago Press, 1992).
36. Paul Ricoeur, *Oneself as Another*, p. 331.
37. Ibid., p. 339. In another place Ricoeur writes: "Let us attempt, in conclusion, to take an overview of the entire range of attitudes deployed between the two extremes of the summons to responsibility, where the initiative comes from the other, and of sympathy for the suffering other, where the initiative comes from the loving self, friendship appearing as a midpoint where the self and the other share equally the same wish to live together," (ibid., p. 192).
38. Enrique Dussel, *Helennic Humanism* was written in France in 1962, but published in Argentina by EUDEBA in 1975, at the time of the military coup d'état. Packages of the recently published work remained hidden in the warehouses of the publishing house. It was only in 1984, when the miliary dictatorship fell, because of the war of the Malvinas, that the book was delivered to the bookstores. My books were not allowed to be sold under the dictatorship because my name was blacklisted. I had been exiled for nine years in Mexico. In the prologue, I wrote: "Following Paul Ricoeur, we can say that it is not only a theoretical view of the world, but also a concrete existential posture, a way of acting and behaving" (*Ethos*) (p. ix). Our intention was "to deal adequately with the actual pre-philosophical world in our contemporary America, which is the ultimate object of our investigations" (p. xii).
39. Dussel, *Semitic Humanism* (Buenos Aires: EUDEBA, 1969), published, paradoxically, before the one that had been written first. In the "Hypotheses of Investigation" we concluded: "We pretend to ground the values of our own culture [a labor] of great need in order to embrace the presuppositions of our own Latin American *world*" (p. xiii).
40. At that time I was not aware of the roots of this tradition in Schelling and Feuerbach.

41. This concept was used by Ricoeur in "Universal Civilization and National Cultures," which I went on to use in many of my later historical descriptions, and which I even used in the *Documents* of the bishops who gathered at Puebla (1979), without recognizing that I introduced this concept departing from Ricoeur into the Latin American philosophical culture.
42. Under the title "Amérique Latine et conscience chrétienne," July-August, 1965. In my article "Chrétientés latino-américaines," pp. 2–20, Ricoeur's influence can be seen when I wrote: "Tout système de civilisation s'organise autour d'une substance, d'un foyer, d'un *noyau éthico-mythique* (valeur fondamentales du groupe), qui peut être mis à jour grâce à l'herméneutique des *mythes de base* de la communauté, la philosophie de la religion étant, à cet effect, un des instruments indispensables" (pp. 3–4). . . . Ce travail de discernement phénoménologique n'a pas été réalisé jusqu'à présent" (p. 5). This article, expanded, appeared as a book, (*América Latina y conciencia cristiana* (Quito: IPLA, 1970), along with a new work, "Hipótesis para el estudio de la cultura latinoamericana" (pp. 63–80). In my work *América Latina: Dependencia y Liberación* (Buenos Aires: García Cambeiro, 1974) are collected my articles from 1964, where the influence of Ricoeur can also be seen in my analyses of Latin American culture.
43. *Esprit*, 7–8, 1965, p. 91. During the sessions of this week, there also spoke Claude Trestomant, Yves Congar, Josue de Castro, Germán Arciniegas (although his work was not published), and others. In 1965, in Ortega y Gasset's journal *Revista de Occidente*, I published "Iberoamérica en la historia universal," April 1965, pp. 85–95), along the same lines.
44. Enrique Dussel, "La civilización y su *núcleo ético-mítico*" in *Hipótesis para una historia de la iglesia en América Latina* (Barcelona: Estela, 1967), p. 28.
45. In rotaprint, Universidad Nacional de Resistencia, 1966. This was later published many times, for example, under the title "Cultura, cultura popular latinoamericana y cultura nacional" in *Cuyo* (Mendoza, Argentina), 4, 1968, pp. 7–40. It also appeared in *Método para una filosofía de la liberación* (Salamanca: Sígueme, 1974), pp. 205ff. In August of 1968, I lectured on "Cultura latinoamericana" (Villa Devoto, Buenos Aires), unpublished, which began: "I. Towards a philosophy of culture. Civilization, nucleus of values, ethos and life style" (pp. 33ff).
46. Enrique Dussel, *El dualismo en la antropología de la cristiandad* (Buenos Airies: Editorial Guadalupe, 1974).
47. We had already given a preparatory course, *Para una destrucción de la historia de la ética*, published three years laters (Mendoza: Ser y Tiempo, 1972). This was to be followed by two volumes on history never published.
48. Dussel, *Para una ética de la liberación latinoamericana* (Buenos Aires: Siglo XXI, 1973, Vols. I and II). The third volume appeared in my Mexico exile, through the publishers Edicol (1977). The fourth and fifth volumes appeared in Bogotá (USTA, 1979–80).
49. Ibid., Vol. 1, Paragraphs 13–19; pp. 97–156.
50. Levinas speaks of the Other (*Autrui*) as "pauvre," but Marx already had done similarly, as we will see, and within the same tradition (originating in the old Schelling and Feuerbach).
51. See Ricoeur, *Oneself as Another*, p. 331.
52. See chapter two of this work, pp. 000.
53. Ibid., p. 339.
54. See my *Para una ética de la liberación latinoamericana*, paragraph 24, "La *conciencia*

ética como oír la voz-del-Otro" (Vol. II, Chap. IV, pp. 52–58). Simple "*moral* conscience" applies (*applicatio* or *Anwendung*) the principles of the established system; "*ethical* conscience" opens itself to the exteriority and has criteria of discernment: "Who will be able to distinguish the master from the executioner, the master who calls for a discipline from the master who requires a slave?" (Ricoeur, *Oneself as Another*, p. 339).
55. See Ricoeur, *Oneself as Another*, p. 331.
56. Herbert Marcuse, *Dialectics of Freedom* (Mexico: Siglo XXI, 1968), p. 190 (cited in *Para una ética de la liberación latinoamericana*, Vol. I, p. 192, n. 425).
57. This is the thesis which I developed in the second volume of *Para una ética de la liberación latinoamericana*, and specifically in *Método para una filosofía de la Liberación*, already cited, pp. 114ff. On the theme see the work of Anton Peter, *Der Befreiungstheologie und der Transzendentaltheologische Denkansatz. Ein Beitrag zum Gespraech zwischen Enrique Dussel und Karl Rahner* (Freiburg: Herder, 1988), where the transition was made from Hegel to Schelling, by Feuerbach, Kierkegaard, Marx, et al., until arriving at Levinas; Roberto Goizueta, *Liberation, Method and Dialogue. Enrique Dussel and North American Theological Discourse* (Atlanta: American Academy of Religion, Scholars Press, 1988); Edgard Moros, *The Philosophy of Liberation of Enrique Dussel: An Alternative to Marxism in Latin America?* (Dissertation, Vanderbilt University, 1984); Jesús Jiménez-Orte, *Fondements Ethiques d'une Philosophie Latinoaméricaine de la Libération: E. Dussel* (Dissertation, Universite of Montreal, 1985); Mariano Moreno, *Filosofía de la Liberación como Personalismo* (Doctoral thesis, Murcia, Spain, 1994).
58. "The Lord of Being (*Herr des Seins*), a much more appropriate notion than that which says that God is Being itself (*tò òn*)" (*Schelling Werke*, ed. Manfred Schroeter, Vol. V (Munich: Beck, 1958), p. 306. This may have inspired Heidegger to speak of Dasein as the "shepherd of Being."
59. See my work *El último Marx (1863–1882)* (México: Siglo XXI, 1990) Chap. 9.2, pp. 336ff. In his thirteenth lecture Schelling says: "It is said that something has been created *out of nothing [aus Nichts geschaffen]*, that means that something has its being due to a divine will" (*Philosohie der Offenbarung* [Frankfurt: Surhkamp, 1977], pp. 179–80). Marx expressed, on the one hand, that the creation of surplus-value for the capitalist "has all the charms of something *created out of nothing [Schöpfung aus Nichts]*" (*Capital*, Vol. 1, p. 325 [*MEGA* II, 6, p. 226, lines 7–9]. And, on the other, Marx also says of living labor, "in exchange for his labour capacity as a fixed, available magnitude, he surrenders its *creative power [schöpferische Kraft]*, like Esau his birthright for a mess of pottage" (*Grundrisse*, p. 307; German [Berlin: Dietz Verlag, 1974], p. 214, lines 29–31), or "What is produced in addition to that [the reproduction of living labour capacities] is not reproduction but rather *new creation*, and, more specifically, *creation of new values [neue Wertschöpfung]*, because it is the objectification of *new* labour time in a use value" (Ibid., p. 359; German, pp. 264, line 44–265, line 1). It reproduces the value of the wage earner, but when working during the surplus labor time, *it creates value out of the nothing of capital*. This theme I have treated extensively in commentaries on the four redactions of *Capital*. This is the unkown, Schellingian current in Marx.
60. In the general introduction to the *Historia de la Iglesia en América Latina* (Salamanca: Sígueme, 1983), pp. 34–36.
61. I have written in *Liberación latinoamericana y Emmanuel Levinas* (Buenos Aires: Bonum, 1975), an explicit presentation of this critique.

62. Enrique Dussel, *Para una ética de la liberación latinamericana* (Buenos Aires: Siglo XXI, 1973).
63. It is here where the philosospher of the periphery feels sadness, pain, and even anger. It was twenty years ago that I published an ethics in five volumes, in "Spanish." This means it is "unpublished" for the philosophy of the "center" (English, German, or French). Many misuntanderding, could have been prevented if my colleagues had read these volumes. But since it is in Spanish, it is as though it had never been published! In French, one can find part of Chap. VI, Vol. II, under the title "Pensée analéctique et philosophie de la liberation" in *Analogie et Analéctique* (Genève: Labor et Fides, 1982), pp. 93–120. A new version of this same thematic is now present in works that have emerged from my debate with Karl-Otto Apel; see Fornet-Betancourt, ed. *Ethik und Befreiung* (Aachen: Augustinos Buchhandlung, 1990) and chapter 2 in this volume. Now, however, it is articulated from a pragmatic perspective, and not solely trans-ontological phenomenological, as was the case in 1971.
64. The question of affirmation as origin of the negation of the negation was clearly articulated by Ricoeur ("Negativity and Primary Affirmation" in *History and Truth*, pp. 305ff). The only difference is that, in contrast to Ricoeur and Nabert, I thought of the affirmation of the Other as Other, as possibility and point of departure of negation and the negation that weighs down on the oppressed as *oppressed* in a system, and on the "I" itself (*soi-même*) as dominator. The analectic moment consists, exactly, in the affirmation of the person of the oppressed as *person*, and out of said "affirmation" to negate, let us say, his negation as "slave," as "sexual object" (dominated woman), as "wage labor" (in capitalism), etc. Chapter VI, "The Method of Ethics" (*Para una ética de la liberación latinoamericana*, Vol. I, pp. 129ff) deals with this theme. And I return to it in *Método para una Filosofía de la Liberación* (Salamanca: Sígueme, 1974), departing out of reinterpretation of the post-Hegelian Schelling of the *Philosophie der Offenbarung* of 1841. See Anton Peter's thesis, already cited.
65. Later this position was gathered my *Philosophy of Liberation*, pp. 158ff.
66. Dussel, *Filosofía ética de la liberación* (1973), Vol. III (Mexico: Edicol, 1977), pp. 1–121.
67. Ibid., pp. 123–227.
68. Dussel, *Filosofía ética latinoamericana*, Vol. IV (Bogota: USTA, 1979).
69. Ibid., Vol. V (Bogota: USTA, 1980).
70. In 1974 appeared my *América Latina: Dependencia y Liberación* (Buenos Aires: Garcia Cambeiro, 1974), which included articles from this period.
71. Enrique Dussel, *Filosofía de la liberación* (Mexico: Edicol, 1977). This work has later editions in Argentina, Mexico, Brasil, the United States, Italy, and Germany. In 1983 appeared my *Praxis latinoamericana y Filosofía de la Liberación* (Bogota: Nueva América, 1983) with articles from this period.
72. The clearest article on this point was "Cultura latinoamericna y filosofía de la liberación (Cultura popular revolucionaria, más allá del populismo y el dogmatismo)," published in different places, among them *Ponencias* (III Congreso Internacional de Filosofía Latinoamericana; Bogotá: USTA, 1984), pp. 63–108. In this work I showed the complexity of many cultures in opposition (transnational culture, national culture, mass culture, Enlightenment culture, popular and working-class culture, ethnic and *campesina* culture, etc.), which in certain situations (like Nicaragua at that time) can become a creating "subject" of new cultures. "Revolutionary popular culture" would become the new matrix of a hermeneutics of

Hermeneutics and Liberation 99

liberation. The "readers" have been differentiated, the "texts" find themselves in contradiction. A philosophy such as that of Ricoeur would need many new distinctions in order to account for the *asymmetrical* complexity of the hermeneutics of peripheral countries, of the South.

73. This becames patently clear from the citations, the bibliographies, and the weakness of the arguments.
74. Concerning these philosophers see Chap. 8 of my work *El último Marx (1863–1882)*, pp. 297–332, "Philosophical Interpretations of Marx's Work."
75. See my *Filosofía de la Producción*, where I developed a whole philosophy of *poiesis* (which ought to be clearly distinguised from *praxis*).
76. See Chap. 15, "The Manuscripts of 61–63 and the Concept of Dependency" in my *El último Marx (1863–1882)*, pp. 312ff; see also *El último Marx (1863–1882) y la liberación latinamericana* (Mexico: Siglo XXI, 1990).
77. Which were: 1) The *Grundrisse* (published successively in 1939 and 1954), 2) the *Manuscripts of 61–63* (published in 1977 and 1982, in the *MEGA* II, 3, 1–6 [Marx-Engels *Collected Works*, Second Series, Vol. 3, parts 1 through 6]).
78. Thus there appeared my three volumes: *La producción teórica de Marx. Un comentario a los "Grundrisse"*, where we carried out a commentary of the first redaction; *Hacia un Marx desconocido. Comentario de los Manuscritos del 61–63*, where we carried out a commentary of the second redaction; *El último Marx (1863–1882) y la liberación latinoamericana*, already cited.
79. *El último Marx (1863–1882)* consists of a commentary on the third and fourth redactions.
80. Note the priority of the practical relation to the poietic or technological relation in Marx, in the following example: "The possession of nature is always already mediated through his existence as a member of a *community* . . . a relationship to other human beings, which conditions his relation to nature." (Karl Marx, *Manuscripts of 61–63* in *MEGA II*, 3.5, p. 1818). On this is based our whole reinterpretation of Marx, and we come to the affirmation that *Capital* is an ethics (see *El último Marx*, Chap. 10.4).
81. Among the possible positions of interpretability we find the "reader-before-a-text," which has been so magisterially described by Ricoeur.
82. See my *Hacia un Marx desconocido*, Chap. 14, for a clarification of the meaning of "science" for Marx (pp. 285–311).
83. Marx, *Manuscripts of 61–63*, in *MEGA* II, 3.6, p. 2239, 20–22; emphasis added. The full German citation reads: "Dieser Verwirklichungsproceß ist ebenso der Entwirklichungsproceß der Arbeit. Sie setzt sich objektiv, aber sie setzt ihre Objektivität als ihre eignes Nichtsein, oder als das Sein ihres Nichtseins—des Capitals." Was not Marx a philosopher?
84. "Poverty in Times of Cholera" is the title of an article that appeared in *Página Uno* (Mexico), 3 March 1991, p. 4, in which it is said that the *Vibrio cholerae* (the cholera virus) began, in the actual epidemic in Peru, in a neighborhood close to the port, in Chimbote, about which we read: "In the last ten years this locality has had an explosive and disorganized growth, due to which 50 percent of the population lacks the most elemental services of water and drainage. . . . The microorganism of cholera has found a favourable environment in which it can spread with incredible speed because of the *extreme poverty that affects large groups of the population*."
85. We will take into account *The Science of Logic: Theorie Werkausgabe*, Vol. 6 (Frankfurt: Suhrkamp, 1969); English: *Hegel's Science of Logic*, 2 vols., trans. W.

H. Johnston and L. G. Struthers (London: George Allen & Unwin, and New York: Humanities Press Inc. 1929); and the *Encyclopedia of the Philosophical Sciences: Theorie Werkausgabe*, Vol. 8 (Frankfurt: Suhrkamp, 1969; English: *Hegel's Logic*, trans. William Wallace (Oxford: Clarendon Press, 1975).

86. In this text we will use "reality" whenever *Wirklichkeit* appears in the original German, even when translations translate it as "actuality."
87. I note that for Marx the entire problem of exteriorization (*Äusserung*) is translated *economically* as objectification (*Gegenständlichung*)—the definitive way of dealing with the question of alienation (*Entfremdung, Entäusserung*), in its cultural or productive aspects. The negative meaning of alienation is expressed through "subsumption."
88. "Surplus value," for example, can have "being" in the product, can "exist" in the commodity, but only becomes "real" in the profit obtained through the selling of said commodity. The profit is the *real* surplus value as *realized*. Existing surplus value, for example, is annihilated if the commodity is not sold; it does not become real.
89. *Hegel's Logic*, § 142, pp. 200–01. (translation slightly modified).
90. Ibid., § 143, p. 202.
91. Above all, "But at this point, Real and Possible being formal distinctions, their relation too is only formal, and consists in this only, that the one as well as the other is a positedness, that is, in *Contingency*." *Hegel's Science of Logic*, Vol. 2, p. 174.
92. Ibid.
93. Ibid., § 144.
94. Ibid., § 145, emphasis added.
95. Ibid., § 146.
96. Ibid., § 147.
97. Ibid., § 148.
98. Ibid, §§ 149–51.
99. Ibid., § 151.
100. Ibid., § 153.
101. *Hegel's Science of Logic*, at the end of the section "Doctrine of Essence," p. 205. The same is said at the end of paragraph 159 of the *Encyclopedia*: "The great vision of substance in Spinoza is only a potential liberation from finite exclusiveness and egotism: but the concept itself realizes for its own both the power of necessity and real freedom" (*Hegel's Logic*, p. 222; see also the *Zusatz* to paragraph 151).
102. In the *Grundrisse*, p. 295–96; German (Berlin: Dietz Verlag, 1974), pp. 203–04; see the commentary in my work *La producción teórica de Marx*, Chap. 7.1, pp. 138ff. In the *Manuscripts of 61–63* (in *MEGA* II, 3, 1, pp. 147–48, also in p. 30; commentary in my work *Hacia un Marx desconocido*, Chap. 3.2. pp. 62ff). In the definitive text of *Capital*, I, Chap. 2, 3 (1867), section 2; Chap. 4, 3 (1873) (German [*MEGA* II, 5], pp. 120ff; English, *Capital*, Vol 1. p. 270ff; Commentary in my work *El último Marx*, Chap. 5, pp. 138ff).
103. *Capital*, Vol. 1, p. 280.
104. *Grundrisse*, p. 295. Italics in original. In 1963 Marx wrote: "The autonomy of the *being-for-itself-of-value* in the form of money.... confronts contradictorily the capacity of living labor.... This absolute separation between property and labor, between value and the value-creating capacity [*Wertschaffendenthätigkeit*], and because of that the *alienation* of the content of labor against labor itself,

manifests itself now as *product* of labor itself, as objectification of its own moments" (*Manuscripts of 61–63*, in *MEGA* II, 3, p. 2238,3–19). This alienation is no longer that which is given in the original situation, but in the final situation, when labor has become alienated *product*.
105. Without the objective "conditions" of labor it is not real, that is, it does not have objectivity.
106. It can exist, but is not real.
107. Hegel uses this expression explicitly: "For Possibility is not yet real *Reality*—no question has yet arisen of *real* and absolute Reality—it is only that Possibility which first occurred—Formal Possibility, which determined itself to be *only* Possibility. (*Hegel's Science of Logic*, p. 177).
108. That is, without "effect."
109. *Grundrisse*, p. 295–96. translation slightly altered.
110. "The *objective conditions* of living labour manifest themselves as values separately autonomous, contradictory to the living capacity as a subjective entity [*Dasein*]. . . . What is reproduced and is produced a*new*, is not only the *entity [Dasein]* of said objective conditions of living labor, but the *alienated entity [Dasein]* of the worker. The material he worked is now *alienated* material. Living labor manifests itself as *alienated*, in contraposition to the capacity of living labor, whose work it is, and from which it is its exteriorized life [*Lebensäusserung*]" (*Manuscripts of 61–63*, *MEGA* II, 3, p. 2284, 5–28). In this case, the "conditions" are not the original ones, but the ones which confront it (living labor) as "capital" every day it returns to work.
111. The theme of the pauper we have developed amply in our commentaries to the four redactions of *Capital*. Consider, for instance, the following citation: "It is already contained in the concept of *free labour*, that he is a *pauper*: virtual pauper. According to his economic conditions he is merely a *living labour capacity*, hence equipped with the nessaries of life. Necessity on all sides, without the objectivities necessary to realize himself as labour capacity. . . . He can live as a worker only in so far as he exchanges his labour capacity for that part of capital which forms the labour fund. This exchange is tied to conditions which are accidental *for him*, and indifferent to his *organic* presence. He is thus a virtual pauper" (*Grundrisse*, p. 604; German, p: 497–98). It is interesting that in the *1844 Manuscripts*, Marx uses the same terminology: *gleichgültigen . . . zufälligen* (*MEW*, EB I, p. 523). For the worker the conditions that capital proposes are contingent, but they are necessary in order to be real.
112. *Grundrisse*, p. 296; italics added.
113. This is one of the determinations that still appears in the fourth redaction of *Capital* I: "a commodity whose use-value possesses the peculiar property of being a *source of value [Quelle von (Tausch-) Werth]*, whose actual consumption is therefore itself an objectification [*Vergegenständlichung*] of labour, hence a *creation of value* [*Werthschöpfung*] . . . existing in corporeality, the living personality [*lebendigen Persönlichkeit*] of a human being, capabilities which he sets in motion whenever he produces a use-value of any kind" (*Capital* I, p. 270; German, *MEGA* II, 5, p. 120; *MEGA* II, 6, p. 183; italics added).
114. Franz Hinkelammert reproduces this critique against Friedrich Hayek and Milton Friedman in his work *Critica de la razón utópica* (San Jose: DEI, 1984). In addition, a similar critique is in order against John Rawls.
115. We have underscored this repeatedly throughout our commentaries on Marx.
116. The word possibility can be *Möglichkeit, Potentia, Macht, dynamis* (Marx frequently

the Greek, as in the *Grundrisse*, p. 297.), *Vermögen*. All have different connotations. In this case real "possibility" would be *potentia* or *Vermögen* (from English: "labor *force*," "labor capacity," and later "labor force").

117. The function of "activity" as mediation between a "thing" and its "conditions" in order to become "real," in Hegel, should be kept in mind.
118. We have insisted in our commentaries that the concept "source" (*Quelle*) comes from Schelling and is different from that of foundation (*Grund*) (see my *El último Marx*, Chap. 9.3: "El trabajo vivo come la fuente creadora del valor," pp. 368–79, in which I use many citations as evidence).
119. Because capital provides labor the conditions of its becoming real, its reality.
120. Labor is possibility, but unreal if the conditions of its realization are not given. On the other hand, capital itself is also unreal without the thing (labor) and activity (labor working); that is, labor itself is the universal (general) possibility of capital's realization.
121. *Grundrisse*, p. 296.
122. "If we consider the original relation, before the entry of money into the self-realization process, then various conditions appear which have to have arisen, or been given historically, for money to become capital and labour to become capital-positing, capital-creating labour, wage labour. (*Grundrisse*, p. 463).
123. *Grundrisse*, p. 296.
124. In the Hegelian sense: entity, thing, real phenomenon which produces effects, has consequences.
125. *Capital* I, p. 677. (German [*MEGA* II, 6], p. 500, 1–3); italics added.
126. Ibid., p. 678; German [*MEGA* II, 6], p. 501, 11–13).
127. Ibid., p. 799; German [*MEGA* II, 6], p. 588, 13–22); italics added.
128. *Grundrisse*, p. 872; German, *Grundrisse*, 755.

6

A "Conversation" with Richard Rorty

> The obvious objection to defining the mental as the intentional is that *pains are not intentional*[1].... *Are you suffering?* This is the ability to distinguish the question of whether you and I share the same final vocabulary from the question of *whether you are in pain.*[2]

On the occasion of Richard Rorty's visit to Mexico, as a guest to the biannual philosophical congress held at the Universidad Autónoma Metropolitana, I wanted to establish a "conversation" with him and to express my point of view concerning his philosophical project as a United States thinker, which is that of a liberal ethos and a progressive,[3] taking into account the radically different point of departure from which liberation philosophy sets out.

6.1 Different Original Situations

By "original situations"—in contrast to Rawls's trascendental version of it—we want simply to indicate different points of departure. Rorty himself describes his "situation":

> The result is to leave American philosophy departments stranded somewhere between the humanities (their ancestral home), the natural sciences.... and the social sciencies.... My story has been one of struggles between kinds of professors, professors with different aptitudes and consequently with different paradigms and interests. It is a story of academic politics—not much more, in the long run, than a matter of what sort of professors come under which deparmental budget....[4]

His struggle is very North American, intra-university. Rorty, who was educated within the Analytic tradition, rebelled against his old philosophical community. At age thirty two (1965) Rorty criticized the philosophers of the "linguistic turn":[5]

> The relatively pessimistic conclusions reached in the preceding sections entail that linguistic philosophers' attempts to turn philosophy into a *strict*

science must fail. How far does this pessimism carry? If linguistic philosophy cannot be a strict science, if it has a merely critical, essentially dialectial, function, then what of the future?[6]

In fact, Rorty departs existentially and institutionally—in his philosophical practice—from a North American academic and universitary medium, especially from the philosophical groups focused on language, which he knows throughly from his lengthy treatment of their problematics. From both, philosophers that advocate an "ideal language" and those who depart from "ordinary language,"[7] it can be understood and accepted "that rational agreement is possible" within the limited sphere of their questions, but that in the last instance they fall into "circularity." That is, Rorty's philosophy departs from its empirical, concrete, and academic history, from its university situation where analytic philosophy is a "game" among many other "language games." Within the university situation the personal Rortyan "position" is critical on two fronts: 1) before its old community of analytical philosophers; 2) before the philosophers who use metaphysical notions (such as traditional Thomism, for example) or universalist rationalizations (which would be Apel's "position"). Or, in other words, skepticism versus analytic philosophy, and versus universalist rationalism. Rorty intends to affirm *solidarity* in the face of "pain" and against "cruelty," a profoundly ethical attitude, which can be assumed, thinks Rorty, without having to appeal to universal reason. Rorty's position is that of someone who stands in solidaristic responsibility before the pain of the abstract Other, from out of the contingency of someone who assumes participartorily the contents of their *Lebenswelt* (daily life).

It should be indicated, in addition, that the Rortyan position in a Latin America where analytical philosophers have "controlled," since the sixties, significant positions of power in the philosophical profession (universities, national congresses, institutions of investigations, magazines and journals, etc., that is, the "material *institutions*" of philosophy's reproduction), is extremely healthy, beneficial, and positive. In the first national colloquium of philosophy in Mexico (Morelia) of 1975, Mario Bunge identified "serious" philosophical knowledge with the possibility of formalization (quasi-mathematization). These "beliefs" are demolished by the post-analytical Rorty (if analytic or linguistic philosophy means "the view that philosophical problems are problems which may be solved—or dissolved—either by reforming language, or by understanding more about the language we presently use"[8]).

We can walk with Rorty a long strech of way, with the critic of analytic thinking, with the democrat (although he does not notice that liberalism and democracy are contradictory logics), with the one who searches for solidarity. But we cannot follow him into the extreme ambiguity of the incommensurability of his ethical principles, in his neopragmatist contextualism, which in the end turns into an accomplice to domination, from our North-South case (which he cannot criticize by definition). Nor can we follow him in his liberal Northamericanism of eurocentric character.

Liberation philosophy, instead, departs from another situation; it places philosophy originally in the context of concrete praxis, in engagement and solidarity with the oppressed (with the exploited *poor* in the periphery of capitalism, women dominated by machism, the racially discriminated Black person, and non-hegemonic cultural and ethnic groups, the ecologically responsible to future generations). It is not a question, first of all, of a reflection *on* the word, language, the "text,"[9] as an external observer. It is a question of a practical, concrete presence in and within popular, femininst, ecological, or antiracist movements; in the face-to-face,[10] immediate relation of the "organic intellectual,"[11] giving obviously priority to communicative action (or the illocutory moment of the speech-act) from out of which philosophical thinking begins its work; that is, philosophical reflection begins its task *as reflection (second act) on praxis itself (first act)*. Mediation through the analysis of a text, whether it be "analytical" (since Rorty's *Linguistic Turn*) or "hermeneutical" (in the manner of Ricoeur's "travail du lecteur"), is *a posteriori* and in some cases entirely absent, as is the case with the praxis of the illiterate who does not express herself or himself through writing. The point of departure is always someone who is suffering ("I suffer . . .), but as an oppressed at the political, erotic, concrete level[12]—not from a university or academic environment, nor solely as a dispute between linguistic or analytic philosophical schools—and who emerges as a *subject of liberation*. Reflection departs from the poor or oppressed, who in her suffering, needing corporeality, works: where there is a priority of developing an economics from the oppressed, from the suffering which is felt as *misery* (*Elend*, Marx would say) of the dominated (this is the ethical moment). This setting out from a "we" lies "beyond" (in an exteriority) the dominating, ruling, hegemonic, central (i.e. center-periphery) "we-intentions" of "liberal irony." Evidently the oppressed (as in the "vision of the vanquished" before the conquest of America) has her language, the "voice of the oppressed," which for the oppressor is a non-language . . . until it is *translated* by a liberal ironist to the language of the dominator (so that he may accept it as language, even as with liberation philosophy itself, which also must be translated into the ruling philosophical languages).

One may depart from *suffering*, as Rorty or liberation philosophy do, but some additional questions still need to be asked. What type of suffering? Which are the *causes*[13] of this suffering?

Liberation philosophy, once it has ethically and rationally received the interpellation of the oppressed, ought to reflect on the entire problematic which is presupposed and determines the praxis of liberation: the praxis of erotic liberation by women, the pedagogy of the son and the people, the political economy of the poor and underdeveloped nations, etc. This is an entire program of reflection and communicative, strategic, and tactical praxis. Philosophy does not end with the reception of the interpellative speech act, which provokes, challenges to action; *it only begins with it!*

Keeping in mind what has been said, and the theoretical positions to which we have referred, we could propose the following minimal schema:

Schema 1. Three Possible "Positions"

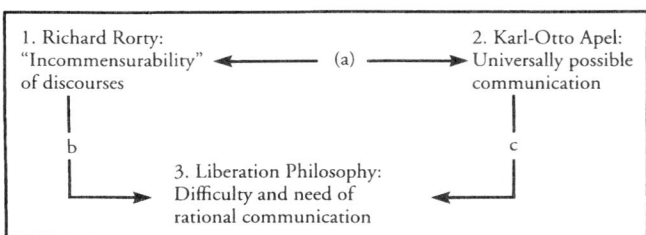

There is, first of all, a confrontation between neopragmatist contextualism and rationalism (a), in which Liberation Philosophy also takes part, but with which we will not deal here; in the second place, there the confrontation between Rortyan neopragmatism with liberation, or that between the incommensurability of intercultural, inter-class dialogues and those of a Rorty (b); and, in the third place, there is the confrontation between hegemonic rationality and the reason of the other, that which is implicit in the subtle developmentalist fallacy which can fullfil the role of a rationalism which frequently is not universal, but European, liberal, capitalist, etc. (c), and with which we have dealt in numerous works.

6.2 Rorty's Philosophical Project

Since Rorty is little known in Latin America, let us go through his main works, first his "Metaphilosophical Difficulties of Linguistic Philosophy."[14] In this work we observe the expert philosopher of the *Linguistic Turn*, where he writes in the introduction: "The history of philosophy is punctuated by revolts against the practice of previous philosophers."[15] For this revolt, the rebellious philosophers use new methods (as in the case of Descartes, Kant, Marx, Husserl, or Wittgenstein). But, essentially, these new methods presuppose certain metaphysical or epistemological theses (metaphilosophical "criteria", says Rorty), and only through the acceptance of the theses can the method obtain validity. Therefore, one falls into "circularity.":[16]

> Since philosophical method is in itself a philosophical *criterion* ... every philosophical revolutionary is open to the charge of circularity or to the charge of having begged the question.[17]

For Rorty, even the great philosophers fall into this same naivete:

> What is particularly interesting is to see why those philosophers who lead methodological revolts think that they have, at last, succeeded in becoming *presuppositionless*, and why their opponents think that they have not.[18]

In the same way, Rorty shows that linguistic or analytic philosophy lacks metaphilosophical criteria, whether it is of those who propose an ideal language (like Carnap, for example) or ordinary language (the second Wittgenstein) as their point of departure, and even the philosophy of empirical linguistics (like that of Chomsky). They have all failed, thinks Rorty, because they could not define intersubjectively valid criteria for knowing, for example, when a "good *analysis*" or a "good *meaning*" have been carried out or conveyed. Rorty destroys one by one the presupposed criteria and arrives at a radical skepticism.[19] Through Quine, Sellars, Davidson, Kuhn, or Putnam, Rorty pulverizes the "dogmas" which were held as valid by prior generations (from Locke to Ayer or even Carnap). Slowly, Rorty will distance himself from the analytic philosophers, in order to get closer to methodological or critical contextualism, neopragmatism, historicism—setting out from the second Wittgenstein on the way toward the second Heidegger, Derrida, and the postmoderns—and all due to the crisis of 1968. Thus, Rorty concludes:

> I should wish to argue that the most important thing that has happened in philosophy during the last thirty years is not the linguistic turn itself, but rather the beginning of a thoroughgoing rethinking of certain epistemological difficulties which have troubled philosophers since Plato and Aristotle.[20]

The university crisis of 1968 allowed young North American intellectuals, among them Rorty, to turn their eyes toward "continental" thinking. It is thus that Kant, Hegel, Marx, Heidegger, and a little latter Foucault's and Derrida's readings will be rediscovered. All of this leads Rorty to write his first and up to now only work to be structured properly as a book: *Philosophy and the Mirror of Nature.*[21]

With reference to the philosophical projects of Wittgenstein, Heidegger, or Dewey—the great "edifying" philosophers (in the sense of *Bildung* or *paideia*)—Rorty writes:

> Each of the three came to see his earlier effort as self-deceptive, as an attempt to retain a certain conception of philosophy after the notions needed to flesh out that conception... had been discarded. Each of the three, in his later work, broke free of the Kantian conception of philosophy as foundational.[22]

Philosophy and the Mirror of Nature is a "therapeutic" book, "like the writings of the philosophers I most admire,"[23]—writes Rorty—and therefore "parasitic" of analytic philosophy. In other words, our philosopher, as a new North American generation, uses the vocabulary of the analytic philosophers' community as *a medium*—in order to prove its inconsistency—and that of continental philosophers—like Nietzsche, Heidegger, or later Derrida—as a goal.[24] In order to accomplish this goal Rorty attacks frontally the "theory of representation" (Kant's *Vorstellung*). It would be interesting here to show some analogies with the thinking of Emmanuel Levinas,[25] who served as inspiration to Derrida,[26] Lyotard, and Latin American liberation philosophy itself. What is certain is that the successors of the great founders of "strict philosophy" (Husserl and Russell), after forty years (from approximately 1910 through 1950), were put in question by their best inheritors (Heidegger or Sartre and Sellars or Quine), and seventy years later (Rorty thinks here of himself) we are again as if at the turn of the 19*th* century: together with Royce and Nietzsche.[27] The overcoming of "representation" as epistemology, as a "mirror" in which we see nature (the ontic, or inner-wordly "objectivity"), opens up for Rorty the possibility to understand the attempt by hermeneutics (from a Gadamer, for example, the existential ontological). Rorty thinks that the path to be followed is that of an "edifying philosophy,"[28] which does not pretend to argue but simply to establish a "conversation."[29] Rorty wants to place himself in a peripheral line of the history of philosophy:

> On the periphery of the history of modern philosophy, one finds figures who, without forming a *tradition*, resemble each other in their distrust of the notion that man's essence is to be a knower of essences. Goethe, Kierkegaard, Santayana, William James, Dewey, the later Wittgenstein, the later Heidegger, are figures of this sort. They are often accused of relativism or cynicism.[30]

It is a question, then, of an entrenched struggle against every form of essentialism, against every form of metaphysics or argumentation. As we will see, liberation philosophy, peripheral philosophy which thinks the periphery itself, does not possess the arrogance of the great systematic philosophies, but it also does not share the desperate or skeptical position of the merely "edifying philosophies"—in Rortyian parlance Liberation Philosophy ought to be equally edifying, as *ethical critique*, but its intention is constructive of liberation, *as politics and strategy*. It does not bother us that Liberation Philosophy may be considered a type of edifying philosophy (as ethics), but it would be certainly rejected for its pretension of being constructive-revolutionary (by responsibility); it would be, in that case, a "great word" in Rorty's vocabulary.[31] Rorty is more Kierkegaardian (who criticized Hegel as "speculative", from *speculum*, mirror—and confronted him with "irony" and from the "absurdity" of "faith") than Liberation Philosophy, although Liberation Philosophy it also departed from Kierkegaard.[32] Rorty wants to maintain the "conversation of humanity" without falling into the rational arguments of systematic philosophy. Rorty's *Denkweg* is the astonishing and passionate critical path of a North American generation which, departing from the analytic style, ends up in the continental, although now its tradition is skeptical, as a critique of metaphysics in the traditional Anglo-Saxon sense.

Shortly after his book *Philosophy and the Mirror of Nature* there appears a collection of articles under the title *Consequences of Pragmatism: Essays 1972–1980*.[33] This work is extremely useful for our understanding of Rorty's philosophical project. In addition, it gives us great insight into the history of North American philosophy (not "American" as it is abusively written, thus cornering Latin Americans into becoming nothing). In fact, Rorty belongs to a philosophical elite, the new generation of postwar youth, which had, for example, Rudolph Carnap and Carl Hempel as its direct teachers.[34] From then until today, his philosophical style will be that of the Analytic philosophers[35]—be they positivists or post-positivists—but we could call it the second generation, influenced already by Quine, the second Wittgenstein, Sellars, or Davidson. In other words, the dogmas of a Hans Reichenbach[36] are no longer acceptable, who despised with an Olympian attitude all non-analytic philosophy.[37] It will be a long evolution that will allow Rorty to discover the value of North American pragmatism or anti-metaphysical continental philosophy (Nietzsche, Heidegger, Derrida). The path was approximately the following:

> 1. Analytic philosophy started off as a way of moving from speculation to science.... 2. The notion of *logical analysis* turned upon itself, and committed slow suicide, in Wittgensteinian *ordinary language*, Quinean, Kuhnian, and Sellarsian criticism of the purportedly *scientific* vocabulary.... 3. Analytic philosophy was thus left without a genealogy, a sense of mission, or a *metaphilosophy*.... 4. This development hardened the split between *analytic* and *Continental* philosophy by moving the study of Hegel, Nietzsche, Heidegger, etc., out of philosophy departments.[38]

In a certain manner Rorty, without renouncing the style of analytic philosohy, open himself up toward a new field, a re-defined pragmatism—in the tradition of Peirce, Dewey, and Charles Morris[39]—and hermeneutics in the broad sense, in Nietzsche's path, Heidegger, Derrida, Foucault, et al. He thus adopts a post-analytic and post-philosophical critical position, in the traditional sense of the term philosophy (postmodern already?).

> On the pragmatist's account, positivism was only a halfway stage in the development of such a culture [the post-philosophical culture]—the progress toward, as Sartre puts it, doing without God.... Pragmatism does not erect Science as an idol to fill the place once held by God. It views science as one genre of literature....[40]

Neither "irrationalism",[41] nor "skepticism"[42] frighten Rorty. On the contrary, he sets them off against analytic philosophy, which he knows so well from "within."[43]

His recent work, *Contingency, Irony and Solidarity*,[44] closes the cycle and is the most up to date synthesis that we have of Rorty's position. Here what is central is the attempt to do justice to two apparently opposed positions: the self-actualization of privacy's autonomy (the "private perfection" of a Kierkegaard, Nietzsche, Heidegger) and public justice (Marx, Mill, Habermas, Rawls).[45]

Liberation Philosophy, it may be considered, although this would be a superficial consideration, would appear to coincide with Rorty in the discovery of the suffering of the Other, which is also one of the themes of his work:

> In my utopia, human solidarity [contra Lyotard] would be seen ... as imaginative ability to see *strange people* as fellow suffers. Solidarity is ... created. It is created by increasing our sensitivity to the particular details of *the pain and humiliation of other*, unfamiliar sorts of people.[46]

This solidarity, however, has its limits since Rorty has to affirm as his only point of reference the "belonging to a particular language community,"[47] which in his case is the North American community.[48] It is thus that, against the rationalist and scientific Enlightenment, Rorty raises the romanticism that re-discovers poetry, culture, and tradition: "The imagination, rather than reason, is the central human faculty."[49]

For Rorty, then, the discovery of the Other, in confrontation with Davidson's "metaphors", is a function of "ethnography, the journalist's report, the comic book, the docudrama, and, especially, the novel,"[50] and not one of philosophy. "Only poets, Nietzsche suspected, can truly appreciate contingency":[51] *contingency of language*. With this gesture he takes away from us reason as a weapon, the very same philosophical reason of our liberation.

Furthermore, "for Freud's account of unconscious fantasy shows us how to see every human life as a poem—or, more exactly, every human life not so racked by pain as to be unable to learn a language nor so immersed in toil as to have no leisure in which to generate a self-description. He sees every such life as an attempt to clothe itself in its own metaphors":[52] *contingency of selfhood*; but incommensurable identity, and even more dangerous still when armed with computerized, highly technical, atomic weapons, as in the Gulf War.

The vocabulary, in the third place, of the rationalist Enlightenment has become an obstacle for democratic societies. It is not a matter of rationally grounding liberalism, but of discovering a more appropriate language (a new metaphor): "The citizens of my liberal utopia would be people who had a sense of the contingency of their language of moral deliberation, and thus of their consciences, and thus of their community":[53] "we liberals." The question is not only of the public, but "the ironist's *private* sense of identification."[54] The ironist Rorty is a skeptic (in the good sense, like Kierkegaard) of "final vocabulary,"[55] and is a liberal ("cruelty is the worst thing they do").

He is a critic of everydayness ("The opposite of irony is common sense"[56]), but falls into it when he affirms it ethnocentrically. In the last instance, Rorty is a critic of the pretensions of the "common sense of the West"[57]—Hegel, for Rorty, was a good "dialectical ironist"—but in a metaphysical sense. Irony cannot be socialized ("Irony seems inherently a private matter"[58]). "The ironist takes the morally relevant definition of a person, a moral subject, to be *something that can be humiliated*. Her sense of human solidarity is based on a sense of a common danger, not on a common possession or a shared power."[59]

Kant was able to awaken in ethics the sense of rationality and duty without dependence on the accidents of history. Rorty, instead, pretends to awaken the sense of "pity for pain and remorse for cruelty,"[60] from out of solidarity with "intersubjective validity" for New Yorkers as well as for the inhabitants of Malaysia:[61] "We can have obligations by virtue of our sense of solidarity with any of these groups,"[62] from out a set of *we-intentions*," as in the pronouncement: "We *all* want . . ." where one's membership is not indicated by an "I want. . . ." That "membership," for Rorty, is the fruit of "certain historical circumstances,"[63] and therefore "we are under no obligations other than the *we-intentions* (Sellars[64]) of the communities with which we identify."[65]

Rorty explains that "the ironist . . . thinks that what unites her with the rest of the species is not a common language but *just* susceptibility to pain and in particular to that special sort of pain which the brutes do not share with the human's humiliation. On her conception, human solidarity is not a matter of sharing a common truth or a common goal but of sharing a common selfish hope."[66]

For Rorty, "pain is non-linguistic: It is what we human beings have that ties us to the non-language-using beasts. So victims of cruelty, people who are suffering, do not have much in the way of a language. That is why there is no such things as the *voice of the oppressed*[67] or the *language of the victims*. The language the victims once used is not working anymore, and they are suffering too much to put *new words* together. So the job of putting their situation into language is going to have to be done for them by somebody else. The liberal novelist, poet, or journalist is good at that. The liberal theorist usually is not."[68]

Solidarity cannot be grounded or justified, according to Rorty, in any metaphysical consideration such as, for instance, the encountering in the Other of something that "resonates to the presence of this same thing in other human beings."[69] One does not need to look for this "commonality" beyond history or institutions. In reality we act in solidarity, says Rorty, "by nothing deeper than *contingent* historical circumstance."[70] But, where does "a moral obligation to feel a sense of solidarity with all other human beings" originate?[71]

Rorty thinks that there is a universality, that of "ironism,"[72] but because of the contingency of language, selfhood, and community this cannot have "universal validity."[73]

Rorty avers:

Our insistence on contingency, and our consequent opposition to ideas like *essence*, *nature*, and *foundation*, makes it impossible for us to retain the notion that some actions and attitudes are naturally *inhuman*.[74]

What remains is "nothing deeper than contingent historical circumstances"[75] in order to act solidaristically. And with this Rorty becomes more and more sensitive to diversity ("It is thought of as the ability to see more and more traditional differences—of tribe, religion, race, customs, and the like—as unimportant when compared with similarities with respect to pain and humiliation—the ability to think of people wildly different from ourselves as included in the range of *us*"[76]). The ethnographic or novelistic description of this suffering or humiliation, and not philosophy, thinks Rorty, is what allows moral progress. Also the marginalized should be included within the horizon of the "we," in order not to be cruel. "It is the ethnocentrism of a *we* (*we liberals*) which is dedicated to enlarging itself, to creating an ever larger and more variegated *ethnos*."[77]

What is important in Rorty is that he does not wish to affirm *too quickly* "human solidarity with the identification with *humanity as such*,"[78] and this because, historically, the "we" that could encompass humanity ought to grow in its "own sensibility to the pain and humiliation *of others*."[79] It is a matter of separating the question "Do you believe and desire what I believe and desire?"—a representational question—from the question "Are you *suffering*?" This means to have consciousness of the distinction between wanting to look for a "final vocabulary" and wondering "if you are in pain."[80]

In any event, if two "we-intentions" confront each other, in which one of them cruelly dominates ("cruelty is the worst thing we do"[81]) the other, Rorty would have some difficulty. In this case there are no "we intentions" which could encompass both, and therefore the solidarity or participation of one group does not have "reasons" in order to include the other (in such a way that they do not form a "we"). What is it that allows the overcoming of our own horizon of "we intentions,"[82] to open ourselves to solidarity with the Other, from another world, people, culture . . .? Rorty may, at the most, demonstrate an *ad intra* solidarity, but never an *ad extra* to other "we intentions." His immanentist contextualism and neopragmatism do not allow it. Even the "Black" is viewed as "one of us: a North American." And the foreign Mexican? To say that she is a "human being," writes Rorty: "is a weak, unconvincing explanation of a generous action."[83] "The position put forward in Part I of this book is incompatible with this universalistic attitude."[84] But that the horizon of a previous "we" could be extended to the people who were a "they" is a contingent and historical happening, thinks Rorty.

6.3 Rorty's Pragmatism and Liberation Philosophy

When reading, listening, and "talking" with Rorty himself, here in Mexico, about the two works to which I will refer, only then did I understand the opinion of some North American friends when they indicated the apparent similarity between Liberation Philosophy and North American pragmatism. It is time to see such a similarity, but also their great differences.

The articles in question are: "Feminism and Pragmatism" (Rorty, 1990) and "Human Hope and History in a Comic frame" (Rorty, 1991). The first of these, which enters because of its thematic (but not by intention, which is always and only the philosophy of language) within women's liberation philosophy,[85] can help us see the similarities. However, we ought not to deceive ourselves. Rorty occupies himself with the problem of feminism in order to show the the advantages that this movement could obtain by adopting his neopragmatism. *In reality, it is a reflection on the philosophy of language*. A text by Catherine MacKinnon is his support point, especially when she writes:

> I'm evoking for women a role that we have yet to make, in the name of *a voice that, unsilenced, might say something that has never been heard.*[86]

From this positive assertion, Rorty will deduce the convenience of abandoning essentialist, representational, universalist, realist, teleological, or rationalist language.[87] It is a question of allowing the "logical" or "semantic space" to grow, until now dominated by males, so that a "femenine language" may be created. What is interesting is that Rorty captures perfectly that the oppressed situation of woman demands not to recognize the masculine semantic horizon as the language which could express the "nature" or "essence" of humanity in general. This leads Rorty to negate all rationality, universality, etc., and to assume a neopragmatic, ambiguous irrationalism:

> This means that one will praise movements of liberation not for the accuracy of their diagnoses but for the imagination and courage of their proposals.... They abandon the contrast between superficial appearance and deep reality in favor of the contrast between a painful present and a possibly less painful, dimly seen, future.[88]

What remains for movements of liberation are, then, "imagination" and "courage," and they ought, therefore, to renounce "reason,"[89] for "the function of philosophy is instead to *clear*" the path that in reality prophets and poets traverse.[90] And taking an expression from Marilyn Frye, Rorty cites that "it takes courage to overcome a mortal dread of being outside the field of vision of the arrogant eye."[91] Rorty ratifies this when he affirms:

> If you find yourself a slave, do not accept your masters' descriptions of *the real*; do not work within the *boundaries of their moral universe*.[92]

This is the question that in Liberation Philosophy we have placed under the thematic Totality-Exteriority. Thus, I think, Rorty steps over the limits of critique when he rejects *every possible reason*, or every sense of reality. The boundaries of his moral world, his reasons, or his descriptions of the real ought not be confused with the ethical and the rational, nor with reality in its critical sense, without falling into metaphysical essentialism which Habermas himself has already clearly superseded.[93] I believe that the background theme to be discussed with Rorty (and with Apel, but precisely in the opposite sense) is that of the reach of "reason." If by reason is understood the *limited* comprehension of the ruling totality, the representational horizon as dominating semantic system, then Rorty has reason in thinking that its pretension to universal validity has to be rejected—because it is no more than a particular reason which has been totalized. But Apel is clearly forewarned of this objection since he takes recourse to a communication community, always already presupposed by every seriously performed communicative speech act (and we leave aside in what sense we mean "argumentative" in order not to exasperate Rorty). In Apel's case, reason does not close upon itself in terms of the *acceptance of the established or valid agreement*. Instead, rationality is essentially played out in the continuous aperture to the "acceptance" of new words, languages, or reasons, which are more valid because they are intersubjectively better proved and justified (in the case of feminism, this will "demonstrate," through its praxis of liberation, the "reasons" of its "reality," constructed historically and with novelty, indispensable and unique, *new*). It is a rationality of "discourse," which emerges from the practical construction of reality (if we speak of "human reality"). It is a rationality which is non-metaphysical, in its naive sense. Apel's "transcendentality," however, can make him lose the need and urgency for a more detailed description of the empirical, always changing, and new implementation of the semantic content of the now and here valid—this would be the "level B," empirical, hermeneutic of the architectonic of his discourse ethics. Liberation philosophy accepts perfectly the non-ultimate (absolute) validity of what is held to be valid, truthful, essential, or universal by the ruling, hegemonic, and dominating Totality, in which we are then in agreement with Rorty, a matter which was demonstrated by Levinas. But we are against Rorty when he thinks that the negation of the universal validity claims of a concrete, dominating (such as "machism" or "bourgeois ideology," which he rejects as a great word) agreement, is at the same time the negation of a dialectical, diachronic concept which unfolds and proceeds from the "rational" to the "real." Women's reality actualizes and manifests itself (in and through historical praxis) historically, not as if it were incrementally revealing aspects of an ahistorical or eternal essence, but inasmuch as it "phenomenizes" itself in a concrete, practical, historical, changing, dialectical world. This is the "realization" (more than mere "production") of what "woman" *becomes as it produces itself* (a *Selbst-herzeugung*, Marx would say).

It is in this way that we may entirely accept Rorty's expression: "What looked like nature [for the oppressing machist language] begins to look like culture [for the feminist]."[94] This, however, instead of negating reason or valid knowledge, only puts in question the alleged "naturalness" of a semantic Totality of the ruling language, from the Exteriority of a person who slowly creates a new language which confronts the prior (the machist) as an historical and cultural product (and not "natural").[95] This then is a dialectical, historical process, just as "reason" itself is.[96] As I wrote almost twenty years ago in my book *Philosophy of Liberation:*

> The ineffable, wordless "saying" . . . that springs from the exteriority of the oppressed questions the fetishist absolutization of a semiotic system. . . .[98] The interjection as exposition *of the pain of the oppressed*,[99] the protest of women's liberation, the rebellion of the young man against his teachers, are messages, words, revelation, or metaphoric apocalypsis, for they take us beyond the spoken word toward the one who speaks as a distinct exteriority. . . . A semiotic of liberation should describe the process of the passage of a given system of signs to a *new order* that surges forth when the *old order* is surpassed.[100]

I think Rorty does not give sufficient reason to abandon the "rational" horizon—which however ought not to be "totalized," in Martin Jay's sense, by the hands of the dominator, so as to not abandon the work of liberation to a few souls filled with a pure sensibility of courage or blind praxis. The negation of "a" certain illegitimate use of reason (essentialist, "metaphysical") and "a" dominating language does not negate the necessity of an affirmation of a "new" moment of rationality's exercise, of a "new" liberating language. Rorty identifies the dominating reason with "historical reason," which is always dialectical, and thus negates its capacity to create new "logical spaces": *liberating* reason continuously opens itself to *new* futures.[101]

But it is now, when going to the second work which Rorty presented in Mexico, "Social Hope and History as Comic Frame," that our philosopher starts manifesting a deep performative self-contradiction or, simply, inconsistencies. In his reflection on women, he took them seriously, and thus saw the need for a new language that would occupy the "logical space" feminist liberation would create. Before the poor, the worker, the exploited peripheral countries, instead of being in solidarity with this new subject and attempting to find a new language to speak its sufferings (*pain*), he closes the door. He does this, interestingly, basing himself on the work of an exiled Argentinian (as I am) who now lives in England, Ernesto Laclau.[102] Rorty's text, selected and perhaps written *ex professo* in order to be read in Mexico, is an apology against marxism in the name of contextualist neopragmatism, which takes as "proof" the "fact" of 1989. Laclau or Kenneth Burke are anti-Marx, Vaclav Havel is the anti-Lenin.

The "narration" begins by considering recent history, starting with the events that were unleashed on 9 November 1989, and arrives at conclusions on the immediate political events as though they were self-evident or irrefutable (since "facts" do not speak by themselves, it is the "interpretation" of these which speaks, as does Rorty's). Rorty's ironical nominalist practice tends to take all meaning away from the "Great Words" of the "Great Narratives"[103] which had been used by the left, such as capitalism, working class, bourgeois ideology:

> Since *capitalism* can no longer function as the name of the source of human misery,[104] nor *the working class* as the name of the redemptive power, we need to find new names for these things. But until some new meta-narrative replaces the Marxist, we shall have to characterize the source of human misery in such untheoretical and banal ways as *greed, selfishness,* and *hatred*.[105]

Rorty finds now a hero, a symbol of this post-1989 epoch: Vaclav Havel.[106] There is no longer the "incarnation of logos," nor "capitalism or bourgeois ideology as the name of *The Great Bad Thing*."[107] Marx's discourse, as so many other apocalyptic narratives, disappears from the Rortyan horizon as if in a certain "End of History"; although Rorty does not accept Fukayama's interpretation, he does accept Laclau's.

Feminists can use terms like feminism, male domination, nature, culture, or Dewey's "masculine experience of things,"[108] while the economically and politically oppressed must resign themselves to "banalize the entire vocabulary"[109] of oppression. In other words, Rorty deploys his entire anti-essentialist argumentation against Marxist terminology, and thus simply leaves the exploited of the "capitalist system" (horrible expression of a "Great Narrative," before which Rorty's irony must feel sorry for such great naivete)—the workers, the marginalized, the poor or miserable masses (in Latin America there are more than 100 million person living under the level of absolute poverty), the peripheral nations—he leaves them, I say, *without words, without language.* The Rortyan radical critique to language does not direct itself against the dominant language (of Hayek's or Friedman's neoliberal and conservative market economy, for example) but, instead, against the beaten, criticized, and stammering language of the poor and exploited (to which Marx has still a lot to say[110]).

Applauding Habermas, Rorty speaks of the "logic of the self-regulation of a market economy."[111] Franz Hinkelammert[112] has shown the disguising and mystifying character of this concept. Now Rorty develops his own narrative on the "Great *Good* Thing" which is called the market economy, but in his ears this is a non-metaphysical, non-essentialist expression. Again, as in the case of feminism, the theme is not that of the liberation from *pain* since 1989 (as is the case in Liberation Philosophy), but that all these events are an occasion for the "narrator" (Rorty) to illustrate an example in the exercise of the philosophy of language; that is, of how a language can dissapear (that of the Marxist left), and how it would take an unacceptable and untenable essentialism to try to revive it. This manifests, as is evident, profoundly political intentions, especially if we consider that Rorty is writing this paper precisely while the Gulf War is being waged, and there is no reference to this event of infinite "cruelty," which demanded from him "solidarity" with those victims of thousands of tons of bombs dropped by "we Americans." The worst is that, in this case, there is no pretension, nor are positive steps taken, toward the reconstruction of language, as in the case of feminism.

A discussion would still be relevant on what "liberal democrat" could mean.[113] We cannot refer to the long tradition that is inagurated by John Locke, and which culminates with John Rawls. Both, in the end, must postulate political equality (freedom of the citizen before the law), but both admit economic inequality (which in Rawls calls for the subterfuge of a second principle of "the difference"). In reality the liberal democrat must overcome this contradiction: How to govern *a majority*, who in economic inequality are "the poor" (Great Word) or the "least lucky" (word of a more "discrete Narrative," that is to say, more liberal)?

In Rorty's narrative he never takes the first person ("I") when he speaks of pain. He also does not consider the suffering corporeality itself of an ethics, of an economics of need—work as reproduction of human *life*. His philosophy always remains as a philosophy of language (pain as a non-representational moment, as a counter-linguistic example!), against every "final vocabulary"; as a provisionary language of narratives; all the same, a "conversation" without great pretensions, apparently.

Liberation Philosophy can thus appreciate that Rorty raises the question, as a central problem: *Are you suffering?*[114] The goal of coming to an agreement with the other as to what vocabulary ought to be employed with respect to the question *Are you in pain?* is a central point in his exposition. A "conversation" between Rortyan neopragmatism and liberation philosophy could be established on the grounds of this theme. But the "intention" of that conversation would immediately distinguish and separate us: for Rorty the conversation ought to deal with *language*; for the Philosophy of Liberation we ought to talk and do something about *the suffering of the Other*, about the *cause* of this pain and the way to abolish it and overcome it.

I think that Rorty, in agreement with his project of the last thirty years (at least since the first article, in 1965), in the end, has remained caught in the net—to talk with Foucault—of his own point of departure: the philosophy of language. Relentless critic from out of the very logic of analytic thinking, his only possibility for philosophical "exercise" is the "conversation," which speaks with some on different themes concerning language itself. Eventually he is critical, in a cutting manner, of certain other languages of the left which are located at the economic and political level: he leaves the poor without words.

"Are you suffering?" If in this conversation the other would respond: "Yes, I suffer . . . I suffer because I am tortured, because I am beaten when our union marches in protest, because I have nothing to eat, because I have nothing to clothe myself with, because I have no roof, because I cannot give my children the possibility of education. Yes I suffer. . . ." I believe that the conversation may, honestly and seriously, only continue thanks to two questions: first, *Why do you suffer?* and second, and inevitable if Rortyan solidarity is to be serious, *How can I help?* But, in order to seriously and honestly ask these questions, it is necesssary to have a disposition to understand, comprehend, reason what the other tells me. It would be necessary to use reason in order to interpret a meaning, a referent. Furthermore, the description of the *type* and the causes (the *why*) of suffering demands to move from personal and private structures (ontogenetic or biographical) to socio-historical and public structures (phylogenetic or economic-political). It is precisely here where we must abandon *mere* conversation with Rorty, and to engage ourselves in the practical use of reason.[115] It seems as though Rorty found himself in the situation of Sartre in *Les Mots*, or as the popular Italian song says: "Parole, parole, parole. . . ." In the peripheral world (the so-called Third World, to which Rorty makes no reference, the 75 percent of humanity!), the poor, the miserable, the marginals of the metropolises in peripheral capitalism in India, Africa, Latin America, every "conversation" cannot evade the fact: "I am hungry! Help me!" Solidarity manifests itself necessarily as action, as praxis, as politics, as strategic and tactical reason—having been in its begining communicative action (for Habermas), face-to-face (for Levinas), from out the perspective of utopia as a transcendental regulative or situational idea of Marx's "community of a free humanity."

No one can banalize or trivialize their own hunger; much less can the "interpellation" that emerges from the suffering of the poor be taken in a comic spirit (the matter is tragic). Nor can the languages which attempt to explain the causes of their suffering (like Marx) and, which above all, strive for their practical elimination be trivialized.

To conclude I will cite a Great Word of a Great Narrative, from Marx, who today is not in fashion in the North American universities:

> Suddenly, however, there arises the voice of the worker, which had previously been stifled in the sound and fury of the production process. . . . You may be a model citizen [exclaims the worker], perhaps a member of the R.S.P.C.A [an association for the protection of animals in England], and you may be in the odour of sanctity as well; but the thing you represent when you come face to face with me has no heart in its breast. . . . I demand the value of my commodity.[116]

I believe this text still makes sense in Chicago (especially if one speaks of an Afro-American) or Los Angeles (especially if one speaks of a Hispanic); in

New Dehli, Nairobi, or São Paulo. This "language" has relevance where there is "capital": that is, where a worker sells his labor for a salary which produces a profit—more precisely, as Marx would say, surplus value. Its effective relevance, its contemporaneity (reality?), encompasses the entire earthly globe (so as to not talk about "universality" and thus awaken the process of anti-metaphysical, anti-essentialist immunization).

Notes

1. Richard Rorty, *Philosophy and the Mirror of Nature* (Princeton: Princeton University Press, 1979), p. 22.
2. Richard Rorty, *Contingency Irony and Solidarity* (New York: Cambridge University Press, 1989), p. 198.
3. Rorty thinks that "liberals are the people who think that cruelty is the worst thing we do" (Rorty, *Contingency Irony and Solidarity*, p. xv). The problem resides in being able to come to an agreement as to what cruelty is. For example, is it cruelty to throw hundreds of tons of bombs on the enemy and to kill thousands of enemies in order to "save lives" ("our boys"), as was the case in the Gulf war of 1991 or in the Panama "invasion" in 1990—this last one an invasion of the same type as the one Iraq carried out in Kuwait? In the first case the United States struggles to "liberate" Kuwait; in the second it occupies Panama without there being a liberator that might throw out the invader? What type of "solidarity" can be ethically demanded by Kuwaitis or Panamanians to United States citizens if these last ones are participants of another "*we intention*"? Perhaps, thinks Rorty, to solve this dilemma means to transform oneself into either a theologian or a metaphysician. Were this the case, then the entire peripheral world (the old Third World) would be criticized by Rorty for being "theological" or "metaphysical" when using reason against the genocide that we suffer today in Latin America, Africa, and Asia.
4. Rorty *Consequences of Pragmatism* (Minneapolis: University of Minnesota Press, 1982), p. 228.
5. Rorty, ed., *The Linguistic Turn* (Chicago: The University of Chicago Press, 1967), p. 9, shows that Bergmann used that expression for the first time.
6. Ibid., p. 33.
7. Ibid., pp. 24ff.
8. Ibid., p. 3. Rorty shows, as we have indicated above, the circularity into which analytic or linguistic philosophy fell.
9. See, for instance, Paul Ricoeur.
10. See, for example, Emmanuel Levinas.
11. See Antonio Gramsci.
12. Ethically, a toothache because one has a cavity is not the same as the suffering which is "produced" by an act of torture (for instance, as when the torturer pulls out a tooth from a political prisoner in order to "produce" a certain "suffering" so as to obtain certain information by atrition, and thus "treason" to his comrades.
13. It is known, and we will return to this theme, that for Marx the "rational" problem consists in knowing the *origin* or *cause* of *pain*, the "misery" of the worker, to which he says: "We saw in Part IV, when analysing the production of

relative surplus-value, that within the capitalist system all methods for raising the social productive of labour are put into effect at the cost of the individual worker; that all means for the development of production undergo a dialectical inversion so that they become means of domination and exploitation of the producers; they distort the worker into a fragment of a man, they degrade him to the level of an appendage of a machine, they destroy the actual content of his labour by turning it into a torment; they alienate [emtfremden] from him the intellectual potentialities of the labour process in the same proportion as science is incorporated in it as an independent power; they deform the conditions under which he works, subject him during the labour process to a despotism the more hateful for its meanness; they transform his life-time into working-time, and drag his wife and child beneath the wheels of the juggernaut of capital. But all methods for the production of surplus-value are at the same time methods of accumulation, and every extension of accumulation becomes, conversely, a means for the development of these methods. It follows therefore that in proportion as capital accumulates, the situation of the worker, be his pay high or low, must grow worse. Finally, the law which always holds the relative surplus population or industrial reserve army in equilibrium with the extent and energey of accumulation rivets the worker to capital more firmly than the wedges of Hephaestus held Prometheus to the rock. It makes an accumulation of misery a necessary condition, corresponding to the accumulation of wealth. Accumulation of wealth at one pole is, therefore, at the same time accumulation of misery, the torment of labour, slavery, ignorance, brutalization and moral degration at the opposite pole, i.e. on the side of the class that produces its own product as capital." *Capital*, Vol. 1, pp. 798–99; *MEGA* II, 6, pp. 587–88. This is the "rational" question par excellence, which would appear not to preoccupy Rorty, but which to us is of the utmost importance, even if we take it in the strictest sense of North American pragmatic philosophy: Marx is *useful* to us because he allows us to respond to the question that "hurt" us in our flesh, the carnality of the poor and exploited, the sick with cholera.

14. Rorty, *The Linguistic Turn*.
15. Ibid., p. 1.
16. Ibid. For Apel this is Rorty's permanent argumentative strategy: "Im Grunde ist Rortys Argumentationsstrategie sehr einfach: Geht es um die Frage der normativen Masstäbe oder Kriterien einer kritischen Beurteilung oder Legitimation moralisch-politischer Ordnungen, so wird diese Frage *als metaphysisches Scheinproblem* zurückgewiesen" (K.-O. Apel, *Diskurs und Verantwortung* [Frankfurt: Suhrkamp, 1988], p. 400; Apel dedicates the entire section 1.3.2 of the last chapter of this book to Rorty. Since metaphysical or essentialist problems are *a priori* discardable, it is concluded that the argumentation of a rationalist or analytic philosopher can just the same be discarded.
17. Rorty, *The Linguistic Turn*, p. 2.
18. Ibid., p. 2.
19. Karl-Otto Apel, in constrast, radicalizes the presupposed criteria and shows how everyone presupposes always already a "communication community." Rorty's method is destructive; Apel's is reconstructive.
20. Rorty, *The Linguistic Turn*, p. 39.
21. Rorty, *Philosophy and the Mirror of Nature* (Princeton: Princeton University Press, 1979).
22. Ibid., p. 5.

23. Ibid., p. 7.
24. The strategy, as it can be seen, is in a certain sense similar to that of Apel. Apel also uses analytic philosophy in order to show its achievements—in contrast to Rorty—but just as well its limits. Apel achieves this by appealing to certain continental philosophers (for example, by articulating Wittgenstein through Heidegger, or Morris and Peirce through Gadamer) in order to arrive at the always already presupposed (the "communication community"), but in an entirely different way to how Rorty uses the "edifying" philosophers.
25. On Levinas's view on Husserl's theory of representation see *The Theory of Intuition in Husserl's Phenomenology* (Evanston: Northwestern University Press, 1973). Against Husserl, Levinas wrote: "But we are far from thinking that one starts with representation as a non-conditioned condition! Representation is *bound* to a very different 'intentionality,' which we are endeavoring to approach throughout this analysis" Emmanuel Levinas, *Totality and Infinity* (Pittsburgh: Duquesne University Press, 1969), (p. 126). This is a point of departure for Liberation Philosophy: the Other as other who is beyond every initial "representation" (see *Philosophy of Liberation* (Maryknoll: Orbis Books, 1989), pp. 39ff (2.4), and pp. 120ff (4.2.). Only through "revelation" or "analogy" (initially) can be "comprehended" the word or speech of the other. Rorty's critique of "representation" has been subsumed by Liberation Philosophy as a critique of the Totality—a critique of *hegemonic* reason, reason of domination, one-dimensionally closed upon itself, to say it with Marcuse—but not as critique of *historical* reason or liberation.
26. See Jacques Derrida, *Speech and Phenomena*: And other Essays on Husserl's Theory of Signs (Evanston: Northwestern University Press, 1973), the chapter on "Meaning and Representation," pp. 48ff. See my work *Para una ética de la liberación latinoamericana* (Buenos Aires: Siglo XXI, 1973), Chap. 6: "El método de la ética" (pp. 129–95).
27. This is presented in Chapter 4 of *Philosophy and the Mirror of Nature* where he deals with Quine and Sellars.
28. Rorty *Philosophy and the Mirror of Nature* Chap. VIII, 2, pp. 365ff.
29. This anti-epistemological concept was suggested to Rorty by M. Oakeshott *The Voice of Poetry in the Conversation of Mankind* [London: Bowes and Bowes, 1957]. For Oakeshott "conversation" is the quasi-poetic act through which a group of persons, mutally conscious of their belonging to a community (*universitas*), are united eventually from out of diverse life paths, in order to traverse a stretch of life in mutual respect and solidarity (without need of either strategic or tactically common interests). It is a gratuitous act.
30. Rorty, *Philosophy and the Mirror of Nature* p. 367.
31. Rorty writes magnificent lines on these themes (ibid., pp. 367–68).
32. See my *Método para una filosofía de la liberación*, paragraph 20: "La primera síntesis de la crítica, pero nuevamente teologizante: Sören Kierkegaard" (pp. 149ff).
33. Rorty, *Consequences of Pragmatism*.
34. Rorty, *Philosophy and the Mirror of Nature* p. xiii.
35. It is noteworthy, however, that Rorty does not articulate the analytic-pragmatic line, represented, for instance, by Austin (in *How to Do Things with Words?*) or Searle (*Speech Acts*). This is important in order to understand Rorty's "closure" within an analytic propositional (of sentences) tradition and not within a pratical-communicative (of statements) one. See chapter 2, above.
36. See for example his work *The Rise of Scientific Philosophy* (Berkeley: University of California Press, 1951).

37. This attitude of "scientific" arrogance also took root in Latin America after World War II, and, as we already noted, assumed control of many educational and philosophical organisms since the sixties, thus coinciding with the military dictatorships, since this type of philosophy possessed a particular "blindness" to philosophy as practice, ethics, or politics, allowing it to "live" without "seeing" the tortures, suffering, injustices, which are taken as mere empirical experiences without philosophical relevance or pertinence to philosophy. Rorty writes: "The great emigrés—Carnap, Hempel, Feigl, Reichenbach, Bergmann, Tarski—began to be treated with the respect they deserved. Their disciples began to be appointed to, *and to dominate*, the most prestigious departments. Departments which did not go along with this trend began to lose their prestige" (Rorty, *Consequences of Pragmatism*, p. 214).
38. Ibid., p. 227.
39. Charles Morris can be considered the first pragmatist philosopher who brings together analytic philosophy and pragmatism. It is possible that the early discovery of Peirce (1961) by Rorty might have led him to view skeptically the whole analytic tradition.
40. Rorty, *Consequences of Pragmatism* 1982, p. xliii.
41. See especially Rorty, *Consequences of Pragmatism*, pp. 160ff.
42. Ibid., pp. 176ff; pp. 181ff.
43. It is clear, however, that the later Habermas's or Apel's critiques would not be so easy to answer since these stem from the continental tradition which Rorty does not dominate as well as the analytic. See Jürgen Habermas, *The Philosophical Discourse of Modernity: Twelve Lectures* (Cambridge: The MIT Press, 1987), pp. 206–207; Karl-Otto Apel, *Diskurs und Verantwortung* (Frankfurt: Suhrkamp Verlag, 1988), pp. 161ff, 176ff, 381ff, 394ff, 399–413, 426ff, where Apel gives Rorty a central position.
44. Rorty, *Contingency, Irony and Solidarity*.
45. "This book tries to show how things look if we drop the demand for a theory which unifies the public and private, and are content to treat the demands of self-creation and of human solidarity as equally valid, *yet forever incommensurable*" (ibid., p. xv).
46. Ibid., p. xvi.
47. This is also Habermas's consideration; *Postmetaphysical Thinking: Philosophical Essays* (Cambridge: The MIT Press, 1992), pp. 135–37. This point is of extreme importance in terms of a North-South dialogue.
48. Apel tells us that during a debate with Rorty in Vienna, he responded to the question about the grounding of moral principles by stating: "*It's just common sense, I am just an American, we have just to persuade the others that our way is the right one*. Then I asked him [Apel], somewhat scandalized: "Could I simply say: I am just German. It's just common sense." With this I wanted to mean that "common sense" was what among us, during the Third Reich, was called the 'healthy feeling of the people.'" Apel, *Diskurs und Verantwortung*, p. 409. For us Latin Americans, the question is even more acute because "immanentist contextualism" is dangerous not because it could *have been Nazi*; rather, it is dangerous because *it is actually* the point of departure of the invasion of Grenada, Nicaragua,
49. Rorty, *Contingency, Irony and Solidarity*, p. 7.
50. Ibid.
51. Ibid., p. 28.
52. Ibid., pp. 35–36.

53. Ibid., p. 61. Commenting on the article "The Priority of Democracy to Philosophy," which orginally appeared in M. Peteson and R. Vaugh, eds. *The Virginia Statute of Religious Freedom* (New York: Cambridge University Press, 1987), and is reprinted in Rorty's *Objectivity, Relativism, and Truth: Philosophical Papers, Volume One* (Cambridge: Cambridge University Press, 1991), pp. 175–96, Apel quotes Rorty: "But such a philosopher [philosopher of liberal democracy] is not thereby justifying these institutions by reference to more fundamental premises, but the reverse: He or she is putting politics first and tailoring a philosophy to suit" (R. Rorty, *Objectivity, Relativism, and Truth*, p. 178). Apel comments, "Here it is hard for me not to make the following comment: approximately that was what many philosophers in fact did during the Third Reich" (Apel, *Diskurs und Verantwortung*, p. 403). Again Apel criticizes Rorty as "Nazi." Apel and Habermas are rationalists before the *terror of nazism*. Liberation Philosophy affirms an anti-eurocentric historical reason before the *terror of North American power* (but also before Latin American *populism*, which coincides with nazism in its profound, anti-rational ambiguity). Rorty, in his immanentist contextualism, turns himself before our eyes into something extremely disquieting, someone may even use a "great word": a liberal democrat in the United States may support the "contras" in Nicaragua and not criticize the invasion of Panama. There is a certain solidarity with the "American way of life" which is deathly, unjust, and tyrannical for a "Latin American way of life." The *Lebenswelt* as such can never be the criterion of rationality (although it may be affirmed reflexively).
54. Rorty, *Contingency, Irony and Solidarity*, p. 68.
55. Ibid., p. 73.
56. Ibid., p. 74: "The ironist is a nominalist and a historicist." He only speaks of *Weltanschauung*, perspective, dialectic, conceptual framework, historical epoch, language game, redescription.
57. Ibid., p. 77.
58. Ibid., p. 87.
59. Ibid., p. 91.
60. Ibid., p. 192.
61. However, he destroys his own bridges to a dialogue with the inhabitants of the Pacific once the "we intentions" of Rorty the "American" are articulated as an incommensurable point of departure.
62. Ibid., p. 195.
63. Ibid.
64. See Sellars, *Science and Metaphysics* (London: Routledge and Kegan Paul, 1968).
65. Rorty *Contingency, Irony and Solidarity*, p. 198. "That is the ethnocentrism of a *we* (*we liberals*) which is dedicated to enlarging itself, to creating an even larger and more variegated *ethos*."
66. Ibid., p. 92.
67. As we will see later, he will contradictorily approve this expression in the mouth of MacKinnon.
68. Ibid., p. 94. This is the historical function of Liberation Philosophy.
69. Ibid., p. 189.
70. Ibid., p. 189.
71. Ibid., p. 190.
72. Ibid., p. xv: "a liberal utopia: one in which ironism, in the relevant sense, is univesal."
73. Ibid., p. 67.
74. Ibid., p. 189.

75. Ibid.
76. Ibid., p. 192.
77. Ibid., p. 198.
78. Ibid., p. 198.
79. Ibid., p. 198.
80. Ibid., p. 198.
81. Ibid., p. 197.
82. See Sellars, *Science and Metaphysics*, p. 222 "It is a conceptual fact that people constitute a community, a *we*, by virtue of thinking of each other as *one of us*, and by willing a common good *not* under the species of benevolence, but by willing it as one of us, or from a moral point of view." Sellars identifies the "we-consciousness" with Christian *caritas*.
83. Rorty *Contingency, Irony and Solidarity*, p. 191.
84. Ibid.
85. See my work "La erótica latinoamericana" in *Filosofía Ética de la Liberación* (Buenos Aires: La Aurora, 1977) Vol. III, pp. 25–121.
86. Cited in Rorty, p. 231.
87. It is interesting to note that Rorty criticizes the position of Hispanic woman, Maria Lugones, as "an example of a feminist theorist who sees a need for a general philosophical theory of oppression and liberation. She says, for example, that 'the ontological or metaphysical possibility of liberation remains to be argued, explained, uncovered' ([Maria Lugones] "Structure/Antistructure and Agency under Oppression," *Journal of Philosophy*, 87, October 1990, p. 502). I should prefer to stick to merely empirical possibilities of liberation." Richard Rorty, "Feminism and Pragmatism" (Tanner Lectures on Human Values, University of Michigan, December 7, 1990). *Michigan Quarterly Review* 30, 2 (Spring 1991), p. 254, note 22). This essay has also appeared in Richard Rorty, et al., eds. *The Tanner Lectures on Human Values*, Vol. 13, 1992 (Salt Lake City: University of Utah Press, 1992), pp. 3–35.
88. Rorty "Feminism and Pragmatism, pp. 239–40.
89. The strategic, tactical, and "decadent" use of *reason* will be that exercised by, for instance, the Pentagon in order to carry out "invasions." Rorty denies that he himself is the "comfort of metaphysics" of the "great words." but with the same gesture he takes reason away from the oppressed.
90. Rorty "Feminism and Pragmatism", p. 240. In any event, just as Rorty, we have always shown that philosophy, in great measure, has the labor of clearing the obstacles that block thinking. I wrote some time ago: "The pertinence of a philosophy can be shown by its *negative critical destructive capacity*. It would seem that the Philosophy of Liberation has a tremendous destructive potential because it can not only assume critical methods, but it can in addition criticize those critical methods. . . . [The Philosophy of Liberation] *clarifies* the praxis of militants in the process of liberation" (*Philosophy of Liberation*, 5.9.5.5, pp. 179–80).
91. Rorty, "Feminism and Pragmatism", p. 240. We have also refered on numerous occasions to the metaphor of the eye. It should also be remembered that Marx spoke of "exteriority" as an eye: See *Manuscripts of 44*, II; *MEW*, EB I, pp. 523–24). On exteriority in Marx's see my *La producción teórica de Marx* (Mexico: Siglo XXI, 1985), pp. 137–48, 337–43; *Hacia un Marx desconocido* (Mexico: Siglo XXI, 1988), pp. 61–68, 290–97, 365–72; *El último Marx* (Mexico: Siglo XXI, 1990), pp. 138–44, 336–85.
92. Rorty, "Feminism and Pragmatism", p. 241. On the back cover of our work

Para una ética de la liberación latinoamericana, Vol. II, we wrote: "The moralities of the past are moralities of the law; they applauded past heroes, and lived from their glories and killed, and continue killing the present and future heroes of future nations. This *anti-ethics* lifts itself, as consciousness, against all of them and declares them immoral." All of what we have written over the last twenty years indicates this theme: the *without sense* (for the ruling morality) of the oppressed's liberation praxis.

93. In Jürgen Habermas *Postmetaphysical Thinking: Philosophical Essays*, pp. 28ff. We can affirm that liberation philosophy has a concept of metaphysics or reality in the Habermasian sense of post-metaphysical. The totality of the system of meanings, of a phenomenal "world," encircles what Rorty denominates "the master's control over the language spoken by the slaves—their ability to make the slave think of his pain as fated and even somehow deserved, something to be borne rather than resisted" (Rorty, "Feminism and Pragmatism", p. 244). In the Totality what appears as real, as the essential (in Rorty's sense) is grounded and justified through the very same ruling semantic system: "The one-dimensionality of everday discourse, the impossibility of discovering a sense other [MacKinnon, for example] than the one that has been imposed [sexist language], the only sense accepted by all, the one *everyone says*, is converted into a gigantic tautology" (Dussel, *Philosophy of Liberation*, 4.2.5, p. 120).

94. Rorty, "Feminism and Pragmatism", p. 232.

95. Apel, for instance, argues even more adamantly. For instance, he will show that *pacta sunt servanda* is an ethical principle accepted factically by every possible *Lebenswelt*. This will show the weakness of Rorty's pretended "strategy of argumentation's immunity" (See Apel, *Diskurs und Verantwortung*, p. 400ff). The "basic consensus" of a *konkrete Lebensform*, or *common sense*, is not sufficient in intercultural dialogue, i.e., North-South. One must look for the presupposed conditions of every cultural everydayness (Totality) which allow for the laying of a bridge for the establishment of rational dialogue. This does not negate but affirms the Exteriority of the Other. It calls for careful solicitude for the other's "interpellation."

96. The problem is that Rorty understand "reason" only in a totalized sense, as the reason of the dominator. He does not admit into the definition of reason, in its content, a dialectical, diachronic, historical sense. For Liberation Philosophy reason is "historical reason." In other words, inasmuch as we reason or argue, reason can open itself up to other "reasons." See chapter 2, above.

97. Levinas speaks of *le Dire* (saying) as a verb, as the other's self-presentation in her carnality, in the possibility of her living trauma, in contrast to *le dit* (the said), as works which express facts, things with sense.

98. This representational Totality is what Rorty negates.

99. It should be kept in mind that the question of pain is central to Rorty's thought, but with a different sense than that it has for the Philosophy of Liberation. For Rorty pain expresses a non-representational realm—it is a question, again, of a *philosophy of language*. Pain for Liberation Philosophy is the reality product of the injustice that is suffered in the carnality of the oppressed. It is thus an ethical question which calls me to be a responsible person (I am the one that ought-to-take-charge [*spondere* in Latin] of the other).

100. Dussel, *Philosophy of Liberation*, 4.2, pp. 123–25.

101. Rorty too quickly dismisses Sabinas Lovibond's position, who refuses to abandon Enlightenment universalism (see "Feminism and Postmodernity," *New Left*

Review, Winter 1989, p. 12; (Rorty, "Feminism and Pragmatism", p. 236). Liberation Philosophy might be able contribute some useful insights to this debate. It would appear that for Rorty "objectivity" necessarily stands in opposition to liberating reason: "We do not pretend to be *objective* concerning this. We are trying to represent woman's *point of view*." From expressions like this, Rorty concludes that it is not necessary to be objective, but instead we must be pragmatic (in Dewey's sense). If objectivity refers to the representational "machist" world, then it is impossible to be in agreement with such objectivity. This, however, does not deny that we ought, through a better established intersubjective agreement, to bring about a new objectivity, which hitherto has not been considered. "The point of view" of the oppressed can never, initially, coincide with the dominating objectivity. In Rorty there is a lack of certain distinctions that Liberation Philosophy has developed and constructed in a "pragmatic" sense (now in an Aristotelian sense).

102. Ernesto Laclau *New Reflections on the Revolution of our Time* (London: Verso, 1990). In his introductory talk, Rorty advised us Latin Americans to abandon Marxist great narratives, at least when we present our thinking to North Americans. This discourse, he suggested, has lost all of its validity. It would be interesting, instead, to compare the book by Laclau with that by Enrique Semo, *Crónica de un derrumbe. Las revoluciones inconclusas del Este* (Mexico: Grijalvo-Proceso, 1991), where he concludes: "The barbarity of Stalinism and the failures of real existing socialism ought not to be translated into apologies of a system, such as capitalism, which multiplies the productive capacities and exults individual freedom, but which consumes and destroys millions of men and women as if they were disposable containers" (p. 235).

103. With respect to feminist prophetism, and with great reason, Rorty did not label it a Great Narrative; instead, he was inspired to his own poetry, prophetism, and courage. Now, in contrast, he uses the same argument in order to destroy all proletarian or Third World "prophetism" (a theme fact entirely non-existent in Rorty, although he knew he was coming to Mexico to read his work).

104. It would be good to know how Rorty arrives at this conclusion, knowing that he is presenting this in a philosophical institute in Mexico, that is, in Latin America, in the periphery which suffers United States imperialism (a "Great Word" for Rorty). Prof. Bolivar Echeverria, who was present at the event, raised a well-aimed and spirited critique against Rorty's presentation. He practically said (with respect to the comparisons Rorty made between Darwin and Sartre, James and Nietzsche) that if, in our university environment, someone were to express such suggestions, they would be dismissed as naive.

105. Rorty, "Social Hope and History as Comic Frame", p. 13. Rorty adds: "One reason why all of us in the international left are going to have weed terms like *capitalism, bourgeois culture* (and, alas, even *socialism*) out of our vocabulary is that our friends in Central and Eastern Europe will look at us incredulously if we continue to employ them" (p. 18). Later he equates "Hitler and Mao—to avoid imitating them" (ibid., p. 25).

106. When Havel came through Mexico in 1991, there appeared in the press (*La Jornada*) an article: "Havel's naivetes." In Mexico he declared that Czechoslovakia admires the people of the United States because they saved his nation on three occasions: in the First World War, the Second, and beginning with 1989. Havel said this in Mexico, a country which in 1848 lost half of its territory to the United States, and a little after the United States (like Iraq in

Kuwait) carried out its Panama invasion. Havel travelled to Nicaragua, where he compared his goverment to that of President Violeta Chamorro, entirely forgetting that Czechoslovakia was invaded by Stalinist tanks and Nicaragua suffered an undeclared war, for ten years, waged by the United States, and not by the Soviet Union. In other words, Chamorro suceeded the Sandinistas, who had struggled against an invasion, just as the Czechs had struggled agains stalinism. *Mutatis mutandis*, it is as though Havel were a Stalinist. But Havel is a great poet, and this is why he is admired by Rorty and all of us, but he is far from understanding rationally (therein lies the danger of a narrative without rationality!)—as Rorty is also—the peripheral world, the Third World, poor and empowered by the "Great Word" of the "Great Narrative," such as is the neoliberal word of market economy, free competition, of which Hayek speaks, or of Nozick's minial state: "The Great *Good* Thing" presupposed in Rorty's every conversation. It is interesting that Rorty says that "he feels a guilty relief by the fact that they were not born [his generation of honorable, white males] women or homosexual, nor black" (Rorty "Feminism and Pragmatism"), but he forgets to add, "nor Latin American, African, or Asian." This negativity does not even cross his imagination.

107. Ibid., p. 26.
108. This last phrase is cited by Rorty, "Feminism and Pragmatism" "Philosophy and Democracy", p. 241 (John Dewey, in *Middle Works of John Dewey* (Carbondale: Southern Illinois University Press, 1976–83), Vol. 11, p. 145).
109. Rorty, "Social Hope and History as Comic Frame" p. 2. "As one argument in favor of such banalization, I can invoke Laclau's claim that *the transformation of thought—from Nietzsche to Heidegger, from pragmatism to Wittgenstein—has decisively undermined philosophical essentialism*" (ibid., pp. 2–3).
110. I asked Rorty at the philosophy institute in Mexico: "Pragmatically, in Dewey's sense, speaking, if someone is in misery, in absolute poverty, with a salary of 50 dollars a month, with five children, living in house made of cardboard, illiterate, living next to garbage dumps, with a daughter turned to prostitution, etc., which language will be, "pragmatically," more useful: either the banalization or the serious consideration of Marx's language which tries to rationally explain the *causes* of their pain, and who pronounced the "law of accumulation" thus: the accumulation of wealth is the reverse of the accumulation of misery?" Rorty could not but answer that Marx's language would be more useful. With this the entire question of Liberation Philosophy becomes clear, at least from the point of view of Dewey's "pragmatism"!
111. Rorty, "Social Hope and History as Comic Frame", p. 12.
112. Franz Hinkelammert in *Critica a la razón utópica* (San José, Costa Rica: DEI, 1990) shows the "metaphysics" (in the essentialist and realist sense of Rorty) that underlie a "market of perfect competition" or the "self-regulation of a market economy."
113. "Merely formal democracy," without an economic project that would supersede the neoliberal market economy, which is dominant today in Latin America, would lead to disaster and more misery. A *rational* discussion on this theme, as a Latin American political philosophy, would be necessary to formulate here, and would show Rorty the ambiguity of calling oneself in Latin America an "American liberal democrat."
114. Rorty *Contingency, Irony and Solidarity*, p. 198.
115. Marx indicates clearly this movement from "conversation" to solidaristic and

responsible "action" in the eleventh of the *Theses on Feuerbach*: "The philosophers have only *interpreted* the world, in various ways; the point is to *change* it" (Marx, *Early Writings*, p. 423; *MEW* 3, p. 7). This would appear to be a strictly pragmatic (in Dewey's sense) slogan. For Marx, it is necessary to change the social structures in order to end the pain of those who suffer, or at least mitigate it. In contraposition, the greatest cruelty a liberal may commit consists, precisely, in proclaiming rights and negating them in fact, as John Rawls does when he accepts as a point of departure the *naturalness* of economic inequalities (this is the "second principle" or "difference principle"), inequalities that ought to be judged as unjust, but which instead are taken as a point of departure in the "original position," where justice will be excercised as impartiality—a *contractio terminorum:* given that it is an impartiality that accepts "partiality," in favor of the rich, as origin. The liberals, Locke or Rawls, set out from inequality as "nature" (at least both Rousseau and Hegel anticipated Marx in questioning this "nature"). Rorty cannot agree with them because of their univeralistic rationalism, but in the last instance, and as a "liberal," he cannot evade their contradictions.

116. *Capital*, Vol. 1, pp. 342–43; German [*MEGA* II, 6], pp. 240–41). We have argued this text with Apel, against whom we emphasized that this "voice" interpellates from beyond the empirical communication community (although the Other can also be situated in the ideal communication community). Now, against Rorty, this text reminds us that the "*new*" word" of the other, in a situation of economic-political exteriority, ought to be able to be accepted within more than just a mere "conversation" in the incommensurable of our *Lebenswelt*.

7

Modernity, Eurocentrism, and Trans-Modernity: In Dialogue with Charles Taylor

I would like to compare Charles Taylor's ethical project of describing the material (or substantive) contents of modern identity, arrived at from a philosophical and historical narrative of the *Sources of the Self* (1989), with the ethical project of the Philosophy of Liberation, which agrees with Taylor's project in many aspects but differs in many others. It is not a question, then, of making a commentary or exegesis of the Canadian philosopher's work, but instead of effectuating a critical confrontation from a clearly defined and situated point of view ("from" the perspective of the Philosophy of Liberation). And as we are also engaged in a debate with Karl-Otto Apel, I would like to refer to him in order to achieve greater clarity in my exposition.

The exposition will be divided into two parts. In the first, we will confront the historical reconstruction of the sources of the modern self that is carried out by Charles Taylor. In the second, we will confront the background question, namely, whether an ethic that attempts to orient itself toward the good, substantively (Taylor), or an ethics which is formal and procedural (Habermas), is necessary or even possible. At both levels the Philosophy of Liberation will adopt its own, differing positions.

7.1 The Project of the Historical Reconstruction of Modernity

During the decade of the sixties, I had the intention of describing the "material contents"[1] of Latin American culture. For methodological reasons, this project transformed itself into a "historical" description—in an analogous manner to that intended by Taylor—of the cultural contents of the Latin American world.[2] I therefore have extreme sympathy for Taylor's project. In fact, in his most important work, *The Sources of the Self: The Making of the Modern Identity*, our philosopher explains his intentions:

That is what I want to try to do in what follows. But to do so is not easy.... Often it will be a question precisely of articulating what has remained implicit.... But there is one great recourse here, and that is history. The articulation of modern understanding of the good has to be a historical enterprise.[3]

This historical journey is "a combination of the analytical and the chronological" (*Sources of the Self*): In fact, it is an analysis of the contents of the modern self through its historical sources. The selections of his exposition, which are inspired from philosophical works (a) departing from Greek philosophers (b) and the later focus on exclusively European thinkers (c) would appear to be an obvious matter or a secondary issue without consequences. I believe this is not so, and will attempt to demonstrate it.

a) I wish to *methodologically* refer to the way in which Taylor attempts to carry out his historical analysis of modern identity, taking into account the sources of the self. For his project, Taylor almost exclusively uses works by philosophers[4] (Plato, Augustine, Descartes, Locke), which are thought through their own discourses, that is, self-referentially. It is as though it were a history of philosophy, from philosophy itself.[5] He writes with a magisterial hand, with knowledge, with a creative manner of obtaining results, but it is only an "intraphilosophical" exploration, which lacks a history, an economy, and a politics—as moments of the "world," in the Heideggerian sense. This methodological limitation will prevent the author from reaching more critical results, as we will see. It would appear as though capitalism, colonialism, and the continuing use of violence or military aggression had no importance.

b) A second aspect consists in underscoring that Taylor departs from Plato in his reconstruction of modern identity. With that, he repeats a long tradition of Western philosophy: the Greeks are taken not only as a point of departure for all philosophical methodology, but also as a privileged example in order to analyze the concrete contents of our culture;[6] in this case, of the ethical articulation directed toward the good (*agathón*). It is a question of a *hellenocentrism* of grave consequences.[7] Toward the end of Taylor's reconstruction, with respect to the concept of the self,[8] it would have been more useful to have recourse to "sources" such as the following: where the dead (in their "carnal" individuality) confront the tribunal (which means an ethical self-reflection of the *Self*) as a person, and assume charge of the acts committed with free responsibility during their temporal existence:

> I have given bread to the hungry man [exclaims the dead as a justification before the gods of the underworld who stand in judgment], and water to the thirsty man, and apparel to the naked man, and a boat to the shipwrecked.[9]

A daily reader in Montreal, Frankfurt, Moscow, or Mexico will find with this text more "familiarity" than with those of Plato. Certainly, this is one of modernity's more remote "sources" of orientation toward the good. In fact, the

Egyptian god Osiris resuscitates the dead;[10] that is to say, personal individuality is attempted to be retained. Hence, the existence of cemeteries, an institution of modern Europe that existed neither in Plato's Greece nor in Indo-European India, for the bodies, sources of evil,[11] were destroyed so that the only positive which counts would remain: the immortal, non-personal soul.[12]

In analogous manner, it would have been more useful to have departed, for instance, from the following tradition:

> By my protecting genius, their brethren in peace are guided: by my wisdom are they sheltered. That the strong may not oppress the weak; that the orphan and the widow may be counselled.

Here, we have already expressed the ethical principles of alterity,[14] which are totally absent in Plato's thought. I think that these traditions are more important to Taylor's hypothesis, inasmuch as it is a question of effective "sources" for the orientation of the later Christian-Mediterranean and Western-Latin culture. Taylor falls into an obvious hellenocentrism. Paul Ricoeur had already demonstrated in *The symbolism of Evil*[15] that the treatment of the tragic myth of Prometheus (that Plato repeats with his doctrine of the *ananke*) is radically opposed to the "Adamic myth," where the structure of "temptation" is given as a dialectic of free will (and certainly within the Adamic tradition we may locate the "sources of the modern self"). Hellenocentrism completely distorts Taylor's investigation.

c) A third aspect. Just as in the case of Hegel—who was philosophically the initiator of this question in the history of philosophy[16]—for Taylor the originary diachronic process of modernity also follows the linear movement Augustine-Descartes-Locke, et al. In short, I argue that this manner of interpreting modern identity is eurocentric, that is to say, provincial, regional, and does not take into account modernity's global significance and, thus, the inclusion of Europe's periphery as a "source," also constitutive of the modern "self" as such.[17] This will allow us to discover certain aspects (and to occlude others) of "modern identity" and the "sources of the self."

Modernity, according to my interpretation (and in this, as is obvious, I would oppose the hegemonic opinion of the Euro-North American philosophical community), may have a first definition that I will call eurocentric, and another that I will denominate worldly (planetary, not universal).[18] The eurocentric definition describes modernity with characteristics or determinations solely European. The worldly or planetary description incorporates determinant moments within the constitution of modernity as *center* of a world process in such a way that the phenomenon of modernity, exclusively attributed to the "development" of European subjectivity, would include determinations (and contra-determinations) of its situation of center with respect to a *periphery* (first colonial, then neocolonial; Third World in the epoch of the cold war, up to the understanding of the structural underdevelopment or the simple "exclusion" from the market or global capitalist system after the so-called revolution of 1989).

To reiterate: modernity is a phenomenon originally European—and it is evident that its sources date back to the Egyptian, Babylonian, Semitic, Greek worlds, but that only in the 15th century it reached worldly implementation; and that it constitutes and reconstitutes itself simultaneously by a dialectical articulation of Europe (as center) with the peripheral world (as a dominated sub-system) within the first and only "world system." Modernity *originates* in the Europe of free cities (within the context of the feudal world) from the 10th century on, approximately, but is *born* when Europe constitutes itself as center of the world system, of world history, that is inaugurated (at least as a limit date) with 1492. The medieval crusades are a frustrated attempt. The Viking "discoveries" in the North Atlantic and the Portuguese in the African Atlantic in the 15th century are its antecedents, but only with the "discovery" (by Europe) or "invasion" (in a non-eurocentric view of the peripheral peoples)[19] of the "New World" will Europe (a particular "ecumene" without evident comparative advantages up to then) enjoy a true springboard that will allow it to supersede and overcome all other ecumenes, regional or provincial systems (especially that of China). In this manner, from 1492 (and not before), "world history" begins as worldly: that is to say, the history of all civilizations or former provincial ecumenes are placed in an effectively empirical relation. The Persian, Roman, Mongolian, Chinese, Aztec, Inca, and other empires were provincial or regional ecumenes more or less *disconnected*, all of them ethnocentric "navels of the world," whose boundaries divided "human beings" from "barbarians"—the Aztecs, for instance, denominated the barbarians "Chichimecas." All the great neolithic cultures were "centers" of civilizing subsystems with their own peripheries, but without any historically significant connection with other ecumenes. Only *modern* European culture, from 1492 onwards, was a center of a world system, of a universal history that confronts (with diverse types of subsumption and exteriority) as *all the other cultures of the earth*: cultures that will be militarily dominated as its periphery.

For philosophers, it has gone unnoticed that, because of this fact, the problem of universality should have been formulated for modernity in a *never-before-undertaken* manner. Eurocentrism consists precisely in confusing or identifying aspects of human abstract universality (or even transcendental) in general with moments of European particularity, *in fact*, the first global particularity (that is, the first concrete human universality[20]). Modern European culture, civilization, philosophy, and subjectivity came to be taken as such abstractly human-universal. A great part of the achievements of modernity were not exclusively European but grose from a continuous dialectic of impact and counter-impact, effect and counter-effect, between modern Europe and its periphery, even in that which we could call the constitution of modern subjectivity. The *ego cogito* also already betrays a relation to a proto-history, of the 16th century, that is expressed in the ontology of Descartes but does not emerge from nothing. The *ego conquiro* (I conquer), as a practical self, antedates it. Hernán Cortés[21] (1521) preceded the *Discours de la méthode* (1636) by more than a century. Descartes studied at La Flêche, a Jesuit college, a religious order with great roots in America, Africa, and Asia at that moment. The "barbarian" was the obligatory context of all reflection on subjectivity, reason, the *cogito*.[22] It is so for Marx Weber, and Habermas indicates it explicitly:

> Weber identifies in retrospect the "universal-historical problem" on which he endeavored throughout his life to shed light;[23] the question of why, outside of Europe, "Neither scientific nor artistic, nor political, nor economic development entered upon that path of rationalization peculiar to the Occident?"[24]

It is this "context" that Weber develops in his thought; that is to say, in the relation center-periphery. Weber searches for the cause of Europe's or modernity's "superiority" within certain determinations (capitalist enterprise, capitalist calculus, organization of labor power, technico-scientific knowledge, systems of bureaucratized control, permanent military power, rationalization of existence at all levels). And Weber concludes:

> A product of modern European civilization, studying any problem of universal history, is bound to ask himself to what combination of circumstances the fact should be attributed that in Western civilization, *and in Western civilization only, cultural phenomena* have appeared which (as we like to think)[25] lie in a line of development having *universal* significance and value.[26]

Weber's eurocentrism consists in presupposing *a priori* that the "cultural phenomena" that were produced in the "soil of the West", *exclusively and from its own evolutionary direction*, had since the 15th century an implicit universality, "from [out of] itself." The reverse question should have been: Is it not the case that the chain of events that led, on Western soil and only there, to the production of cultural phenomena that (*against* what we always imagine) given the conquest of a *central* position at the origin itself of the history of the *world system*, the modern West achieved comparative advantages that lead to the imposition of its own culture on the remaining others, and in addition with pretensions of universality?

Why was it Europe and not China that conquered the center of the emerging world system? China, which knew the coasts of the south of Kenya in Africa, and up to Canada in America, did not have any interest in expansion to America. For Europe—specially for Venice—it was essential to be able to reach India, but they had to circumvent the Turkish-Muslim blockade. There was, therefore, interest in risking an Atlantic voyage. The conquest of America was easy (there were no iron weapons in the New World). For this reason, the first European periphery was Latin America[27]—Africa and Asia resisted militarily until the 19th century.[28] Latin America gave to Europe the first *comparative advantage* that explains, in part (but it is a part of the explanation that is never considered in the interpretations of modernity), the triumph over the Muslim world, vanquished at Lepanto in 1571 (25 years after the discovery and the beginning of the exploitation of the Zacatecas silver mines in México and the Potosí silver mines in Bolivia), and over China, which "closes" upon itself until the 20th century. Even the phenomenon of rationalization is an effect-cause of a world centrality that allows for the discovery of "other worlds," which then have to be dominated with "universal" management. We could thus undertake another reconstruction of modernity.

It is thus that a small text of Taylor is not innocent:

> This is in fact merely one example of a general process by which certain practices of Modernity have been imposed, often brutally, *outside their heartlands*. For some of them this seems to have been part of an irresistible dynamic. It is clear that the practices of technologically oriented science helped endow the nations where they developed with a cumulative technological advantage over others. This, combined with the consequences of the new emphasis on disciplined movement which I described earlier, gave *European armies a marked and increasing military advantage over non-Europeans from the seventeenth* until about the mid-twentieth century. And this combined with the consequences of the economic practices we call capitalism allowed the European powers to establish a world hegemony *for a time*.[29]

It may appear as an insignificant question. But, to situate in the 17th century the beginning of the new comparative advantage is to have left to the side the conquest of Latin America (end of the 15th century and all of the 16th century). However, it is in this moment (which I have denominated the proto-history of the *ego cogito*) where the domination over indigenous America is achieved—from Mexico to Peru for the most part—and from it, as a springboard (before the emergence of Bacon, Newton, or Descartes), the structuration of the differential advantage over the Afro-Asiatic cultures. In other words, what was perhaps already the "consequence" of the Europe *centrality* over a world *periphery* (a cultural, economic, scientific, etc. centrality that was based, in its sources, in a technical-military superiority over the American Indian, and *not* over the equal or superior, from a scientific or "rationalization" point of view, Afro-Asiatic cultures, such as, for instance, the Muslim Mongolian, and Chinese worlds), was instead presented as the "consequence" of rationalization, science, and the "modern self". In this historical interpretation (and for that reason analytical), Weber as much as Taylor may have been totally mistaken.[30]

The same takes place with Habermas. In fact, the philosopher from Frankfurt, writing about critical counter-discourses, expresses exactly the type of eurocentrism I have been discussing, as is shown by the following texts culled from *The Philosophical Discourses of Modernity*:

> The change of paradigm from subject-centered to communicative reason also encourages us to resume once again the counterdiscourse [*Gegendiskurs*] that accompanied Modernity from the beginning. Since Nietzsche's radical critique of reason cannot be consistently carried out along the line of a critique of metaphysics or of a theory of power, we are directed towards a *different* way out of the philosophy of the subject. Perhaps the grounds for the self-critique of a Modernity in collapse can be considered under other premises such that we can do justice to the motives, virulent since Nietzsche, for a precipitous leavetaking of Modernity.[31]

Or as in this other remark:

> The New Critique of Reason suppresses that almost 200-year [!] old counterdiscourse inherent in modernity itself which I am trying to recall in these lectures.[32]

And still:

> Modern Europe has created the spiritual presuppositions and the material base of a world in which this mentality has usurped the place of reason—this is the true nucleus of the critique of reason that dates back to Nietzsche. But, who else but Europe could extract from its own [*eigenen*] traditions the penetration, the energy, the will to vision and phantasy. . . . [33]

In these texts we can see, clearly, what I call eurocentrism. Also evident is the "developmentalist fallacy."[34] In first place, Habermas situates in time the beginning of this "counterdiscourse": there at the beginning stands Kant (we would therefore be only two hundred years old!). Yet, in historical reality, from a non-eurocentric point of view of modernity (that is to say, worldly), this *counter-discourse* is already five centuries old: it began on the Hispaniola Island when Antón de Montesinos attacked the injustices that were being carried out against the Indians, and from there it reached the classrooms of Salamanca (since it is there that the critique of 1514 is continued with the theoretical and practical labor of Bartolomé de las Casas, and it is there also where this counter-discourse will be expressed in the university lectures of Francisco de Vitoria concerning *De indiis*). As is always the case with Central-European philosophers, and especially Germans, the 16th and 17th centuries do not count, and Latin America much less.

Furthermore, modernity being a world phenomenon (the first epoch that involves all the cultures of the planet, in the manner of a metropolitan center in Europe or as a colony or world impacted by Europe in the periphery), this counter-discourse, precisely this and no other, could emerge within the European critical reason that opened itself and co-constituted itself from the dominated, exploited alterity: the hidden Other of dominating Europe (that always will pretend to negate such counter-discourse). But that European counter-discourse (European because of its geographical implantation) is the fruit of the European-center and the dominated-periphery. Bartolomé de las Casas would not have been able to criticize Spain without having resided in the periphery, without having heard the cries and lamentations, and without having seen the tortures that the Indians suffered at the hands of the colonizing Europeans. That Other is the origin of the European counter-discourse. It is evident that Europe, as the visible part of the iceberg, had cultural hegemony (economic and political[35]), "information," and would be the privileged place on the planet for the "discussion" of world and also philosophical problems. But this intellectual production, when it is anti-hegemonic, although still European (for instance Montaigne, Pascal, Rousseau, or Marx), is not only European. It is so neither because of its exclusive origin nor because of its significance. In addition, in the periphery there existed also an intellectual production (and philosophical; for instance Francisco Xavier Clavigero, 1731–87,[36] in Mexico, a contemporary of Kant), but as *counter-discourse* before the European hegemonic world vision, and only with provincial *sources*. Clavigero cannot publish his work in Castilian, but only in Italian. The peripheral cultures were kept isolated and without contact among themselves. They only communicated through Europe, being thus reinterpreted through center-Europe. "European" philosophy is not the *exclusive* product of Europe. Instead it is the product of the humanity located in Europe, and with the contribution of the peripheral cultures that were in an essential co-constitutive dialogue.

To say that such a "counter-discourse" is *immanent* to modernity could be accepted, if modernity were defined worldly, but in this case modernity would have to include its peripheral alterity. It would be hegemonic modernity and a dominated colonial peripheral world as a world-system. As a matter of fact, inasmuch as modernity is defined as an exclusively European horizon, it is pretended that the counter-discourse is also an exclusively European product. In this manner, the periphery itself, in order to criticize Europe, will have to europeanize itself, because it would have to use a European counter-discourse in order to show Europe its own contradictions, without being able, once again, to contribute anything new and having to negate itself.

If, instead, this counter-discourse is already the dialectical product (affirmation of alterity as principle of negation of the negation: analectical movement) of a critical dialogue with alterity, it cannot be said that it is exclusively and intrinsically European, and least of all that Europe is Europe the only one that can "retrieve from its *own* traditions" the continuation of such counter-discourses. On the contrary, it is likely that it is only outside Europe where this counter-discourse may develop more critically, and not as continuation of a strange or *exclusively* European discourse, but as continuation of a critical labor that the periphery has already stamped in the counter-discourse produced in Europe and on its own peripheral discourse (in fact and almost integrally, when it is non-eurocentric it is already counter-discourse).

From this it follows that the study of thought (traditions and philosophy) in Latin America, Asia, and Africa is not an anecdotal task or a task with parallels to the study of philosophy as such (without-anything else coming to bear). Instead, it is a question of a history that *rescues* the non-hegemonic, dominated, silenced, and forgotten counter-discourse, namely, that of the constitutive alterity of modernity itself. Kant (hegemonic-central philosopher) or Marx (European counter-discourse) and Clavigero (peripheral philosopher) will be studied as the two faces of one epoch of human thinking. Certainly, Kant, because of his hegemonic position, produced a critical philosophy that confronts the best of the world intellectual production (located empirically in Europe), and because of that Kant can be the point of departure of philosophy in all the world during two centuries. Kant, in this strict sense, is not exclusively a European thinker, but a thinker to whom the task fell, because of his historical, political, cultural, and economic situation, of producing a critical philosophy with world relevance. But the philosophical thought of Clavigero, with only regional importance hitherto (and because it is a region or dominated periphery[37], rapidly falling into oblivion even in its own Mexico), is the Other face of modernity, or of the world totality modernity/alterity, and for this very reason has equal "world" relevance. In the future we will have to study seriously what was produced philosophically in the peripheral world in order to have a common vision. Kant/Clavigero are part of a center/periphery world philosophy in the 18th century. The future history of philosophy will have a new *world* vision of philosophy and will deepen aspects thus far unsuspected, when the rich thematic of the *refraction* of the center of the system (which produced in Europe a center-philosophy, which up to now is the only one taken as "philosophy") in, or by, the periphery (which produced a peripheral-philosophy) is discovered. The center-philosophies and the peripheral-philosophies are the two faces of philosophy in modernity, and the counter-discourse (as much in the center as in the periphery) is a bequest from all the philosophers of the world, and not only from European ones.

This is essential for our philosophical project. The Philosophy of Liberation is a counter-discourse, a critical philosophy, that is born in the periphery with world pretensions. It has *explicit* consciousness of its peripherality, but at the same time it has a planetary claim (a claim to *mundialidad*). It confronts consciously a *European* philosophy (as much postmodern as modern, procedural as well as communitarian) that conflates and still identifies its concrete Europeanness with its unknown functionality of center-philosophy during five centuries. To distinguish among a) concrete Europeanness (its own European *Sittlichkeit* or *Lebenswelt*), b) the functionality of "center" that was Europe's place to exercise, and c) strict universality would produce an awakening of European philosophy from a deep sleep in which it has been immersed from its very modern inception: its eurocentrism has celebrated, exactly, five centuries.

It would have to be necessary to have *explicit* consciousness of this always present "horizon," of the colonial Other, of the barbarian, of the cultures in asymmetrical positions, dominated, "inferior,"[38] as an essential source in the constitution of the identity of the modern self, permanent source, co-constitutive. The non-consideration of this Other in the constitution of the modern self practically invalidates Taylor's entire philosophical analysis, given its eurocentric character.[39] This analysis yields only the discovery of an aspect of self-centered modern identity. Is not the identity of modernity constituted dialectically from a negated alterity (placed or posited *gesetzt*, in the Hegelian sense, as a non-identity[40] with itself, alienated), from the Other face of modernity?[41]

Finally, we should indicate that the Latin American historical reconstruction will require in addition that it be formulated from the standpoint of universal ethical criteria. Therefore, without abandoning the empirical level of "being-in-the-world" or the Husserlian *Lebenswelt*, the Philosophy of Liberation developed universalizable categories, beyond every historical-concrete *telos*.[42]

7.2 Taylor's Ethics of the Good

Our argumentative strategy will follow two paths: in a) we will present the ultimate "contents" (the "material" or "quasi-metaphysical" of Kantian ethics, in order partly to agree with Taylor and to prepare the way for our critique of Habermas and Apel); in b) we will consider Hegel's critique to a certain extent (and that of Heidegger) of all formalisms, and thus therefore of Taylor's critique of Habermasian formal proceduralism; in c) we will present the habermasian critique of Taylor (and thus implicitly of Hegel and Heidegger); in d) we will consider the critiques of the Philosophy of Liberation to the ontological ethics of the *Sittlichkeit* (Hegel, Heidegger, Taylor, MacIntyre) from the oppressed or alienated (which we will call the *principium oppressionis*) within the Totality that strives after the good; and in e), lastly, we will consider the critiques to Habermas and Apel that are attempted by the Philosophy of Liberation from the exteriority or "exclusion" of the Other (the *principium exclusionis*), of the poor, the oppressed woman, the child, future generations, the discriminated races. In this short work, we will only "point to" the argumentative architectonic without being able to deepen it.

a) Always, as with all "formal" ethics, there is in Kant an ultimate "content" (quasi-metaphysical). In a first formulation of the categorical imperative, Kant appeared to be purely "formal";

> So act that the maxim of your will could always hold at the same time as the principle of a universal [*allgemeinen*] legislation.[43]

In this sense the moral law is "merely formal ... it abstracts from all matter [*aller Materie*]."⁴⁴ At this moment, we do not want to insist on this point; nor do we want to focus on the problem of the application (*Anwendung*) of the principle.⁴⁵ We would like here, instead, to show the "content" (beyond the purely "formal") in a second moment:

> Act in such a way that you always treat humanity, whether in your own person or in the person of any other, never simply as a means, but always at the same time as an end.... ⁴⁶ Without doubt the person is broad enough, but the humanity in his person (*Person*) ought to be sacred to him. In all of creation ... only the person, and with him every rational creature, is an end in itself.... Its personality is the only thing that makes them be ends in themselves.⁴⁷

The inevitable question is: Why is the person an "end in itself"? An answer to this question *inevitably* leads us to a quasi-metaphysical discussion. But it is this answer which can clarify the reason why I must have "respect" for the law. In fact, given that the person belongs to "both worlds" (to the intelligible and the empirical), "she ought to consider her being referring to her second and supreme destination with veneration (*Verehrung*) and its laws with the greatest respect (*Achtung*)".⁴⁸

That is to say, in the last instance, "respect" for the law is deduced from respect for the *dignity of the person*. Strictly:

> The ground [*Grund*] of this principle [the categorical imperative] is: Rational nature exists as an end in itself.⁴⁹

This ultimate content is also encountered in Habermas or Apel. In both, as with Kant,⁵⁰ the communication community (be it ideal or transcendental) has an ultimate reference to the "personhood" of all the participants and all those affected, as persons with equal rights. It is evident that in all "validity claims," the personhood of the Other is a required reference, just as when we say that we "comprehend illocutorily the (acceptable) attempt to establish an interpersonal relationship (*interpersonele Beziehung*)."⁵¹ That is to say, the illocutory moment of the speech-act always already (*immer schon*) presupposes the existence of the Other, of another person, who is respected as an equal; and thus, in the "ideal speech act" arguments must be used, and the irrational force of violence is simply not to be exercised or deployed. Similarly, Karl-Otto Apel presupposes the dignity and equality of the person as an ultimate transcendental moment:

> Who argues has already attested *in actu*.... This means that the ideal rules of argumentation in an, in principle unlimited, communication community of *persons* who *recognize each other reciprocally as equals*, represent normative conditions of possibility of the decision on ethical validity claims [*ethischen Geltungsansprüchen*] through the formation of consensus.⁵²

This already assumed "person of the Other" as a presupposition is, exactly, the taking charge of the "ethical" par excellence:[53] the ethical *content* of every formal morality (or the hidden and always implicit foundation of every "formalism," be it Kantian, Habermasian proceduralism, or Apelian transcendentalism). Is the presupposed relationship with the Other an *intrinsic* moment of the theoretical-argumentative reason, or is it a previous moment of *ethical reason* (strictly *practical* or as *will*) as foundation of the theoretical-argumentative reason?

b) On the other hand, Hegel's critique of Kantian "formalism" dates back to his first intuitions as a student. I am of the opinion, with respect to the theme that is our present concern, that Taylor is inspired by Hegel's critique of Kant.[54]

As a matter of fact, the first hegelian critique of Kant is an ethical critique.[55] Hegel had studied a cold and scholastic theology in Tübingen, and was thus affected by the pedagogical rebellion of the young Schiller, who in 1795 published *The Aesthetic Education of Humankind*. Hegel had read Kant's *Religion within the Limits of Reason Alone* and the *Critique of Practical Reason*. Hegel was inspired by Schiller in his understanding of reason (*Vernunft*) as the vital faculty of synthesis; while understanding (*Verstand*) determines its object, separates it, kills it. In the *Spirit of Christinaity and Its Fate*, Hegel writes:

> In the Kingdom of the Heavens he [Jesus] shows to them [his disciples] not the elimination of the law, but instead that these will be fullfilled through a justice, one which will be different and greater than the justice as is obtained from the mere fidelity of duty [Kantian].[56]

For the young Hegel, still a theologian, Kant is the Old Testament of the formal law (morality, *Moralität*); Jesus is the New Testament, the subsumption (*Aufhebung*) of the unilateral in the *pléroma* (the future ethical life, *Sittlichkeit*). There is not only formal universal law, but also equally inclination, love, synthesis (*Synthese*):

> The most comprehensive principle may be called a tendency to execute what the law commands, unity of inclination [*Neigung*] and law, thanks to which this loses its form as law; this agreement with the inclination is the *pléroma* of the law.... The same is true with this tendency, a virtue [*Tugend*], is a synthesis in which the law loses its universality (in virtue of which Kant always named it objective), the subject its particularity, and both their contradiction [*Entgegensetzung*].[57]

In this text of 1798, we already have the definitive Hegel (and in him, in some way, the intuitions of Taylor and MacIntyre). The objective law that commands from *without* is sublated by the synthesis of the subject-object (as community or concrete people), and now as a "second nature."[58] What in "morality" commands, in "ethical life" (*Sittlichkeit*) operates through love, through inclination, through *ethos*: "Agreement [*Übereinstimmung*] is life, and as such relation of the different: love."[59] That is to say, "the Kingdom of God ... is a living community,"[60] and not the isolated individual called for by the objective law that kills.[61] It would be fitting to underscore many aspects, especially the Hegelian critique of the impossibility of the effective universalization of the maxim without contradictions (which the consensual proceduralism of Habermas optimizes);[62] and the empirical possibility of the adequate "application" of the principles;[63] but with what has been said, it is enough in order to proceed with our theme.[64]

Heidegger, similarly, also departs from a critique of Kant. He, however, does it in an ontological manner (and not ethical).[65] The subjectivity of the Kantian subject already "ex-sists" in the "world" as it constitutes objects (also when constituting practical objects). The "world" is openness to the "comprehension" of Being.[66] *Being and Time* and also *Kant and the Problem of Metaphysics* are subsumptions of modern subjectivity (and therefore also of Kantian practical reason) in "being-in-the-world." The point of departure, therefore, is "facticity," and re-reading Aristotle, we can translate:

> Virtue is a habitual mode of dwelling in the world (*héxis*) which confronts elective possibilities (*proairetiké*) knowing how to determine the just medium between them in view of the fundamental pro-ject, thanks to an interpretative circumspection, such as would locate it within the existential horizon of the authentic man (*hó frónimos*).[67]

In my case, I reconstructed, departing from Heidegger, an *ontological ethics*, from the critique of Kant, at the beginning of my work *Towards an Ethics of Latin American Liberation*, Chap. 1.[68]

In what does Taylor's attempt consist? At the beginning of his major work, our philosopher explains that "I didn't feel I could launch into this study without some preliminary discussion of these links" (p. x). Here he develops his position, in the axiological terminological "style."[69] In fact, the fundamental intention of the *Sources of the Self* is to show the origin, the content, and identity crisis of the modern self, impossible to discover in a mere moral or abstract formal ethic. The ethical life can only be reconstructed in its concrete horizon, oriented by "intuitions" toward the good, toward "hypergoods" that presuppose a "moral ontology" based, in the last instance, in a "respect for life." "Strong evaluations" are at the base of the "respect for Others," of the "sense of one's own dignity," that have been placed in question by a horizon of "disenchantment," as a "dissipation of our sense of the cosmos." In reality there is something like a "quest" (as MacIntyre has put it) for an "articulation" of life, as an affirmation of "ordinary life." The identity of the self presupposes the recognition and affirmation of the historical moral sources of modernity, implicit but always apparent: the deism of the Christian God, the self-responsibility of the person as a subject, the romantic belief in the goodness of nature. But as these sources are not recognized, or have been forgotten, modernity finds itself in crisis. In order to be able to awaken an operative ethical "motivation," we would have to count on an aesthetic impulse. It is not argumentation that motivates to the realization of the good life, but aesthetic narrative, as expressed in the tradition of a *pathos*, such as that of Schiller, Nietzsche, or Benjamin. In conclusion:

> The intention of this work was one of retrieval, an attempt to uncover buried goods through rearticulation—and thereby to make these sources again empower, to bring the air back again into the half-collapsed lungs of the spirit. . . . There is a large element of hope. It is a hope that I see implicit in Judaeo-Christian theism . . . and in its central promise of a divine affirmation of the human.[70]

In *The Ethics of Authenticity*, the theme is deepened, arriving at new results. The three malaises of modernity (individualism, the primacy of instrumental reason or technological capitalism, and the despotism of the system,[71] produce a "loss of meaning," an "eclipse of ends," and a "loss of freedom" in bureaucratized societies. But in the midst of so much "dis-articulation," an "ideal of authenticity" opens up. The original "source of identity," born of a "disengaged rationalism" of a "self" that has to think reflexively about itself, child of the romantic epoch, as an "atomism of the community"[72] is the "inwardness" of a self-determined and autonomous will that attempts being true to itself.[73] This authenticity is "dialogical,"[74] departing from the "significant other,"[75] where identity as much as "difference" before them is affirmed. This difference emerges from a common "horizon." "Our identity requires recognition by others."[76] And therefore "to deny recognition is a form of oppression."[77] This allows Taylor to make a nice description of authenticity as the right to creation, to invention, discovery, and originality; of the opposition to the rules of society.[78] He concludes:

> A fragmented society is one whose members find it harder and harder to identify with their political society as a community. This lack of identification may reflect an atomistic outlook, in which people come to see society purely instrumentally.[79]

The theme of the "universal recognition of difference,"[80] is the object of the work entitled "The Politics of Recognition,"[81] where we encounter sketches of a more concrete political horizon. Now Taylor broadens the horizon of modernity.[82] It is a question of a "continuing dialogue and struggle with significant others."[83] And now, the philosopher of the center, exclaims:

> There are other cultures. . . . It is reasonable to suppose that cultures that have . . . articulated their sense of the good, the holy, the admirable, are almost certain to have something that deserves our admiration and respect. . . .

It would take a supreme arrogance to discount this possibility apriori.... But what the presumption requires of us is not peremptory and unauthentic judgements of equal value, but a willingness to be open to comparative culture study.... What it requires above all is an admission that we are very far away from that ultimate horizon from which the relative worth of different cultures might be evident.[84]

From these preoccupations that are our own concern, Taylor criticizes Habermas's philosophy for its pretension to construct a consensual, universalist formalism, which in fact is grounded in a concrete (and material) horizon of orientations toward the good; in a "good life," with substantive contents:

It seems that they are motivated by the strongest moral ideals, such as freedom, altruism, and universalism. These are among the central moral aspirations of modern culture, the hypergoods which are distinctive to it.... They are constitutionally incapable of coming clean about the deeper sources of their own thinking.[85]

It is, somehow, the repetition (*Wiederholung*) of the Hegelian and Heideggerian critiques to Kant: the subject is always already immersed in a *Sittlichkeit* (Hegel) or in the *Welt* (Heidegger). And Taylor cannot but be partly right.

c) We will consider now, in a few words, Habermas's critique of Taylor.[86] For the Frankfurt philosopher, for instance in his work *Justification and Application: Remarks on Discourse Ethics*,[87] the fundamental distinction between "strategic" reason (oriented to ends, as in Aristotle, and in some way in Taylor), "ethical" reason or the concrete *Sittlichkeit* (the level in which Taylor is situated in order to "motivate" an ethics of authenticity), and "moral" reason (the formal universality which Habermas and Apel put forth), tends to revitalize the Kantian problematic, albeit now "transformed" through a "communication community" (pragmatic paradigm of speech acts), beyond solipsism and the paradigm of consciousness. Habermas indicates that contemporary practical philosophies give priority to the question of formal "justice" (as in Rawls) or to the "good life" (Aristotle's *eu bios*). Taylor puts forth an ethics within a strategic horizon (toward good), of strong evaluation and oriented toward the modern concept of the "good life," which "motivates" the self in order to retrieve, affirming its own forgotten identity, an identity which is sought out of its oldest and most antique sources.[88] For Habermas, this is not the intent of a moral philosophy. In addition, such an ethic does not possess the criteria that would allow it to judge the morality of its own life world and, least of all, to establish a dialogue between the morality of the ethos of different cultures. Neither can aesthetics serve as a therapy that motivates authentic ethics, a path attempted by Adorno without any success.

d) We need to take the last two steps. In the first, it is a question of carrying out, if it were possible, the critique already performed many years ago to the pretensions of every ontological ethics.[89] I would like to denominate *principium oppressionis* that pronouncement in which the Other is considered as oppressed *"in" the Totality*, as a "functional part" (and not as subject), *whose different interests are negated in the "system."*[90] It is a matter of the theme of alienation[91] itself (the reification of the Other).

In every life world, communication community, or ethics oriented to ends (ontological horizon with virtues and values), there is always an Other who is *oppressed*, negated. The oppressed is justified by the good, the end (the *telos*), virtues, values as the non-existing, or at least as the not-yet seen, not-discovered, hidden. More than twenty years ago, I wrote:

> To see, to comprehend, to know, to calculate, to think, the *noêin* or the *gnosis* [today I would say: to argue] are supreme modes of being human in the Totality.[92] Such is perfection for Plato and Aristotle, and equally the *authentic* for Heidegger [for Taylor also?]. In this case *authenticity* does not have any ethical life whatsoever, since the Totality itself, being identity, grounds the intra-world or ontological morality, itself amoral, non-ethical; or ontological ethics as ontology of the Totality. Properly, there is no ontological good or evil. There is only a fundamental structure tragically unmovable [the ethos of our culture] to which we can approach through a certain type of *gnosis* [or aesthetics] (*authenticity, Eigentlichkeit*). The foundation is *as it is* and nothing else."[93]

In a world, in a culture (because all cultures are ethnocentric[94]), in an ethos, in a *real* communication community, negation *a priori* of an Other never stops. In slavery, the slave was not "human" for Aristotle; in feudalism, the serf was not *simpliciter*, part of the *civitas* for Thomas of Aquinas; the wage-earner (who sells his labor) was not the owner of the fruit of his/her labor for Adam Smith (and this because of a second "state of nature,"[95] superior to the primitive state of nature); in machismo, women are sexual objects, obedient housewives; in ecologically predatory cultures, future generations also do not have rights. All of these Others, invisible in every Totality, life world, or given *ethos* (also the "central" modern ethos that Taylor analyzes), negate the Other without "ethical conscience;" By necessity,[96] the *telos* or good of a culture, of a Totality, cannot be the last foundation of the morality of our acts. It will only be "for now," while the negated Other is not discovered in this type of system.[97]

It is in this context that the Philosophy of Liberation attempted to overcome the incommensurable relativity of the given systems, and attempted a formal-historical transcendentality that skirts the difficulties of the communitarians, without falling into relativism. The imperative is: "Liberate[98] the person unworthily treated in the oppressed Other!" This *principium oppressionis* is absolute, it holds for *every* existential or functional system,[99] and it is always concrete, not abstract.[100] The negated Other is discovered *from the concrete ethos*, from the Hegelian Sittlichkeit, the Heideggerian world, the daily life of Taylor. The "slave" cannot be discovered as a transcendental, abstract, or universal negated person. The Philosophy of Liberation attempts to describe the logic of a Totality as a totalization (an ontology of the "closed society" as is Popper's), and to describe the logic from which the discovery of the Other as oppressed is possible (the logic of alterity).

Aristotle's Hellenic heroes hunted slaves with "tranquil," "good" conscience, just as the hero of modern authenticity conquered the Amerindian, enslaved Africa, exploited Asia—everything justified by the "good" and the "hypergood," just as Hegel said of the English *gentleman*:

> The English become the missionaries of civilization in the entire world.[101]

Hegel justified colonialism (negation of the peripheral Other) with complete authentic consciousness. Here is the ambiguity of *every ontological ethics*— inevitably also true with Taylor—criticized for a long time by the Philosophy of Liberation!

e) The second step that we should take consists in beginning a critique of the universal morality or the pragmatic formalism of Habermas, where Taylor's[102] formulation of the "recognition" of differences[103] will be of use, in yet another problematic context, (which we have already presented in the first version of my work *Toward an Ethics of Latin American Liberation* of 1970, since Levinas anticipated it explicitly). Now it is necessary to refer, after the linguistic turn, or out of the pragmatic paradigm, to the *principium exclusionis*: the Other as the "affected" in the exteriority,[104] as the excluded "of" the Totality, or alterity (the Other as nothing[105]). As with Hegel, Heidegger, or Taylor, we depart from the factical, concrete situation, of a world or present, given, *Sittlichkeit*. The empirical is not abandoned ideally or transcendentally (as Habermas does from an "ideal speech situation," or as Apel does in a "transcendental pragmatics," i.e., ideal communication community); instead the horizon of the system is "perforated" ("transcended"[106]) in search of the excluded Other.

The problem is enunciated in the following manner: the fundamental distinction for Habermas between "morality" (universal) and "ethics" (concrete),[107] although it refers to Kant, still tends to discover the real conditions in the problem of the application of principles of universality, thanks to the consensual community:

> What in a moral sense is justified, every rational being must be able to will.... Discourse ethics replaces the Kantian categorical imperative by a procedure of moral argumentation. Its ["D"] principle postulates, only those norms may claim to be *valid* that could meet with the consent of *all affected* in their role as participants in a practical discourse.[108]

Which is mediated by the procedure (U):

For a norm to be valid, the forseeable consequences and side effects of its general observance for the satisfaction of each person's particular interests must be without coercion acceptable *to all*.[109]

To which Apel adds a "principle of formal complementarity (C)," which helps in the "realization of the conditions of the application of (U), taking into account the situational and contingent conditions."[110] The minimal real conditions are: the survival of the real communication community, the participation of *all* possibly affected. But, when taking into account what we could call the *principium exclusionis*, the "all the possibly affected" becomes ethically problematic. In fact, all the affected can never become real participants:

There will always be excluded-affected from and by every possible real communication community.

Which confronts us with a contradiction: a) although all the affected always have the right (implicitly at least) to participate in the real communication community, b) there are always excluded-affected; that is to say, it is factically impossible that there be none.[111]

This places the problem of validity, of the morality of the agreement (*Verständigung*), in a new perspective. Every agreement is not only provisional and falsifiable, but also ethically defective (has an "originary" defect). "Procedurally," the first question that should be asked by the "participants" in a real communication community is: Whom could we have left "out"—without recognition—and this "excluded"?

Furthermore, since at this level no one can be excluded, it is necessary to recognize transcendentally or ideally each "participant" as a distinct person; the Other of everything else, the principle of every possibility of "dissent" (and origin of a new discourse). This respect and recognition at the transcendental or ideal is the point of departure that allows the Other "participation" in the community into which she has factically irrupted as a *new* Other.[112] Respect and recognition of the Other, ideally or factically, is the ethical moment (and as such ethical and rational) *par excellence*. This is what is presupposed in every "explication" (epistemological) or "assent" (argumentative) by and to the argumentation of the Other. For to "respect" and to "recognize" the *new Other* (as a subject of "dissent" of a "new Other," distinct[113]) is the ethical act or the practical rationale *kath'exokhén*, since it is the "giving place to the Other" so that she may intervene/participate in the argumentation as an equal, with rights.

The essential difference between discourse ethics, which finds itself practically in the position of the "inapplicability" (*Nichtanwendbarkeit*) of fundamental moral norms in exceptional situations, and the Philosophy of Liberation, is located precisely at that boundary moment in which which discourse ethics discovers its own limit(s):

Revolutions—writes Albrecht Wellmer—against unjust claims should be considered as morally *exceptional* situations; and in such a manner that the foundations of a reciprocity morally understood have been abolished, because moral duties of one side can no longer have correspondence with the moral pretensions of the other side.[114]

These limit situations are precisely the matter of greatest concern for the Philosophy of Liberation (wars, revolutions, the process of women's liberation, of the oppressed races, of popular cultures, of the majorities without rights in the periphery or the colonial world that by definition find themselves in a structure of oppression). The concrete principle of "Liberate *hic et nunc* the oppressed!" or "Make the affected-excluded participate!" demands procedural realization, but not properly an "application" of the transcendental in the empirical.[115] What are "exceptional situations"[116] of application for discourse ethics are normal situations of determination for the Philosophy of Liberation. With reason Levinas begins his work *Totality and Infinity* with the expression:

> The state of war suspends morality; it divests the eternal institutions and obligations of their eternity and rescinds ad interim the unconditional imperatives.[117]

In this case, for the impoverished world periphery (inheritor of modern, ethically irrational colonialism), for woman (always within a machist system of violation), for the oppressed races (such as the Jews in Hitler's Germany and African slaves in the United States, or apartheid in South Africa), for the minorities, such as the Palestinians in Israel, or the great majorities, such as the wage-earners in capitalism, for all of them the "exceptional case" prevents the "application" of transcendental moral norms in their concrete cases. Of what good is such a morality?[118]

7.3 Conclusions

We may conclude that in a certain manner the ontological critique of Hegel (Taylor) against Kantian formalism (Habermas, Apel) is repeated once again, an issue which is at the very origin of the Philosophy of Liberation itself.[119] It is obvious that between the real Hegel and us there mediates a century and a half of history; there we find the old Schelling, Marx, Levinas, and many others. The debate, thus, is located between 1) a "formal morality," 2) a "concrete ethical life," and 3) a *tertium quid* not considered in the Euro-North American debate, and much less if it is placed in the perspective of an impoverished, exploited, and excluded world periphery (the absent affected), that is to say, from a "world ethical alterity" that attempts to supersede formal "morality" (Kantian or profoundly "transformed" by Apel and Habermas) as the substantive "ethical life" (Hegelian, Heideggerian, or the communitarian of a Taylor or MacIntyre). "Alterity" allows the superseding of the formal universality of morality, on the one hand, and, on the other, the concrete substantivity of an ethical life, from a horizon of a new problematic. The position of the Philosophy of Liberation would appear to be in agreement with Taylor's call for a reclaiming of the positivity of a life world oriented toward the good[120] (against Habermas and Apel); but, at the same time, discovers "formal" criteria that allow the critique of every ontological, systematic totality or *Sittlichkeit* (against Taylor), from the ethical principle of the alterity of the Other (beyond Habermas and Apel).

The project of liberation *of the oppressed* and the *excluded* opens up from the exteriority of the Other, beyond (*jenseits*) every given situation. The construction of alternatives, even if it were also necessary (which cannot be discarded *a priori*), the construction of an historical utopia or a new society, is not only a product of the "application" of a model, or ideal, or transcendental situation. Nor is it the authentic accomplishment of a given life world (be this the modern world or another), much less when thought of as the defectless movement of a necessary logic (such as Hegel's teleology or historical reason or *standard* Marxism or Stalinism), but a responsible "dis-covering" as an answer to the "interpellation" of the Other, in a prudent and slow movement (where the theory of a real communication community, which arrives rationally and procedurally at consensus with intersubjective validity, helps us better understand the elective development of a *frónesis* of liberation), where the philosopher (as the "organic intellectual" of Gramsci) ought to take seriously (with Taylor) the ethical motivations of the liberation of the oppressed and excluded.

Notes

1. With this I intend to indicate that Taylor enters into a "positive" description of the "substantive" moments of the modern self and does not remain at a purely formal level. I have, for a period of ten years, attempted to describe in a "positive" manner the Latin American experience, having for a method the hermeneutic of Ricoeurian inspiration; I abandoned the project for methodological reasons (concerning the critique of this position, see my work "Más allá del 'culturalismo'" in *Historia de la Iglesia en América Latina*, I/1 (Salamanca: Sígueme, 1983), pp. 34ff; consult also Hans Schelkshorn, *Ethik der Befreiung* (Freiburg: Herder, 1992) the chapter titled "Faktizität versus Universalismus der Moderne" (pp. 48ff) and the following sections.
2. In Schelkshorn's work, "Neudefinition des weltgeschichtlichen *Ortes* Lateinamerikas" in *Ethik der Befreiung*, pp. 58ff, and the following paragraphs.
3. Charles Taylor *Sources of the Self: The Making of the Modern Identity*, (Cambridge: Harvard University Press, 1989) 103. Taylor tells us in the preface: "In part, it was because of the very ambitious nature of the enterprise, which is an attempt to articulate and write a history of modern identity" (ix).
4. Although Taylor also counts with the help of writers, theologians and other thinkers of the human sciences.

5. Alphonse de Waehlens use to say to us that "philosophy thinks the non-philosophical" (*La Philosophie et les expériences naturelles* [La Haya: Nijhoff, 1961]).
6. In my work, originally written in 1961, but published much later, *El Humanismo Helénico*, I attempted an interpretation of the Semitic *ethos* in opposition to the Greek (also presented in another work, *El Humanismo Semita*, where we studied the thesis formulated above).
7. Modern Western culture has attempted and achieved a "kidnapping" of classical Greek culture as an exclusive European moment. There is no clear consciousness of the fact that classical Greece, and even the Byzantism, is as much Arab-Muslim as it is Latin-Christian. In *Eurocentrism*, the Egyptian thinker Samir Amin shows this correctly. Aristotle was studied in Baghdad (the very same bombarded Baghdad of the 20th century!) during the 10th century, A.C., when he was still unknown in the Latin-Christian world.
8. For Taylor the "self" is as much the *ego* as it is the *person* (see the entire first section, "Agency and the Self", in *Human Agency and Language: Philosophical Papers, vol. 1* (Cambridge: Cambridge University Press, 1985), 13–114 and *Sources of the Self*, 25–51.
9. *Book of the Dead* in Papyrus Nu (London: Routledge & Kegan Paul Ltd., 1960), p. 372. The translation has been slightly altered: "mariner" is not consonant with the boats that were common for the Nile. This text, present in the Christian New Testament (but absent in the Old Testament), speaks to us of the presence of Egyptian culture in the consciousness of the founder of Christianity, who suffered political exile in this country during his infancy.
10. This mythological belief is of Bantu origin, from Black Africa, the south of the first cataract of the Nile.
11. The *próton kakón* of Plotinus's *Enneads*. See my work on "Plotino, genio reflexivo indoeuropeo" in *El dualismo de la antroplogía de la christiandad*, (Buenos Aires: Guadalupe, 1974) Chap. IV, pp. 137ff.
12. The soul is one for the whole universe, un-created, immortal, divine. It has nothing to do with the personal "self." Instead, the "dead" or the "flesh" of the Egyptian is personal-individual and pretends perpetuation as such. It is the proto-anthropology of modernity. With respect to this, see my *El dualismo en la antropología de la Christianidad*, Chap. II "Antropología cristiana y humanismo helénico," § 4, "La resurrección como doctrina del hombre."
13. Hammurabi, King of. Babylon, *The Hammurabi Code and The Sinaitic Legislation* trans. Chilperic Edwards (Port Washington, New York: Kennikat Press, 1971), pp. 73–74.
14. See my *El dualismo en la antropología de la cristiandad*, el § sign 85, "Hacia el descubrimiento de la persona come exterioridad" (pp. 279ff).
15. Paul Ricoeur, *The Symbolism of Evil* (New York: Harper and Row, 1967).
16. Taylor's works about Hegel, in my opinion, influenced him to give central importance to the concept of ethical life (*Sittlichkeit*), a "substantive" and not merely "formal" position with respect to ethical questions. But, at the same time, he absorbed from Hegel's eurocentrism. See my recent work *The Invention of the Americas: Eclipse of the Other and the Myth of Modernity* (New York: Continuum, 1995) with respect to the theme of "eurocentrism". Hegel wrote,"Europe is absolutely the center and end [*das Zentrum und das Ende*] of universal history" *(Die Vernunft in der Geschichte, Zweiter Entwurft* (1830), in *Sämtliche Werke*, ed. J. Hoffmeister, (Hamburg: 1955), p. 235). In my Frankfurt conferences, we could all "laugh" (more than two hundred participants in all) at the quasi-comical

ingenuities of Hegel's racist and superficial eurocentrism (with respect to the interpretation of Europe in universal history, and the denial of historicity to Latin America and Africa, and the localization of Asia in an "infantile" stage, merely preparatory to European history). The commentators (Taylor himself, *Hegel* (Cambridge: Cambridge University Press, 1975) 3ff never refer to Hegelian eurocentric contempt for Latin America, Africa, and Asia, nor to his way of justifying European colonialist violence: "Against the absolute right that it [the dominating people of the world: *Weltbeherrschende*] has because of its function as the bearer of the development of the world spirit, the spirit of *other peoples does not have any right [rechtlos]*" (*Enzyklopädie*, § 347).

17. This is the central thesis of my *Towards the Origin of the Myth of Modernity*.
18. That is to say, the extremely elaborate characterization by Taylor, as well as that of Weber (which inspired Habermas), or Lyotard's critique—all of them ignore an essential determination, a "source of the self": European "centrality," since the late-18th century, in the planetary human experience that we denominate world history (*wordly*, *mondiale*, and not universal, *universelle*).
19. See the third part of my work on 1492 *The Invention of the Americas*, "From the Invention to the Discovery of the Other."
20. We have to distinguish between "concrete universality" (imposed by modern European domination in the world system, in the periphery) and the "worldliness" or totality of concretely existing cultures. A "trans-modern" project proposes a new "worldliness" as a full realization of future humanity, where all cultures (not only the modern European one) can affirm their alterity, and not merely a process of modernization where the Euro-North American culture is imposed upon them or its abstraction (an "abstract" modernity that is no more than very same Euro-North American modernity from which some disturbing characteristics are taken away).
21. See "Toward a phenomenology of the *Ego Conquiro*," Chap. 1 of *The Invention of the Americas*.
22. See Tzetan Todorov's work, *Nous et les autres* (Paris: Seuil, 1989).
23. Jürgen Habermas, *Theory of Communicative Action. Volume One: Reason and the Rationalization of Society* (Boston: Beacon Press, 1983) p. 157.
24. Ibid., p. 157.
25. Here Weber opens the door to our suspicion of it being an ungrounded, partial, provincial, and eurocentric representation.
26. Max Weber, *The Protestant Ethic and the Spirit of Capitalism* trans. Talcott Parsons (New York: Charles Scribner's Son, 1958), p. 13; German: "Vorbemerkung" in *Die protestanstische Ethik*, I (Hamburg: Siebenstern Taschenbuch Verlag, 1973), p. 9 (emphasis added). The question is not, as Habermas thinks, whether that universality has universal validity "for us" (Habermas, *Theory of Communicative Action. Volume One*, p. 179).
27. This is the not yet invalidated thesis of Immanuel Wallerstein, *The Modern World-System* (New York: Academic Press, 1974). See my work *The Invention of the Americas*, the third lecture.
28. The conquest of Africa was organized during the Berlin Congress of 1884–85, a century ago.
29. Taylor, *Source of the Self* 207. That "for a time" is the last 500 years, and not only until the middle of the 20th century, but until the Gulf War and its consequences in 1993. Perhaps Taylor thinks that the United States replaces Europe in world hegemony, but philosophically and culturally they are the "same."

30. Taylor's text indicates that colonialism or the domination of the periphery has only a posterior and quantitative effect: "This has obviously had tremendous importance for the *spread of these practices*..."; but not as preceding moments to its constitution. Taylor does not understand the eurocentric sense of his following phrases; in any event, he recognizes this "won't figure in my analysis, except at the boundaries." Like Ginés de Sepúlveda, Taylor believes that the domination of Europe over its periphery "has had a crucial effect on the development of both [!] European and non-European societies, and the prestige [!] of the self-understandings associated with them has a fateful importance for the development of cultures." In such a manner all of this process has to be interpreted culturally. And what if the development of modern violence and barbarism, such as slavery and colonialism, were the structural underdevelopment of all the cultures of the South? This type of conclusion is fruit of a method that only takes into account philosophical "ideas." Would this be that which some call *idealism*?
31. Jürgen Habermas, *The Philosophical Discourse of Modernity: Twelve Lectures* (Cambridge: The MIT Press, 1987), p. 301.
32. Ibid., p. 302, 309. Taylor extends modernity a bit longer: "The whole modern era from the seventeenth century is frequently seen as the time frame of decline" *The Ethics of Authenticity* (p. 1).
33. Habermas, *The Philosophical Discourse of Modernity*, p. 367.
34. The *entwicklungsideologische Fehlschluss*.
35. The universities, the publication of books, etc. presuppose economic development and the accumulation of wealth acquired in the peripheral colonial world, which are the material conditions of what Gramsci will call the "material apparatus" of culture (and philosophy, of course).
36. Born in Veracruz (México); died in Bologna (Italy); he was exiled from Mexico in 1767, by Borbonian expulsion. He knew in addition to Castilian, Greek, Latin, Nahuatl (Aztec), and Mexteco, which he practiced during his youth. He was professor in the college of San Gregorio de México, in Puebla, Valladolid (later Morelia), and Guadalajara. He carried out a systematic critique of Buffon and De Pauw, defending the dignity of the American indian: "We were born of Spanish parents and we have no consanguinous affinity with the Indians, nor can we from their misery expect any reward. And thus with no other motive than love for truth and jealousy for humanity, we are made to abandon our own cause in order to defend *another's* [the Other] with less danger of erring" (*Disertaciones*, V, "Constitución física y moral de los mexicanos," in the work by Clavigero, *Historia antigua de México*, which he had to translate from Castilian to Italian in order to be able to edit it in 1780 in Italy. Porrúa, [ed. Mexico 1976, pp. 503–24]). In addition Clavigero wrote a *Historia de la Antigua y Baja California*, edited in Venice, 1789. See also from Clavigero, *Antología*, introduction by Gonzalo Aguirre Beltrán (Mexico: Sep-Setentas, 1976). Another work that should be considered is Miguel Léon Portilla's *Recordación de Francisco Xavier Clavigero. Su Vida y su Obra* (Mexico: Porrúa, 1974). Clavigero chooses, then, a historical, hermeneutical-political line in order to reconstruct regional Mexican particularity against Spain, and because of that he writes a pamphlet on the Virgin of Gaudalupe (flag of Mexican political emancipation from Spain), and indicates a path of reconstruction of that which is Mexican against the abstract universality of the European Enlightenment, a true *"positive* philosophy," just as that of Schelling's *History of Mythology*. See my work *Método para una filosofía de la*

liberación. Superación analéctica de la dialéctica hegeliana (Salamanca: Síguemen, 1974): "Del Hegel definitivo al viejo Schelling," pp. 116ff. In fact, Clavigero wrote about these themes at least fifteen year before Schelling wrote *The Positivity of the Christian Religion* (1795–96).
37. This is the sense of Augusto Salazar Bondy's hypothesis in his work *Existe una filosofía en nuestra América?* (Mexico: Siglo XXI, 1967).
38. See Tzvetan Todorov's work, *Nous et les autres* (Paris: Sevil, 1989).
39. Let us consider only a quantitative factor, which really does not indicate much, but gives us an idea of the proportions. Today, in 1993, Western Europe, the United States, and Canada (that is the *exclusive* cultural and philosophical horizon of Taylor's work) constitute only 15 percent of humanity (750 million among the 5,000 million). Can the remaining 85 percent feel itself expressed in this type of historical analysis? Has not Euro-North American philosophy itself become provincial and regional?
40. It is for that reason that the entire work of Clavigero in the 18th century, like the Philosophy of Liberation in the 20th century, departs from the affirmation of an "identity" (of the negated Aztec world by the conquest of modern man: Hernán Cortés) that is the negation of the modern "identity" as "modernization"; modernization which presupposes the negation of the peripheral culture as Other, distinct, as an in-itself. The peripheral "self" departs from the negativity of the "hegemonic modern self." The entire analysis by Taylor is only the first chapter of the "making of the Modern Identity." It is evident that there the entire irrational violence of the modern self, with respect to the periphery, violence that is justified in the name of civilization, does not make its appearance; and this is what I call the "myth of modernity". This "myth" has neither been discovered nor analyzed. See *The Invention of the Americas*, fifth lecture, "Critique to the Myth of Modernity," which is as much a critique of Lyotard as it is of Habermas, or Taylor, from the debate of Valladolid in 1550, where Ginés de Sepúlveda (a modern argumentative rationalist), who opposed Bartolomé de las Casas (the founder of an explicit philosophical "counter-discourse" in the *world-modernity* as a project of a "trans-modernity" from its "other face," from the Other, Latin America, Africa, and Asia, women oppressed by machismo, the destroyed Land as a capitalist "means of production").
41. In the way that the "other face" of the moon although never seen is always a constitutive part of the terrestrial satellite.
42. In the work by Schelkshorn already cited (pp. 69ff), especially "Die Ethizität der menschlichen Existenz," pp. 97ff.
43. Immanuel Kant, *Critique of Practical Reason and Other Writings in Moral Philosophy*, p. 142. *Kritique der praktischen Vernunft (KpV)*, A 54; see also *Grundlegung zur Metaphysik der Sitten (GMS)*, BA 52; in my *Para una de-structión de la historia de la ética* (Mendoza: Sei y Tiempo, 1972) pp. 100ff.
44. *KpV*, A 197.
45. This "application" (the *application* of the "moral conscience" of the ancients) is a function of the "practical faculty of judgment," *praktische Urteilskraft* (see *Kritik der Urteilskraft*, B xxvi, A xxiv). See the excellent work by Albrecht Wellmer, "Derecho natural y razón practica" in Karl-Otto Apel, Adela Cortina, et. al. eds., *Ética comunicativa y Demócracia* (Barcelona: Editorial Critica, 1991), pp. 154–169, although Wellmer is partial in his critique of Marx.
46. Immanuel Kant, *Groundwork of the Metaphysics of Morals*, p. 96; *GMS*, BA 66–67.
47. *KpV*, A 155–56.

48. Ibid., A 155.
49. *Groundwork of the Metaphysics of Morals*, p. 96. *GMS*, BA 66.
50. About the "community" in Kant as "kingdom of God," as *corpus mysticum*, as "kingdom of ends," see my work *Para una de-strucíon de la historía de la ética*, pp. 108ff.
51. Jürgen Habermas "Was Heißt Universalpragmatik?" in *Vorstudien und Ergänzungen* (Frankfurt: Suhrhamp, 1984), p. 407; English version "What Is Universal Pragmatics?" in *Communication and the Evolution of Society*, pp. 1–68.
52. Apeln, "Notwendigkeit, Schwierigkeit und Möglichkeit einer philosophischen Begründung der Ethik im Zeitalter der Wissenschaft" in P. Kanellopoulos, ed., *Festschrift für K. Tsatos* (Athens: Nomikai Ekdoseis Ant., 1980) p. 264. Emphasis added.
53. Not inasmuch as it is empirical or a life world, but as the "ethical" (the practical as person-to-person relationship), the moral is made universal and the life world is *ethical*.
54. For instance, in Charles Taylor, *Hegel* (Cambridge: Cambridge University Press, 1975) 369ff.
55. See the exposition of this theme in my *Método para una filosofía de la liberación*, pp. 64ff.
56. G. W. F. Hegel, in *Frühe Schriften, Theorie Werkausgabe*, Vol. 1 (Frankfurt: Suhrkamp, 1971), p. 326. This is from the fragment titled *The Spirit of Christianity and its Fate*.
57. Ibid.
58. Aristotle's *deutera physis*, of virtue as *héxis* (*Nicomedean Ethics* II, 1: 1103 to 18ff; specially II, 6, 1106 b 36ff). The Hegelian *Sittlichkeit* is precisely this "second nature" (*als eine zweite Natur*) (*Rechtsphilosophie*, § 151; in *Theorie Werkausgabe*, vol. 7, p. 301).
59. Hegel *The Spirit of Christianity*, p. 327.
60. In *Grundkonzept zum Geist des Christentums*, in *Frühe Schriften*, Vol. 1, p. 312. This formula of *lebendige Gemeinschaft* is used by Karl Marx in his *religion exam*; "lebendige Gemeinschaft" (*WEB*, EB 1, p. 600), and is found in the radical foundation of his communitarian paradigm. See my essay presented in the seminar on Marx in the context of the debate with K-O. Apel, 1992, at the Goethe University in Frankfurt: "Relektüre Marx aus Lateinamerikan," Chap. 3 "Toward a North-South Dialogue."
61. Everything else is known, just as much as the descriptions of *Sittlichkeit* in the *Phenomenology of Spirit* (VI), in the *Encyclopedia* (§§ 513ff), in the *Philosophy of Right* (§§ 142ff); etc.
62. I wrote in 1969: "Kant himself, when writing his *Critique of Practical Reason*, had no full self-consciousness that his thinking, in the end, was the thinking of the Prussian bourgeois *ethos* of the XVIII century. Could he have written, if he had had such a critical consciousness, that 'neither in the world, nor outside the world in general, is it possible to think anything that may be considered as good without restriction, but perhaps only as much as a good will [*ein guter Wille*]'[*Grundlegung zur Metaphysik der Sitten*, I, BA 1]? Does this position betray the tragic ethic of a chained Prometheus or a blinded Oedipus? Would these principles accept the Tlacaélel ethic, the foundation of the Aztec empire? Is not this principle only understandable within the Western Christian tradition, and especially of Spencer's pietism?" (*Para una de-structíon de la historía de la ética*, p. 9.)

63. Kant himself recognizes that "the question how the law in itself and immediately be the foundation for the determination of the will (which is, however, the essence of every morality) constitutes an irresolvable problem [*unauflösliches*] for human reason, and identical to the knowing of how a free will is possible" (*KpV*, A 128). For the problem of *Anwendung* see *KpV*, A 119ff.
64. Hegel considers this theme when commenting on and criticizing Fichte in his *Difference of the Philosophical Systems of Fichte and Schelling* (1801): "Reason and freedom as being reasonable are no more reason or freedom if not being oneself.... If the community of reasonable entities were essentially limitation of true freedom, this would be in itself and for itself tyranny.... In the living relation there is no freedom if only in the measure in which this implies the possibility to be subsumed and to enter in relationship with others..." (*Frühe Schriften* in *Theorie Werkausgabe*, Vol. 2 (Frankfurt: Suhrkamp, 1970), pp. 82–83. On the contrary, in "the community under the domination of understanding [*unter der Herrschaft des Vertandes*] (83–84), the "rational" or living moment is the superation of that limiting determination as domination.
65. My *Para una ética de la liberación latinoamericana*, § 1, Vol. 1, pp. 33, deals with "La fundamentación subjectiva de la moral moderna," which is superseded by "La comprensión existencial" (Vol. 2, pp. 38ff).
66. This "com-prehension" is a "possibility-for-Being" (*Seinkönnen*), a *telos* in the Aristotelian sense. See my work *Para una de-structión de la historia de la ética*, § 3, "El ser como eudaimonia" (pp. 32ff).
67. *Nicomachen Ethics*, II, 6; 11–6, b 36. My citation is an explicitly Heideggerian translation-interpretation.
68. One would have to note there how I carried out this Heideggerian reconstructive labor; and it was there, also, that I discovered the *limits* of the early and late Heidegger.
69. See my critique of axiology in *Para una de-strucción de la historia de la ética*, IV, pp. 126ff. I think that Heidegger, in *Brief über Humanismus* (Frankfurt: Klostermann, 1947), proleptically made a critique of that "style." I have in Louvain studied the Husseral archives, thanks to van Breda, and I have read the axiological manuscripts of Husserl (see *Para una ética de la liberación latinoamericana*, Vol. 1, "Manuscritios éticos de E. Husserl que se encuntran en el Husserl-Archiv de Lovaina," pp. 193ff), from the *F I 20* (1890ff) until de *B I 16* (1931–34). Kant was the ethicist most studied by Husserl, and in particular *The Critique of Practical Reason*. The critiques to Scheler's formalism (*Der Formalismus in der Ethik und die materiale Werkethik*, Bern: Francke, 1954) and of Nicolai Hartmann (*Ethik*, Berlin: de Gruyter, 1962) have been studied in the above cited work. Because of its "style," Taylor's philosophical position owes tremendously to the axiologists, but just the same to the ontological philosophers like Aristotle, Sartre, or Heidegger, from Anglo-Saxon philosophy attentive to the linguistic turn. It is something like "axiological-existential-linguistic."
70. Taylor, *Sources of the Self*, 521.
71. Taylor, *The Ethics of Authenticity*, 1ff.
72. Ibid., 25.
73. Ibid., 29ff. In a Philosophy of Liberation this "being true with oneself" (solipsistic, atomistic moment) becomes the "being true with an oppressed and excluded people" (communitarian, historical moment) of the hegemonic identity (as with Clavigero, for instance).
74. Taylor, *The Ethics of Authenticity*, 33.

75. See George H. Mead, *Mind, Self, and Society* (Chicago, University of Chicago Press, 1962), pp. 67ff.
76. Taylor, *The Ethics of Authenticity*, 45.
77. Ibid., 50. We will see that the oppressed within systems and the excluded ones in communication communities are already politically, economically, sexually, and pedagogically oppressed, and, therefore, by definition, not recognized. It is not that their non-recognition is cause of their oppression; on the contrary, the non-recognition is a condition of the "reproduction" of the system of their oppression and exclusion.
78. Taylor, *The Ethics of Authenticity*, 66. In the Philosophy of Liberation all of these themes are not affirmed from the standpoint of atomistic "authenticity" but from the right to the dignity of the persons excluded from the community of humanity, of the oppressed classes, of women oppressed by machismo, of the child without rights before adult society, and so on. It is something deeper, greater in number, more ethically relevant, without taking importance from that "authenticity" described by Taylor in the central and hegemonic countries.
79. Taylor, *The Ethics of Authenticity*, 117.
80. Ibid., 50.
81. Charles Taylor, "The Politics of Recognition" in Amy Gutmann, et. al., eds. *Multiculturalism* (Princeton: Princeton University Press, 1992).
82. "It is held that since 1492, Europe has projected an image of such people as somehow inferior, uncivilized, and through the force of conquest have often been able to impose this image on the conquered" (Ibid., 26). This is new! But from this hypothesis all of his work *Sources of the Self* is in question.
83. Taylor, "The Politics of Recognition" 37. This is precisely the theme formulated by the Philosophy of Liberation more than twenty years ago: the significant other is the Indian (15 million killed in the first holocaust of modernity), the African slaves (thirteen million enslaved from the 16th to the 19th century, the second holocaust), the exploited peripheral nations of colonialism and neocolonialism (more that 80 percent of humanity), the working classes dominated under a salary-and-production-of-surplus regime (even in the countries of central capitalism), etc. The Philosophy of Liberation, since 1970, expressly formulates the "encounter," the "dialogue" with the *significant other* (see *Para una ética de la liberación latinoamericana*, Chap. 6, "El Método de la ética": "El rostro del pobre indio dominado, del mestizo oprimido, del pueblo lationamericano es el tema de la filosofia latinoamericna. Este pensar analectico [to be read: dialogico], porque parte de la revelación del Otro y piensa su palabra, es la filosofía lationamerica, única y nueva, la primera realmente posmoderna [I would write in 1970 much earlier than Derrida y Lyotard. Today I would have to write: transmodern and superseder of modernity]" (Vol. II, p. 162).
84. Taylor, "The Politics of Recognition" 72–73. It is interesting that almost five centuries after Bartolomé de las Casas, a philosopher from the Anglo-Saxon world repeats his words, which *in a unique manner*, written in Guatemala in 1536, showed that the American Indians had dignity and deserved to be treated in the *only manner* humanly possible, with rational arguments and not with the violence of the war (from the conquest of Mexico in 1519, until the Gulf War in 1992, that still continues in 1993). See my work *The Invention of the Americas*, lecture 5.3.
85. Charles Taylor, "Language and Society", in Axel Honneth and Hans Jonas, eds., *Communicative Action: Essays on Jürgen Habermas's The Theory of Communicative*

Action (Cambridge: The MIT Press, 1988), pp. 23–35, and "Le juste et le bien" in *Revue de Metaphysique et de Morale*. 93, 1 (1988), 33–56.
86. See especially Jürgen Habermas, *Justification and Application: Remarks on Discourse Ethics* (Cambridge: The MIT Press, 1993), pp. 124 ff, and 69–76; and *Faktizität und Geltung* (Frankfurt: Suhrkamp Verlag, 1992), pp. 640ff.
87. In Habermas, *Faktizität und Geltung*, see concerning Taylor pages 226, 313, 325, and 607, but on themes that do not strictly touch on what we are debating.
88. Habermas, *Justification and Application*, pp. 69–76. The critique of A. MacIntyre, especially his work *Whose Justice? Which Rationality* (Notre Dame: Notre Dame University Press, 1988), also applies to Taylor (pp. 96–105). Although in the case of MacIntyre, I think that Habermas does not adequately formulate the question when he negates the necessity, in all dialogue of cultures, to attain a *sufficient* knowledge of the other tradition, or of the culture of the Other in order to be able to "argue rationally." In other words, to be able to belong to both in some way. For Habermas this is not possible, except as a dialogue as an application of one's own point of view through the process of convergence of perspectives. I ask: To what extent does Habermas (as every philosopher of the periphery, who experiences Europe as something his/her own because of a long learning processes of the "other culture," as is the case with Latin Americans) have experience of "other" worlds? Can one think philosophically the problem of intercultural dialogue without having for years lived in *other cultures*? Eurocentrism is here a bad adviser.
89. This was, precisely, the moment of birth of the Philosophy of Liberation. See the move from Chap. 2 to 3 in my work *Para una ética de la liberación latinoamericana* (Vol. 1, pp. 97ff); or *Método para una filosofía de la liberación*, Chap. 4, pp. 115ff, "Superación europea de la dialectica hegeliana." See especially "La no-eticidad de la autenticidad gnostica del heroe tragico y moderno" (*Para una ética de la* Vol. 2, pp. 22ff).
90. Niklas Luhmann, in his consideration of the subject as functional part of the system, correctly describes that it is not "persons" but "functions," autopoietic and self-referential moments (see Niklas Luhmann, *Soziale Systeme* (Frankfurt: Suhrkamp Verlag, 1988), pp. 30ff, "System und Funktion"). A. Gehlen had seen this clearly with his definition of "institution": "Man kann anthropologisch den Begriff der *Persönlichkeit* nur im engsten Zusammenhang mit dem der Instituionen denken"; *Anthropologische Forschung* (Hamburg: Rowohlts, 1961), p. 72.
91. See in *Philosophy of Liberation*, "Alienation," 2.5.
92. Here Totality can be as much the Heideggerian world, as the modern world (Taylor), or even still the "*real* communication community" (that of the effective *arguers*).
93. *Para una ética de la liberación latinoamericana*, Vol. 2, pp. 14–15. It is impossible here to repeat what has been written, given that it would require going through the concept of evil in Kant (a question which has not being brought up by any of his modern readers, and I am referring to the "root of Evil" [*die Wurzel des Bösen*]", in *Die Religion innerhalb der Grenzen der blossen Vernunft*, I,III, B 32–39, a 29–36, until note 1), Schelling, Hegel (i.e., *Rechtsphilosophie*, § 139; *Enzyklopädie*, § 570), Nietzsche, etc.
94. But modern European culture is the only one that has been ethnocentric and *center of world history*, in such a way that it has constituted all other cultures as a *dominated* periphery an *a-symmetrical* situation unique in history.
95. "In the primitive and rough state of society, which precedes the accumulation of capital ... the integral product of work belongs to the worker.... Though as

soon as capital is accumulated in the power of determined persons, some of them attempt to regularly hire them in given work to laborious peoples, providing them with raw materials, food, in order to extract a benefit" (Adam Smith, *Wealth of Nations*, I, Chap. V). In a similar manner Rawls, in his second principle, defines "the *social and economic inequalities* will have to be arrange in such a way . . ." (*A Theory of Justice*, II, 11). The question is: How can there be "social and economic inequalities" in a "state of nature" or in an "original situation"? How do such inequalities exist from the very point of departure?

96. "By necessity" until consciousness of the negated other is finally acquired, and this may take centuries or millennia, centuries: How many millennia did humanity practice slavery until it finally acquired consciousness of its immorality in the 19th century? How many millennia did machismo oppress woman until the 20th century? *Before* the *historical* discovery of the negated Other, "by historical necessity," factically, the *telos*, the good, virtue, and values of the prevailing system justify, implicitly or explicitly, the oppression of the other.

97. "System" in a broad sense, and not exactly in the sense of Luhmann.

98. Liberation is the action, the practical process through which the non-free becomes a factical subject of freedom.

99. It is evident that it becomes operative when "it has discovered" a new type of oppressed Other, for example, when certain religious communities struggle against slavery, or capitalism discovers that a free wage earner is more efficient than a slave. From the moment of "discovery" of the Other as *oppressed*, the dominator becomes factically culpable.

100. That is to say, the "slave" is a *"concrete* manner" of negating human dignity discovered by certain Protestant communities or by capitalism; the "wage-earner" is another *"concrete* manner" of the negation of human dignity discovered by Karl Marx, etc.

101. "Missionarien der Zivilisation in der ganze Welt" (Hegel, *Vorlesungen über die Philosophie der Geschichte*, IV, 3, 3, in *Theorie Werkausgabe*, Vol. 12 [Frankfurt: Suhrkamp, 1970], p. 538). The term missionaries gives a sacred character, and "civilization" evidently refers to modern Europe—but with that he leaves clear his ingenious and provincial eurocentrism.

102. See Taylor, "The Politics of Recognition", 1992 b, p. 65. "One of the key authors in this transition is undoubtely the late Franz Fanon, whose influential *Le Damnés de la Terre* argued that the major weapon of the colonizers was the imposition of their image of the colonized on the subjugated people." Fanon is a Latin American, from Martinica, from whose work the Philosophy of Liberation makes its departure in the decade of the sixties.

103. Which I have termed "dis-tinction" in order not to be confused with Derrida's "di-fference" (see my *Philosophy of Liberation*, 2.4.3; "Dis-tinction" is not "Difference" [2.2.5]. For all of these themes see Hans Schelkshorn's *Ethik der Befreiung*.

104. See *Philosophy of Liberation*, 2.4, "Exteriority."

105. "Nothingness," as much in Levinas as in Marx (see on this question my work *El Ultimo Marx (1863–1882)*, Chap. 10).

106. It is not the *a priori* "transcendentality" but the "transcendentality" of the one who goes "beyond" the horizon of the world, of the system, of the "good" of our culture.

107. In our works we have given to *ethics* (for example, in *Toward an Ethics of Latin American Liberation*) the sense of the formal critical, while to "morality" (for example, in bourgeois morality, as in Marx) the sense of Hegelian *Sittlichkeit*. Simple clarification is in order to prevent confusions.

108. Jürgen Habermas, *Erläuterungen zur Diskursethik* (Frankfurt: Suhrkamp, 1991), p. 12; for the English version see "Morality and Ethical Life: Does Hegel's Critique of Kant Apply to Discourse Ethics?" in Jürgen Habermas, *Moral Consciousness and Communicative Action*, p. 197. Translation slightly altered.
109. Habermas, *Erläuterungen zur Diskursethik*, p. 12.
110. "Limites de la ética discursiva?" in A. Cortina, *Razón comunicativa y responsabilidad solidaria* (Salamanca: Ediciones Sugueme, 1985), p. 261. On the theme of "application" (*Anwendung*), see Matthias Kettner, "Drei Dilemmata angewandter Ethik" in Karl-Otto Apel and Matthias Kettner, eds. *Zur Anwendung der Diskursethik in Politik, Recht und Wissenchaft* (Frankfurt: Suhrkamprerlag, 1992), pp. 9–27; K–O Apel, "Diskursethik vor der Problematik von Recht und Politik" in ibid, pp. 29–60.
111. We can not problematize here the entire theme of how, "procedurally," one assumes consciousness of the oppressed and excluded. The description of the *logic* of the "oppression" and "exclusion" of systems is the first theme of the Philosophy of Liberation, in order to allow for the "assuming-of-conscience" (*conscientization*). To this assuming-of-conscience there follows the "organization" of the oppressed and excluded. Only when, because of a *process of liberation*, which has to describe and justify ethically the affected-oppressed and excluded of the real communication community at the hands of the *hegemonic* participants, have "negotiating power" or "effective participation" (that is reached *at the end of a process of liberation*), then, and only then, can the exercise of ethical-argumentative reason be began on an equal footing. The affected-dominated and excluded are not minorities: they are the great majority of humanity. The richer 20 percent of humanity consumes 82 percent of said goods; see *Human Development Report 1992*, United Nations Program (UNDP) (New York: Oxford University Press, 1992). The excluded and affected are the 50 percent of humanity (women); the 40 percent (children); the 20 percent of the poor in rich countries; the discriminated races; etc. That is to say, if we were to make a mathematical calculation, not even 5 percent of actual humanity would belong to the real hegemonic communication community (which is the real "participant"): men, white, adults, western culture, "central" capitalism, the power groups (economic, political, intellectual), etc. But is this not also the case with Taylor's modern *Self* (male, white, adult)?
112. See my lecture "La razón del Otro. La *interpelación* como acto de habla" in Raúl Fornet-Betancourt, ed., *Diskusrethik oder Befreiungsethik?*, pp. 106ff, "La Exterioridad y la comunidad ideal de comunicación."
113. To recognize in the slave a person, hidden in slavery as a non-person and, therefore, *excluded-not-affected* (for in order to be affected it is necessary to be-a-person; and it would be good to problematize this from an ecological philosophy) is the *radical* point of departure of every possible argumentation with the *ancient* slave and the *new* Other, now recognized as a "participant."
114. "Derecho natural y razón practica" in Apel, et. al. eds; *Etica Communicativa y Democracia* p. 29. Apel himself acknowledges that "under finite conditions, the principle of development of morality never [*niemals*] can reach–inasmuch as it is a principle of historically responsible application of ethics—moral reality, because a new rational beginning *of all man* cannot be obtained on the grounds of the ideal validity of the discursive principle" (*Diskurs und Verantwortung*, p. 465).
115. The Philosophy of Liberation departs from the situation of the negated dignity of the person within a system or a Totality (for instance, when Freud says that "the masculine comprehends the subject, the activity and the possession of the

phallus; the feminine integrates the object and passivity" (*Die infantile Genitalorganisation*, in *Studiensausgabe* Vol. 1 [Franfkurt: Fischer, 1970], p. 241); or when Marx says "the real subsumption of living labor under capital is developed in all of those forms that produced surplus value..." a definition of alienation of the person in the Totality capital (*Manuscripts of 61–63, MEGA* II, 3, p. 2190 [Berlin: Dietz Verlag, 1982]). Methodologically, the Philosophy of Liberation moves upwards from the "functional part" (the women-object in the machist system, wage labor in capitalism, etc.) toward the foundation, the ground, the being, the *telos* of the system (see *Philosophy of Liberation*, 5.2), and from that horizon the causes of "oppression" are explained. To negate this negation of the oppressed person is the "just," "good" praxis. This is the theme of Vol. II of *Para una ética de la liberación latinoamericana*, already cited. In volumes III (erotics), IV (politics), and V (anti-fetishism), the analytical path of the ethics of liberation is traversed at different levels.

116. If to situations of impossible "direct" application we add the restriction that every application is "partial" and "approximate," and that it cannot be realized in situations of revolution, war, or lack of rights, it can be discovered that it can *never* be applied in concrete and really. This is what we call the "inapplicability" (*Nichtanwendbarkeit*) of this transcendental ethic. Furthermore, the ideal situations (Habermas) are "models of impossibility" (as has been shown by Franz Hinkelammert in *Critica de la razón utópica*) that cannot appropriately "ground" but only "delimit" the horizon of the "possible" (by the "absolute empirical principle of impossibility," as when Einstein proposed an impossible model [the *perpetuum mobile*] that does not "ground" but *opens* the field of "possible" or "empirical" mechanics. This is treated at greater length in a work under preparation.

117. Emmanuel Levinas, *Totality and Infinity*, p. 21; French: *Totalité et Infini. Essai sur l'exteriorité* (La Haye: Nijhoff, 1968), p. x.

118. With reason H. Schelkshorn objects that the Philosophy of Liberation, which is so "strong," is for "exceptional" situations (that are "normal" in today's world), but is less operative in normal situations. It would not be hard to show that the normal situations are constructed on the foundations of institutions of permanent oppression (for example, in capitalism the wage earners who produce surplus value) or of exclusion (for example, the *pauper*, the unemployed or marginal).

119. See *Para una ética de la liberación latinoamericana*, Vol. 1, Chap. I, pp. 35ff.

120. In our case these may be trans-systematic "projects of liberation" (see my *Para una ética de la liberación latinoamericana*, Vol. II, "El bien ético como justicia," pp. 34ff). The practical relation with the Other we call "love-of-justice" (thus bringing together the rectitude of justice and the "love" of the good).

Part Two

8

Response by Karl-Otto Apel: Discourse Ethics Before the Challenge of Liberation Philosophy

8.1   The Prehistory of the Contemporary Discourse

Before I can turn to the theme itself, it seems necessary to introduce some preliminary remarks concerning the prehistory of the thematic. In November of 1989 there took place in the Catholic Academy of the Archdiocese of Freiburg a seminar on the "Foundations of Ethics in Germany and Latin America" [*Begründungen von Ethik in Deutschland und Lateinamerika*].[1] This seminar was organized by Raúl Fornet-Betancourt as a continuation of the "First German-Iberoamerican Ethics Session" (Buenos Aires, 1985). I received an invitation to present there the transcendental pragmatic grounding of discourse ethics. I did this with a contribution bearing the title "Discourse Ethics as an Ethics of Responsibility: A Post-Metaphysical transformation of Kantian Ethics."[2]

One can recognize from the title itself that I, with all innocence so to say, wanted to introduce and explain the theme, as if among ourselves, from the perspective of European intellectual history. In view that the rest of the German participants who dealt with the critical discussions on discourse ethics also presented their argumentation within this same historical frame of reference, what could have resulted would not have been much different from any other seminar of this sort that is organized in Germany. In such a case, the publication of the contributions under the title *Ethics and Liberation* would have been very difficult. I say this, although I am convinced that the exigency of an approximate realization of the ideal communication community (which constitutes, with reservations, the prospective dimension of discourse ethics) certainly has to do with liberation, with liberation taken in a universal sense, and not limited to Europe or the First World.[3]

We know well, though, that the "informative content" of concepts (and especially the concepts of philosophy and theology), based on *alienation* and *provocation*, stands in need of having to be continuously renewed. This is especially valid in the case of the informative content of the word *liberation*, in a society in which the actuality of the skeptical-pragmatic attitude of appeasement determines the proper philosophical tone. Obviously we cannot overlook that, around the time that the Freiburg encounter took place, the significative content of the word liberation was the object of a renewal in the concrete political sense in Germany and eastern Europe. I must return later on to this point. But it is necessary to recognize that it was but thanks to Enrique Dussel's contribution that the title "Ethics and Liberation" acquired its particular connotation. Dussel's contribution was presented as a commentary to my own contribution, which was later published under the title "Community of Life and the Interpellation of the Poor."[4] This intervention constituted, in my opinion, the main and most interesting challenge from the Freiburg seminar. Therefore, after some preliminary remarks, I will attempt to offer an answer to the problems formulated by his contribution.

(In my case, these preliminaries were indispensable because I was forced to disclose gradually the different levels that Dussel's intervention formulated against my own European understanding, especially West German, and, in the last instance, against my transcendental-pragmatic conceptual understanding (this last with the help of other writings by Dussel, and in particular of the synthetic exposition of the *Philosophy of Liberation*.[5])

In the first part of this attempt at an answer, I will first characterize (from my perspective) the central thematic points of a necessary and possible discussion of the philosophical *pretensions* of Liberation Philosophy. In order to accomplish this, I am forced to introduce certain suppositions (or, if it is preferred, certain *prejudgments*) linked to the philosophical position that I hold. The second part of my work will discusss in greater depth and detail those parts of the text of Dussel's intervention in Freiburg which appear relevant. In a third and final part I will attempt to clarify the consequences of all of this for a continuing dialogue between discourse ethics and Liberation Philosophy.

8.2 The Themes of the Dusselian Challenge

My first approach to Dussel's position and to the challenge to discourse ethics formulated by it was determined by two moments that provoked in me two diverse, spontaneous, and in fact contradictory reactions. On the one hand, Dussel's thesis that approximately 75 percent of humanity, precisely those masses who do not belong to the adapted elites of the Third World, find themselves practically excluded from what is called the real communication community, constituting thus the "exteriority of the other" (in Levinas's sense) in relation to our Euro-North American "we" and its "world." On the other hand, Dussel's affirmation that because we read too little, or without care, Marx's *Das Kapital*, we are not prepared to understand the meaning of his theories in relation to a possible liberation of the Third World.[6]

The first of these points appears to me in essence correct and, above all, so important that I want to see in this "interpellation" of the "other" made to our discourse by Dussel the central theme, still pending, of the global application of a discourse ethics, parallel but at the same time fundamentally linked to the ecological crisis (fortunately the theme of the threat of nuclear war that for such a long time occupied a central place in our preoccupations does not appear to be so actual).[7]

Nevertheless, at the same time, I am convinced that the problem of the *interpellation of the excluded from discourse*, as articulated by Dussel as a base for the concepts of a communicative ethics, does not challenge the transcendental pragmatic focus of discourse ethics. On the contrary, I believe that this presents a characteristic problem of *Part B* of discourse ethics.[8] The central question of this part of discourse ethics is precisely: How should we act under the presupposition (to a great extent realistic) that the conditions of application of an ethics justified (in *Part A*) through an *ideal communication community* (always anticipated counterfactually) are to great extent not given?

In relationship to this, in Dussel's articularion of *Part B* of discourse ethics, the question of the adequacy of the maxims of conduct valid for all who have good will is formulated. That is, as much for those who find themselves excluded from discourse (or for their representatives), as well as for those who belong to a privileged communication community, because, in reality, these last ones find themselves obliged in principle, according to the grounding *Part A* of discourse ethics, to an advocatory representation of the interests of *all the affected*, and not only of the *participants* in the discourse (for instance, the representation of the interests of the generations that will succeed us, as it concerns the conservation of an inhabitable planet and the preservation of its resources).

Furthermore, they also find themselves obliged, in view of the grounding *Part B* of discourse ethics, to collaborate in the establishment in the long run of conditions that will allow for the application of discourse ethics. But this means nothing else than: those conditions in which, at the minimum, no adult or mentally healthy person would be excluded from the relevant discourses (discourses in which their own interest could be discussed).

In our discussions in Freiburg, as well as in those in Mexico, Dussel seemed to share the opinion that his preoccupation with the "exclusion of the other" could be considered as a theme of *Part B* of discourse ethics.[9] However, the formulation of his opinions in relation to this point in the published version of his Freiburg intervention (and even more in the older expositions of the *Philosophy of Liberation*) have given me reason to examine with greater detail the supposition of a dialogue based on discourse ethics. We cannot accept as given, as a "gift," something that ought to be seen as object of controversy.

In the grounding of theoretical and practical philosophy, I have taken as a point of departure that in *argumentative discourse* (in which humans do not fight against each other, but instead let arguments confront each other) the motives for conflict can be exposed in a more radical manner than is possible in *real* conflicts, that is, than it is possible, through either overt or covert violence, to resolve in the conflicts of the life world.[10] Because of this reason argumentative discourse can also lead, according to the possibility in principle, to more "in depth" solutions of conflicts than are possible in any other sphere or plane of human interaction or communication (for example, in strategic negotiations). This possibility of a post-conventional era of human cultural revolution ought, at the least, to be defended and adopted by philosophers.

With respect to Dussel's *second* thesis, the first impression that I had of it in Freiburg, in November of 1989, was that it was something like an *anachronism*. At this point, the doctrine of *Capital* would appear, even before the eyes of those who in the two prior decades had been its new receptors in Germany, in the sense of a non-orthodox Western marxism, and in the face of the even more evident collapse of the totality of the socialist system, as something definitively discredited. However, through a more detailed analysis of the Latin American background of Dussel's formulations, and a more distanced observation of the eastern European events, it appears to me that Dussel's reference to Karl Marx's work, at first sight disconcerting, acquires a contemporary significance.

With this I am not suggesting that after the following reading of Liberation Philosophy I would come to share the economic-political presuppositions and hopes of its author. However, it appears to me that in his writings, a perspective of alienation or distancing [*Verfremdungsperspektive*] is manifested, which, with respect to the necessary and distanced reconstruction of the history of marxism-leninism, and the evaluation of contemporary global problems, can be of great use for us Europeans. What would be the object of a contemporary reconstruction of the history of marxism-leninism? And where could we locate the significance of the Latin American perspective of alienation and distancing, given the consequences of the failure of this conception which we are forced to acknowledge?

(In the following I am only concerned with a very tentative exposition of the political-economic background problematic of the intended coming to terms with Enrique Dussel, and, thus, in no way does it deal with him directly.[11] My concern is to articulate the different *possible* perspectives and positions, rather than to take a stand in terms of a "definitive" position. This definitive position would also, as a *direct* derivation of the justification of discourse ethics, not be possible; for this, as a foundation of ethics, seeks to make explicit the essential normative conditions of the possibility of intersubjectively valid argumentation, conditions that must be presupposed in all life-worldly-*centric*-perspectives in all possible valid-logical questionings.)

8.3 European Perspective on the Collapse of Marxism-Leninism

In first place, it is a matter of formulating the correct questions about the causes of the collapse of marxism-leninism. We cannot, within the context of our problematic, detain ourselves over the question of the possible perversion of eastern state socialism by Stalin and stalinism. This is a difficulty that still determines Gorbachev's conception of *perestroika*. Although one could concede that the history of the Soviet Union would have been different without the elimination of the *kulaks* carried out by Stalin as a continuation of Lenin's "new political economy," what Stalin did was in essence but to carry out the Leninist-Bolshevik program and the politics inherent to the dictatorship of the proletariat through the party. Still, the "voluntaristic" realization of the Russian revolution by Lenin, that is, in a country in which the socioeconomic conditions required by Marx were not present, and the option for a dictatorship of an elite Communist party corresponding to it, cannot be considered as the determining cause of the failure of marxism-leninism. This failure ought to be explained in the sense of the socioeconomic conditions of political history described by Marx as deeper causes. Such causes ought to be looked for, in the last instance, in the Marxist conception of a possible substitution of the capitalist market economy by a socialization of the means of production and the distribution of goods.

Part of this Marxist- social utopia, and its correponding beliefs, that a market economy based on the exchange of commodities and the private ownership of the means of production can, in the long run, only lead to the destruction of human life and nature, is clearly still shared by Dussel. However, this suffices to weaken Dussel's position, notwithstanding his own assurance that with respect to what is relevant to Liberation Philosophy's recourse to Marx, this has *nothing* to do with "standard Marxism-Leninism."[12] It seems to me that today's attempt at a critical reconstruction of the history of marxism must also include the demand for a certain fairness toward the representatives of "standard marxism," including Lenin. In the last instance, Lenin was through Marx himself confronted with the unavoidable problem of the anticipated superseding of the market economy through a socially "transparent" planned and somehow organized distribution of products under the conditions of the—provisional—dictatorship of the proletariat (according to Marx's intimations, Lenin had to structure this problematic as a theoretical task[13]).

In the following attempt at coming to terms with the Philosophy of Liberation, I would like to consider the essential alternative to the issues at hand, namely, whether today it is possible to hold to the Marxist vision of the dissolution, in the sense of overcoming, of the capitalist market economy (especially with respect to its unquestionably implied *institutional mediation*, and that means the partial "objectification" of interhuman relationships); or, whether it is a matter of having to understand anew what Adam Smith, and even Marx himself, recognized as the enormously advantageous effectiveness of the (to use contemporary language) functional differentiation of the social subsystem of the market economy; and also in the sense of a *framework order* of the economy, reformable from all sides, which demands democratic acceptability on a world scale, and which is thus subordinated to indirect control through the rationality of the human discoursive community.[14] That this last conception, in view of the North-South problematic and the ecological crisis, calls for the drastic task of a, perhaps unrealizable, transformation of today's market economy (with respect to its political-legal framework) will not be debated; rather it would have to be further underscored.

What the history of state socialism has shown in the Soviet Union, and also in China, (in which there was an acknowledgment by the regime itself), would appear to be, above all else: the bureaucratic management of the economy, meaning: the annulment of a market economy directed by "price signals" and its corresponding competition in favor of a command economy, is not able to mobilize the power of humans. State socialism must compensate for this motivation deficit, or, if it is preferred, the absence of the specific and natural brutality of capitalist competition must be compensated for through the direct political means of violence or restrictions of freedom, that is, through recourse to pre-capitalist relations and conditions. In addition, violence from above, as well as its inherent restriction of freedom, must keep under control the growing tendencies toward an informal economy [*Schattenwirtschaft*], as well as the parasitic behavior of the disillusioned "comrades." The political perversion of socialism from above is "explained," then, in great measure by perversion from below, that is, by the absence, the non-appearance of the "new men" anticipated by the communist utopia.

Here we have the key that refers us to the *internal* affinity between the Marxist and Leninist conceptions of revolutionary socialism, even if, in reality, Marx could have imagined not even in his dreams the necessity for the Leninist measures for the realization of the revolution and the dictatorship that these entailed. What is fundamental here is that Marx, imbued with a belief in the historical validity of dialectical laws, considered the capitalist system of market economy as not reformable. What is fundamental is that in his early writings,[15] Marx finds himself disposed to abandon this system (which he considers extremely effective[16]) together with its corresponding achievements such as liberal rights, political democracy, and even the bourgeois morality. All of that in favor of a *social utopia* which transcends this system: a society without classes to be realized by the proletariat in a "realm of freedom" in which there is no longer any state monopoly of violence.

Indeed, in the second period, the so-called period of maturity of his thought,

Marx had dedicated all of his efforts to present this conception, which at the beginning only had an ethical-anthropological and eschatological-visionary character, through a dialectical reconstruction, empirically supported, of the necessary development of capitalism as a quasi-value-free result of scientific analysis. However, this scientistic transformation, that not even in *Capital* itself is capable of disguising the moral-critical commitment and the utopian-eschatological passion, had as an effect the reinforcement of the determination (as much in Marx *as in* Lenin) to reject any reformist tendency in the sense of the trade union movement and "social democracy." The belief in a scientifically demonstrated necessity of a revolutionary substitution of capitalism by socialism and, in the last instance, by a "realm of freedom," had no other effect but to reinforce the political will to realize the revolution, as well as the utopian-eschatological hope of a "new man."

In relation to this point, it is necessary to make the anticipatory remark that, at least in Dussel's *Philosophy of Liberation* (originally published in Mexico in 1977), aside from a convincing ethical (or ethical-religious) commitment, there predominates the spirit of an empirically and pragmatically undifferentiated rejection of any possibility for North-South cooperation on the bases of a—possibly reformed—capitalist system. This is what is meant, for instance, on page 173: "The system of the capitalist company, with hereditary ownership of capital by some and the selling of their work by others, which originated slowly in the Middle Ages in the associations of masters and apprentices, and which experienced a fundamental change thanks to the colonial accumulation of capital, and which once again was redefined through the industrial, financial and monopolistic revolution, can no longer be imitated in the periphery. The liberation of the working and farming classes requires a complete economic revolution. The philosophy of economy must clarify this problematic, namely that of the transition to another world system, already without periphery, beyond the capitalist mode of production."[17] Behind this conception is present, as in Marx, an unconditional belief in the possibility of the realization of a concrete social utopia which would include the elimination of all the institutionally created alienating dimensions of human communal living. It is to this context that Dussel's "metaphysics of proximity" (the relation of the face-to-face between humans) belongs, which obviously has to be understood from a Levinasian as well as a Marxian perspective. Proximity means: "The first, archeological proximity [something like the mother-child relationship] anticipates the last, the eschatological. The last is located beyond all aspiration; as the unfulfilled but always desired; as the realized infinite. It is a desire for proximity without distance, without economy, without contradictions, without war.... It is the utopia that keeps us expectant."[18] And, in another place: "When alienated work liberates itself from capital, when it creates the community of *free* humans, face-to-face, human life objectified in commodities can be subjectified in justice. The feast, the enjoyment, the satisfaction, the singing are now possible."[19]

Later on I will return to this problem of utopia. For the moment, I will deal with, in first place, the delineation of a point in relation to which the Marxist critique by Dussel constitutes, even in the actual moment, that is, after the evident collapse of marxism-leninism, a challenge to the philosophical discourse of the First World.

It is possible to arrive at the following summary of the European, and in particular the German, experience with the history of the political confrontation with socialism in this century. The strongest argument against marxism-leninism can be found for Europeans, especially for Germans, not so much in the economic failure of state socialism in the Soviet state. Rather, it is found in the circumstance that, finally, the long-term triumphs of social democracy and of the labor union movements of restructuring the social state of western democracies have not only strengthened it, but have also made it appear, thanks to social services, as something more attractive than the states of "real socialism." We are thus justified in making the following general judgment. The path of *social reform* has been the correct path not only because of the preservation of political freedom, but also because of the interest in the approximative realization of the Welfare State (so as to not say simply: of social justice). This path has not only been able to maintain parliamentary democracy without essential modifications; it has also known how to preserve the market economy system, placing, through a reform of the "political system" of the conditions of the system itself, the efficacy of this system at the service of social politics, instead of directly intervening in the economic system itself.

On the thread of this summary it would be probable to establish in Western Europe a broad and trans-party consensus concerning these opinions. It was precisely this empirically saturated probable consensus that provided the reason why Dussel's "interpellation," and more precisely his appeal to Marx, in the Freiburg seminar, sounded like an anachronism.

However, it is on this point as well that the actuality of the "crucial" arguments of Latin American Liberation Philosophy, inasmuch as they are arguments of the Third World, prove important. It is a matter, in the first place, of an adequate argument in order to question the *eurocentric* perspective of the contemporary discussion, that attempts to make once again valid the Marxist and even Leninist critical perspective on capitalism. I think here of the so-called *theory of imperialism*, initiated by Hilferding, Rosa Luxemburg, and Lenin—but also by the liberal, Hobson—[20] and which was later developed from the Latin American perspective as the *theory of dependence*.[21]

The theory of dependence, which encompasses a varied spectrum of positions, could be characterized through a dual dependency thesis with regard to the economic development of the Third World, on one side, and with regard to the First World, on the other side. With regard to the Third World it maintains that the causes of continuing under-development are maintained through dependence on the dominating economy (as well as politics) of the First World. Thus, it contradicts the older "theories of modernization" which considered under-development to arise primarily from *internal* causes, in the sense of a theory of developmental phases valid for all societies. However, the theory of dependence maintains—among a series of different important arguments—that one of the causes for the under-development of the Third World is its dependence on the advancement and always growing wealth of the capitalist countries of the "center" of the world market system. To that extent, however, the following objections, formulated pointedly and succinctly, can be derived from the theory of dependence against my own summary of the European experience with the social welfare state within reformed capitalism (for example, in the "social market economy" of the Federal Republic of Germany).

The success of the northern democracies (success from the point of view of the Third World), of or to put it more precisely, the development just described which has led through social reforms to a relatively attractive solution to the social question; this success could only have been accomplished thanks to the *neocolonial* exploitation of the natural resources and cheap labor (the real "proletariat" of today) of the Third World. The key to the clarification of this complementarity situation of economic prosperity and social consolidation of the North and the permanent under-development and pauperization of the the Third World may be found, accordingly, in the framework conditions [*Rahmenbedingungen*] of the political order of the global economic system dictated by the North. These framework conditions, it is said, are neocolonial to the extent to which the political-economic elites of the developing countries are led, through violence or corruption, to collaborate at the expense of the exploited masses of the South with the multinational companies which represent the interests of the North.

According to this, it would be impossible, in principle, under the capitalist conditions (and now this means *neocolonial imperialistic*) of a global economic system, to overcome the progressive impoverishment of the masses of the Third World. These conditions determine the *terms of trade* of the exchange of goods between the North and the South, thus both causing and defining the debt crisis. In addition, growing pauperization would have to turn against the First World itself, thus bringing to an end the reprieve that capitalism had won for the metropolises of the North through its exploitation of the South. This last expectation, which reestablishes the connection between the theory of dependence with the older theory of imperialism, is strengthened in our days by two additional arguments. First, through the northward emigration that the impoverished masses of the South have undertaken. Second, and above all, through the consideration that, due to growing poverty, the South is forced to alter even more its environment, thus making more acute the threat to the ecosphere. How can we begin to answer to this global argument?

8.4 Methodological Gains of the Theory of Dependence

Before I attempt to enter into the arguments of the economists of development—with examples from the relevant literature—I would like to underscore one of the main merits of the theory of dependence, which in my opinion is of fundamental significance for understanding the structural presuppositions of a critical-historical reconstruction of the contemporary situation; and, which is also important—as it will be shown later—for the problematic of a historically dependent application of discourse ethics.

The attempts at a reconstruction of the human cultural revolution[22]—and in its context the closely linked attempt by Max Weber at a reconstruction of the *rationalization processes*[23] or *theory of modernity*[24]—are in a certain sense unavoidably thrown upon an "internal history" (I. Lakatos) of their presupposed object realm and the acknowledgment, in the face of all (empirical) explanation of history through "external" factors, of the methodological priority of this quasi-construct.[25] The reason for this methodological necessity lies, so it seems to me, in the situation that the historical-reconstructive sciences must be able to consider the inspection of their own conditions of possibility—in the last instance, the inspection of the normative conditions of the univeral validity of their argumentative discourse—as a factum or quasi-*telos* of the history to be reconstructed, in such a way that they must be able to make understandable the state of affairs of this factum as result of an "internal" history. Were this necessity to be ignored, and instead were one to want something like an explanation of history totally out of "external" causes (in the sense of a naturalistic or materialistic "reductionism"), this would mean that the historical-reconstructive sciences could not *re-trace* [*einholen*] the historical understanding of their own presuppositions and consequently, in the last instance, would fall into a (performative) contradiction against their own universal validity claims (understandibility, truth, truthfulness, and rightness, in the sense of morally fundamental norms of discourse).

I have called this the self-catching-up-principle [*Selbsteinholungsprinzip*] of the critical-reconstructive social and historical sciences,[26] and I would defend the thesis that one must, in light of this principle, generalize a thesis that Lakatos made valid for the history of science, namely, the methodological priority of "internal" in opposition to "external" history; and must apply this generalized thesis to the reconstruction of the whole of cultural evolution.[27] A particularly elucidating example of a reconstructive program in this sense is provided by the attempt to apply the ontogenetically dependent developmental logic of levels of moral-judgment competences to the critical reconstruction of phylogenesis, and to that extent, to cultural evolution.[28]

However, it is to be understood from the outset that all attempts at a reconstruction of the internal rationalization dimensions of human cultural evolution are very problematic. This is even more the case the farther removed the object realm of reconstruction is from the paradigm of a specific rationality type (such as, for example, logical-mathematical rationality; the causal or functional-analytical rationality of science; means-ends rationality as technical-instrumental and as strategic-action rationality, or communicative rationality).[29] This distance is unquestionably of a more disproportionate measure, in the case of political or economic history, than with something like the history of science (especially the exact sciences) or the history of technology.

Every program of a purely *internal* reconstruction of a particular process of rationalization is complicated by the fact that the simultaneous consideration of every other type of rationality may appear as a consideration of *external* factors (as is the case, for example, with the explanation of the motivation for mathematical discoveries in a reconstruction of the internal rationalization processes of mathematics in terms of external factors, just as the motivation for the Newtonian theory of "absolute space" is explained through his theosophical speculations or through the religious motivation of a "purposive rational life conduct" of the Protestant founder of capitalistic economy in Weber's sense). Furthermore, every program of an internalistic reconstruction of rationalization processes will be rendered even more suspect by the fact that all *abstractive* forms of rationality (more precisely: all forms of rationality that do not stand at the service of the communicative understanding of validity claims) could place their motivation at the service of non-rational forces and usually do so. This is particularly valid for the forms of means-ends rationality (technical-instrumental and strategic rationality).

The consideration of the motives of human action external to reason must clearly play an essential role in every "materialistically" oriented development theory—and thus also to a *dialectical-historical* as well as in an *evolutionary systems theory* of the economy. Here the scope of the possible internalistic reconstruction of rationality and rationalization processes will always shrink in relation to the realm of only-causally-explainable historical contingency. One could then only go beyond the reconstruction of subjectively describable rationality of action and suppose in a *dialectical* manner processes of objective rationalization (in the sense of the "determinate negation" of existing social constradictions), or in a systems-theoretical manner, suppose processes of objective rationalization of a functional rationality system (something like the "invisible hand" of the market system in Adam Smith's sense).

These methodological complications of the the program of an internalistic reconstruction of rationalization processes may be supplemented with general reflection on the situation that every attempt (in the sense of the *Selbsteinholungsprinzip*) at a reconstruction of the teleological process of history's progress is threatened by the danger of confusing the historically contingent conditions (including ethnocentric idiocyncracies) of a particular social situation with the historically realized conditions of the possibility of universal validity claims of scientific discourses. Where someone believes in the reconstruction of a process of progress of human rationality (or at least in the evolution of the systems-rationality of social subsystems), there he/she may in truth only deal with the factual development path of his/her own culture, which was subject to numerous—and still unclarified—non-rational external motivations or even contingent causes.

Out of this critical consideration it does not follow in any way that the *Selbsteinholungsprinzip* of a self-consistent historical reconstruction, or even the presupposition of the universal validity claims of argumentative discourse, would have to be abandoned (as Rorty and the postmodernists suggest[30]), for that would mean the end of philosophy and science, and with them, the end of rational self-critique. It does follow however, that every reconstruction program must be held open to the *communicative-hermeneutical confrontation with foreign cultures*, and must expose itself to *the self-application of the critique of ideology* with the help of quasi-naturalistic explanation methods. (This is precisely what did not happen any longer, for example, with the orthodox Marxist discourse on historical reconstruction, which immunized itself from all critiques of ideology through its absolutized ideology critique on all positions of "bourgeoise science," in which every possible counter-argument was *a priori* reduced to simple historically explainable factors external to discourse.)

After these—very vague—methodological remarks on the problem of the reconstruction of the cultural evolution, it appears possible to make understandable the main service provided by the *theory of dependence* within the problem context of the reconstruction of history. Here is disclosed, in my opinion, if we depart from the exemplary case of the history of economics, a deficit of historical reflection of the eurocentric theories of rationalization and modernization, which, as far as I can see, has determined and characterized the pursuit of science in the North. Two moments of the reflection deficit may be distinguised.

First of all, the rationalization and modernization theories of the North set out implicitly from a non-critical reflection and therefore potentially eurocentrically narrowed version of the *Selbsteinholungsprinzip*. That means, coarsely put: these theories depart, with reason, from the presupposition that Western (better: the in-the-West-factually-developed) philosophy and science are, in principle, in a legitimate position to act as advocates for argumentative discourses with universal validity claims, and that they have obtained through these discourses a unique advantage over other cultures.

This is even valid in the sense of the modern differentiation of scientific rationality in opposition to Asiatic high cultures, which have in common with Western culture their roots in the "Axial Period" (roots which in our case are traceable to the Greeks, on the one hand, and the Christian-Jewish tradition, on the other),[31] namely, the breakthrough to philosophy and/or world religion. This is even more valid in opposition to all other cultures which have not reached this breakthrough (for instance, Africans south of the Sahara) or were near this breakthrough when they were rendered "decapitated sunflowers" (O. Spengler), like the Indian high cultures of South and Middle America. It becomes clear here that Latin American Liberation Philosophy's often-assumed claim of "authenticity," in opposition to Europe, can reasonably be drawn only with reference to the originality (autonomy) of its internal concern, for example, the advocative representation of the "non-white" cultures of South and Central America, and thus cannot link its rationality concept to non-European origins.

The *foreshortening* of the justifiable claims of the *Selbsteinholungsprinzip* by the theories of rationalization and modernization of the North, resides precisely in that the potential eurocentrism of the respective reconstructive formulations would immunize themselves against questioning from non-European standpoints. This came about in particular through the demand that one must always depart methodologically only from a *comparison* between the development of non-European cultures with one's own developmental path, and hence must only measure their development against the European one. In this case, it is a matter not only of the concrete, historical *interdependence* relationship between the cultures, which since the begining of the so-called modern epoch, and irreversibly, has been determined through the political and economic, but also the scientific and technical, dominance of the North.

However, it is this overlooked interdependence relationship that has to a certain extent made it impossible to compare, and match one against the other, the development path of the North and of non-European cultures, and thus to *objectively* determine the "respectively attained levels" of development. For the "respectively attained levels" of development belong to a complex general situation of global development, which since the time of colonization has been determined through the interdependences between cultures of comparable development.

This—at least partial—impossibility to compare the theoretical levels of the developmental paths, which is brought about through the historical interdependence of concrete developments, points to the *second* moment of the reflection's deficit of eurocentric rationalization and modernization theories.

This second moment—which seems hardly refutable in its core—has been disclosed in an exemplary fashion by the theory of dependence through its reference to the development of a world economic system. At least up to today, there has been no refutation of the possibility that the solution to the social question attained in the reformed capitalism of northern democracies cannot serve as a model, and thus as a prototype, for the development (modernization) of the Third World, because such a development would be prevented by the dependence of the countries of the Third World on the North. Indeed, the economic prosperity of the "prototypical North" may be directly predicated on the maintenance of the world system of economy (for instance, its terms of trade), in which the remedial development [*nachholende Entwicklung*] of the South would be hindered by the North.

This argument against the possibility of a "remedial development" would be considerably strenghtened through the ecological argument that the imitation of the northern path of development by the countries of the Third World—something like an economic growth based on similar resource squandering and the emission of noxious substances, as today characterizes the industrialized North—*should* absolutely not take place, because this would not be compatible with the preservation of the general human ecosphere.

(Within this nexus one could find proof for the fundamental insight of the theory of dependence—in the sense of a global interdependence, as I made explicit—in an almost macabre situation, namely, in the fact that the contemporary export industry of the North—a special case would be the German auto industry—plagued by recession, looks hopefully at the growth "boom" of the rising Chinese markets, while ecologists imagine with horror what it will be like when so many millions of people replace their bicycles with automobiles. This is also the case—in a smaller measure—with the positively assessed economic development of Mexico under Salinas Gostary: more jobs, more autos, and more pollution, especially for the 18 million inhabitants of Mexico City. In all such cases, the interdependence of the economy of the First and the Third Worlds appears to be disclosed in a way where even the positive developments, in the sense of "bourgeois" *and* Marxist development economy, allow themselves to be represented as ambiguous in the sense of the ecological assessment.)

However, after this very global and macroscopic appraisal of the basic insights of the theory of dependence, it is time to attempt a more empirical-pragmatic assessment, keeping in mind the recent discussions. The fact that the *theory of dependence* has lost many of its supporters in the last decade, and that "theories of modernization," together with neoclassical economics, disavowed by almost all, have gained a new footing, should be considered with special care.[32]

8.5 The Skeptical-Pragmatic Problematization of the Grand Theories of Political Development

What has to be done first, to use an expression of Habermas, is to indicate the "new unsurveyability" [*neue Unübersichtlichkeit*] of the discussion on the North-South conflict and the "politics of development."[33] The "grand leftist theories," it is said in the contemporary North in relationship to this thematic, have been shown to be inadequate simplifications of a far more complex problematic. Consequently, the theory of dependence long ago exceeded the highpoint of its plausibility. We can affirm, in fact, that for each of the premises that underlies this theory, counter-examples can be elaborated, for instance, against the global historical-geographic presupposition of its validity claims as a theory of the North-South *conflict*. The relations and conditions of the different Latin American, Asian, and African countries have been and are far more diverse than is suggested by talk of a Third World and of dependence on the First World. This is valid not only in referring to the those aspects of difference that can be explained from the historical reconstruction of the history of colonialism (of the Iberian in Latin America, of the English in North America, Australia, and New Zealand, and of the French in Africa and Oceania, as well as the essentially Russian and English colonialism in Asia; see D. Ribeiro, 1985); it is also valid in relation to those aspects that the theory of dependence does not consider or underestimates.

Thus, for instance, the argument of the North that the crises of the South are in great measure home-made does not entirely lose its force before the theory of the corruption of the elites of developing countries, that is, before the forced and irresponsible political dependency on the North, because, in fact, these minority groups have acted in different ways. The differences rest on ethnic and socio-cultural presuppositions of the greatest variety, entirely independent of the relation of subordination of the South to the North. This is also valid with respect to the differences of ethnic and cultural presuppositions during the colonization period. Such presuppositions ought to be considered in the explication of the different degrees of economic success of the older colonial territories. More precisely: it is necessary to consider the distinct predispositions, existing to our day, toward the successful adaptation to the economic forms of capitalism. With this I also refer to the results of the hermeneutic reconstructions of the economic ethics of distinct cultural traditions, in the spirit of Max Weber.[34] Such reconstructions suggest that the functioning of capitalism depends also on a religiously conditioned motivation and on the disposition to a corresponding rationalization; for instance, on the disposition to strictly separate the rule of law from company, private, and family interests.

In an interesting study, the "Ethic of the 'mafiosi' and the Spirit of Capitalism,"

Pino Arlacchi analyzed the differences between the development of North America and Western Europe in this sense, on the one hand, and, on the other, Latin America and Southern Europe (in particular the south of Italy).[35] This corresponds partially with the explication (close to the theory of dependence), offered by Darcy Ribeiro, of the differences between poor and rich in Brazil, in the first place, and between Brazil and the United States, in second place. These are phenomena that result from the distinction between two different stages of the colonial period: commercial Iberian capitalism and Anglo-American industrial capitalism.[36]

Furthermore, there is much to be said in favor of the thesis that the notable economic success of certain territories of eastern Asia (particularly, South Korea, Taiwan, Hong Kong, and Singapore), which suffered Japanese imperialistic colonialism, can be explained from the socio-cultural and ethno-demographic conditions peculiar to these regions. Evidently, the success of Japan itself can be explained in terms of the theory of dependence, that is to say, if one departs from the independence that was maintained by Japan during the colonial period, in contradistinction to what took place in India. But, in relation to this, it is also possible to affirm that ethnic and socio-cultural conditions also play a fundamental role.

The relative economic stability of China, which has surpassed the Soviet economy by some years, and that of its satellite states, is also supported in the same measure, by the specific cultural tradition of the family, and the typically industrious character of this numerous people, as by the relative independence (reestablished thanks to the Communist takeover) of the country in relationship to the global capitalist system. Finally, with respect to Black Africa, in conjunction with Bengal, Bangladesh, and the north of Brazil and the indigenous territories of Latin America, which exhibit the greatest impoverishment, we can also speak of the clash of attempts at explaining the notorious failure of the politics of development. On the one hand, we have the argument in relation to economic exploitation during the colonial period and its neocolonial continuation in the states that emerged out of the older colonies—states that, to say truly, are artificially constituted and find themselves frequently divided by tribal conflicts. In opposition to this we have the argument that the impoverishment is due partially to socialist experiments and the successive civil wars (Ethiopia, Somalia, Tanzania, Mozambique, Angola), but, above all, to the insufficient socio-cultural predisposition of tribal societies with respect to the framework conditions of capitalist economic forms. As a support for this thesis is frequently cited the fact that the standard of living of the population, including the Black population, is higher in South Africa, where the control of the state is in the hands of the white population.

With this it is shown, then, that the historic-geographical presuppositions (globally simplifying) of the theory of dependence prove to be problematic.

In a narrower sense, its economic *premises* are equally questionable.

Now, is it necessary to affirm that the economic-structural characteristics put in relief by the theory of dependence (such as the high consumption of luxury goods by the dominant states, the export orientation of monocultures linked to a low integration with the internal market, and, consequently, a higher degree of "structural heterogeneity" of the social economy in its totality, and, above all, the "marginalization" and growing poverty of the majority of the population) constitute a distinctive characteristic of the Third World economy? Or, put differently, Is this "peripheral capitalism" distinguished not only in comparison to the actual economic and social structure of the First World, but also with respect to the *non-dependent* development of Europe once industrialization was initiated? Can we then, on the "diversity conditioned by dependence," base the thesis of the, impossibility (in principle) of a progressive development of the socioeconomic structure of the Third World under the conditions of a global capitalist system dominated by the North?

Interestingly, a critique of the historic-economic premises implicit in the theory of dependence can be found in Thomas Hurtienne, who can be considered a Marxist sympathizer in the questioning of the normal paradigm of the neo-liberal theory of development.[37] Hurtienne notes that the structural characteristics of Third world peripheral capitalism, which we have just mentioned, also characterized English economy and, later, the German-Prussian economy of the 19th century. Hurtienne also shows a frequently overlooked fact, namely, "that the great mass of workers and farmers of these regions, had a lasting participation in the 'fruits' of economic growth, but only after a hundred years of capitalist industrialization."[38] After reconstructing English development during the 18th and 19th centuries, Hurtienne notes that "as a result we can conclude that the English industrialization, despite its having early achieved a high degree of capitalistically induced production relations and the relative modernity of the social structure (small farmers and craftpersons had lost all social and political weight), is characterized, at least up to the First World War, that is, until approximately 130 years after the initiation of the industrial revolution, by certain central traits of a *structural heterogeneity*: namely, by extreme inequality in the distribution of income, minimal importance of the industrial production of goods of general consumption, absolute and extreme poverty, social marginalization...."[39]

I cite here the conclusions of a study strongly inclined toward marxism, because it can help us as a point of reference in questioning the position sustained by the theory of dependence in relation to the impossibility of the South's developing within the framework of capitalism. The economist of development Albert O. Hirschmann has reflected, in a pragmatic and non-dogmatic manner, on all the important and relevant theories of this type.[40] His work contains more detailed questionings and problems of the neo-liberal and Keynesian presuppositions of the Western politics of development after 1945, as well as of the presuppositions that underlie the theory of dependence. Although Hirschmann on occasion is a participant in the critiques of Western politics of development, he arrives at a positive conclusion about the real possibilities of social reform in Latin America. A very important point of support for his comes from the fact that with the end of the cold war, that is, with the disappearance of the fear of a Communist revolution, the United States finds itself no longer obliged to continue its repressive "backyard" politics. In the face of such positive expectations in Latin America, the panorama that presents itself in the post-Soviet Union countries is naturally extremely obscure concerning economic and social reforms. In these countries the reintroduction of a capitalist social order after more than 70 years would appear to encounter obstacles of a greater magnitude than those in many of the peripheral capitalist countries of the Third World. The social sacrifices after *perestroika* (conceived, in reality, as a reform of state socialism) could be of a proportional magnitude.

What consequences can we extract from these considerations, which are selective and, without doubt, insufficient with regard to the inherent problems, of the theses of the theory of dependence? Do we obtain an entirely negative result with regard to the situational valorization on which Dussel bases his Liberation Philosophy? In my opinion, the answer is negative, in spite of all the arguments that we have offered with respect to the problematic character of the theory of dependence.

8.6 The Ethically Relevant Facts of the Relationship between the First and Third Worlds

Dussel's Liberation Philosophy presents itself, above all, as an *ethical* challenge to the philosophy of the North. Therefore, it is not convenient to prejudge the situational valorization that essentially underlies it, from a theoretical point of view (that is, its economics of development and social scientific justification). Instead, it ought to be assessed in terms of empirical facts, which give rise to its "interpellation" in the name of the "poor" of the Third World, and which, in my opinion, justify it fully. To this interpellation there belong, as recognized even by divergent theories, the following facts, which form part of the background of the North-South conflict, especially of its manifestation in Latin America, and which find themselves causally conditioned by the historical expansion of Europe at a global scale during the modern period, and that even in our day have visible effects:

1. Approximately around the year 1500 the indigenous populations of America, Black Africa, and great sections of Asia were uprooted, generally in a violent manner, from their natural and socio-cultural conditions of life, and were decimated or simply exterminated. These cultures were also partly

stripped of their advanced cultures, as well as of their social order. They were enslaved and, in any event, condemned to become an extremely poor marginal group of humanity; a group, in addition, economically and culturally dependent on the North. These observations prove to be particularly appropriate with reference to the aboriginal populations of America and its tribal cultures, who were the object of almost near extermination through violence, forced labor and sickness. In relation to the advanced state cultures of Middle, Central, and South America, the antecedent judgments are fair in the sense of political and socio-cultural control and economic-social corruption, which even today in Mexico, a country were the indigenous populations have been officially vindicated, have not been fully modified.

2. It is important to note in this context that the liberation of the English, Spanish, and Portuguese colonies in America carried out, in the name of the Enlightenment and liberalism, did not improve the conditions of life of the indigenous population nor of the slaves and their descendants (who were used to replace the progressively depopulated natives). In fact, in some cases, liberation worsened their conditions (the European metropolises of the colonial powers had to some extent defended the interests of the autochthonous populations before the exploitative interests of the white colonizers and Creoles). The fate of the last Brazilian indigenous tribes, especially in the Amazon zone, is in our day particularly tragic. Their extermination would appear inevitable to the extent that the proletarian-farmer groups see their only opportunity for survival in the exploitation of the Amazonian forests. In actuality the government seems as incapable of controlling the deforestation of the jungle by immigrants, gold hunters, and rubber gatherers as of dealing with illegal immigration and the construction of *favelas* in the marginal zones of Sao Paulo and Rio de Janeiro. Understandably, the approximately 50 million poor in the country, the majority of Black origin, constitute, for the government and public opinion, a problem worthier and of greater political importance than the salvaging of the country's last tribes of Indians.

3. The Blacks, more robust than the Indians (it would seem for biological reasons), together with the American and African mestizos, bore the greater weight of enslavement in the Third World, but they survived, thus constituting (thanks to the development of medicine in the North) the principal source (with India, Indonesia, and China) of the ecologically problematic overpopulation of the planet.

4. In what corresponds to the deep socioeconomic structure of the North-South relationship, it is possible to verify, for example, the following facts, leaving aside diverse theoretical and ideological interpretations. The fundamental situation of South-North dependence (to which in our day belong Western Europe, North America, and Japan), created by European colonial expansion, has not been modified in essence; not even in the countries of the

Near East, which through membership in OPEC enjoy extreme wealth. All of this becomes particularly evident in the *framework conditions* of contemporary late capitalism's *terms of trade*, which after the collapse of state socialism maintain worldwide domination. Furthermore, phenomena like the *debt crisis*, the *deterioration of the third world environment*, and, above all, the *internal relation* between both symptoms of crisis, are evidence that these conditions do not constitute, as liberals pretend, *eo ipso* a "social market economy"[41] (a system of exchange that guarantees, thanks to a division of labor and an unconstrained freedom of commerce, the reciprocity of advantages). (In fact, to want to establish the reciprocity conditions of the justice of exchange contracts without consideration for the socially presupposed position of contracting parties, as is the case in contract negotiations, which could be of more or less equality or even of extreme inequality, would amount to a complete philosophical naivete).

In support of what has been presented above, I would like to cite here two recent and synoptic situational analyses free of ideological biases, but nevertheless possessing political pertinence. One is the book of the German-Iranian Hafez Sabet, *Die Schuld des Nordens* [*The Debt of the North*], which is based on economical statistics;[42] the other is the book by the director of the Institute for European Environmental Politics [*Instituts für Europäische Umweltpolitik*], Ernst-Ulrich von Weizsäcker, *Earth Politics, Ecological Realpolitik at the Threshold of the Century of the Environment* [*Erdpolitik, Ökologische Realpolitik an der Schwelle zum Jahrhundert der Umwelt*].[43]

Hafez Sabet documents the development of the debt crisis. The sum total of the foreign debt of the South with respect to the North is approximately $1.3 billion U.S. Under the actual framework conditions, this debt could not be paid in even 100 years. For Sabet, the causes of this crisis have to do with *external* factors such as: colonialism and its consequences; the shock of the price of petroleum for non-OPEC Third World countries; the weight the interest on the debt and the increase of the interest rates; the slump of the prices of raw materials; the deterioration of the terms of trade, as well as the protectionism of northern countries. On the other hand, however, as *internal* factors, Sabet lists: errors of political economy in the utilization of foreign credits; corruption and the peculiar behavior of elites, in addition to the flight of capital and talent ("brain-drain"); and excessive expenditure on armaments by the countries of the South. Sabet then makes a counter-assessment to the official version of the debt of the South, registering the interest payments, which have resulted in a flux of resources toward the North between the years 1956 and 1990, based on the framework conditions and the existing terms of trade. From this investigation of the deep structure of the world economic system, Sabet finally concludes that if economic relations had been more just, the North would owe more than 40 times the $1.3 billion that the South is indebted to the North, that is, approximately

$50 billion. In view of the consequences, Sabet arrives at the further conclusion that either the actual global economic order must be replaced by a new order, or the crisis of the South will necessarily strike back at the North in the form of a massive northward emigration and through the global consequences of the destruction of the environment brought about by poverty.

The situational analysis of von Weizsäcker has only confirmed and supplemented the results of Sabet, for example, in Chapter 8 of his book, which is dedicated to the Third World as a center of ecological destruction. Here one would have to note, however, in relationship to this point, that the richest part of the global population, which constitutes only 10 percent of humanity, consumes and uses directly or indirectly the greater part of the natural resources (energy, soil, water, air, etc.). Von Weizsäcker also confirms, in relationship to this, the "global division of labor" between the industrialized North and the Southern exporters of raw materials. This relationship has been long an object of praise by economists, but, according to Eduardo Galeano, actually means that "some specialized in gaining, while others specialize in losing."[44] According to von Weizsäcker, this relationship has led to "the dispossession of nature and of the majority of developing countries":

> For, in fact, how do developing countries pay the interests and the repayments? In reality, in addition to the natural resources, these countries do not have anything else that could be sold in the world markets. To an extent, developing countries "sell" also their air, their hydraulic resources, and their soil to the North. This takes place, for instance, when Japanese, European, or North American garbage industries migrate into the Third World, when Europeans import products from the tropics, whose cultivation we consider a loss or extremely expensive for the fertile European soils, or also when we send directly our special despoils to the Third World.[45]

Among the direct consequences of the global division of labor, we also find, according to von Weizsäcker, the fact that due to the "cutting down of entire woods, and the conversion of cultivable surface area into cattle-rasing areas and growth of fruits for exportation, rain water can no longer be absorbed as before by the soil, which can lead to floods in the lower regions, while in the dry seasons the aquatic sources dry up, great expanses of territory become sandy."[46] Finally, basing himself in the Brundtland Report (*Our Common Future*) of the World Commission on the Environment and Development,[47] von Weizsäcker reports that (approximately since 1985, "*circa* 40 million U.S. dollars have flowed from the developing countries to the North." Of this quantity, the greater part went to cover the costs of debt, mainly interest, and only a minuscule proportion toward repayment. It has to be noticed that the total transfer of capital from the North to the South, in the form of "development help," is significantly smaller than the flow of capital and values from the South to the North.[48]

The distinctive emphasis of von Weizsäcker's analysis, in contrast to the analysis of the majority of development economists (including the representatives of the theory of dependence), resides in making evident the following point: the objective consequences, regardless of the form of its realization, of a "remedial"[*nachholenden*] development of the countries of the Third World—that is, a development that would pretend to imitate for a population of a 1,000 million the model of the First World—is illusory and self-destructive from a purely quantitative and ecological point of view.[49] The planet would not be able to sustain an ecological pressure of this type. I will return to this point of view.

After this *Exkurs*, whose objective consisted in making explicit the most important ethical phenomena of the contemporary North-South relationship, we can concern ourselves with the discussion of the situational, socioeconomic, and political presuppositions of the Dusselian challenge to eurocentric philosophy. It ought to be made clear, since nothing is farther from my intentions, that I do not want to trivialize the fact of the "marginalization" and "exclusion" of the poor of the Third World from the community of life [*Lebensgemeinschaft*], as conditioned by the global economic system and the social order. But, obviously, we ought to add that we cannot reflect and elaborate on such facts on the basis of rhetorical-metaphysical simplifications. Instead, the base of our reflection ought to be exclusively the critical collaboration, in an ethically relevant manner, of philosophy with the empirical sciences. In the sketch I have presented only a very incomplete representation of this mediation between philosophy and the empirical sciences was transmitted.

I am in fact of the opinion that with the end of the cold war, and after the reduction of the danger of a nuclear war, *the number one problem* of world politics, and of its corresponding macro-ethics of the co-responsibility of all human beings, is and will be the question of the relationship between the First and the Third Worlds due to the insoluble connection between the ecological crisis and the socioeconomic crisis. (The dissolution of the so-called Second World has but accented this problematic, in addition to having made even more evident that the desperate attempt of the successor countries of the ex-Soviet Union to maintain themselves as industrial states is also intimately linked to a growing lack of concern with problems relating to the environment. This is also characteristic of Third World countries with threshold economies [*Schwellenländer*], such as the industrial center of Brazil, the area of Sao Paulo, or Taiwan.)

Thus far I have wanted to localize, within the limits of my capacities, the perspective of distantiation and alienation which can be brought about through Dussel's questioning of eurocentrism. It appears clear to me that, for instance, every tendency that pretends to reduce (as is frequently the case in the Western world) ethics to a conservation or a reinforcement of the "customary"

[*Üblichkeiten*], reduced to our cultural tradition, in view of the already presented world situation, amounts to irresponsible escapism. At the most minimum, the equal co-existence of different cultures, whose particularities have to be preserved, requires a *universalist* macro-ethics of humanity.[50] Only this type of ethics is capable of taking into account the "interpellation of the other" as formulated by the poor of the Third World. In our world situation, it would be either cynical or naive to reduce the problem of an ethically relevant justification of norms [*Normenbegründung*] to a technical-instrumental (means-ends rationality) problem of the investigation of adequate means and strategies for the attainment of "supreme objectives" [*Oberzwecke*], in which participants in negotiations do not have recourse to trans-subjective principles of justice; that is, in which, without consideration for the absent interests of third parties, adversaries or interested parties could reach an agreement thanks to a calculus of interest.[51]

Nevertheless, before I directly enter my coming-to-terms with [*Auseinandersetzung*] Dussel on the possibilities of discourse ethics, and with the goal of doing justice to his claims, I must first conclude my confrontation with marxism's inheritance. In other words, I must attempt to summarize my evaluation of the importance of marxism's inheritance in light of the foregoing reflections and in relation to the utopian element of the ethics of liberation.

It appears to me that the questioning, inspired by marxism, that the theory of dependence makes of the standard models of Western development, be they neoliberal or Keynesian, has at least established that a critique of the contradictions of the capitalist economic system, at a global level, is something that has neither been refuted nor whose critical potential has been exhausted. This opinion can be maintained even if one is convinced that the capitalist economic system is reformable and, from the ethical point of view, more acceptable than the variants of bureaucratic or state socialism that have been realized.[52] I justify this conclusion above all on the circumstance that it is precisely the presuppositions of the Marxist system of thought, on which the so-called *sublation [Aufhebung] of utopia by science*, rests, that ought to be abandoned or completely transformed.

This thesis refers to three fundamental elements of Marxist thought:

1. The theory of "alienation" or "reification," inasmuch as it is essentially referred, in Marx, to the positive, basic concept of "living labor," and not primarily to the relation of reciprocity of interaction, which in the life world is complementary to work. This reference is also present to the extent that this theory does not distinguish between an *uncircumventable exteriorization* or an objectification of human subjectivity (or more explicitly, of immediate intersubjectivity), *and* the *self-alienation and reification* of subjectivity, or respectively, of the inter-subjective relation.

2. The marxist labor theory of value and surplus, inasmuch as it rests, in the last instance, on the theory of alienation as referred to work and the utopian ideal of the annulment of alienation.

3. The historical-determinist theory of the unconditioned prediction of the substitution of capitalism by Communist socialism that would actualize the "utopia of the realm of freedom."

ADDENDUM 1

With respect to the theory of *alienation*, developed by the young Marx through his confrontation with Hegel and the young Hegelians, and which in a certain measure also constitutes the characteristic background of the theory of work in *Capital*, it appears to me indispensable to distinguish two things:

A) First, we must supersede, in a more fundamental sense than Marx and Hegel did,[53] the limitations of the point of departure in "living labor" as a *relation humaninty-nature* (the self-creation of humans through the exteriorization and re-appropriation of "human essential powers"). This tradition dates back to the dominant modern tradition of *object-subject philosophy*. This sublation ought, furthermore, to take place in the sense of a distinction of and reflection on the complementarity between work and interaction, that is, linguistic communication. The problematization of exteriorization or alienation would have to be developed, then, by making reference to the *relation of complementarity* between labor and interaction, that is, communication, which in turn is already anchored in the life world. This would have to take place in such a way that institutionalized exteriorization and tendential alienation are not understood primarily as the exteriorization and alienation of an autarkically thought autonomous subject (nor of a "species subject"), but instead primarily as the exteriorization and alienation of the relationship of reciprocity of acting subjects and their linguistic communication. Only then it is possible to analyze the emergence of social *institutions*, and functional-structural *social systems*, in opposition to the exteriorization of labor in works or products, namely, as a supplement of labor as a phenomenon of tendential alienation.[54] To that degree there is, on the one hand, a certain harmony between my attempt at differentiation and certain tendencies, present in Marx and Hegel and, above all, in Dussel's basic concept of *proximity* (understood as the relation to the "other," the neighbor [*Nächsten*][55]), while, on the other hand, there is disagreement when my position suggests that, original to all human interactions there is also a *strategic* relationship, delegitimated from the outset by both Dussel and Marx. The consequence of this delegitimation resides in that for both Marx and Dussel, all anticipated and potential "objectifications" in the market system can no longer be understood by recourse to the relationship of the *exchange of commodities* susceptible to legitimation *within the sphere of consensual communication*, and the assumed *essential* consideration of the *use-value* of goods.

B) Seconds, the suggested differentiation, in the sense of a supplementation, finds itself linked to the greater complexity of the problem of alienation, which in turn leads to Marx's central idea of the utopia of the total, the "emancipatory" *sublation of the alienation of human praxis*, as present in the market economic system, on the one hand, and, on the other, to the overcoming of the system of state power. If we do not adopt the attitude of orienting ourselves exclusively (as the young Marx did) to the creative production process of the craftperson or artist (exteriorizes and at the same time reappropriates herself in her products), but instead orient ourselves to the *temporal mediation of interaction and communication through institutional or systemic means*, inherent in language but fully winning its quasi-autonomy only in the non-linguistic media of social systems (for example, *money* and *power*),[56] then, the following, at the minimum, would become clear. The notion of a complete sublation of the alienation and objectification of the unmediated relation of *proximity* between humans (in the sense of the structural-functional quasi-nature of social systems), which unquestionably has characterized the human condition, would imply by necessity something practically equivalent to a regression/dismantling [*Rückgängigmachung*] of *cultural* evolution. For all the differentiation of functional systems that began with rituals and archaic institutions, through which human praxis *unburdened itself from* initial execution, that is, creative action in favor of effective automatism (thereby deploying itself in time), would be converted into something superfluous in the Marxist "realm of freedom." Such an imaginable realization of the Marxist utopia would not be equivalent to state socialism, which does nothing but replace the self-regulative functional system of market economy by the regulative system of state power. Indeed, it would be equivalent to the regressive utopia of Pol Pot. What is now clear is that the "realm of freedom," which according to Marx would find its realization in communism, is differentiated from Hegel's "progress in the consciousness of freedom," precisely through the fact that here it is a matter of a *real sublation of alienated praxis by revolutionary praxis*, and not that philosophy sublate (*aufhebt*) the exteriorization and alienation of the subjective spirit in the *objective spirit* by understanding both of these moves as *necessary conditions of self-consciousness*.

In view of this *trans-cultural utopian dimension* of Marxist "liberation philosophy," it would be suggestive to return to a position that, as it were, has its point of departure between Hegel and Marx. It is not a matter, in any way whatsoever, of annulling totally the Marxist concretization of the problematic of alienation and to return to Hegelian idealism. Nevertheless, it appears necessary to differentiate, partially reverting to Hegel, between the *exteriorization* (understood as something necessary) of human praxis (of work, as well as of interaction and communication) in social institutions and systems (as a cultural quasi-nature) *and* unconditionally avoiding the total *alienation* of praxis.

This raises the problematic of the adequate relation (scientifically informed and ethically responsible) of humans with institutions or functional systems; something unquestionably important in our days. This means, on the one hand, that we ought to recognize the necessity to differentiate systems of action of quasi-automatic functioning, such as the economic social system and the state under the rule of law, and, to this extent, that we ought to take into account the ideas of systems theory inasmuch as this counts as social science.[57] For the effectiveness of social systems depends in great part on the adequate consideration of these ideas; in an analogous manner, technology's effectiveness in controling nature depends on the causal-analytical perspective of the natural sciences. Nevertheless, we must resist system theory's suggestion of *functional reductivism*, just as much as physicalism was resisted as a previous form of reductivism.

To put the matter in a positive and programmatic sense: *linguistic communication*, which is equiprimordial with humanity's Dasein and is complementary to work (inasmuch as this is a re-elaboration of nature), and which attains its reflection in *argumentative discourse* in philosophy and science[58] this *meta-institution* of all institutions—must capitulate before neither social systems which have achieved their differentiation nor the so-called system constraints. It must not capitulate, that is, in the sense that its bearers [*Träger*] let themselves be persuaded that philosophical reflection (for example, the reflection on the intersubjective validity of truth claims and the normative correctness claims of morality) can be *reduced* to the "self-reference of an autopoietic social system" (something like the system of science), out of many other functional system of this type.[59] Rather, the human communication community, which through argumentative discourse arrives at a consciousness of its *meta-institutional* responsibility, must retain effective practical control and organizational initiative before any functional system. This means, for example, that this community must retain an effective capacity for the critique and reform of the *framework conditions of the market economy*, just as is the case with the democratic state in what refers to the system of regulation of power.

Naturally, the difficulty of this task lies not only in that it would have to be resolved (as happens in the democracies that we know) within the framework of a system of national-state self-affirmation, but also within the framework of a "civil and legal world order" [*weltbürgerlichen Rechtsordung*] (Kant). The problem lies, in addition, in the circumstance that the meta-institutional discourse of any human communication community ought by necessity, at the same time, to *institutionalize* itself, as *real* discourse, and to this extent submit itself to the conditions of functional systems. However, to question the fact that, in the service of the postulated task, we have a responsibility to use technical communications media as well as the communicative disposition of the experts of science and technology, as well as that of those who are politically responsible, would be not only irresponsible defeatism but a complete distancing from reality.

It is precisely this that takes place today in thousands of congresses, commissions, etc, which concern themselves, at least according to their public pretensions, with the *regulation of human problems in the sense of an advocatory representation of the interests of all the affected.* In so far, then, with respect to the publicly effective, the regulative principle of a *discourse ethics* is already complied with here (or more precisely, Part A of the grounding of this type of ethics is already claimed, although it should be made clear that the participating representatives of political and economic systems of self-affirmation in most cases continue, or see themselves obliged by responsibility, to follow in praxis Lübbe's model of *negotiations oriented at success,* or even see themselves obliged to follow it out of responsibility, in the sense of Part B of discourse ethics.[60] Nonetheless, and owing above all to the pretension that it is publicly effective, this type of ethics does not absolutely exclude an approximative accomplishment of the task of a meta-institutional or meta-systemic discursive responsibility as I have postulated it. I would like to underscore here that the only realistic and responsible possibility of having, through politically mediated *reforms,* some influence on *the framework conditions of the global economic system* and of transforming, perhaps in the long run, this system, in the sense of the realization at a global scale of social justice, is already given in the "function" of discourse that I have been suggesting.

ADDENDUM 2

The critique or transformation, just sketched, of the Marxist theory of alienation and its complete sublation in reality, suggests, to a certain extent, a critique to Marx's labor theory of value. As is evident in the critique that follows, I will only indicate the most general aspects of its philosophical heuristic.

When one reads with impartiality the passages in *Capital* where Marx formulates his theory of value, one cannot help but be surprised at the *way* Marx distinguishes between use-value *[Gebrauchswert]* and exchange-value [Tauschwert]:

> The usefulness of a thing—according to Marx—makes it a use-value. But this usefulness does not dangle in mid-air. It is conditioned by the physical properties of the commodity, and has no existence apart from the latter. It is therefore the physical body of the commodity itself, for instance iron, corn, a diamond, which is the use-value or useful thing. . . . Use-values are only realized [*verwirklicht*] in use or in consumption. They constitute the material content of wealth, whatever its social form may be. In the form of society to be considered here they are also the material bearers of . . . exchange-value.[61]

Here one is surprised that for Marx use-value, that is, the *usefulness* of a thing (which, as he correctly observes, "does not dangle in mid-air") finds itself *exclusively* conditioned by the "physical properties of the commodity." Undoubtedly it is correct to say that "without this" (i.e., the commodity as a physical body) usefulness could not exist, but we ought to also ask ourselves if such usefulness does not find itself conditioned as well by *people's needs*; more precisely, by the demands of potential users or consumers. Perhaps, however, Marx held this latter determination as self-evident. But if this were the case, the *demand in exchange* would also have to be, in the last instance, an expression of usefulness, that is, of the exchange-value of things inasmuch as they are goods. Use-value is constituted, so to speak, in the life world ("Use-values are only realized in use or consumption"), and in that sense they distinguish themselves, undoubtedly, from the *exchange-value that is referred to price*. But the use-value would have to be also *co-constitutive*, that is, it would also have to be a significant factor in the constitution of exchange-value in the economic system, for the simple reason that this is already a significant factor, co-constitutive, of the demand of the buyer. It is precisely this that Marx seems to call into question. Marx accomplished a radical *abstraction* when he introduced exchange-value as referred to a system.

As is evident from the Marx citation, use-values are *only* "the material bearers of exchange value." "Exchange-value appears first of all as the quantitative relation, the proportion, in which use-values of one kind exchange for use-values of another kind. This relation changes constantly with time and place...." Nevertheless, "the valid exchange-values of the same commodity express something equal," and the "relation of exchange," between "let us now take two commodities, for example corn and iron. Whatever their exchange relation may be, it can always be represented by an equation.... What does this equation signify? It signifies that a common element of identical magnitude exists in two different things, in 1 quarter of corn and similarly in x cwt of iron."[62] But, "this common element cannot be a geometrical, physical, chemical or other natural property of commodities. Such properties come into consideration only to the extent that they make the commodities useful, i.e. turn them into use-values. But clearly, the exchange relation of commodities is characterized precisely by their abstraction from their use-values.... As use-values, commodities differ in quantity, while as exchange-values they can only differ in quantity, *and therefore do not contain an atom of use-value*."[63]

With this *supra-abstraction* Marx has eliminated every co-constitution of exchange value through use-value; Marx is now ready to introduce what can be called his *absolute labor theory of value*:

> If then we disregard the use-value of commodities, only one property remains, that of being *products of labour*..... With the disappearance of the useful character of the products of labour, the useful character of the kinds of labour embodied in them also disappears. They can no longer be distinguished, but are all together reduced to the same kind of labour, human labour in the abstract.[64]

Marx's supra-abstraction is confirmed with the following determination that he makes of abstract human labor:

> A use-value, or useful article, therefore, has value [=exchange-value in the economic system] only because abstract human labour is objectified [*vergegenständlicht*] or materialized in it. How, then, is the magnitude of this value to be measured? By means of the quantity of the "value-forming substance," the labour, contained in the article. This quantity is measured by its duration, and the labour-time is itself measured on the particular scale of hour, days, etc. . . . The total labour-power of society, which is manifested in the values of the world of commodities, counts here as one homogeneous mass of human labour-power, although composed of innumerable individual units of labour-power [among themselves different]. [Because] each of these units is the same as any other, to the extent that it has the character of a socially average unit of labour-power and acts as such, i.e. only needs, in order to produce a commodity, the labour time which is necessary on an average, or in other words is socially necessary.[65]

This average time "changes with every variation in the productivity [*Produktivkraft*] of labour."[66]

After Marx has reduced the value of commodities in the capitalist economic system to the labor power of work (or of workers) expended during a certain time, he can introduce his theory of "surplus," which has fundamental importance for the critical reconstruction of capitalism and in particular for the theory of class struggle [*Theorie des Klassengegensatzes*]:

He shows, first of all, that the formation of *surplus*, without which neither the formation nor the utilization of capital is possible, cannot be obtained through an exchange of equivalents in the realm of the normal circulation of commodities. Nor can it emerge through the fact that buyers and sellers cheat each other, since this would represent nothing else than the redistribution of existing capital.[67] Marx then shows that under the historic-social conditions of capitalism, the solution resides in that "in order to extract value out of the consumption of a commodity, our friend the money-owner must be lucky enough to find within the sphere of circulation, on the market, a commodity whose use-value possesses the peculiar property of being a source of value, whose actual consumption is therefore itself an objectification of labour, hence a creation of value."[68] This "specific commodity" represents "the capacity for labour, in other words the labour-power" of the wage-worker.[69] The value of this labor power that the capitalist buys is generally greater than the value of the wage that ought to be paid for the reproduction of the labor power of the workers (including the reproduction of their kind in their descendants), in this way the capitalist appropriates the *surplus* that allows him the utilization of capital.

Given this reconstruction of the grounding of the Marxist labor theory of value, we cannot be surprised that the *unilateral* (or *supra-abstraction*) determination of exchange-value that we have been underscoring has been the object of strong critiques since the beginning. Eugen Böhm-Bawerk, for instance, the representative of the theory of "marginal utility" [*Grenznutzentheorie*], has criticized the neglect of the value of "natural resources" [*Naturgabe*] as well as of the function of "use-value" and, in general, of the "game of supply and demand" in the investigation of the influence that the quantity of employed labor has on the lasting form of the "price of goods."[70]

The representative of revisionist marxism, Eduard Bernstein, who wanted to consolidate the Marxist theory of value with the limit of utility theory, criticized the onesidedness of the theory in the sense we have indicated.[71]

A particularly concise critique, from the view point of our heuristic of the complementarity of work and interaction, is that of George B. Shaw.[72] According to him, the unilateral aspect of the Marxist theory resides precisely in the fact that Marx's analysis of the commodity, which "wants to investigate the points in relationship to which commodities are commensurable with one another, considers, nevertheless, exclusively only one of them, that is, their character as *product of abstract human labour*." In opposition to this there is the theory of "marginal utility," that "commodities are commensurable with each other in proportion to their *abstract utility*, and that the comparison that is made in praxis with a view to an exchange of commodities is not a comparison of their cost in abstract human labour, but instead is a comparison of their *abstract desirability*."[73] However, this depends directly on the degree of the satisfaction of needs through the commodities that are offered.[74]

In my opinion, the unilateral character of the reduction of the "essence" of the "value" of goods (objectified already, as the "exchange-value" of "commodities") to inverted *work*, and, consequently, to the *labor-time* employed, can only be understood when one takes into account, as I have indicated, that Marx does not from the beginning relate the alienation of human praxis (which finds its objectified expression in the capitalist economic system) to the whole life complex of praxis—that is, to the relation of complementarity between work and interaction or communication. Instead, Marx refers such an alienation to work, that is, the production of goods, in accordance with modern subject-object philosophy and, in particular, with the tradition of the labor theory of value of the classics of economy.

If Marx had also referred from the beginning, and in a consequential manner, to the original reciprocity of human relations (which Dussel refers to as "proximity"), in the context of the problem of exteriorization, of alienation, and of the "cancellation" of objectified praxis in the capitalist system, he could not have overlooked that in the explication of economic relations of exchange, and, therefore, also the exchange-value of commodities, we cannot be completely abstract from the "use-value" of goods, thus entirely attributing it to (the "usefulness in relation to human needs") to the pre-economic status of natural things. Marx would have had to note and consider in a consequent manner that not only is "abstract work" (the labor-power employed, that is, the cost of production of a commodity) constitutive of the value of goods, but the reciprocity of supply and demand as well. And that this depends on the *abstract utility for the buyer*, something that, in turn, depends not only on *the natural qualities* of goods but also on the *not-satisfied needs* of the buyer and, in this manner, on the *degree of the scarcity* of goods.

Summarizing, Marx would have had to locate differently the rupture between the praxis of the life world and its alienation in a quasi-objectified system, considering fully the complementary character of *work* and *interaction* in the life world and the economic system. Not only "living labor," as *production of goods*, ought to have its origin in the life world, such as this is imagined before the differentiation of an economic system; also the *exchange relation* between humans—not exclusively between producers of goods, but equally between those who dispose of the resources (think, for example, of the exchange of land and women)—ought to have the same origin. The institutionalization of morality and law, and with it the development of the indispensable framework of social order for all possible economic systems, ought to be developed out of the linguistically articulated and reflected *relation of reciprocity*, as is implicit in (economic) exchange (*Tausch*), and not exclusively on the basis of the potential value-creating capacity of the production of goods through work. In addition, the institutionalization of morality, as conventional morals [*Sittlichkeit*], as well as the institutionalization of law [*Recht*] in the *power system of the state*, represent necessary processes in the *externalization* and, consequently, in the tendential *alienation* of life praxis, which in turn constitutes a necessary presupposition of the effective functioning of the economic system.[75]

From this system of correlations and connections we can extract the following conclusion. The attempt to overcome the alienation and objectification of worldly life praxis, which is inherent to the capitalist economic system, through the exclusive consideration of the "productive forces" and "production relations," that is, by appealing to the socialization of the property of the means of production, is equivalent to either a simple regressive utopian suppression of culture or, as Max Weber[76] anticipated with relation to marxism, to an unforeseen bureaucratization and paralysis of the economy due to the state system. In any event, the necessary efforts to mobilize the productive forces, that is, to ensure the efficient management of scarce resources in a system of production with a division of labor, cannot be guaranteed simply by the "free association" (proximity) of the producers, which constitutes in a certain sense, for Marx[77] and for Dussel, as far as I can see, the utopian dimension of the "realm of freedom."

ADDENDUM 3

The third fundamental element of the Marxist thought system that must be abandoned is historical determinism, or "historicism" in Popper's sense,[78] taken together with Hegel's dialectical method and used by Marx at least at the macroscopic level of his thought, and applied by him in contrast to Hegel) in his "scientific" predictions of the future. This historical-dialectical formulation, in combination with the claims of a thematization of social being and of the consciousness that develops with it, that is, of the superstructure (and consequently, of scientific consciousness as well), has led to the adoption, not only by Marx, but above all by the "orthodox" Marxists, of a curious *meta-position* with regard to the normal world discourse of science. This has inevitably led to an almost total immunization of their position before any type of critique. On the basis of the dialectical-historical perspective, one could adopt a standpoint from which it seemed to be possible to localize any scientific-philosophical claim in a dialectical-historical fashion, and to explain it, consequently, objectively. This has led to the elimination in practice of the possibility of participating in (virtually unlimited) argumentative discourses, inasmuch as this last one is the *meta-institution* responsible for the *justification* or *critique* of all theories and any type of institutionalized science. Not discourse proper, but the dialectical-historical explanation of the objective necessity of factual discourses, as well as its results, appeared as something transcendentally uncircumventable [nicht hintergehbar] for all argumentation. The questioning of this point by a non-Marxist theory was no reason for the Marxists to have recourse to an impartial decision, that is, to an argumentative discourse, in order to confront it, but instead to formulate the problem of "explaining" the theory in question in conjunction with its social context as the outcome of a determined phase in the development of bourgeois thought.

This tendency to "historicism," which has been fatal for the universalist undertaking of progressive science, culminated in "ethical historicism" or "futurism" (Popper). This has resulted in practice, With Lenin, Stalin, and Mao Tse Tung, this created a situation in which Marxist intellectuals advanced from secretaries of parties to "philosopher kings" in the Platonic sense. These thinkers found themselves in a position that allowed them to impose politically (at least within the sphere of their influence) the meta-position of the instance of the uncircumventable decision before any other different validity claim. In this way, not only was *truth* what the politburo had to certify in accordance with the dialectical vision of the necessary path of history, but also what had to be considered as the *good* and the *just*, inasmuch as in *accordance with the path of history* these had to be the object of determination. The consequences of all of this are well known: the repeated determination of the party line, as well as the inevitable "purges" of the party and the state.

In view of the above, it appears understandable that all the anti-orthodox Marxists (among them also the author of Liberation philosophy) have distanced themselves from this historicism. For Dussel, Marx (even he of *Capital*) is primarily an ethical thinker,[79] in the sense, let us say, of the "categorical imperative" which the young Marx elaborated in his *Introduction to the Critique of Hegel's Philosophy of Right*, where he writes; "The criticism of religion ends with the doctrine that *for man the supreme being is man*, and thus with the *categorical imperative to overthrow all conditions* in which man is a debased, enslaved, neglected and contemptible being."[80]

The acknowledgment of the actual meaning and validity of this imperative, which is inevitable if we do not want to fall in to cynicism when considering the problem of the Third World, leads us also, in our day, to the imperative necessity of facing the problem of *historical progress with regard to the political-moral*. Hence, we are not allowed to bring too far our critique of the *historicism* of the 19th century *maitres penseurs* (Glucksmann), so as to negate even the moral duty—previously affirmed by Kant—of conceiving as possible moral progress in history, and to contribute to the effort of resisting its frustration, or to contribute in any way to its realization.[81] It is not acceptable, then, to accept the postmodern affirmation of a definitive dissolution of the "unity of human history" and of the solidarity (anticipated counterfactually in argumentative discourse) of the *We*.[82] Nor can it be satisfactory to comply with the quiescent slogan of German neo-pragmatism that would like to subvert Marx's eleventh thesis on Feuerbach in the following manner:

> Hitherto philosophers have only changed the world, where instead it is a question of letting it be in peace.[83]

All of expressions can be considered as typically eurocentric from Dussel's perspective.

Now, how does it present itself to us: the actuality of the legitimate problem of an ethically grounded answer to the "interpellation of the other," to the interpellation of the permanently impoverished masses of the Third World, to the interpellation of those who do not effectively participate in the relevant discourses of the dependent metropoleis and their elites in peripheral capitalism? How does it present to us, this problematic under the conditions that today, as I have expounded, can be acceptable? These conditions require that *the path for replacing market economy imagined by Marx is unrealizable*. Or, said more philosophically: *the vision of a complete sublation of the tendential "exteriorization," objectification, and "alienation" of human praxis (that is, of its subject-object and of its subject-co-subject dimension) in a functional-structural social system, such as the global market-economy system constitutes, is in the worst of senses a utopia*. This Marxist idea contradicts, inasmuch as it is a postulate which refers to the institutional relations among free human beings and with nature, conceptions about the possibility of cultural evolution.

Obviously, we have affirmed that the human discursive or communication community, to which the interpellation of the other, of the poor, is directed, retains its place as *meta-institution of all institutions*, i.e., of all other *functional systems*, as long as we are capable of examining and discussing *interpellations*, such as the one Dussel presents in the name of the Third World. In accordance with this—and this is the provisional answer that I offer Enrique Dussel—what is important, and ought to be important to us, is politically and ethically to influence the *institutional-framework condition* of the economic system, something that requires considering the political-legal conditions of a system at the national and international level, with the goal of doing justice to the interpellation of the poor of the Third World.

What can *discourse ethics* contribute to this, as an ethics that as we have indicated, requires for its application conditions that do not yet exist in the contemporary world? I will attempt an answer to this question within the framework of a more detailed and text-based discussion in connection with Enrique Dussel's program.[84]

Notes

1. See Fornet-Betancourt, ed. *Ethik und Befreiung* (Aachen: Ausgustinus Buchhandlung, 1980).
2. Ibid., pp. 10–40.
3. Compare with the continuation of this "preliminary consideration" in its second part, "Diskursethik vor der Herausforderung der lateinamerikanischen Philosophie der Befreiung" in Raúl Fornet-Betancourt, ed. (forthcoming).
4. Fornet-Betancourt, ed. *Ethik und Befreiung* (Aachen: Augustinus Buchhandlung, 1990), pp. 69–96.
5. E. Dussel, *Philosophy of Liberation*. See also his "Philosophie der Befreiung" in R. Fornet-Betancourt, ed., *Positionen Lateinamerikas* (Frankfurt: Materialis-Verlag, 1988), pp. 43–59; and "Les quatre rédactions du Capital" in *Concordia*, 19, 1991, pp. 65–75, as well as the "The Reason of the Other. *Interpellation* as a Speech Act" (above), contribution to the congress "Transcendental Pragmatics and the North-South Ethical Problems," Mexico, March 1991.
6. Dussel has intensively occupied himself with the work of Marx, having published three volumes on the theoretical production of the Marx of the *Grundrisse* (*La Producción Teórica de Marx*), on the "Unknown Marx" of the 1861 to 1863 manuscripts (*Hacia un Marx Desconocido*), and on "Late Marx and Latin American Liberation" (*El Ultimo Marx [1863–1882] y la Liberación Latinoamericana*). See the reviews by R. Fornet-Betancourt in *Concordia*, 11, 1987, pp. 101–03; 15, 1989, 99–100, and 19, 1991, 108.
7. Compare with V. Hösle, *Philosophie der ökologischen Krise* Munich: C. H. Beck Verlag, 1992, as well as his *Praktische Philosophie in der modernen Welt* (Munich: C. H. Beck, 1992), pp. 131ff. See also Karl-Otto Apel, "The Ecological Crisis as a Problem for Discourse Ethics" in A. Öfsti, ed. *Ecology and Ethics: A Report from Melbu Conference, July 1990* (Trondheim: Nordland Akademi forkunstog Vitenskap, 1992), pp. 219–60.

8. See Karl-Otto Apel, *Diskurs und Verantwortung*, and "Diskursethik als Verantwortungsethik—eine postmetaphysische Transformation der Ethik Kants," in Eornet-Betancourt, *Ethik und Befreiung*.
9. See E. Arens's report on the congress in Mexico, *Orientierung* (Zürich), 19, 55, Sept. 1991, pp. 193–95.
10. See K.-O. Apel, "Harmony through Strife as a Problem of Natural and Cultural Evolution" in Shu Hsien Liu/R. E. Allison, eds., *Harmony and Strife. Contemporary Perspectives East and West* (Hong Kong: The Chinese University Press, 1988), pp. 3–19.
11. The isolated publication of these "prelimiary considerations" in Fornet-Betancourt's *Diskursethik oder Befreiungsethik* (pp. 16–54) has clearly led to a misundertanding. Thus, for instance, Franz Hinkelammert ("Die Marxsche Wertlehre und die Philosophie der Befreiung: einige Probleme der Diskursethik unter der Marxisumskritik Apels," manuscript), confused these "preliminary considerations" with an unpublished lecture which I gave in 1991 in Mexico. Dussel, similarly, misunderstood my position, as is evident from his "Erste Erwiderung an Karl-Otto Apel und Paul Ricoeur" (Porto Alegre lecture, September 1993), and "Re-Lectüre Marx: Aus der Perspective der lateinamerkanischen Philosophie der Befreiung" in *Bremer Philosophica*, 5, 1992, pp. 1–10). In this revised and expanded version of my "preliminary considerations" I will go into the positions of Dussel and Hinkelammert; see notes 74 and 75 of this essay.
12. See E. Dussel, "Re-Lectüre Marx," p. 1.
13. See especially *Capital*, Vol. 1, Chap. 1, Section 4: "The Fetishism of the Commodity and Its Secrets" (New York: Penguin Books, 1990 [1976]), pp. 170ff.
14. Compare my debate with J. M. Buchanan's and K. Homan's conception of a democratically legitimated market economy in Karl-Otto Apel, "Institutionenenethik oder Diskursethik als Verantwortungsethik? Überlegungen zur Begründung der Wirtschaftsethik" in J. P. Harpes, *25 Jahre Diskursethik. Anwendungsprobleme der Diskursethik in Politik und Wirtschaft* (forthcoming).
15. See especially K. Marx, "Zur Judenfrage" (1843), in S. Landshut, ed., *Karl Marx: Die Frühschriften* (Stuttgart: Körner, 1953), pp. 171–206.
16. See "Manifest of the Communist Party"; see note 15, pp. 525–60, and, especially, 527–31.
17. Enrique Dussel, *Philosophy of Liberation*, paragraph 4.4.8.6. Translated from the Spanish.
18. Dussel, *Philosophy of Liberation*, paragraph 2.1.6.3; p. 20.
19. Ibid., paragraph 2.6.9.5.
20. See R. Hilferding, *Das Finanzkapital* (Vienna: Europa Verlag, 1919); J. A. Hobson, *The Evolution of Modern Capitalism* (London: Allen & Unwin, 1949); R. Luxemburg, *Die Akkumulation des Kapitals. Ein Beitrag zur ökonomische Erklärung des Kapitalismus* (Leipzig: Franke, 1921); V. Lenin, *Der Imperialismus als höchste Stadium des Kapitalismus* (Berlin: Verlag Neuer Weg 1946).
21. See especially Immanuel Wallerstein, *The Modern World-System* (New York: Acaolemic Press, 1974); *The Capitalist World-Economy* (New York: Cambridge University Press, 1979); André Gunder Frank, *Capitalism and Underdevelopment in Latinamerica*, rev. ed. (New York: Monthly Review Press, 1969). In addition, see T.T. Evers, and P. v. Wogau, "Lateinamerikanische Beiträge zur Theorie der Unterentwicklung" in *Das-Argument*, 79, 1973, pp. 303–404; I. Sotelo, *Soziologie Lateinamerikas* (Stuttgart: Kohlhammer, 1973). D. Senghaas, ed., *Imperialismus und Strukturelle Gewalt. Analysen über abhängige Reproduktion* (Frankfurt: Suhrkamp, 1972), and by the

same editor, *Abhängigkeit und die strukturelle Theorie der Unterentwicklung* (Frankfurt: Suhrkamp, 1974). F. Cardoso and E. Faletto, *Abhängigkeit und Unterentwicklung in Lateinamerika* (Frankfurt: Suhrkamp, 1976; original Spanish, 1969). See with respect to this thematic the following essays by Dussel, which show how in its quintessence the theory of dependence is derived from Marx: "Marx's Economic Manuscripts of 1861–63 and the 'Concept' of Dependency" in *Latin American Perspectives*, Issue 65, Vol. 17, 1990, pp. 62–101, as well as "Die Essenz der Dependenz: Die Beherrschung unterentwickleter durch hochentwickelte Bourgeoisien und die Übertragung des Mehrwerts" in *Dialektik*, 2, 1993, pp. 99–105.
22. Compare J. Habermas, *Zur Rekonstruktion des Historischen Materialismus* (Frankfurt: Suhrkamp Verlag, 1976). This has been partly translated by Thomas McCarthy in *Communication and the Evolution of Society* (Boston: Beacon Press, 1979).
23. W. Schluchter, *Die Entwicklung des okzidentalen Rationalismus. Eine Analyse von Max Webers Gesellschaftsgeschichte* (Tübingen: Mohr 1979). See also J. Habermas, *Zur Rekonstruktion*, and *Theory of Communicative Action* 2 volumes (Boston: Beacon Press, 1983, 1987).
24. Compare J. Habermas, *The Philosophical Discourse of Modernity: Twelve Lectures* (Cambridge: The Mit Press, 1987).
25. Compare I. Lakatos, "Die Geschichte der Wissenschaft und ihre rationalen Nachkonstruktionen" in W. Diederich, ed., *Theorien der Wissenschaftsgeschichte* (Frankfurt: Suhrkamp, 1974), pp. 55–119.
26. *Selbsteinholungsprinzip* also suggests the following ideas: a retracing, as well as a giving an account of one's own positions through historical reconstruction; literally, to catch up with oneself. Karl-Otto Apel's principle wants to elucidate and formalize the general intuition that historians since Hegel have, namely, that a historical discourse must be able to justify its own argumentative position, as well as that of its opponents, in terms of the internal logic of its very own theoretical constructs. [Translator's note]
27. Compare K.-O. Apel, *Diskurs und Verantwortung*, Index; "Rationalitätskriterien und Rationalitätstheorien" in G. Meggle and A. Wüstehube, eds., *Pragmatische Rationalitätstheorien* (Berlin: de Gruyter, 1994); "The Hermeneutic Dimension of Social Science and Its Normative Foundations" in *Man and World*, 25, 1993, pp. 247–70 (expanded version in K.-O. Apel and M. Kettner, eds., *Mythos Wertfreiheit?* (Frankfurt: Campus, 1994).
28. Compare J. Habermas, *Zur Rekonstruktion*, and K.-O. Apel, *Diskurs und Vesantwortung*.
29. Compare K.-O. Apel, "Types of Rationality Today: The Continuum of Reason between Science and Ethics" in Th. Geraets, ed., *Rationality Today* (Ottawa: University of Ottawa Press, 1979), pp. 307–40, and "Rationalitätskriterien und Rationalitätstypen," in G. Meggle and A. Wüstehube, eds. *Pragmatische Rationalitätstheorien*.
30. Compare K.-O. Apel, *Diskurs und Verantwortung*, especially pp. 154ff and 370ff, and "The Challenge of a Totalizing Critique of Reason and the Program of a Philosophical Theory of Types of Rationality" in D. Freundlieb and W. Hudson, eds., *Reason and Its Other* (Oxford: Berg, 1992), pp. 23–48.
31. Compare K. Jaspers, *Vom Ursprung und Ziel der Geschichte* (Frankfurt: Fischer, 1955). Shmuel N. Eisenstadt, ed., *Kulturen der Achsenzeit I. Ihre Ursprünge und ihre Vielfalt* (Frankfurt: Suhrkamp, 1987), and by the same, *Kulturen der Achsenzeit II. Ihre institutionelle und kulturelle Dynamik* (Frankfurt: Suhrkamp, 1992).
32. See U. Menzel, *In der Nachfolge Europas. Autozentrierte Entwicklung in den*

ostasiatischen Schwellenländern Südkorea und Taiwan (Munich: Simon and Magiera, 1985), *Auswege aus der Abhängigkeit.* Die entwicklungspolitische Aktualität Europas (Frankfurt: Suhrkamp Verlag 1988). D. Senghaas, *Von Europa lernen. Entwicklungsgeschichtliche Betrachtungen* (Frankfurt: Suhrkamp Verlag 1982); U. Menzel and D. Senghaas, *Europas Entwicklung und die Dritte Welt. Eine Bestandsaufnahme* (Frankfurt: Suhrkamp Verlag 1986). T. Hurtienne, "Die Globale Abhängigkeitstheorie in der Sackgasse? Plädoyer für historisch-strukturelle Abhängigkeitsanalysen" in Blätter des *IZW*, 154, 1989, pp. 31–35. G. Hauck, "Modernisierung, Dependencia, Marxismus—was bleibt?" in *Peripherie*, 39/40, 1990, pp. 68–81. See also the literature mentioned in note 34.
33. See, for example, U. Menzel, "Das Ende der 'Dritten Welt' und das Scheitern der grossen Theorie. Zur Soziologie einer Disziplin in auch selbskritischer Absicht" in *Politische Vierteljahresschrift*, 32, 1991, pp. 4–33, with references to the critique to the theory of dependence as presented by H. J. Puhle (ed.), *Lateinamerika. Historische Realität und Dependencia-Theorien* (Hamburg: Hoffmann & Campe, 1977); T. Smith, "The Underdevelopment of Development Literature: The Case of Dependency Theory" in *World Politics*, 31, 2, 1978 pp. 247–88; D. Seers, ed., *Dependency Theory. A Critical Reassessment* (London: Pinter, 1983).
34. See M. Weber, *Die protestantische Ethik*, I, ed. J. Winkelmann (Munich/Hamburg: Siebenstern, 1967), as well as volume II, *Critiques and Anti-Critiques*, by the same editor, 4th rev. ed. (Munich/Hamburg: Gütersloher Verlaghaus, 1982); C. Seyfart and W. Spronde, eds., *Religion und gesellschaftliche Entwicklung. Studien zur Protestantismus-Kapitalismus These Max Webers* (Frankfurt: Suhrkamp, 1973); W. Schluchter, ed., *Max Webers Studie über Konfuzianismus und Taoismus* (Frankfurt: Suhrkamp, 1983), *Max Webers Studie über Hinduismus und Buddhismus* (Frankfurt: Suhrkamp, 1984), and *Max Webers Sicht des Islam* (Frankfurt: Suhrkamp, 1987).
35. P. Arlacchi, *Mafiosiethik und der Geist des Kapitalismus* (Frankfurt: Cooperative, 1989).
36. D. Ribeiro, *Amerika und die Zivilisation. Die Ursache der ungleichen Entwicklung der amerikanischen Völker* (Frankfurt: Suhrkamp, 1985).
37. T. Hurtienne, "Peripherer Kapitalismus und autozentrierte Entwicklung-Zur Kritik des Erklärungsansatzes von Dieter Senghaas" in *Prokla*, 44, 1981, pp. 105–36. D. Senghaas later abandoned the theory of dependence, see the works cited under note 32.
38. Ibid., p. 107.
39. Ibid., p. 121.
40. A. Hirschmann, *Entwicklung, Markt und Moral* (Munich: Carl Hanser, 1989).
41. See, for example, the study by G. Radnitzky, "Markwirtschaft: frei oder social?" in G. Radnitzky/H. Bouillon, eds., *Ordnungstheorie und Ordnungspolitik* (Berlin: Springer Verlag, 1991), pp. 47–75.
42. Hafez Sabet, *Die Schuld des Nordens* (Bad Köning: Horizonte, 1991).
43. E. U. von Weizsäcker, *Erdpolitik, Ökologische Realpolitik an der Schwelle zum Jahrhundert der Umwelt*, 2nd rev. ed. (Darmstadt: Wiss. Buchgesellschaft, 1990).
44. Ibid., p. 117. Galeano as cited in *State of the World 1990. WorldWatch Institute* (New York: W. W. Norton, 1990), p. 140.
45. E. U. von Weizäcker, *Erdpolitikp, Ökologische Realpolitik an der Schwelle zum Jahrhundert der Umwelt*, p. 120.
46. Ibid., p. 120.
47. German edition by V. Hauf, *Unsere gemeinsame Zukunft* (Greven: Eggenkamp, 1987).

48. von Weizäcker, *Erdpolitik, Ökologische Realpolitik an der Schwelle zum Jahrhundert der Umwelt*, p. 122.
49. Ibid., p. 123.
50. See K.-O. Apel, "A Planetary Macro-ethics for Humankind: The Need, the Apparent Difficulty and the Eventual Possibility" in E. Deutsch, ed., *Culture and Modernity: East-West Philosophical Perspectives* (Honolulu: University of Hawaii Press, 1991), pp. 261–78. See also K.-O. Apel, *Ethics and the Theory of Rationality. Selected Essays Volume Two* (Atlantic Highlands: Humanities Press, 1996).
51. See H. Lübbe, *Philosohie nach der Aufklärung* (Düsseldorf: Econ Verlag, 1989), pp. 198ff, and "Sind Normen methodisch begründbar? Rekonstruktion der Antwort Max Webers" in W. Oelmüller, ed., *Transzendentalphilosophische Normen-begründungen* (Paderborn: Schöningh, 1978); as well as my discussion of Lübbe in K.-O. Apel, *Diskurs und Verantwortung* (Frankfurt: Suhrkamp, 1988), pp. 60ff; and the polemic with Lübbe on the theme "Ist eine philosophische Letztbegründung moralischer Normen nötig?" in K.-O. Apel/D. Boehler/G. Kadelbach, eds., *Funkkolleg Praktische Philosophie/Ethik: Dialoge* (Frankfurt: Fischer, 1984), pp. 54–81.
52. See A. Przeworski, "Warum hungern Kinder, obwohl wir alle ernähren könnten? Irrationalität des Kapitalismus-Unmöglichkeit des Sozialismus" in *Prokla*, 78, 1990, pp. 138–71.
53. It is unquestionable that both Hegel and Marx dealt with the problematic of intersubjectivity, that is, of the alienation of human relationships. Nevertheless, this did not lead to a recognition of the paradigmatic and simultaneously complementary distinction between *object-subject and subject-co-subject* relations. See J. Habermas, "Arbeit und Interaktion. Bemerkungen zu Hegels Jeneser 'Philosophie des Geistes'" in his work *Technik und Wissenschaft als Ideologie* (Frankfurt: Suhrkamp, 1968); and his *Theory of Communicative Action*.
54. J. Habermas, *Theory of Communicative Action*.
55. See E. Dussel, *Philosophy of Liberation*, paragraph 2.1.
56. See A. Gehlen, *Urmensch und Spätkultur* (Bonn: Athenäum, 1956), First Part: Institutionen. See also my critical observations in "Arnold Gehlen 'Philosophie der Institutionen' und die Metainstitution der Sprache" in K.-O. Apel, *Transformation der Philosophie*, Vol. 1, pp. 197–222; and also my commentaries in K-.O. Apel/D. Böhler/K. Rabel, eds., *Funkkolleg Praktische Philosophie/Ethik, Studientexte* (Weiheim/Basel: Beltz, 1984), pp. 42–65.
57. See J. Habermas, *The Theory of Communicative Action*.
58. Language [*Sprache*], that is, linguistic communication, is differentiated from any other form of human praxis in that, on the one hand, like other forms of praxis it is dependent on its being institutionalized as a "functional-structural system" which as a semantical system always unburdens the individual from the authentic intentionality of self-expression and world-interpretation through its providing all members of the linguistic community with a common interpretation, which in turn results in a "reduction of the complexity of meaning," but which, on the other hand, participates in the capacity of the human mind for self-reflection, in such a way that it is capable of articulating and making conscious, in an intersubjectively valid manner, its own exteriorization and objectification in a system, as well as in every other systemic exteriorization of human action. This peculiar function of language constitutes the ground on which also rests the possibility, in principle, of recognizing, in the argumentative discourse of the social sciences and philosophy, the institutional and systemic exteriorizations of human praxis as something inevitable but susceptible of control.

59. This is what is suggested, at least as far as I understand it, by systems theory, in the sense Niklas Luhmann has elaborated it as a substitute for the "old European philosophy." See N. Luhmann, *Soziale Systeme*. and *Die Wissenschaft der Gesellschaft*.
60. See note 7.
61. Karl Marx, *Capital* Vol. 1, p. 126.
62. Ibid., pp. 126–27.
63. Ibid., pp. 127–28. Emphasis added.
64. Ibid., p. 128. Emphasis added.
65. Ibid., p. 129.
66. Ibid., p. 130.
67. Ibid., pp. 266ff.
68. Ibid., p. 270.
69. Ibid., p. 270.
70. Eugen Böhm-Bawerk, "Zum Abschluss des Marxschen Systems" in O. Freiherr von Boenigk, ed., *Staatswissenschaftliche Arbeiten*, Festgaben für Karl Knies (Berlin, 1896).
71. E. Bernstein, "Allerhand Werttheoretisches," Vol. II: "Vom reinen Arbeitswert," in E. Bernstein, *Dokumente des Sozialismus* (Frankfurt: Saver & Auvermann, 1968), Vol. V, in particular p. 270; vol. III, "Vom Wesen und Wert des Wertbegriffes," pp. 369 and 464; Vol. IV, "Vom Wert des Wertbegriffes," pp. 557ff.
72. G. B. Shaw, "Wie man den Leuten die Werttheorie aufherrscht" in E. Bernstein, *Dokumente des Sozialismus*, Vol. II, pp. 84ff.
73. Ibid., p. 86.
74. F. Hinkelammert (see note 11) believes that my remarks reflect a "fundamental misunderstanding of the marxist theory of value" but he confirms simultaneously that they express the opinions of the "marginal use" theoreticians and also Böhm-Bawerk (p. 4). My misunderstanding of the Marxist theory of value is said to lie in that I reproach Marx "with abstracting from use-value in his explanation of market-prices," whereas in fact not Marx but the market itself abstracts from the use-value and hence is the "subject of abstraction" (p. 2) The reference to "marginal-use" theory, on the other hand, is said to have lost its relevance today because its opinions have been proven false. It was proven by, for instance, Edgeworth and Pareto, that the "measurability of use-extent" (in contrast to the measurability of labor time) is impossible, which within neoclassical economic thought led to the conclusion of having to abandon value-theory entirely because, in light of this, it was denounced as "metaphysical."

To both of these points I would like to address myself in the following remarks:

Addendum 1. I believe, in fact, like the "marginal-use" theoreticians, that Marx has incorrectly assumed that an explanation of how market prices are determined ought to abstract from "(abstract) utility"—and from the "use-value" of goods—because the market mechanism (as Marx correctly assumed) of price determination abstracts from the "concrete use-values" of goods. This abstraction is indeed also confirmed by bourgeois theoreticians like Paul Samuelson and M. Weber (see Hinkelammert, p. 14ff). The point of this critique of marxism lies in that it can possibly open a perspective to the indispensable achievements and benefits of the market mechanism (especially price signals) that were not considered by Marx (such as, for example, the discovery and mediation of needs and resources): benefits, which, under the presuppositions of an appropriate "framework" (i.e., a "social market economy" on a world scale), could build a deciding counterweight to the admittedly often disastrous "external effects" of the capitalist market system. Were this to be the case, then there would be an alternative to the Marxist presupposition that the market economy must destroy "humanity and nature." On this point, Hinkelammert is still in basic agreement with Marx, but he simultaneously declares "that we today must take as obsolete and utopian the marxist solution of the overcoming the capitalist system" (p. 8). I do not know, then, how he can arrive at an ethically engaged philosophy of economy.

Addendum 2. I do not believe that the now clarified critique of the Marxist labor theory of value must be burdened with all the special assumptions which Hinkelammert supposes I should be committed to; assumptions such as, for instance, the "measurability of use-extent" or the adoption (corresponding contrapuntally to the Marxist utopia) of a bourgeois utopia of an "ideal price system," or, similarly, a deterministic system of equilibrium of "perfect competition" (pp. 8ff). I hold, as Hinkelammert does, that the attempt of the 19th century to understand economy as an exact, value-free, nomological science, in analogy to classical physics, was essentially a project that failed; just as Karl Marx's attempt to understand the "laws" of the economy, in the sense of a macroscopic-dialectical insight into the "necessary path of history"—which in turn implied the possibility of "an unconditional prognosis" (Popper)—also failed.

Hinkelammert is right when claims that the "overcoming of capitalism [would have to be] necessary and inevitable," if one had to suppose, with Marx, that "the capitalist production of commodities created wealth in which the sources of wealth, humanity and nature, are themselves destroyed" (p. 26). However, this presupposition by Marx represents an "unconditional prognosis" of the future of history, something that in my view is methodologically no longer admissible. Furthermore, the implied theory of the "impoverishment" of the proletariat has been contradicted in the leading industrial countries of the North, and this is essentially due to the fact that Marx's presupposition of a free market with respect to the specific commodity, labor power, has been canceled through the intervention of labor unions. There is thus in principle the possibility that the capitalist system of the market economy could be reformed socio-politically, that is, with respect to the "frame-work" conditions, in historically unpredictable ways. (Here lies, in my opinion, the possible starting point for an ethics of the economy.) Admittedly it is this possibility that has—on a world-scale—not been redeemed. Why is this the case?

With this type of questioning, I have introduced the *theory of dependence* as an innovative and earnestly received theory, while also attempting to develop for myself, through a *pro* and *contra* discussion of the literature, a picture of its relevance. For the unbiased reader, one could hardly talk of a "throw-away critique" (Hinkelammert), although one could just as little talk of a definitive assessment. This far I am not yet.

75. I hope in the context of these "preliminary considerations," to have made clear that, in contrast to Dussel's assumption (in his "Response to Apel and Ricoeur," below), for me it is not a question of disputing something like the relationship of the Marxist conception of "living labor" to a "community," but that, instead, it is a matter of suggesting that the life-worldly basis of intersubjectivity that is supposed by Marx—the basis of a *community of producers*—is insufficient for an understanding of the constitution of any market-economic relationships of commodity

exchange. The "essential" presupposition of this last should be, in my view, more complex than it is presupposed by either Marx or Dussel. In the philosophical undercutting of this complexity there lies, however, the dangerous, illusionary and very utopian anticipation of a possible dissolution of the market economy of commodity exchange through a direct (self-transparent) distribution of goods by the community of producers. It is solely in light of this conception, which Dussel clearly shares with Marx (despite the reservations expressed by Hinkelammert), that I have assessed Dussel's "marxism" (and not, as Dussel supposes, by imputing to him some sort of dogmatic marxism-leninism).

However, this discussion shows that, with regard to the concepts of utopia, regulative ideas, ideal models, and "transcendental" (philosophy), or a "transcendental economy," as Dussel once postulated, clarification is still required: one which, in the context of these preliminary considerations, cannot be undertaken.

76. M. Weber, *Gesammelte Aufsätze zur Soziologie und Sozialpolitik* (Tübingen: Mohr, 1924), pp. 508ff. See also W. Schluchter, *Aspekte bürokratischer Herrschaft. Studien zur Interpretation der fortschreitenden Industriegesellschaft* (Frankfurt: Suhrkamp, 1985).
77. I am here basing myself especially on the following section from Vol. 1 of *Capital* ("Fetishism of the Commodity and Its Secret"), which is very telling with regard to what Marx had in mind as an economic system which would come after the overcoming of the capitalist market economy of commodity exchange:

> Let us finally imagine, for a change, an association of free men, working with the means of production held in common, and expending their many different forms of labour-power in full self-awareness as one single social labour force.... The total product of our imagined association is a social product. One part of this product serves as fresh means of production and remains social. But another part is consumed by the members of the association as means of subsistence. This part must therefore be divided among them. The way this division is made will vary with the particular kind of social organization of production and the corresponding level of social development attained by the producers. We shall assume, but only for the sake of a parallel with the production of commodities, that the share of each individual producer in the means of subsistence is determined by his labour-time. Labour-time would in that case play a double part. Its apportionment in accordance with a definite social plan maintains the correct proportion between the different functions of labour and the various needs of the associations. On the other hand, labour-time also serves as a measure of the part taken by each individual in the common labour, and of his share in the part of the total product destined for individual consumption. The social relations of the individual producers, both towards their labour and the products of their labour, are here transparent in their simplicity, in production as well as in distribution. (*Capital*, Vol. 1, pp. 171–72)

78. Karl R. Popper, *The Poverty of Historicism* (London: Routledge and Kegan Paul, 1957); and *The Open Society and Its Enemies: The High Tide of Prophecy*, Vol. 2. (Princeton: Princeton University Press, 1991).
79. See E. Dussel, "Les quatre rédactions du Capital" (see note 5, as well as the works cited in note 6).
80. Marx, *Early Writings*, p. 251.
81. I. Kant, "Über den Gemeinspruch: Das mag in der Theorie richtig sein, taugt aber nicht für die Praxis," *Akademie-Textausg.*, Vol. VIII, pp. 308ff.
82. See Jean-François Lyotard in *Critique*, 456, May 1985, pp. 559ff.

83. O. Marquard, *Schwierigkeiten mit der Geschichtsphilosophie* (Frankfurt: Suhrkamp, 1982), p. 13.
84. Karl-Otto Apel, "Discourse Ethics before the challenge of Liberation Philosophy: Second Part", trans. Eduardo Mendieta Forthcoming in *Philosophy and Social Criticism*, vol. 22, no. 2, pp. 1–25.

9

Response by Paul Ricoeur: Philosophy and Liberation[1]

I have entitled my intervention "philosophy and liberation" and not "philosophy of liberation" so as to not pronounce an *a priori* judgment on the success of the confrontation between those two terms, for I consider their link as problematic. As a justification for my reservation I provide two motivations. First, I admit that every philosophy has liberation as its ultimate goal. This term has received more than one meaning in the course of history, as is demonstrated by Spinoza's philosophy, which assumes that the third type of knowledge is to be considered as liberation, par excellence, of the imagination and of the passions. As a second motivation, it is not only the thematic of liberation which is problematic, but also the situations from which these different positions on liberation are articulated and developed. Thus, the Latin American philosophies of liberation depart from a precise situation of economic and political pressure which puts them in direct confrontation with the United States. However, in Europe our experience of totalitarianism, in its double aspects, nazism and Stalinism—eight million Jews, thirty or fifty million Soviets sacrificed, Auschwitz and the Gulag—serves as a different point of departure.

With respect to the recent history—still underway—of Central and Eastern Europe, it belongs to the annals of a monstrous history. Today, this adventure is lived under all of its aspects as an experience of liberation, as demonstrated by the fall of dictatorships in Germany, Italy, Spain, Portugal, and Greece. No one can deny that it is a question of the experiences of liberation.

It is therefore necessary to consider different thematics, and different original situations. We can talk with this intention, of a plurality of histories of liberation. The question now resides in knowing what it is that each can teach the other, and what one can learn from the other.

With respect to this point, a corollary seems important to me: the philosophies and theologies of liberation that do not depend on this history can no more express themselves in the same terms before and after the collapse of Soviet totalitarianism and after the failure of its supposedly socialist and revolutionary bureaucratic economy.

If I insist on the heterogeneity of the histories of liberation, it is in order to prepare our spirits to admit not only that these experiences are diverse, but perhaps even incommunicable. Furthermore, the self-understanding that is attributed to the one creates obstacles to the full comprehension of the other, and a certain controversy with respect to this intention is perhaps insurmountable for us as well.

I had to make these preliminary clarifications before entering fully into the theme, which will be more philosophical than political, although here political philosophy occupies a broad space, albeit precisely as philosophy. The theme that I would like to discuss is this: What can Western thought contribute of greater and better solidity to a debate in which it accepts being only one of the partners? Here, we are only presupposing the agreement on the search for and reception of the better argument, as is suggested by Apel's and Habermas's discourse ethics. Because, we are by hypothesis in the realm of discourse, although we are not always aware of it, and are conscious that we proceed in a world of struggles that are not precisely struggles of discourses, but of force and violence.

I

I will not take up directly the question of hermeneutics and liberation, to which Domenico Jervolino and Enrique Dussel have allocated ample space. I will come to it only in my concluding observations. Instead, I would rather situate this discussion in which I am implicated too directly, against a broader background whose accent will be on those great Western thematics that are a legacy of a historical experience of liberation. I will remain within the limits of modern philosophy, which Hegel opposes to that of the ancients, defining it in general terms as the philosophy of subjectivity in opposition to the philosophy of substance, which Hegel had the ambition to reunite dialectically. Which elements of this philosophy of subjectivity (from Descartes through Locke, Kant, and Fichte) are bequeathed at the same time as cause and effect of the experience of liberation? It can be said for the moment, and in a general form, that it is to the extent that this has produced an indivisible ethical and political conception of freedom. With respect to this philosophy, I will refer shortly to its limits, but I will underscore above all the reason that demands that I declare that I have no shame of Europe. I will distinguish three components of this ethico-political conception of freedom.

1. Above all, the critique of the sovereign and sovereignty, conceptualized as transcendence, whether in a religious sense or not. This critique of sovereignty, demystified as domination, has extracted its effective experiences from the Enlightenment liberation of the formation of the Italian or Flemish free cities, the establishment and development of the British Parliament, and the

French Revolution. With respect to this, the contractualism of Rousseau and Kant will allow us to understand it as a critical arm: everything appears before its eyes as if power were born of an agreement freely assumed concerning the abandonment of savage freedom in favor of a civilized freedom. This contains a formidable force of subversion.

In fact, there exists in the center of power an opaque point, and around it an aura almost sacred, which Hannah Arendt liked to relate to the distinction Roman thinkers made between *potestas* and *auctoritas*: "Power is with the people. Authority with the senate." In the same way, there is in Spinoza, in his political philosophy, a comparable distinction between *potentia* and *potestas*. Its limit leads to the nakedness of power, which could be the desire to live within a historical community. But this origin is forgotten, and can—within another being who is only symbolically represented through higher forms which is suggested by the word *auctoritas*—augment the public potency which comes to less. From this there comes a struggle without end for the reduction of domination to authentic power; a reduction which is resisted by a residual sacredness that is manifested in the personal access to power and in general in the personalization of power. To which it is necessary to add the slow learning of the separation between the political and the religious, and toward the religious, of the distinction between the ecclesiastical community of the people of God and the authoritarian and hierarchical instance that surrounds it. This first historical experience presents a disquieting paradox: If the critique of domination had not had success, would power, now rendered naked, be feared and believed? It is required that we admit that democracy is the first political regime that knows itself poorly founded because it must be continually justified. With respect to this, the best that Western thought can offer is the crisis of its foundational notions. Perhaps it is the only thought that is at the same time foundational and critical, or better, self-critical.

This affirmation is probably not indifferent to the goals of our debate with Liberation Philosophy, to the extent that this puts the main emphasis on the economic dimension of oppression, more than on its political dimension. As for myself, I see the necessity for a serious warning. If the critique of political and social oppression does not go through the critique of political domination, and if it is pretended to judge economic liberation by any political path, this condemns it to a terrible vengeance by history. Leninism is the example for the left. For the West the path through political liberation appears unavoidable, as has been continuously taught by the totalitarian catastrophe.

2. I would like now to emphasize the search for and crisis of the *concrete universal* in the thinking and in the historical experience of Western Europe. This is a problem that supersedes and comprises the prior, namely, the question concerning the sovereignty of the state. This concerns the rationality of historical experience. In order to introduce the problem I will successively call

up the historical-political writings of Kant, especially the *Idea of a Universal History from a Cosmopolitan Point of View, Conjectures on the Beginnings of Human History* and *Perpetual Peace: A Philosophical Sketch*, and Hegel's *Philosophy of Right*. The notion of universal history is here treated as the regulative idea under which it is possible to think humanity as developing one history, and not inasmuch as it constitutes only one species, albeit this does not reach a universal political institution.

This investigation of the *concrete universal* has halted because of a specific crisis. In order to comprehend this formulation, I will suggest the transfer to the realm of language the attempt by the Kantian and post-Kantian philosophical projects to formulate the universal at the level of the rational plane. Language constitutes a good territory for this exercise, to the extent to which, on the one hand, language does not exist but through the plurality of natural languages, and, on the other hand, its fundamental unity is disclosed thanks to the phenomenon of the possibility of universal translation. This is an *a priori* when we establish that any language can be translated into any other. It is the only way in which we can affirm the universality of language. Now, that which applies at the level of language, applies equally at the level of the moral and political. At the level of the moral, we can easily conceive that a duty is an imperative only if it can be, in one way or another, considered universal. On the other hand, moral life exists only under conditions of cultural contexts that we denominate customs. Between the universality of duty and the historicity of customs there persists a caesura. This fissure is reflected in the element of language, as is evidenced in the contemporary discussion between Rawls and Habermas. The first formulates a purely procedural conception of justice which ignores the historical conditions of its realization. The second projects, within the framework of a universal pragmatics, the idea of an "ideal communication community" which regulates the ethics of the better arguments. But the question remains nevertheless of knowing which contents can be attributed to either one of these ideas, be it to this purely procedural idea of justice, or be it to the conditions of possibility imposed by universal pragmatics. To put it more simply: Which arguments are exchanged in a post-conventional morality? Is it not through the passions, the sentiments, the interests, and the convictions that is shaped what Kant called the maxim of action? I would like to insist on the last term of the preceeding enumeration, the convictions, since it is in through them that conflicts are introduced into discussion, without which negation and the need for arbitration would not be even an issue.

With respect to this, the more respectable convictions that emerge from historic experience generate irreducible controversies. It would appear now that the sign of universality can only be found in the formation of fragile compromises that weave the net of conflicts of the dangerous slope of imminent civil war. Perhaps, with reference to this question, this may be one of the major contributions of Western Europe, namely, the learning of the resolution of conflicts and the invention of the procedure of negotiations and compromise. It will be objected that not everything is discourse. Habermas, not too long ago, evoked the phenomenon of "systematic distortion of communication" under the pressure of money and power. This is true. But the mediation of discourse, of debate and argumentation, remains as our only recourse. It is equally relevant that although the North-South debate derives from relations of domination of another order, that is to say, of an order that is not ethical-political, it would be, just the same, one day or another, a conflict that will need to be arbitrated and treated. Either discourse or violence, as was taught by in testimony by Eric Weil. The consequences of the implications are unavoidable: from the practice of negation to the logic of argumentation, and from this to the ethics of discussion.

3. I would like now to proceed to a third aspect, namely, that of *right* (*diritto*) and *juridical institutions*, which concerns the crisis of the concrete universal, paying close attention to the regulative idea of "justice." The investigation of the principles of justice has a long history, which is also marked by a crisis of great importance. It can be said, although in a general way, that juridical thinking constitutes the condition and the horizon for the formation of a state of the rule of law, and of the practice of negotiation or compromise I mentioned in the preceding paragraphs. I am not only thinking of the considerable labor of passing from reason to action in the elaboration of penal right (to establish the proportional punishment to according to the crime), but also of something that is much more interesting, namely, of civil right (when repairing the damages caused to others by the effects of culpable action). We find that the birth of the idea of responsibility consists in that each one is disposed to render account of their actions, to assume the consequences of their actions, and thus to recognize being obliged to repair the damages caused to others and to suffer the penalty of culpability for something that is considered a crime by society. One cannot but be impressed by the formidable juridical edifice of law codes which have been born out of juridical practices (written laws, courts of law, institutions of judgment of individuals invested with the power to decide the right of particular situations, dispensers of sentences, the monopoly of legitimate violence). Should we denounce the hypocrisy of the law? One may certainly do so. The relations of power and violence do not let themselves be occluded. But, in whose name is the law denounced if not in name of a better justice, in the name of the exigency of more independent and honorable judgments, that is, with the hope of an institution of justice that conforms better to the idea of justice?

This idea leads to an internal critique and to its crisis. Since Aristotle we have distinguished between arithmetical justice, strictly egalitarian, and geometric justice, proportional to merit, which regulates unequal divisions. This distinction continues to impose itself, to the degree that, despite the extension of the sphere of egalitarian justice (equality before the law, right of expression, of gathering, freedom of the press and opinion, etc.), the problem of unequal and unfair (unjust) divisions, operated according to other rules of distribution, remains the central paradox of social justice.

This problem is treated by John Rawls's *A Theory of Justice*. In his purely procedural conception of justice, that of a social contract accomplished under the "veil of ignorance," the idea of justice divides in two: civil and political justice defined as equality before the law, and social and economic justice for the unequal distribution which lends ear to the principle of "maximin" (the principle by virtue of which the increase in privilege of the more favored ought to be compensated by a decrease in the disadvantages of the less favored. Thereof the expression maximin: to maximize the minimum.)

The difficulty is immediately apparent: the heterogeneity of the social goods to be distributed, the aleatory state of every concrete system of distribution, the always contestable character of every order of priority assigned to the satisfaction of goods at the expense of others (productivity, citizenship, education, security, health, etc.). From the dispute provoked by this difficulty, there comes the bifurcation between "procedural universalism" and "contextual communitarianism" which characterizes the contemporary discussion concerning the idea of justice. It will be objected that this discussion concerns only the internal dispute of Western social-democracy. I accept this objection voluntarily. This dispute is the best that we have to offer in this third register of the politics of freedom. I would suggest that it is to the extent that we have been propelled to maximize the resources of social-democracy, with its contradictions and conflicts, that we may be able, inasmuch as one is a valid interlocutor before the protagonists, to select other ways of development (against the simplistic schema of linear development and the search for an arborescent schema of development). Our complex and confused history only allows us to warn our partners in discussion against the temptation to any foreshortening of history. Rawls displays an exemplary firmness in this proposal: one cannot economize the first principle of justice (civil and political equality before the law) and confront with any political means the problem of social and economic justice. Equality before the law is the political condition for economic-social liberation. Do we find ourselves now in a tragic return to leninism?

In the conclusion of this first part, I want to insist on the equivocations of the term liberation. As I said at the beginning, there exist many histories of liberation that do not communicate. If Latin America is confronted by a specific problem which inscribes itself within the framework of North-South relations, Europe is the inheritor of the struggles which have culminated with the liquidation of totalitarianism as illustrated by the words Gulag and Auschwitz. Does this history constitute an obstacle for understanding the Latin American projects of liberation? What is needed is that Europeans admit that the totalitarianism that Latin Americans confront is of a different nature from that which has been known in Europe. These questions ought to remain open. But the reserve and silence that impose themselves should not impede warning our friends that they ought to extract all the lessons from the failure of bureaucratic economy in Eastern Europe, and that they ought not to set aside political freedom in favor of any increase in technological and economic productivity, which ought to be seen instead as components of economic and social liberation.

II

Against this background I would like to return to the *controversy*, hermeneutics-liberation, in which we are greatly implicated, although I will insist more on the problems than on the solutions (mine among others). In essence, we agree with Domenico Jervolino. It is in light of his contribution that I will take up some problems formulated by Dussel.

It is true that the hermeneutic problematic would appear to be extraordinarily distant from the problematic of liberation, in whatever sense this is understood. Is it not from the closure of the text that we have departed? I want to speak with great caution on the legitimacy of the textual transition, even in the situation in which we take liberation as presupposed. It is despite everything, with the favor of an inscription, that writing is the most notable expression, that the past experience of our predecessors comes to us in the form of a received inheritance, of transmitted traditions. It is, in another time and now, under the textual form that the great changes between the past of the tradition and the future of our most alive hopes, according to which our utopias require that they be considered, are founded. I will add now that hermeneutics consists of a struggle against textual closure. With respect to this, Domenico Jervolino has underscored the importance of the functions of the recognition exercised by texts at the level of effective human action. Thanks to this process of recognition, textual critique reinscribes itself at the center of the philosophy of action, which I also consider the great engagement of every investigation relative to language. That which we mentioned about the exchange between tradition and utopia (in the text and through it) has its equivalence in the philosophy of history under the form of the exchange between what Koselleck calls the "space of experience and horizon of hope."

In conclusion, one cannot talk of hermeneutics without situating the process of interpretation within the relation text and reader. With respect to this a critique of reading provides an element of an answer to Dussel's main objection, according to which the producer/produced relation encompasses (*enveloppe*) the author/text relation. In this short-circuit, the vis-à-vis relation that constitutes a critical reader, who may ask about the pertinence of the preceding equation and denounce the relation of domination which is masked in the process of transmission and tradition, is forgotten. The most important phenomenon for our purposes is not so much inscription or writing or, said differently, the *transition from the text to action*, but rather the critical relation of reading that makes possible the *transition from action to the text*.

This transition from the text redirects hermeneutics to ethics, more precisely to an ethics which assigns a central place to the phenomenon of alterity. I allow myself to point out that this is a place for diverse philosophies of alterity: asymmetric for Levinas, reciprocal for Hegel. Here there is also a place for diverse figures of alterity: corporeality, the encounter of the Other, the search for interiorized moral consciousness. Here one may also find the diverse figures of others, others qua face-to-face encounter; others such as the "each one" of the relations of justice. I accept in good will that these figures of alterity, and of the other, may come to be summarized and to culminate in the moment of alterity in which the other is the poor. It is here that the philosophy and theology *of* liberation search for and find themselves.

Note

1. This text is based on the transcript of Ricoeur's answer to Dussel's presentation, occasioned by the seminar "Hermeneutics and Liberation" (chapter 5 above) in Naples, 16 April 1991. The translation is based on the published version, *Filosofia e Liberazione. La sfida del pensiero del Terzo-Mondo* (Lecce: Capone Editore, 1992), pp. 108–15.

10

Response by Enrique Dussel: World System, Politics, and the Economics of Liberation Philosophy

The "fact" that they have reacted to my questions in a critical manner—Karl-Otto Apel orally, in March of 1991, in Mexico, and later in writing,[1] and Paul Ricoeur,[2] at the program of North-South dialogues in Naples—is a novelty. Both are estimable colleagues, and to have accepted a dialogue places them as pioneers in this type of philosophical exchange. Ricoeur's answer was an improvised and extemporaneous reaction to one of my essays (written in Spanish and read in French), where I presented some points on which dialogue might be possible.[3] Apel's answer, on the other hand, was the fruit of a dialogue that began in November 1989[4] continued in Mexico in 1991,[5] and was followed up in August of 1993 in Moscow (at the XIX World Congress of Philosophy), and in September of the same year in Sao Leopoldo (Brazil). That is to say, Apel's text, the first part of a much longer work, is the fruit of a specific type of reflection, on the taking charge of a new problematic by the philosopher from Frankfurt, which in turn puts in evidence his "openness" and creative capacity. The North has not paid any attention to the philosophies of the South when the former departs from its own problematics, from its own reality, and in this Apel is ahead of his own time. Those "excluded" from the hegemonic philosophical communication community are sensible to this "gesture" of acknowledgment, essential for the constitution of the "new philosophical age."

Both texts, Apel's and Ricoeur's, find themselves within the environment of a certain euphoria of the North before the sudden defeat of real socialism in the East. Both pretend to "teach" us people from the South not to *repeat* the political-economic errors already superseded by European history. It would thus appear that I situate myself outside the prevailing "good philosophical tone," when I *return* to superseded, anachronistic, questions. Both authors, however, ought to grow accustomed to the fact that our "reasons" do not form part of the events that lead to the failure of the East, but instead that these reasons, which have existed for five centuries, have their origin in the South. But European and North American philosophers are not used to "listening" to these reasons beyond, or outside, their own horizon of problems. These reasons suggests the benefit of a "provocation," as Apel recognizes.

Ricoeur makes an initial declaration: "I will underscore above all the reasons that demand that I declare that I have no shame of Europe."[6] Apel, on the other hand, with greater experience in the North-South dialogue, writes:

> In my case, these preparations were indispensable because I was forced to disclose gradually the different levels that Dussel's intervention formulated against my own European understanding, specifically West German, and, in the last instance, against my transcendental pragmatic conceptual understanding.[7]

Apel is much more aware of "eurocentrism" than the majority of Euro-North American philosophers, and this awareness is noticeable in his text.

I ought to explain that with both philosophers I have used the strategy of the respectful dialogue "with . . . and beyond":[8] "with Apel . . . beyond Apel,"[9] "with Ricoeur . . . beyond Ricoeur."

10.1 The World System[10] as a Philosophical Problem

Ricoeur states clearly that

> the Latin American philosophies of liberation depart from a precise situation of economic and political pressure which puts them in direct confrontation with the United States. *However, in Europe* our experience of totalitarianism, in its double aspects, nazism and Stalinism [is our point of departure]. . . . It is therefore necessary to consider different thematics, and different original situations. We can talk, with this intention, of a *plurality of histories of liberation*. The question now resides in knowing what it is that each can teach the other, and what one can learn from the other. . . . If I insist on *the heterogeneity of the histories of liberation*, it is in order to prepare our spirits to admit not only that these experiences are diverse, but perhaps even incommunicable. Furthermore, the self-understanding that is attributed to the one, *creates obstacles to the full comprehension of the other*, and a certain controversy with respect to this intention is perhaps insurmountable for us as well.[11]

That is, for Ricoeur the "precise Latin American situation of economic and political pressure" is an "original situation" different from European totalitarianism; they are "incommunicable," or do not "communicate." The contradiction North-South does not touch Europe, and its "totalitarianisms" (Nazi or Stalinist), and, therefore, the Latin American philosophies of liberation have a certain incommensurability with the European ones, even with the recent East European experiences of emancipation. This hermeneutics of incommunicable histories leaves the dominator from the metropolitan center in total innocence with respect to all the cruelties committed in the periphery during the whole of modernity.[12] A French person will recognize that French colonists in Algeria have something to do with France; but just as well the Boers of South Africa with Holland, the *conquistadors* of Mexico and Peru with Spain, those of Brazil with Portugal, the Dutch merchants in Indonesia with the Low Countries, those of Haiti or Martinique (of Franz Fanon) with France, and the Company of the East Indies with England. Not to acknowledge that modernity begins with the expansion and "centrality" of Europe in the history that is thus inaugurated as "worldly"—before civilizations were regional, provincial—is to forget the violence of the European colonization. The colonial period is followed by the neocolonial (for Latin America approximately since 1810). Later on, the modernizing and industrializing processes initiated by the peripheral "populisms" (Vargas in Brazil since 1930, Perón in Argentina, Nasser in Egypt, Sukarno in Indonesia, the Congress Party in India) pretended, thanks to a protectionist nationalist capitalism, to emancipate themselves from the empire. German nazism and Italian fascism in the "center" and the populisms of the periphery are similar economic-political phenomena of the world system inaugurated centuries before by the so-called discovery of America by Europe (for the Amerindians it was the invasion of the continent[13]). Nazism, fascism, and populism attempted "national" liberation within a capitalist regime (for instance, Germany or Italy within the center; Brazil and Egypt within the periphery).

In turn, although in the 16th century Russia was not yet properly a periphery of Europe,[14] the processes of modernization introduced by Peter the First (taking capitalism as his model) and later by Lenin (taking socialism as the model) ought to be interpreted as projects of nations "external" to central Europe (industrialized since the 18th century), and which needed to overcome their backwardness through industrialization and development.

It would be long, but not difficult, to show, *within the modern world system* (that is, since the 15th century), that the populisms (from 1930 to 1955 as a pretension to emancipation by a peripheral capitalism exploited by post-colonial or colonial Europe)[15] have a lot to do with nazism and fascism (capitalist nationalism without "sufficient" colonies in Africa or Asia, in competition with other capitalist nations of the North, which had preceded them in the process of industrialization, such as England and France). Stalinism plays a very well-defined role, if Russia's historical semi-peripheral position is taken into account (it having arrived relatively late to the process of industrialization). Since 1945 (Yalta), the United States has exercised hegemony over world capitalism (including Western Europe and Japan), and therefore the so-called dictatorial regimes of National Security in Latin America (since 1964) have a lot to do with North American domination, not without European complicity, over the world periphery in the era of the transnationalization of capitalism's productivity. If the world hermeneutical "key" of these phenomena is not discovered, and thus is declared incommunicable, then the relation between Nazi or Fascist nationalism (capitalist nationalism in the center), populisms (competing capitalist nationalism in the South)—which Ricoeur does not treat—Stalinism (a model of development of a European semi-periphery), and the Latin American regimes of national security (military totalitarianism which makes viable a dependent capitalism[17]) cannot be seen or surveyed. All of these are different actors, in different scenarios, of a great common horizon: the world system, within the space of the global market, geopolitically dominated by certain states[18] (today, the United States, Western Europe, and Japan), and under the complete military hegemony of the United States.[19]

Schema 1. Some Political Regimes

Forms of Democracy	Capitalism		Socialism	
	Center	Periphery A	Center	Periphery B
Modernizing development without formal democracy	1933 Nazism and European fascism	1930 + Populisms	1917 USSR	
				1959 Cuba
With formal democracy, B	1945 + Postwar European democracies	1955 + Developmentalism		
Dictatorships		1964 + Dictatorships of national security		
Neoliberal formal democracies, B		1983 + Alfonsín (Ar.) Sarny (Br.)	1989	

Clarifications of Schema 1: A, only Latin America; B, electoral democracies with competitive plurality of various political parties; + approximate dates, or only noting the beginning of processes.[20]

The world system is a philosophical problem because Europe confused the evolution of subjectivity within the limits of Europe not only with universality (as much in the morality of Kantian autonomy, as in the supposed post-conventional stage[21]), but also with globality. That is, what Europe came to realize as a center of a world-system (using not only economic wealth, but cultural information) was attributed to its autonomous creativity as a self-enclosed, self-referential, autopoietic system. It not only elevated as universality its European particularity (speaking like Hegel), but it also pretended that the work of humanity "in it" (Europe) was the product of its autonomy and exclusive creativity. Modernity, and modern philosophy with it, never abandoned its eurocentric dream. It never defined itself as a hegemonic center where information is controlled, where the learning of humanity is processed, and where political institutions (political, economic, ideological, etc.) which permit greater global accumulation of wealth in the center (economic, cultural, and all other types of wealth), thus "systematically" exploiting the periphery, are created. Is there a relationship between the wealth of the few and the poverty of the majority? Are these worlds that cannot communicate? Is there no commensurability that may be applied with the goal of establishing poverty as a *factum*, or point of departure, for an ethics, for a practical philosophy? This is exactly the origin of Liberation Philosophy, since it is necessary to co-relate "worlds" apparently uncommunicable in order to obtain a world vision, universal, in relationship to humanity.

The *ego cogito* (of Descartes from 1636) was not the original philosophical expression of modernity. Before, the *ego conquiro* ("I conquer," in first place with Hernán Cortés in 1519 in Mexico) had to undergo the practical experience of Europe's "centrality," of its superiority, which was also expressed in the philosophical debate of Valladolid in 1550. Ginés de Sepúlveda, the modern philosopher par excellence, justified the superiority and violence of modern subjectivity over other cultures. Bartolomé de las Casas, on the other hand, begins the counter-discourse of modernity, not from Europe, but instead from the world periphery. The path had been opened and it would have to be traversed.[22] A complete philosophical historical reconstruction of modernity is necessary,[23] from a world and non-eurocentric perspective. It is for this reason that we indicated that the world system is a philosophical problem, because in it, on the threshold of the 21st century, is deployed the minimal concrete and historical horizon of contemporary philosophical reflection.

10.2 The Pretension to Globality and the Fundamental Insight into the Question of Dependence

Liberation philosophy, in my case, has undergone six moments, which I would like to indicate in order to proceed with this critical reflection. In the first moment (1) the Latin American philosophy student of the 1950s was eurocentric without knowing it. He travelled to Europe in order to be filled with the "wisdom" that he had already studied in books in Argentina. When he arrived in Europe (2), to first Spain (later France and Germany, going through Israel; ten years without returning to Latin America, from 1957 to 1967), he understood immediately place that he was "not European." He discovered himself as Latin American when he left the boat that had brought him from Buenos Aires. This promptly inaugurated the third moment (3) under the perennial question, What does it mean to be a Latin American? And later, how can this *being* Latin American be clarified positively and narratively (historically-philosophically)?

He tried for more than ten years to answer this question (1957–70). The fourth moment (4) constituted the discovery that *being* is intrinsically dominated, and therefore that it was an ethical responsibility to engage in its liberation and to develop theoretically this theme from its negated positivity. This was the first stage of Liberation Philosophy (from 1970 to 1989, approximately). The fifth moment (5) consisted in discovering Europe and the United States (named originally as North Atlantic and later as center) as eurocentric. Although this was suspected since the beginning (1957),[24] now, for the first time, it assumed the clarity of a philosophical theme (ontological, inasmuch as it is a "closure" of the modern world; ethical, insofar as it is always negated with "innocent conscience"). The first work where this theme began to be developed is *The Invention of the Americas: Eclipse of "the Other" and the Myth of Modernity* (university lectures presented in Frankfurt, 1992).[25] It is thus that the sixth moment opens up (6): If Europe is eurocentric without consciousness of being such, this means it has become a provincial, regional culture with a "false consciousness" of its universality. We, from the "periphery," conscious of being thus, and therefore in a situation in which we situate the United States and Western Europe as center, open ourselves for the first time to a globality [*mundialidad*] where Europe and the United States and the peripheral cultures develop a unique *world* history on our small planet. World, global, planetary are the new horizons, which stand beyond eurocentrism and the regionalism of the liberation philosophy of one periphery (only of the periphery or of Latin America[26]). This sixth moment, then, is a "de-centering" of Liberation Philosophy's reflection from the world periphery (from the oppressed woman, the repressed son or daughter, the discriminated races) in order to place itself now in a world "perspective" (a "point of view," a lens, like a microscope or telescope). The "liberation" of which Liberation Philosophy will speak, from this sixth moment on, is no longer solely *Latin American* because of its pretension, but worldly, global; and as philosophy, it is now *philosophy as such, without anything else*, albeit always from the oppressed, the excluded, the discriminated; that is, from the *dis-tinción* (which others have called *differance*), the "exteriority," the "alterity" of the Other.

It is for this reason that Karl-Otto Apel, at the beginning of his critical article already cited,[27] fundamentally believes that he is developing a critique of the so-called Theory of dependence,[28] in whose scientific pretensions (as a "great theory of the left") Apel deciphers as liberation philosophy's point of departure. I have in an *explicit* way denied the theory of dependence's status as a theory, since I demonstrated that it was never formulated as a theory (it does not even use coherent Marxist categories), and, therefore, could not be falsified:

> We can now affirm that in the debate concerning the question of dependence, Marx was frequently notorious in his absence.[29]

No Latin American "dependency" authors explained this phenomenon as a "transfer of value" according to the "law of value"—in Marx's sense—and therefore there never was such a theory. I speak of a concept of dependency, but not of a theory, and of Marx himself.

This means Liberation Philosophy departs from a fact whose "explanation" can be discussed. It concerns a massive fact: the misery of the periphery, which is what Franz Hinkelammert recently called the "goal of knowledge" (*Erkenntnisziel*)[30] of the question of dependency. The contemporary name of the question is the world system, with center and periphery (a *differentiated* periphery, for instance, in the petroleum-producing Arab countries, the "Asian Tigers," Brazil, and Mexico, but, in the last instance, diverse *types* of periphery). What is relevant is that Apel writes now:

> *The number one problem* of world politics and of its corresponding macroethics of the co-responsibility of all human being is and will be the question of the relationship between the First and the Third Worlds due to the insoluble connection between the ecological crisis and the *socio-economic* crisis.[31]

This was the point of departure for Liberation Philosophy since the seventies, given that for it, it was an empirical *factum*. It was always sufficient for us that it was an *empirical* fact, and that nothing more than this was needed, since this was an essential moment of non-philosophical *reality*, from out of which, as peripheral humanity, we ought to philosophize.[32]

With the world system as reality, the planetary claim of Liberation Philosophy departs from an irrefutable fact: the misery of the majority of humanity, 500 years after the "birth" of modernity. Ricoeur himself ends his intervention noting:

> I accept in good will that these figures of alterity, and of the other, may come to be summarized and to culminate in the moment of alterity in which the other *is the poor*.[33]

These agreements, between and with Apel and Ricoeur, serve as an introduction to my approach to the background question.

10.3 Why Marx? Toward a Philosophical Economics

We have had recourse to Marx in our critical texts in the dialogues with Apel and Ricoeur,[34] not because of some fashion—because Marx is no longer in fashion—nor because of some superficial rebelliousness, nor because of a simple anachronism or stubborn dogmatism. On the contrary, up until 1975 we numbered ourselves among the thinkers with strong objections against marxism. The matter concerns the philosophical exigency of coherence with the "reality" of the periphery of world capitalism, such as that of Latin America, which sinks further and further into misery, as both Apel and Ricoeur recognize. A "transcendental pragmatics" is pertinent in a world where science is a relevant phenomenon.[35] A "hermeneutics of the text" is essential to a culture of "cults," of literates, of "readers."[36] I do not deny this. I approve of it. I study it and take advantage of it. Apel and Ricoeur recognize that in the peripheral world of capitalism, 80 percent of humanity, according to the United Nations report on development of 1992, consume 18 percent of the income of the planet. In these immense majorities (I do not speak of minorities) poverty, misery, and the simple reproduction of *life* are perennial problems to be resolved each morning, each day. This brutal, real, irrefutable empirical fact demands not only a transcendental pragmatics, not only a hermeneutics, but *also* an economics (not an "economy": *économie* or *Wirtschaftswissenschaft*, but *économique* or *Oekonomik*), as a fundamental moment (transcendental for Apel, universal for Habermas, ontological for Ricoeur, "metaphysique" for Levinas). It is thus that the objections of Apel and Ricoeur, both of whom depart from the *a priori* that Liberation Philosophy studies Marx because he is Marxist, are erroneous presuppositions and occlude why today we must again have recourse to Marx. The "poor" (lacking institutional and historical means for the reproduction of life[37]) of the planet *demand* (theoretical and ethical demand) a philosophical "economics." That is all!

It is for this reason that we cannot accept the critiques of leninism and *standard* marxism, which Ricoeur as well as Apel impute to me without sufficiently knowing my work. Now I would like to examine Apel's critiques[38] and, in passing, those of Ricoeur.

When Apel and Ricoeur speak of Marxism, they refer to a *standard* marxism I have criticized since the beginning.[39] I thus reject conclusively the expression *Marxist* liberation philosophy. Analogously, when I write that "*Capital* is an ethics," I am not referring to the pedestrian notion of ethics. In my case ethics is a critique of bourgeois morality (and of the bourgeois political economy since Smith) from the exteriority of the Other (from the living labor as person, as poor, as creative source of value).[40]

The question could be formulated thus: Is an analogous reconstruction of Marx's *economics*, such as is being carried out in *pragmatics* (Apel, Habermas, Searle, et al.), possible?

For Liberation Philosophy, Marx is a classic of "economic philosophy" (in addition to being an economist for the economists), a philosophy which was developed as a critique of a capitalist life world whose fundamental structure (and not only as a system) are obstacles to the reproduction of human life. Therefore, Marx departs in his critique from an ideal *community* of producers, out of which a real alienated *society* of producers (capital) is deconstructed. For Marx the essential is not the relation subject of labor/object-nature, but the relation subject/subject as a practical, ethical relationship. His *economics* is a critique from the perspective of an "ideal community" of a capitalist "real society." I have already cited in other works this text:

Response by Enrique Dussel

> Production by an isolated individual *outside society*.... is as much of an absurdity as is the *development of language without individuals living together and talking to each other.*[41]

Just as the speech act presupposes a community, so does production. This is the meaning of the "three stages" in the *Grundrisse*.[42] In an analogous manner, paragraph 4 of Chap. 1 of vol. 1 of *Capital* (1873), the last text to be published during Marx's lifetime, concerns four examples located in two levels (an ideal or transcendental, and another empirical or historical):

> As the foregoing analysis has already demonstrated, this fetishism of the world of commodities arises from the *peculiar social [gesellschaftlichen] character* of the labour which produces them.[43]

The "social" character is not communitarian. Marx departs in his analysis from the critique of solipsism in the Robinson Crusoe mythologies (Schema 2, level A1);[44] that is, it is a question of a critique to an "ideal model," just as presupposed by Smith, which in some way anticipates the "original position" of Rawls (but in the economy). In the second place, Marx goes deeply into "medieval Europe, shrouded in darkness"[45] (Schema 2, level B1). The Robinsonian utopias are ideal models. The Middle Ages are an empirical reality. In the third place, Marx writes:

> Let us finally imagine, for a change, an association of free men, working with the means of production held in common, and expending their many different forms of labour-power in full self-awareness as one single social labour force.[46]

We find ourselves at the level of abstraction of a model, and not of a "future historical moment" (level A2, and not level B3). This is the "third stage" of the *Grundrisse*.

Schema 1. Five Levels in Marx's Critique of Economy

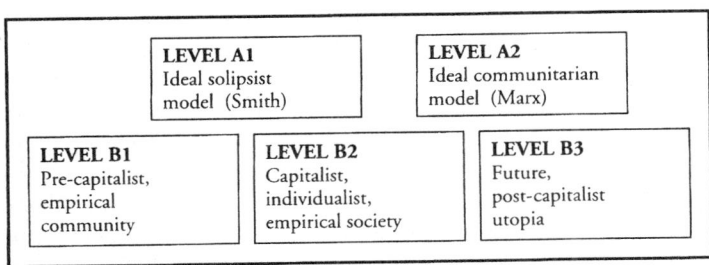

In the same manner, in the classical text on the "realm of freedom," from *Manuscript I*, of Vol. III, from 1865, we ought to locate ourselves at level A2:

> The realm of freedom in fact begins there where work is not determined by necessity or special considerations of efficacy; with respect to the nature of the matter, therefore, it is beyond the sphere of actual material production.[47]

This "realm of freedom," this ideal model (level A2), is transcendental (beyond *all possible modes of production* = empirically or factically impossible). But, in addition, Marx represents it as a community which is presupposed in every act of effective and rational work:

> Freedom in this territory can only consist in that socialized men, *associated producers*, rationally regulate their material exchange with nature, and bring it under their communitarian [*gemeinschaftliche*] control.... But this always remains the realm of necessity. Beyond [*Jenseits*] this begins the development of human capacities... the true realm of freedom... The reduction of the work day is its basic condition.[48]

That is to say, the "perfect community of producers," with zero labor time, is a model, a regulative idea, a type of ideal (level A2), from which real or empirical societies are criticized: capitalism (level B2). In a similar manner, that expression from the *Critique of the Gotha Program*, "From each according to their capacities, to each according to their needs!"[49] is precisely a "model of impossibility."[50] In other words, it is impossible to accomplish this perfectly at an empirical level even with the mediation of institutions (level B3); and if there were such institutions, it would be just as impossible to attempt a numerical approximation between "capacity" for and obligation to work and "necessity" and right to consumption, because we would need an infinite intelligence with infinite speed (Popper) in order to apply this ratio. We would need Kant's *intellectus archetypus*. This also means that a *perfect* capacity for planning would be presupposed, which is impossible, and this is precisely "the transcendental illusion" (to use Hinkelammert's expression). To attempt as factically "possible" (level B3) an "impossible" model (level A2) is precisely to fall into this illusion, into which the great majority of *standard* marxisms fell, and into which stalinism also plunged dogmatically (this, incidently, has nothing to do with Liberation Philosophy, which nevertheless can sustain the opinion that in peripheral capitalism there is no possibility for self-centered and sustainable-from within and without anything else- development). Marx himself denied resolutely that he had proposed a philosophy of history which demanded the necessary fulfillment of determined stages that could be anticipated. Only one example will suffice. Mikhailovskii in 1877 criticized Marx because of his historical-philosophical vision, to which Marx replied:

> He absolutely insists on transforming my historical sketch of the genesis of capitalism in Western Europe into *an historic-philosophical theory* of the general course *fatally imposed on all peoples, whatever the historical circumstances in which they find themselves placed*, in order to arrive ultimately at this eco-

nomic formation which assures the greatest expansion of productive forces of social labour, as well as the most complete development of man. But I beg his pardon. That is to do me both too much honour and too much discredit. . . . By studying each of these developments separately, and then comparing them, one may easily discover the key to this phenomenon. But success will never come with the master-key of a general historico-philosophical theory, whose supreme virtue consists in being supra-historical.[51]

This vision of Marx is unknown by the *standard* marxism of Apel and Ricoeur, but it is precisely the one I have been able to obtain from re-reading Marx as a classic critic of capitalism, so necessary for a liberation philosophy of the poor and excluded yet nevertheless affected.

We now may consider a second level of Apel's critique, namely, the question of value.[52] Apel cites a few lines which are the beginning (*Anfang*, in the Hegelian sense) of the critique of the entire system of categories of bourgeois political economy:[53]

In order to extract value out of the consumption of a commodity, our friend the money-owner must be lucky enough to find within the sphere of circulation, on the market, a commodity whose use-value possesses the peculiar property of being a *source* of value, whose actual consumption is therefore itself an objectification of labour, hence a *creation* of value.[54]

The possessor of money confronts the possessor of labor, establishing thus a practical relation (level B2 from Schema 2) between two persons who are not members of a prior "community" (level B1) but instead are isolated, free, and equal.[55] This confrontation, this face-to-face (think of Levinas and Liberation Philosophy), between him who has money and the "poor," refers us back to the original situation from which Marx departs (and not in John Rawls's sense), which is and real historical and stands in opposition to Adam Smith, when he writes:

[1] In that early and rude state of society which precedes both the accumulation of stock and the appropriation of land. . . . In this state of things, the whole produce of labour belongs to the labourer. . . . [2] As soon as stock has accumulated in the hands of particular persons, some of them will naturally employ it in setting industrious people to work.[56] Every man is rich or *poor* according to the degree in which he can afford to enjoy the necessaries, conveniences, and amusements of human life. But after the division of labour has once thoroughly taken place, it is but a very small part of these with which a man's labour can supply him. The greater part of them he must derive from the labour of other people, and he must be rich or *poor* according to the quantity of that labour which he can command, or which he can afford to purchase.[57]

This theme is treated by Marx, systematically, an at least six other occasions.[58] He deals with the conditions of possibility of "contract,"[59] and describes the confrontation between two owners as unequal, non-equivalent, the product of a previous violent history.[60] This is a matter of the practical question of interpersonal relationships,[61] from which Marx describes the alienated situation of labor. It is for this reason that he placed so much importance on the presuppositions of contract:

> The separation between the property [of money] and [the property of] labor appears as the necessary law of exchange between capital and labor. As *non-capital, non-objectified labor*, the capacity for labor appears: 1) Negatively, as non-raw material, non-instrument of work.... This complete denudation is the possibility of private labor of all objectivity.[62] The capacity for labor as *absolute poverty* [*als die absolute Armuth*].... 2) Positively.... Work not as an object, but as activity, as living source of value [*als lebendige Quelle des Werths*].... Work, which on the one hand is absolute poverty as object, on the other is the universal possibility of wealth as subject and activity.[63]

The poor (for Smith and Marx), before being wage-earners and subsumed by capitalism, are the condition of the possibility of the existence of capitalism itself. Capital is, in the last instance, a "social *(gesellschaftliche)* relation (level B2), non-communitarian (level A2), justified by the legitimating model of capitalist political economy (level A1, which includes Rawls and, in part, Ricoeur and Apel, inasmuch as both are not critical of this model).

The practical "relation" between the owner of capital ("rich" for Smith) versus the owner of labor ("poor") is a quasi-natural relation for the philosophy articulated by capitalism; it is a *factum* of practical reason which is not questioned (and to which the "maximin" is applied). For Marx, instead, this relation is a fruit of the historical structures which determine it. The point of departure is not something natural. It is a *historical* point of arrival. For Latin America, a continent of "poor,"[64] just as with Africa and Asia, this question is central, essential. The "poverty" of our continents is not a point of departure (due to some uncongnizable self-incurred immaturity[65]), but the point of arrival of five centuries of European colonialism (within the world system, in which the United States is today hegemonic), of which Ricoeur, I think, should be ashamed (the holocaust of 15 million Amerindians, 13 million African slaves; Asians, objects of colonial wars, the Opium War. Algeria, South Africa). At the individual level the poor are "alienated" (subsumed) in capital as an instruments, as a mediation of the "valorization of value." At the world level, the poor are the exploited periphery. There are diverse ways of accumulating value (as surplus value or as transference of value from the periphery to the center). This "social relationship" (level B2; non-communitarian, level A2) in the interpersonal is the relation that informs the relations between isolated individuals in daily life (*Lebenswelt*) prior to any Habermasian system. Marx locates himself at the constitutive level of the life world (*Lebenswelt*) itself, which explains his relevance as a philosopher of daily life in capitalism. To conclude this point, I would like to repeat that for Marx is the person-to-person relationship is essential:

> The possession of nature is always already mediated through his existence as a member of a *community* ... a relationship to other human beings, which conditions his relation to nature.[66]

Now we can touch on the objection of Apel, who departs from Marx's following text:

> As use-values, commodities differ above all in quality, while as exchange-values they can only differ in quantity, and therefore do not contain an atom of use-value."[67]

The page which contains this text of 1872–73, included in the second edition of *Capital*, Vol. 1, indicates a new distinction which had not been made clear in the first edition of 1867. In the first edition Marx had written, in note 9:

> In the following, when we use the word *value* without any other additional determination, we refer always to *exchange-value*.[68]

In the second edition, note 9 is eliminated, and in its place the distinction between "value" and "exchange-value" is made for the first time in the theoretical life of Marx:

> The progress of the investigation will lead us back to exchange-value as the necessary mode of expression, or form of appearance, of value. For the present, however, we must consider the nature of value independently of its form of appearance [*Erscheinungsform*].[69]

This means that in 1873 Marx distinguishes the following levels:

Schema 3. Labor as the "Substance"[70] of Value

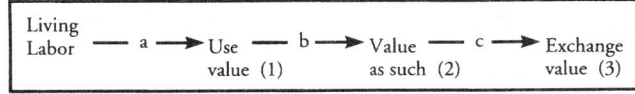

In this schema, concrete labor (or nature) produces (a) *materialiter (stofflich)*, material use value (1), as the concrete quality of a thing. Abstract human labor (already in the *social* relationship of capital, without a presupposed community) produces (b), as a *formaliter* objectification, value as such (2). The *potentialiter* value appears (c) as exchange value (3) in exchange, in the actual relation with another person (person-to-person relationship, intersubjectivity) in the market, as a moment of the commodity in the interpersonal relationship. In this case, the exchange value is a "mode of expression" or "form of appearance" (*Erscheinung*= phenomenon for Kant or Hegel) of value in the "world[71] of commodities."

The commodity, as a thing (*Sache*), has a quality (the relation between the *material* constitution of a thing and human necessity, namely, utility, (*Nützlichkeit*). Otherwise, this quality is a *material* determination (*determinatio* for Spinoza) of a thing as an object of need.

Value (2), as objectification (*vergegenständlichung*) of labor (*potentialer*), can appear or present itself in the actual *social* relationship between persons (*formaliter*), in the world of commodities, as an exchange value (3). However, in *a strict sense*, these levels cannot be confused. Therefore it is necessary to distinguish the aspects: the exchange value (economic) does not have an atom (formally) of useful use value (materially).

But it is evident that value, as the formal objectification of abstract labor, has a material bearer (*materiellen oder stofflichen Träger*): in first place the thing, in second place the use value.[72] Without use value there is no commodity. But the material level of use value (as a thing) is not the formal level of exchange value (social, economic level). Hence the metaphor which has been used: exchange value does not have *formally* any atom of use value. Both levels are formally different.

In addition, Apel confuses the semantic content of "utility" (*Nützlichkeit*) in Marx with that of later commentators such as William Jevons, Karl Menger, Leon Waldras, or Eugen Böhm-Bawerk. For Marx utility is primarily (*materialiter*) established in the following sequence:

Schema 4. Sequence from Labour to Consumption

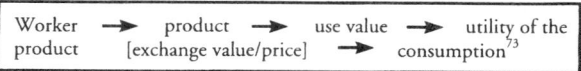

The later commentators reversed the sequence (pure *formaliter*):

Schema 5. Sequence from Labour to Consumption

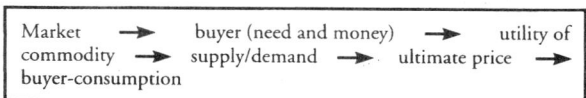

W. Stanley Jevons, in *The Theory of Political Economy* (1871, four years after the first volume of *Capital*), writes:

> The science of Political Economy rests upon a few notions of an apparently simple character. Utility, wealth, value, commodity, labour, land, capital, are the elements of the subject.... Repeated reflection has led me to the somewhat novel opinion, that value depends *entirely upon utility*. Prevailing opinions make labour rather than utility the origin of value; and there are those who distinctly assert that labour is the *cause* of value."[74]

The formation of value depends entirely on the "pleasure or pain,"[75] the "feeling" of the buyer:[76] the greater the pleasure, the greater the utility, the greater the value, the greater the price (it is an increase in "demand"). It is thus that there is a "degree of utility" (*Nützlichkeitsgrad*)[77] which determines value. As can be seen, the categories depart from already given capital, from the market and the buyer. It is a tautology from the pre-existence of capital. The worker, the producer, has disappeared and only leaves a trace of itself as "human capital," as "wage" (a number among many: the person of the worker, the principally "affected" has been "excluded" from the community of economic decisions).

For Marx, on the contrary, utility is the use value of the product (a thing as such, before it becomes a commodity) of work for the *needs of the worker* (this is Adam Smith's first situation of a state of nature [A1], Schema 2). In this case utility is determined by the *anthropological* need of the worker, prior to capital. For Apel, as for Böhm-Bawerk, utility is that of the buyer,[78] and this is measured by the intensity of preference or desirability (*Wünschbarkeit*) of the buyer in the market. In this case utility is determined as a moment of capital: "from out of the market."

It is evident that for the Amerindian of the *encomienda* and the Black slave of the *Ingenios*, for the colonies in the Third World, for over-exploited workers (as shown by Mauro Marini in Latin America[79]), Marx has categories and perspectives which are far more relevant and pertinent to the development of an "economics" (ethical-philosophical economics) than do the commentators or the neo-liberals, who affirm as an empirical fact "the market's tendency to equilibrium" (Hayek). On the contrary, the market shows profound instabilities and lack of equilibrium, which become even more abysmal between the center and the periphery, and which the capitalist system can make only make more acute and deeper.[80] Utility constituted from the desirability of the buyer is always in equilibrium or tends to it (in neo-liberal ideology), apparently. The ethical question begins when we formulate the massive fact of the "basic needs" of the miserable majorities of the planet who are not solvent, who cannot be part of any market.

10.4 There is No Economics without Politics nor Politics without Economics

With reason does Ricoeur insist that an economics is not possible without a politics. I have always held this to be a given.[81] But if in front of Apel, Habermas, Ricoeur, and other philosophers of the center I expound the importance of economics, it is because the hegemonic philosophies (phenomenology, analytical philosophy, hermeneutics, pragmatism, etc.) do not deal with economics.[82] What is the cause for this forgetfulness? In the center, Habermas expresses it explicitly:

> In advanced capitalist countries the standard of living has, in any cases, risen to such an extent, at least among broad strata of the population, that the interest in the emancipation of society can no longer be articulated directly in *economic* terms. *Alienation* has been deprived of its palapable economic form as *misery*.... thus today Marx would have have to abandon his hope that theory can become a material force, once it has taken hold of the masses.[83]

This is Apel's position as well. Ricoeur, in contrast, has other reasons. In our conversation at Chicago, prior to our dialogue in Naples, I asked him why he had not undertaken, as in hermeneutics, the "circuitious way" (*voie longe*) of an economics? To which he responded that economics is a difficult science, with its own presuppositions, and one to which he had not been able to dedicate a lot of time. I believe there is something else. Ricoeur has carried out a titanic work of interpretation of the "text." But to the reproduction of life, at its economic and productive levels, he has never dedicated an important work. In *Du text à l'action* it would appear that he is going to deal with the theme in a final reflection. He even makes a schema on ethics, politics and economics.[84] There he deals with the question in approximately the same terms as those of the critique, or warning, which he made to us in Naples:

> This reduction of the political to the economical is responsible for the lack of interest, so accentuated in marxist thinkers, for the specific problems which are formulated with the exercise of power: a problem eminently political.[85]

That is, Ricoeur struggles against the economicism of *standard* marxism, and defends the importance of the political. I agree with Ricoeur's position. However, he does not answer my critique, namely, why Ricoeur has not developed an economics.

For Ricoeur, what pertains to economics is abstract, is a sub-system of the political (has he perhaps not fallen into a politicism?):

> In a certain sense, the economic-social plan is an abstraction in the measure to which the economic life of a nation is incorporated in the political by the decisions taken by the state.[86]

Is there not a partial consideration of the economic in Ricoeur? Is there no need for a more precise reflection on the logic of human "life," the person-to-person relations at the level of the reproduction of history as life, of labor, the concrete economic structures as such, etc.?[87]

The same takes place in Habermas. At the beginning of *The Theory of Communicative Action*, he indicates why sociology[88] is of greater interest to his philosophical reflection than economics:

> *As* political economy, economics still held fast at the start to the relation to society as a whole that is characteristic of crisis theories. It was concerned with questions of how the dynamic of the economic system affected the

orders through which society was normatively integrated. Economics as a specialized science has broken off that relation. Now it concerns itself with the economy as a subsystem of society and absolves itself from questions of legitimacy. From this perspective it can tailor problems of rationality to considerations of economic equilibrium and questions of rational choice.[89]

Exactly; political economy is what Marx called economics (*Oekonomik*); this was later transformed into the science of economics (*Wirtschaftswissenschaft*). What I am speaking of, since the beginning of the dialogue with Apel and Ricoeur, is that economics which has a relation to global society (*Lebenswelt* and system), but not just inasmuch as it is a theory of crisis, but also as the foundation for "everything pertaining to the economic": from an anthropology, and an ethics, to an ideal community of producers, level A2, which can criticize the factical society of the capitalist system (and equally, Stalinist real socialism).

In an Apelian manner, I have expressed it in the following manner, in the work "Toward a North-South Dialogue":

> Who *works* can be led to recognize or be convinced through self-reflection that, as a producer, he or she necessarily has recognized an ethical norm. This ethical norm can be made explicit in the following manner: who *works* has already attested *in actu*, and with that has recognized that practical reason is responsible for human action; that is, that the claims to *justice* can be and ought to be satisfied through *acts-of-work*, which are not only technically adequate, but also practically *just*.

For Liberation philosophy, which begins with massive *misery* (a point of departure very different from of Habermas's, which is the late capitalism of a "minority" of humanity), it is essential to develop an economics which integrates ethics as a founding moment of its development—and not, as is the case with the "science of economics" (for example in Friedrich Hayek), for which the death of entire peoples who cannot compete in the world market is of no moral concern, and which leaves it entirely immune from any responsibility because marginality does not fall within the sphere of the "science of economics."

I accept Ricoeur's suggestions and warnings. In fact, I presupposed them, and I think that an economics without politics is irrational, a totalitarian economicism, unjustifiable for a liberation philosophy. But, at the same time, I am "warned" of a certain "politicism" in Habermas, Ricoeur, et al. This politicism is also frequent in Latin America, but for other reasons. It is thus that my insistence on the economic has two fronts: the European and the Latin American. In fact, during the phase of national security dictatorships (see Schema 1), a certain theory[90] for and consensus in favor of "democracy" gestated (sustained as much by the left, in crisis, as by the bourgeois, discarded by the military, since the neo-liberal and transnational project did not need an alliance with the peripheral national bourgeois). Thus there emerges a strong current of theoretical reflection on democracy in Latin America,[91] but, in general, without links to an innovative economic project, since it continues to support the neo-liberal military project, which continues to increase the growing impoverhsment of the majority. With the election of Alfonsín in Argentina in 1983 there begins a period of democracy in the eighties. But governments elected popularly have not modified the economic project of the dictatorships. On the contrary, they have propelled a certain neo-liberalism (as with Salina de Gortari, Menem, Fujimori, de Mello, Carlos Perez), and have dismantled the institutions of the populist and developmentalist welfare states, plunging deeper into poverty greater masses of people than during the dictatorships. This reason why, after ten years of *formal* democracies, the claim and call for a concern with the economic level is philosophically, ethically, and objectively relevant. On the other hand, the unpayable external debt incurred by the military dictatorships and deeply corrupt civil governments, and the painful mechanisms of the transnational banks in the central countries, require a certain "legitimacy" of the paying governments. The people were made responsible for electing democratical governments in order to pay a debt which they did not contract and from which they derived no benefit. *Formal* democracy, of which we must applaud many positive aspects, covers up also a great injustice.

It is for this reason that Latin American political philosophy ("politics"), when this is responsible and ethical, ought to be articulated (studying its *mutual conditionality*) through an economic philosophy ("economics").

Today in Latin America, to speak of democracy or politics is not enough. What is necessary is a social or material-economic democracy, and a political philosophy articulated adequately through an economic philosophy.

Now we can understand what it can mean to a philosopher of the periphery when the "warning" or "suggestion" is enunciated in the following manner:

> Our complex and confused history only allows us to warn our partners in discussion against the temptation to any foreshortening of history.[92]

We can only make some remarks. In first place, if the history of Europe is complex and confused, ours, for being colonial (that is, has its own history, but is nevertheless determined by foreign metropoleis) is even more complex and confused. In the second place, it is a question of not repeating the five centuries of modernity (so as to arrive in the year 2500 at the European present).[93] Instead, it is necessary to be able to undertake *one's own path of development*, different from the European (because up to the present we have been the other face of the same system, but the exploited, dominated, dependent face); and therefore, structural and in-depth changes cannot be ruled out *a priori*.[94]

Notes

1. See "Die Diskursethik vor der Herausforderung der *Philosophie der Befreiung*. Versuch einer Antwort an Enrique Dussel" in Raúl Fornet-Betancourt, ed., *Diskursethik oder Befreiungsethik?* (Aachen: Augustinus Buchhanollung 1992), pp. 16–54. Chapter 8, above, is a revised and expanded version of this essay. The program of dialogues was organized and coordinated by Raúl Fornet-Betancourt.
2. See Paul Ricoeur, "Filosofia e Liberazione" in *Filosofia e Liberazione. La sfida del pensiero del Terzo-Mondo* (Lecce: Capone Editors, 1992), pp. 108–15. In this book, chapter 9.
3. See chapter 5, above.
4. See Fornet-Betancourt, ed., *Ethik und Befreiung* (Aachen: Augustinos Buchhandlong, 1990).
5. Fornet-Betancourt, ed., *Diskursethik oder Befreiungsethik?*
6. See "Filosofia e Liberazione," p. 109.
7. Apel, "Die Diskursethik vor der Herausforderung der 'Philosophie der Befreiung,'" in Fornet-Betancourt, *Diskursethik oder Befrelungsethik* pp. 17–18.
8. Apel speaks of "with Popper against Popper," "with Habermas, against Habermas." I do not wish to speak of against, but instead of beyond, that is, departing from their own presuppositions in order to transcend them (which is in *great part* possible with Apel and Ricoeur, and which is not the case with Rorty, for example). Liberation Philosophy, because of its having its own point of departure, can use different discourses for its own goals (this does not mean eclecticism, but the selection of other discourses in order to incorporate them to an architectonic that is its own, and has its own autonomy and logic).
9. Apel attempts to do this when he locates me at the level of "the complementarity principle C," but we will see how the dialogue proceeds.
10. This is I. Wallerstein's phrase *The Modern World-System* (New York: Academic Press, 1917, Passim). "World system" (*Weltsystem* or *Système-monde*) indicates a category similar to that of the "universal concrete" in Hegel, as when it is spoken of as *Weltgeschichte*; *Welt* is not *Allgemeinheit* (abstract universality) but the "planetary," a "concrete" that is the sum of all nations but also supranational and international.
11. See Ricoeur in this book, chapter 9, pp. 205–6. Emphasis added. Ricoeur will give us philosophers from the South some "advice," although it is not clear what he has learned from the South. Not to be "shamed" by Europe would appear to have led him not to have learned anything outside Europe. And in this sense he will add later on: "As I said at the beginning, there exist many histories of liberation that do not communicate. If Latin America is confronted by a specific problem which inscribes itself within the framework of North-South relations, Europe is the inheritor of the struggles which have culminated with the liquidation of totalitarianism as illustrated by the words Gulag and Auschwitz. Does this history constitute an obstacle for understanding the Latin American projects of liberation? What is needed is that Europeans admit that the totalitarianism that Latin Americans confront is of a different nature from that which has been known in Europe. These questions ought to remain open. But the reserve and silence that impose themselves should not impede warning our friends [here a certain eurocentric paternalism is made evident] that they ought to extract all the lessons from the failure of bureaucratic economy in Eastern Europe, and that they ought not to set aside political freedom in favor of any increase in technological and economic

productivity, which ought to be seen instead as components of economic and social liberation" (p. 114).
12. This is the background *philosophical* thesis in my work *The Invention of the Americas: Eclipse of "the Other" and the Myth of Modernity* (New York: Continuum, 1995). A translation of the first chapter has appeared in English in John Beverly and José Oviedo, eds., *The Postmodernism Debate in Latin America: A Special Issue of boundary 2*, 20, 3, Fall 1993 (Durham: Duke University Press, 1993).
13. See Dussel, *The Invention of the Americas*, fifth lecture.
14. I. Wallerstein documents this very well in his work in *The Modern World-System* title Vol. 1, Chap. 6.
15. See my "Estatuto ideológico del discurso populista" in *Praxis latinoamericana y Filosofía de la Liberación* (Bogota: Nueva America, 1983). pp. 261–305.
16. This model failed, but it attempted by less developed nations, such as Russia, which tried to industrialize themselves within an instrumental rationality very similar to that of capitalism, with the disadvantage that once the market was eliminated, and thus competition, they did not have at their disposal a mechanism for technological innovation. Furthermore, they imprisoned themselves within the vicious circle of an excessive anti-democratic bureaucratization.
17. Whereas "populism" is an it attempt at an *autonomous* capitalism (where its principal enemy was England before World War II, as it was later for nazism), the military dictatorships, since 1964, organized, an anti-nationalist capitalism or one "dependent" upon North American hegemony.
18. This global "politics" is invisible to the "political" analyses of European-North American philosophers, from John Rawls to Jürgen Habermas. These States are, on the one hand, the inheritors of colonialism initiated in the 15th century under the diachronic hegemony of Portugal, Spain, Holland, France, England, and lastly the United States (shared with the former USSR from 1945 through 1989). A "political philosophy" cannot forget this concrete-historical horizon with "global" reach, lest it turn unconsciously eurocentric.
19. This aspect is ignored in all European-North American political philosophies. My *Philosophy of Liberation* begins by talking of war as "the father of everything" since Heraclitus and up through von Clausewitz and Kissinger (Dussel, *Philosophy of Liberation* (Maryknoll: Orbis Books, 1985) p. 1.
20. See some of my works on political philosophy: my doctoral thesis in political philosophy, which I defended at the University of Madrid, *La problemática del bien común, de los presocráticos a Kelsen*, v. I–III (Madrid, 1959); Vol. IV of *Filosofía ética latinoamericana*; and the following articles: "Pobreza y civilización" (Paris, 1962), in *América latina, dependencia y liberación*, pp. 144–51; "La propiedad en crisis" (París, 1963), in: *América Latina, dependencia y liberación*, pp. 178–89; "Democracia latinoamericana, socialismo y judeocristianismo" (Paris, 1964), in *América Latina, dependencia y liberación*, pp. 152–60; "Hipótesis para el estudio de latinoamérica en la historia universal" (1966) (Universidad del Nordeste [Resistencia], reprinted in *Método para una filosofía de la liberación*, pp. 213ff; "Cultura, cultura popular latinoamericana y cultura nacional" in *Cuyo* (Mendoza) 4, 1968, pp. 7–40; "De la secularisation au sécularisme de la science, de la Renaissance au XVIIIe siècle" in *Concilium* (París), 47, 1968, pp. 81–101; "Elementos para una filosofía de la política latinoamericana" in *Revista de Filosofía latinoamericana* (Buenos Aires), 1, 1975 pp. 60–80; "La divinización del imperio o de la filosofía de la religión de Hegel" in *Nuevo Mundo* (Buenos Aires), 9–10, 1975, pp. 81–101; "Church-State Relations in Peripheral Latin American Formations" in *The Ecumenical Review*

(Geneva), 29, 1977, pp. 24-34; "Hipótesis para elaborar el marco teórico de la historia del pensamiento latinoamericano. Estatuto del discurso político populista," Conclusiones del Seminario sobre categorías políticas tenido en el Centro de Estudios Latinoamericanos (Mexico: UNAM, 1976), in *Ideas y Valores* (Bogotá, Universidad Nacional), 1977, 50, pp. 35-69; "Filosofía de la liberación y revolución en América Latina" in A. Cuevas, E. Dussel et al., *La filosofía y las revoluciones sociales* (Mexico: Grijalbo, 1978), pp. 25-53; "La chrétienté moderne davant celui que est autre. De l'Indien 'rudo' au 'bon sauvage'" in *Concilium* (Paris) 1978, pp. 65-76; "Basic Rights, Capitalism and Liberation" in *Human Rights. Abstracts of Papers from the Tenth Interamerican Congress of Philosophy*, Tenth Interamerican Congress of Philosophy 18-23 Octubre 1981 (Tallahassee: Florida State University, (1982), p. 33; "Un rapport sur la situation du racisme en Amérique Latine" in *Concilium* (Paris), vol. no. 1982, pp. 89-97; "Christians and Marxists in Latin America," síntesis publicada por *Newsletter from CAREE*, Bulletin 24, 1984; "Cultura latinoamericana y filosofía de la liberación. Cultura popular revolucionaria más allá del populismo y del dogmatismo" in *Ponencias, III Congreso Internacional de Filosofía Latinoamericana* (Bogotá: USTA,1985), pp. 63-108; "El nacionalismo: Hacia una teoría general" (1992), published in the minutes of the philosophy weekly, *Pontevedra* (España), 1992; "Europa, Modernidad y Eurocentrismo" (1993), forthcoming in *Filosofar Latinoamericano* (Montevideo), y Istituto Filosofico (Napoli), 20, p.

21. A certain European-North American "conventionality" and "contractualism" (with all the naivete that these presupposed, what Marx referred to as the utopias of Robinson Crusoe) are thus sustained, which make themselves evident at all moments, especially when it is attempted to "descend" to the level of the "application" (*Anwendung*) of basic norms, and the necessary conditions for it are not given.
22. In the second conference of, *Toward the Origin of the Myth of Modernity*, I develop this argument philosophically and historically.
23. See chapter 7 above.
24. Between 1959 and 1961 I spent two years in the Middle East (especially in Israel where I studied Hebrew). In 1961 I wrote *El humanismo semita* (Buenos Aires: EDUEBA, 1969), in contraposition to my other work from the same period, *El humanismo helénico* (Buenos Aires: EUDEBA, 1976). As a Latin American, it was necessary to supersede hellenocentrism in order to liberate the possibility of a Latin American philosophy. When I now read the work of Martin Bernal, *Black Athena. The Afroasiatic Roots of Classical Civilization*, Vol. One (New Brunswick, N.J.: Rutgers University Press, 1987), I discover something that I had intuited since my first stay in Europe: the German romantics (since Winckelmann, Goethe, Humboldt, Schlegel, and certainly Hegel) needed to "invent" an Aryan, autopoietic Greece. They displaced the African Egypt, and constructed the Indoeuropean myth which grounds the ideology which culminated in nazism (where the University of Berlin and the Gymnasium acted as mediators). This is an entire "construction" that does not precede the 18th century, and of which philosophy, just as it is taught presently, is the fundamental ideological axis.
25. Enrique Dussel, *The Invention of the Americas: Eclipse of "the Other" and the Myth of Modernity* trans. Michael D. Barber (New York: Continuum, 1995)
26. My ethics, published in 1973, carried the title of "Toward an Ethics of *Latin American* Liberation." This indicated the maximum horizon of claim or validity. It was an ethics that emerged from Latin American regional culture and did not yet have (although it suspected it and put it in evidence) a "world claim."
27. See chapter 8, above, p. 163-204.

28. On the "theory of dependence" see Chap. 15, "Los *Manuscritos del 61–63 y el concepto* de dependencia" in my *Hacia un Marx desconocido*, pp. 312–62; translated as: "Marx's Economic Manuscripts of 1861–63 and the 'Concept' of Dependency" in *Latin American Perspectives* (Los Angeles), 17, 2, 1990, pp. 61–101.
29. Ibid., p. 312.
30. From Franz Hinkelammert see "Die Marxsche Wertlehre und die Philosophie der Befreiung: einige Probleme der Diskursethik und der Marxismuskritik Apels," unpublished (San José, 1993), p. 21, under the question: "Was aber ist das Erkenntnisziel der Dependenz-theorie? Apel fragt nicht einmal danach. Er unterstellt ihr seine eigenen Erkenntnisziele und fragt dann, ob sie darauf antwortet. Tut sie es nicht, so gilt sie nicht."
31. Ibid., p. 37.
32. With respect to the refutation of Apel's most important objections against the theory of dependence, I cede the word to the philosopher and economist Franz Hinkelammert, in the work cited, and to Hans Schelkshorn, in his contribution presented at the seminar which we organized in Frankfurt, December, 1992. This is still not published.
33. Ibid., p. 115.
34. See some of my already cited works: "La introducción de la *Transformación de la Filosofía* de K.-O.Apel," paragraph 4.3, in Karl-Otto Apel and Enrique Dussel, eds., *Fundamentación de la ética y Filosofía de la Liberación* (Mexico: Siglo XXI, 1992), pp. 71ff. The expression "life community" disconcerted Apel. For this reason, I returned to the topic again and again: see chapter one, section four; chapter two, section four; chapter three, section four; and chapter five, section four; and Chap. 8 of *Las metáforas teológicas de Marx*, entitled "De la económica a la pragmática." Here we only intend to answer some fundamental aspects of Apel's objections, and some of Ricoeur's.
35. See, for instance, by Apel, "Notwendigkeit, Schwierigkeit und Möglichkeit einer philosophischen begründung der Ethik im Zeitalter der Wissenschaft" in P. Kanellopoulos, ed., *Festschrift für K. Tsatsos* (Athens: Nomikai Ekdoseis Ant. 1980), pp. 215–75. In this essay he wrote: "With respect to *the ecological crisis*, which today represents the greatest problem for humanity . . ." (p. 215). Today we see that the number one problem is poverty linked to the ecological question.
36. In addition, the great universal religions (Christianity, Islam, Judaism, Buddhism, Hinduism) are religions of the "text," and Ricoeur knows this very well.
37. The concept of pauper, frequently written in Latin by Marx, is not a metaphorical, religious, or folkloric category; it is an analectical-economic concept for Marx. It is the person, the "living labor" inasmuch as it is excluded in its relation to capital, once his traditional possibilities for the reproduction of life have been destroyed: *ante festum* when he has yet not obtained work; *post festum* when he is unemployed. It is an "ethical" category par excellence, which is here related to Schelling and Feuerbach, and is later elaborated by Levinas and Liberation Philosophy.
38. In "Die Diskursethik vor der Herausforderung der *Philosophie der Befreiung*" pp. 38–54.
39. Consider this critique in the four volumes which we have written between 1985 and 1993 on Marx; *La producción teórica de Marx; Hacia un Marx desconocido, El último Marx (1863–1882)* and *Las metáforas teológicas de Marx*.
40. This question is extensively treated in *El último Marx (1863–1882)*, Chaps. 9 and 10 (pp. 334–450), and also in *Hacia un Marx desconocido*, Chap. 14, paragraph 14.2, "Critique from the Exteriority of Living labor" (pp. 290–97).

41. Karl Marx, *Grundrisse*, p. 84. Emphasis added.
42. Ibid., p. 75. The first stage is feudal "community." The second is the social (*gesellschaftliche*) relation of isolated individuals without community in capitalism. The third stage, as we will see, is a "model of impossibility" or simply "ideal." This last is not a historical moment. We have studied some texts pertaining to this interpretation in "Toward a North-South Philosophical Dialogue," Chap. 3.
43. Karl Marx, *Capital: A Critique of Political Economy*, Vol. 1, p. 165; *MEGA*, II, 6, p. 103.
44. Ibid., p. 169.
45. Ibid., p. 170.
46. Ibid., p. 171.
47. *MEW*, 25, p. 828. This is from Chap. 28 "The Trinitarian Formula," Section VII, "Revenues and Their Source." Translated from the German.
48. Ibid.
49. *MEW*, 19, p. 21. "Jeder nach seinen Fähighkeiten, jedem nach seinen Bedürfnissen!"
50. Franz Hinkelammert, *Critica de la razón utópica* (San José: Costa Rica: DEI, 1990), has studied the theme of the "models of impossibility," such as the *perpetuum mobile* of physics. Einstein shows that perpetual motion is impossible (just as is, in Marx, "the higher stage of communist society, when subordination would have disappeared..."), but it is a regulative idea, from it are deduced the laws of modern thermodynamics. Just the same, the "realm of freedom" is empirically impossible, but this allows the critique of empirical society.
51. See my detailed discussion of this citation and the entire debate with Mikhailovski in *El último Marx (1863–1882)*, pp. 252–55. Marx's citation can be found in Rubem César Fernandes, *Dilemas do socialismo. A contravérsias entre Marx, Engels e os populistas russos* (Rio de Janeiro: Paz e Terra, 1982), pp. 167–68, or in K. Marx-F. Engels, *Escritos sobre Rusia. II* (México: Cuadernos de Pasado y Presente, Number 90, 1990), pp. 64–65. emphasis added. For an English translation see Teodor Shanin, ed. *Late Marx and the Russian Road: Marx and "the peripheries of capitalism"* (New York: Monthly Review Press, 1984) p. 136.
52. See Apel, chapter 8, above, pp. 189ff.
53. Marx uses different expressions, all of great richness: "the general critique of the whole system [*Gesammtsystem*] of economic categories" (*Manuscripts of 61–63, MEGA* II, 3, p. 1385); Or, in 1858, "present the system of bourgeois economy critically" (*MEW* 29, p. 550); or "to conceptualize the process of the configuration in its different forms" (*Manuscripts of 61–63*, p. 1499); or "develop genetically the different forms" in order to be able to realize the "genetic presentation" of the concept of capital (ibid.). See my *Hacia un Marx desconocido*, pp. 300ff.
54. *Capital*, Vol. 1. p. 270.
55. The themes of freedom, equality, property, etc. are dealt with by Marx in the *Grundrisse*, I, pp. 151–62 (see my commentary in *La Producción de Marx*, pp. 109ff), as well as in his later writings, such as *Capital*, Vol. 1 (1873), at the end of Chap. 6: "The sphere of circulation or commodity exchange, within whose boundaries the sale and purchase of labour-power goes on, is in fact a very Eden of the innate rights of man. It is the exclusive realm of Freedom, Equality, Property and Bentham." *Capital*, Vol. 1, p. 280. (Today we could say: John Rawls.)
56. Adam Smith, *An Inquiry into the Nature and Causes of the Wealth of Nations*, Vol. I, p. 65, chap. VI, paragraphs 1–5.
57. Ibid., p. 47; Chap. 5. For F. Hayek, M. Friedman, and John Rawls himself, the fact that there are rich or poor is a quasi-natural fact, a matter of fortune. This

matter is not the object of philosophical analysis or critique. Evidently, this is not Marx's position.

58. In the *Grundrisse*, November 1857 (*MEGA* II, 2, p. 216); in the *Urtext*, 1859 (*Grundrisse* [Berlin: Dietz Verlag, 1974], V. II, p. 215); in the *Manuscripts 61–63*, August 1861 (*MEGA* II, 3, 1, p. 148); in the lost text of Vol. 1 of *Capital* of 1863; in the lecture on *Wage, Price, Profit*, 1865 (*MEW* 16, pp. 129–32); and in the text cited from *Capital*, I, Chap. 2 (1867), Chap. 4 (1873).

59. In this case we would have to carry out an entire analysis of every form of "contractualism" (to which Ricoeur refers, who accepts as John Rawls's analysis or at least, is not as critical as the case calls for). In fact, Rawls's second principle, which is the economic principle, admits "inequality" as a quasi-natural fact: "Second: social and economic inequalities are to be arranged . . ." (*A Theory of Justice* [Oxford: Clarendon Press, 1972], Chap. 2, paragraph 11, p. 60). To distinguish the political-liberal equality of "basic liberties" from these inequalities, he later adds: "While the distribution of wealth and income *need not be equal*, it must be to everyone's advantage . . . ," p. 61. Why is political equality demanded and economic inequality admitted? This is what Marx puts in question with his critical theory of contract (dealt with in Chap. 4 of *Capital*, Vol. 1, 1873).

60. In the same way that in argumentation the "non-freedom" of the one who argues questions all relations as irrational, in the economic contract the fact that one of the contract partners is violently coerced makes the contract unjust (and also irrational): "It is forgotten, on one side, that the *presupposition* [*Voraussetzung*, a word much liked by Apel] of exchange value, as the objective basis of the whole of the system of production, already in itself implies compulsion over the individual, since his immediate product is not a product for him, but only *becomes* such in the social process, and since it *must* take on this general but nevertheless external form; and that the individual has an existence only as a producer of exchange value, hence that the whole negation of his natural existence is already implied; that he is therefore entirely determined by society. . . . It is forgotten. . . . What is overlooked . . ." (*Grundrisse*, p. 247–48).

61. Apel, like Habermas with respect to his critique of "productivism" in *Philosophical Discourse of Modernity*, thinks that Marx gives a fundamental importance to the relation person-work-nature: "The theory of 'alienation' or 'objectification,' inasmuch as it is essentially referred, in Marx, to the positive basic concept of 'living labor' [*lebendige Arbeit*], and not primarily to the relation of reciprocity with the interaction, which in the life world is complementary to labor" (Apel, "Die Diskursethik vor der Herausforderung," p. 39. But it is not like this. For Marx the essential was the practical Hegelian relationship person-to-person.

62. See the philosophical Hegelian reflection on these categories which we presented in "Hermeneutics and Liberation," chapter 5, section 5, above.

63. Karl Marx, *Manuscripts of 61–63*, in *MEGA* II, 3,1, pp. 147–48. See my *Hacia un Marx desconocido*, pp. 62ff.

64. And now as an "analectical" category of economics, and not as a socio-folkloric metaphor or allegory.

65. This is Kant's definition of *Aufklärung*, in his *Beantwortung der Frage: Was ist Aufklärung?* (A 481): "Aufklärung ist der Ausgang des Menschen aus seiner selbst verschuldeten Unmündigkeit."

66. Karl Marx, *Manuscripts of 61–63*, 4, 5, in *MEGA* II, 3,5, p. 1818.

67. *Capital*, Vol. 1, p. 128.

68. *MEGA*, II, 4, 5. p. 19.

69. *Capital*, Vol. 1, p. 128.
70. "Substance" in the sense of Hegel's *Logik*: a real thing that produces an effect.
71. For Marx "world" means the same as, in Hegel's *Logik*, that which refers to the "totality of phenomena" in economics: the "*world* of commodities," where the commodity is a being (thing) (*Dasein*) in which the essence of capital manifests (*erscheint*) itself, i.e., value.
72. "Use-values are only realized [*verwirklicht*] in use or in consumption. They constitute the *material content* of wealth, whatever its social form may be [level B1, B2, etc.]. In the form of society to be considered here [level B2] they are also the material bearers [träger] of ... exchange value." *Capital*, Vol. 1, Chap. 1, p. 126, *MEGA* II, 6, p. 70.
73. This with respect to the first moment of its description in Vol. I of *Capital*. Later Marx deals with the question of the transition of value to price, thanks to competition in the abstract, that is, the transition of value to the price of production. In Vol. 3 of *Capital*, Marx only arrives at the price of production. Only in a separate treatise after *Capital, Competition*, would he have dealt with the final problem of supply and demand, the ultimate price, and therein the buying and consumption of commodities. That he did not reach this problematic does not mean that we should not attempt to develop this discourse from within Marx. P. Sraffa attempts in his work *Production of Commodities by Means of Commodities. Prelude to a Critique of Economic Theory* (Cambridge: Cambridge University Press, 1960), to avoid this transition of value to price. On the polemic of this "transfer" of value, see J. Steedman, *Marx after Sraffa* (London: New Left Books, 1981), and J. Steedman, P. Sweezy, A. Sheikh, eds., *The Value Controversy* (London: New Left Books, 1981). In Raúl Rojas, *Das unvollendete Projekt. Zur Entstehungsgeschichte von Marx' "Kapital"* (Hamburg: Argument, 1989), the German version of this debate can be observed.
74. W. Stanley Jevons, *The Theory of Political Economy* (London: MacMillan and Co., limit, 1924), p. 1.
75. Ibid., p. 28.
76. Ibid., p. 29.
77. On this depends the "final degree of utility" (Ibid., p. 52), the point of departure for future marginalism, i.e., marginal use.
78. We ought to remember that the "poor" are people who have "needs" but no money (because they have no wage, or because the objective conditions for the reproduction of life in their traditional modes of production have been destroyed or displaced). This means the "poor" are not solvent: they are not part of the market. The poor are miserable, and with them the cynical calculus of market techniques and science can dispense. In Bangladesh or Sub-Saharan Africa they become the "excluded" of the world market.
79. Mauro Marini, *Dialéctica de la dependencia* (Mexico: ERA, 1973).
80. I leave to Franz Hinkelammert, "Die marxsche Wertlehre und die Philosophie der Befreiung," the refutation of a critical political economy.
81. See note 21 for some of my work on political philosophy. Note especially Vol. 4 of *Filosofía ética latinoamericana*, which deals with Latin American politics, written in 1974, before my intensive Marx studies. In the "Latin American Seminar" in Paris, 1964 (published in 1965 with works by Ricoeur and myself in *Esprit*), the debate was strictly "political."
82. In Latin America there are other reasons why the hegemonic political philosophies do not deal with "economics." The defense of the neo-liberal formal democracies (such as those of Alfonsin, Sarney, Salinas de Gortari) need to de-couple the political

problem (democracy) from economics (the misery of the majority, which increases day to day). We will deal with this question later.
83. Jürgen Habermas, *Theorie and Practice*, trans. John Viertel (Boston: Beacon Press, 1973), pp. 195-97. (*Theorie und Praxis* [Frankfurt: Suhrkamp, 1982], pp. 228-29. Emphasis added.
84. Paul Ricoeur, *Du text à l'action* (Paris: Seuil, 1986), p. 393ff.
85. Ibid., p. 396.
86. Ibid., p. 395.
87. Perhaps for the same reason Ricoeur does not understand my objection. I do not say that the "text" is in reality the "product" of labor. This would be an unjustifiable hermeneutical economism. What I indicated in my critique was that, just as a product is achieved through work, and a worker can be dominated by another (e.g., *conquistador*)—and injustice here means the robbery of the value of the work of the dominated—in an analogous manner, the dominator (the conqueror of the Mexican Yucatan) who has written a "text" (for example, the Christian New Testament), does not live by the rules of hermeneutic justice, first, when they impose on the Mayas of Yucatan a "*foreign* text" under threat of violence, and second, when they ignore the "*dominated* text"—for example, the Popol Vuh of the Mayas. That is, and this is the question not answered by Ricoeur; Is not hermeneutics *implicated* with concrete historical cases such as those of the conquest of America by the Spaniards or of Canada by the French? To what an extent can the dominated read the "text" of the dominator, or the dominator the "text" of the dominated? Which are the hermeneutical difficulties, the categories that would have to be developed in order to be able to analyze these cases which are our interest in Latin America? It concerns, then, developing hermeneutical themes not developed in the center, but of great interest for the periphery. Not more, not less. Feuerbach, in *The Essence of Christianity*, trans. George Eliot (New York: Harper Torchbooks, 1957) Chap. 27, at the end, writes: "Bread and wine are, as to their materials, products of Nature; as to their form, product of man ... Eating and drinking is the mystery of the Lord's supper; eating and drinking is, in fact, in itself a religious act; at least, ought to be so." p. 276-277. It would appear that Ricoeur reads the "text", but he has no "Bread and Wine" to eat and to drink. His text has "sense", but it is without carnal ("flesh") content. *Hermeneutics without economics is empty; economics without hermeneutics is blind!*
88. And therefore his dialogue partners are Weber, Mead, Durkheim, Parsons, et al. If he were to have a dialogue with the economists Smith, Ricardo, Malthus, Marx, Jevons, Marshall, Keynes, or Hayek, he would have to make more complex his concept of rationality when incorporating the *material-technical* mediation of the product of the practical-economic relationship, which is very different from that of language in the practical-pragmatic relation.
89. Jürgen Habermas, *The Theory of Communicative Action: Reason and the Rationalization of Society* (Boston: Beacon Press, 1983), pp. 3-4.
90. See for instance the works of Guillermo O'Donnell, "Apuntes para una teoría del Estado" in *Revista Mexicana de Sociología*, 40, 4, 1978, pp. 1157-99; *El Estado autoritario-burocrático* (Buenos Aires: Ed. Belgrano, 1982). Pablo Gonzalez Casanova, *La democracia en México* (Mexico: ERA, 1965); Norbert Lechner, *El proyecto neoconservador y la democracia* (Santiago, Chile: FLACSO, 1981), and *Estado y política en América Latina* (Mexico: Siglo XXI, 1981); Daniel Camacho, ed., *Autoritarismo y alternativas populares en América Latina* (San José: FLACSO, 1982); Daniel Camacho, ed., *Autoritarismo y alternativas populares en América Latina* (San

José: FLASCO, 1982); Tomás Moulian, *Democracia y socialismo en Chile* (Santiago, Chile: FLACSO, 1983).

91. With respect to this debate see the essay by Marcos Roitman Rosenmann, "La Política y las opciones de la Democracia en América Latina," unpublished presentation at Pontevedra, 10 April 1991; Franz Hinkelammert, *Democracia y Totalitarismo* (San José: DEI, 1987). By various authors, *El control político en el Cono Sur* (Mexico: Siglo XXI, 1978); also Norbert Lechner, *Los patios interiores de la democracia: subjetividad y política* (Santiago, Chile: FCE, 1990); Guillermo O'Donnell, *Transiciones desde un gobierno autoritario* Vol. I–IV (Buenos Aires: Paidos, 1986), and *Notas para el estudio de procesos de democratización política* (Buenos Aires: Centro de Estudios de Estado y Sociedad, 1979). By various authores, "Movimientos políticos, sociales y populares en América Latina" in *América Latina: entre los mitos y la utopía* (Madrid: Universidad Complutense, 1990), pp. 247–360; José Coraggio and Diana Dere, eds, *La transición difícil* (Mexico: Siglo XXI, 1986); Agustín Cuevas, *Las democracias restringidas en América Latina* (Ecuador: Ed. Planteta, 1988); Torcuato Di Tella, "Reform and the Politics of Social Democracy" in *Latin American Politics* (Austin: University of Texas Press, 1990), pp. 142–76; Pablo González Casanova, "La democracia en América Latina. Actualidad y perspectiva," presentation at the Seminario Internacional, Madrid, 15–20 April 1991, and *El poder al pueblo* (Mexico: Océano, 1985). Also Peter Hengstenberg, *Profundización de la democracia, Estrategías en América Latina y Europa* (Caracas: Nueva Sociedad, 1989); Julio Labastida, ed., *Los nuevos procesos sociales y la teoría política contemporánea* (Mexico: Siglo XXI, 1986); David Lebmann, *Democracy and Development in Latin America* (Philadelphia: Temple University Press, 1990); Carlos Matus, "La gobernabilidad de un sistema social" in *Diseños para el cambio* (Caracas: Nueva Imagen, 1989); Ronaldo Munck, *Latin America: The Transition to Democracy* (Atlantic Highlands: Humanities Press, 1989); Orlando Nuñez and Roger Burbach, *Democracia y revolución en las América* (Managua: Ed. Vanguardia, 1986); Carlos Pereyra, *Sobre la Democracia* (Mexico: Cal y Arena, 1990); Juan Carlos Portantiero, *La producción de un orden: ensayos sobre democracia entre el estado y la sociedad* (Buenos Aires: Nueva Visión, 1988); Marcos Roitman and Carlos Castro Gil, eds., *América Latina entre los mitos y la utopía* (Madrid: Ed. Complutense, 1990); and with others (eds.), *Quel avenir pour la démocratie en Amérique Latine?* (Paris: CNRS, 1989).

92. Paul Ricoeur, in this book, page 431.

93. The "developmentalist fallacy" consists precisely in suggesting to other cultures or peoples to follow the European path of development. The expression "shortening of history" is ambiguous. Does it mean to follow the same slow European path or the impossibility of a rapid revolutionary path or one's own path? It is rational to attempt to save time, within a realist project, in order to evade the "vicious circle" which necessarily leads to failure (as can be the case with a neo-liberal project of development, whose fruits will never reach "development" due to the international structure of exploitation which prevents sufficient national accumulation in order to attain a real "take off").

94. This is what I, in my first dialogue with Apel, called the "historically possible communication community" (in Apel-Dussel, eds., *Fundamentación de la ética y Filosofía de la Liberación*, pp. 78ff). It is a "project of liberation" that demands knowing how to "govern" the permanent crisis of peripheral countries, but which does not declare *a priori* as impossible that there could be a revolutionary change (although the actual circumstances are far from permitting it, but only situated political prudence can evaluate it).

Bibliography

Amin, Samir. *Eurocentrism*. New York: Monthly Review Press, 1989.
Apel, Karl-Otto. *Die Idee der Sprache in der Tradition des Humanismus von Dante bis Vico*. Bonn: Bouvier, 1963.
———. *Transformation der Philosophie*. 2 Volumes, Frankfurt: Suhrkamp, 1973.
———. *Towards a Transformation of Philosophy*, trans. Glyn Adey and David Frisby. London: Routledge Kegan and Paul, 1980.
———. "Notwendigkeit, Schwierigkeit und Möglichkeit einer philosophischen Begründung der Ethik im Zeitalter der Wissenschaft," in P. Kanellopoulos, ed., *Festschrift für K. Tsatsos*. Athens: Nomikai Ekdoseis Ant., 1980.
———. *Understanding and Explanation: A Transcendental-Pragmatic Perspective*, trans. Georgia Warnke. Cambridge: The MIT Press, 1984.
———. *Diskurs und Verantwortung. Das Problem des Übergangs zur postkonventionellen Moral*. Frankfurt: Suhrkamp, 1988.
———. *Ethics and the Theory of Rationality: Selected Essays, Volume 2*, ed. Eduardo Mendieta. Atlantic Highlands: Humanities Press, 1996.
———. "The Challenge of a Totalizing Critique of Reason and the Program of a Philosophical Theory of Types of Rationality," in D. Freundlieb and W. Hudson, eds., *Reason and Its Other*. Oxford: Berg, 1992), pp. 23–48.
———. "Rationalitätskriterien und Rationalitätstheorien," in G. Meggle and A. Wüstehube, eds., *Pragmatische Rationalitätstheorien*. Berlin: de Gruyter, 1994.
———. "The Hermeneutic Dimension of Social Science and Its Normative Foundations," in *Man and World* 25 (1993), 247–70. Expanded version in K.-O. Apel and M. Kettner, eds., *Mythos Wertfreiheit?* Frankfurt: Campus, 1994.
Apel, Karl-Otto, Enrique Dussel, Raúl Fornet-Betancourt, eds. *Fundamentación de la ética y filosofía de la liberación*. Mexico: Siglo XXI, 1992.
Apel, Karl-Otto, and Matthias Kettner, eds. *Zur Anwendung der Diskursethik in Politik, Recht und Wissenschaft*. Frankfurt: Suhrkamp, 1992.
Austin, John. *How to Do Things with Words*. Cambridge: Harvard University Press, 1962.
Beverly, John, and José Oviedo, eds. *The Postmodernism Debate in Latin America: A Special Issue of Boundary 2*, Vol. 20, 3 (Fall 1993).
Böhme, Gernot and Hartmut. *Das Andere der Vernunft. Zur Entwicklung von Rationalitätsstrukturen am Beispiel Kants*. Frankfurt: Suhrkamp, 1983.
Bondy, Augusto Salazar. *Existe una filosofía en nuestra América?* México: Siglo XXI, 1968.
Chomsky, Noam. *American Power and the New Mandarins*. New York: Vintage Books, 1967.
Cortina, Adela. *Razón comunicativa y responsabilidad solidaria*. Salamanca: Sígueme, 1985.
Derrida, Jacques. *Speech and Phenomena: And Other Essays on Husserl's Theory of Signs*, trans. David B. Allision. Evanston: Northwestern University Press, 1973.
Dussel, Enrique. *El humanismo Semita*. Buenos Aires: EUDEBA, 1969.

---. *El dualismo de la antroplogía de la christiandad.* Buenos Aires: Guadalupe, 1974.
---. *América latina, dependencia y liberación.* Buenos Aires: García Cambeiro, 1974.
---. *Método para una Filosofía de la Liberación. Superación analéctica de la dialéctica hegeliana.* Salamanca: Sígueme, 1974.
---. *El humanismo helénico.* Buenos Aires: EUDEBA, 1975.
---. *Filosofía ética latinoamericana.* Vol. 3. México: Edicol, 1977.
---. *Filosofía ética latinoamericana.* Vol. 4. Bogotá: USTA, 1979.
---. *Filosofía ética latinoamericana.* Vol. 5. Bogotá: USTA, 1980.
---. *Philosophy of Liberation*, trans. Aquila Martinez and Christine Morkovsky. Maryknoll: Orbis Books, 1985.
---. *Para una de-strucción de la historia de la ética.* Mendoza: Ser y tiempo, 1972.
---. *Praxis latinomaericana y Filosofía de la Liberación.* Bogotá: Nueva América, 1983.
---. *Filosofía de la producción.* Bogotá: Nueva América, 1983.
---. *Para una ética de la liberación latinoamericana.* 2 Vols. Buenos Aires: Siglo XXI, 1973.
---. *La producción teórica de Marx. Un comentario de los Grundrisse.* Mexico: Siglo XXI, 1985.
---. *Hacia un Marx desconcido. Un comentario a los Manuscritos del 61–63.* Mexico: Siglo XXI, 1988.
---. *El último Marx (1863–1882) y la liberación latinoamericana.* Mexico: Siglo XXI, 1990.
---. "Marx's Economic Manuscripts of 1861–63 and the "Concept" of Dependency," in *Latin American Perspectives* 17, 2 (1990), pp. 61–101.
---. *Las metáforas teológicas de Marx.* Navarra, Spain: Editorial Verbo Divino, 1993.
---. *The Invention of the Americas: Eclipse of "the Other" and the Myth of Modernity*, trans. Michael D. Barber. New York: Continuum, 1995.
Dussel, Enrique. ed. *Hacia una Filosofía de la Liberación.* Buenos Aires: Bonum, 1973.
Fornet-Betancourt, Raúl, ed. *Ethik und Befreiung.* Aachen: Augustinus Buchhandlung, 1990.
Fornet-Betancourt, Raúl, ed. *Diskursethik oder Befreiungsethik?* Aachen: Augustinus Buchhandlung, 1992.
Fukayama, Francis. *The End of History and the Last Man.* New York: The Free Press, 1992.
Gadamer, Hans-Georg. *Truth and Method.* Second, revised edition, trans. Joel Weinsheimer and Donald G. Marschall. New York: Continuum, 1993.
Goizueta, Roberto S. *Liberation, Method and Dialogue: Enrique Dussel and North American Theological Discourse.* Atlanta, Georgia: Scholars Press, 1987.
Habermas, Jürgen. *Zur Rekonstruktion des Historischen Materialismus.* Frankfurt: Suhrkamp, 1976.
---. *Communication and the Evolution of Society*, trans. Thomas McCarthy. Boston: Beacon Press, 1979.
---. *The Theory of Communicative Action.* 2 volumes. Trans. Thomas McCarthy. Boston: Beacon Press, 1983, 1987.
---. *The Philosophical Discourse of Modernity: Twelve Lectures*, trans. Frederick G. Lawrence. Cambridge: The MIT Press, 1987.
---. *Vorstudien und Ergänzungen zur Theorie des kommunitakiven Handelns.* Frankfurt: Suhrkamp, 1984.

———. *Moral Consciousness and Communicative Action*, trans. Christian Lenhardt and Shierry Weber Nicholsen. Cambridge: The MIT Press, 1990.

———. *Postmetaphysical Thinking: Philosophical Essays*, trans. William Mark Hohengarten. Cambridge: The MIT Press, 1992.

———. *Faktizität und Geltung*. Frankfurt: Suhrkamp, 1993.

———. *Justification and Application: Remarks on Discourse Ethics*, trans. Ciaran P. Cronin. Cambridge: The MIT Press, 1992.

Hinkelammert, Franz. *Crítica de la razón utópica*. San José, Costa Rica: DEI, 1990 (1984).

Hösle, Victorio. *Philosophie der ökologischen Krise*. Munich: C.H. Beck Verlag, 1990.

———. *Praktische Philosophie in der modernen Welt*. Munich: C.H. Beck Verlag, 1992.

Honneth, Axel, Thomas, McCarthy et al., eds. *Philosophical Interventions in the Unfinished Project of Enlightenment*. Translations by William Rehg. Cambridge: The MIT Press, 1992.

Jevons, W. Stanley. *The Theory of Political Economy*. London: MacMillan and Co., Limited, 1924.

Kanellopoulos, P., ed. *Festschrift für K. Tsatsos*. Athens: Nomikai Ekdoseis Ant. 1980.

Kant, Immanuel. *Critique of Practical Reason and Other Writings in Moral Philosophy*, trans. and ed. with intro. by Lewis White Beck. Chicago: The University of Chicago Press, 1949.

———. *Groundwork of the Metaphysics of Morals*, trans. and analyzed by H.J. Paton. New York: Harper Torchbooks 1948.

———. *Political Writings*, ed. with intro. and notes by Hans Reiss; trans. H.B. Nisbet. New York: Cambridge University Press, 1990.

Kellner, Douglass. *Herbert Marcuse and the Crisis of Marxism*. London: MacMillan, 1984.

Levinas, Emmanuel. *The Theory of Intution in Husserl's Phenomenology*, trans. André Orianne. Evanston: Northwestern University Press, 1973.

———. *Totality and Infinity: An Essay on Exteriority*, trans. Alphonso Lingis. Pittsburgh: Duquesne University Press, 1969.

Lorenzen, Paul. *Normative Logic and Ethics*. Mannheim-Zürich: Hochschultaschenbücher Verlag, 1969.

Luhmann, Niklas. *Soziale Systeme*. Frankfurt: Suhrkamp Verlag, 1988.

———. *Die Wissenschaft der Gesellschaft*. Frankfurt: Suhrkamp, 1990.

Marx, Karl. *Capital*. Vol. 1, trans. Ben Fowkes. New York: Penguin Books, 1990 (1976).

———. *Capital*. Vol. 3. New York: International Publishers, 1967.

———. *Early Writings*, trans. Rodney Livingstone and Gregor Benton. New York: Penguin Books, 1992 (1974).

———. *Grundrisse*, trans. Martin Nicolaus. New York: Penguin Books, 1993 (1973).

Mead, George Herbert. *Mind, Self, and Society in Works. Volume 1*. Chicago: University of Chicago Press, 1962.

Øfsti, Audun ed. *Ecology and Ethics: A Report from Melbu Conference, July 1990*. Trondheim: Nordland Akademi for Kunst og Vitenskap, 1992.

Rawls, John. *A Theory of Justice*. Oxford: Clarendon Press, 1972.

Ricoeur, Paul. *The Symbolism of Evil*, trans. Emerson & Buchanan. New York: Harper & Row, 1967.

———. *From Text to Action: Essays in Hermeneutics, II*, trans. Kathleen Blamey and

John B. Thompson. Evanston: Northwestern University Press, 1991.

———. *The Conflict of Interpretations: Essays in Hermeneutics*, ed. Don Ihde. Evanston: Northwestern University Press, 1974.

———. *Oneself as Another* trans. Kathleen Blamey. Chicago: The University of Chicago Press, 1992.

———. *History and Truth*, trans. Charles A. Kelbley. Evanston: Northwestern University Press, 1965.

———. *Freud and Philosophy: An Essay on Interpretation*, trans. Denis Savage (New Haven: Yale University Press, 1970.

———. *Time and Narrative*, 3 Volumes. Trans. Kathleen McLaughlin and David Pellauer. Chicago: University of Chicago Press, 1984–88.

Rorty, Richard. *Contingency, Irony and Solidarity*. New York: Cambridge University Press, 1989.

———. *Consequences of Pragmatism*. Minneapolis: Minnesota University Press, 1982.

———. *Philosophy and the Mirror of Nature*. Princeton: Princeton University Press, 1979.

———. "Metaphilosophical Difficulties of Linguistic Philosophy," in Introduction to *The Linguistic Turn* (Chicago: The University of Chicago Press, 1967), pp. 1–39.

———. "The Historiography of Philosophy: Four Genres," in *Philosophy in History* (Cambridge: Cambridge University Press, 1984) pp. 49–75.

———. "The Priority of Democracy to Philosophy," in M. Peterson and R. Vaughn (eds.), *The Virginia Statute of Relious Freedom*. Cambridge: Cambridge University Press, 1987.

———. "Feminism and Pragmatism" (Tanner Lectures on Human Values, University of Michigan, December 7, 1990). *Michigan Quaterly Review* 30, 2 (Spring 1991).

———. "Social Hope and History as Comic Frame" (April 29), unpublished manuscript of 29 pages, read on 4 July 1991 at the Institute of Philosophy (UNAM, Mexico). A version of this manuscript has appeared under the title "The Intellectuals at the End of Socialism," *The Yale Review* 80, 1&2 (April 1992), pp. 1–16.

Schelkshorn, Hans. *Ethik der Befreiung. Eine Einführung in der Philosophie Enrique Dussels*. Freiburg: Herder, 1992.

Searle, John *Speech Acts. An Essay in the Philosophy of Language*. Cambridge: Cambridge, 1969.

———. *Intentionality. An Essay in the Philosophy of Mind*. Cambridge: Cambridge Univerity Press, 1983.

Sellars, Wilfred. *Science and Metaphysics*. London: Routledge and Kegan Paul, 1968.

Shanin, Theodor, ed. *Late Marx and the Russian Road: Marx and "the Peripheries of Capitalism."* New York: Monthly Review Press, 1984.

Smith, Adam. *An Inquiry into the Nature and Causes of the Wealth of Nations. Volume One*. Oxford: Clarendon Press, 1976.

Taylor, Charles. *Hegel*. Cambridge: Cambridge University Press, 1975.

———. *Hegel and Modern Society*. Cambridge: Cambridge University Press, 1979.

———. *Human Agency and Language. Philosophical Papers, Volume 1*. Cambridge: Cambridge University Press, 1985.

———. *Philosophy and the Human Sciences. Philosophical Papers, Volume 2*. Cambridge: Cambridge University Press, 1985.

———. "Language and Society," in A. Honneth and H. Jonas, eds. *Communicative Action*. Cambridge: MIT Press, 1988, pp. 23–35.
———. "Le juste et le bien," in *Revue de Metaphysique et de Morale* 93, 1 (1988), pp. 33–56.
———. *Sources of the Self: The Making of the Modern Identity*. Cambridge: Harvard University Press, 1989.
———. *The Ethics of Authenticity* Cambridge: Harvard University Press, 1992.
———. "The Politics of Recognition," in Amy Gutmann et al, eds., *Multiculturalism and the "Politics of Recognition"* Princeton: Princeton University Press, 1992.
Wallerstein, Emmanuel. *The Modern World System. Capitalist Agriculture and the Origins of the European World Economy in the Sixteenth century*. New York: Academic Press, 1974.
———. *The Capitalist World-Economy*. Cambridge: Cambridge University Press, 1979.
Weber, Max. *The Protestant Ethic and the Spirit of Capitalism*, trans. Talcott Parsons. New York: Charles Scribner's Sons, 1958.
Zea, Leopoldo. *The Role of the Americas in History*, trans. Sonja Karsen. Savage, Maryland: Rowman & Littlefield Publishers, Inc. 1992.

Index

Adorno, Theodor W., 3, 38n. 19, 143
Albert, Hans, 16n. 21, 65
Alienation, 6
Alterity, 50, 54, 147
Althusser, Louis, 84
Amin, Samir. xxi, 30, 149n. 7
analectical, 6
Analytic philosophy, xxiv, 103ff., 109
Apel, Karl-Otto, vii, viii, ix, x, xvi, xviii, xxi, xxii, xxiii, xxiv, xxv, xxvi, xxxn. 29, 4, 13, 14, 19ff., 27ff., 30, 31, 36n. 1, 37n. 6, 42n. 48, 43nn 49–53, 44n. 60, 45n. 69, 46nn. 77, 85, 47n. 86, 49ff., 57, 62n. 41, 66ff., 93, 120nn. 15, 20, 122n. 48, 123n. 53, 129, 138ff., 206, 213ff., 227ff.
Aquinas, Saint Thomas, 77, 144
Arendt, Hannah, 207
Aristotle, 17n. 24, 33, 60n. 22, 65, 76, 107, 144, 209
Arlacchi, Pino, 178
Augustine, 76, 77
Austin, J. L., ix, xxi, 65

Bellah, Robert, xiii
Bernstein, Eduard, 192
Bernstein, Richard, xviii
Bloch, Ernst. xvii, 3, 7, 11, 12
Bloom, Harold, xiii
Boff, Leonardo, xv
Böhm-Bawerk, Eugen. 192, 226, 227
Bolívar, Símon, xviii
Bondy, Augusto Salazar, xvi, xix, xx, xxi, 79, 86
Borda, Fals, 79
Buber, Martin, xvii, 17n. 25, 78
Burke, Kenneth, 115

Cardoso, xxi
Carnap, Rudolph, 4, 109
Casas, Bartolomé de las, xviii, xxii, 41n. 40, 52–53, 135, 136, 217
CELAM, xix

Chomsky, Noam, 73n. 34
Clavigero, Francisco Xavier, 136ff., 151n. 36
Code of Hammurabi, xxiv
Coletti, Lucio, 84
communication community 14, 19, 21, 25, 27ff., 36, 49, 54ff., 88, 139, 165ff.
Cortés, Hernán, 20, 133, 217
Cuban revolution xix, xx, 2
cynical reason, ix, 67ff. *See also* Peter Sloterdijk

Davidson, Donald, 107, 109, 110
dependency theory, xvi, xix, xxi, 170ff., 218ff.
Derrida, Jaques, 4, 17n. 23, 20, 107, 109
desarrollismo, xx. *See also* developmentalist fallacy
Descartes, René, 13, 77, 131, 133, 217
developmentalist fallacy, 4, 5, 17n. 23, 135, 239n. 93. *See also* desarrollismo
Dewey, John, xin. 2, xiii, 107
Dilthey, Wilhelm, 12
discourse ethics, xxii, xxiii, xxv, 19, 64ff., 70, 163ff., 189ff. *See also* Karl-Otto Apel and Jürgen Habermas

economics, 12ff., 18n. 38, 35ff., 45n. 65, 83ff., 87ff., 219ff., 229. *See also* transcendental economics
Engels, Friedrich, 84
exteriority, x, xvii, xviii, 4, 6, 17n. 24, 21ff., 27ff., 53ff., 114ff.

face-to-face, xvii, 22, 33, 84, 169
Faletto, xxi
Fanon, Franz, 3
Feuerbach, Ludwig, xvii, 11, 17n. 25, 39n. 20, 238n. 87
Feyerabend, Paul, 28, 43n. 53
first philosophy, xvi, xvii, 7, 149. *See prima philosophia*

245

Fornet-Betancourt, Raúl, vii, xix, 163
Foucault, Michel, 4, 67, 107, 109
Frank, Andre Gunther, xxi, xxv
Fraser, Nancy, xviii
Frege, Gottlob, 4
Freire, Paulo, 10, 21, 54, 69
French Revolution, xxiv
Freud, Sigmund, 9, 30, 54
Freye, Marilyn, 113

Gadamer, Hans-Georg, 3, 12, 33, 55, 76, 85
Galileo, 29
Gauthier, Paul, xv
Goethe, Johann Wolfgang von, 108
Gramsci, Antonio, x, 70
Guevara, Ernesto Che, xix
Gutiérrez, Gustavo, xix, xx

Habermas, Jürgen, ix, x, xviii, xxii, 3, 4, 5, 14, 15n. 13, 19, 20, 27, 30, 31, 39n. 20, 41n. 38, 43n. 49, 45n. 70, 50, 51, 53, 57, 66ff., 84, 93, 114, 116, 125n. 93, 133, 134ff., 138ff., 143ff., 156n. 88, 177, 206, 208, 209, 227ff.
Havel, Vaclav, 115, 116, 126n. 106
Hayek, Friedrich, ix
Hegel, G. W. F., xvi, xvii, 3, 11, 17n. 25, 28, 51, 81, 88ff., 107, 109, 111, 131, 138, 140, 145, 149n. 16, 186, 195, 212, 231n. 10
Heidegger, Martin, xvi, xxi, 3, 4, 19, 33, 38n. 19, 55, 75, 77, 85, 107, 108, 109, 141, 145
Hempel, Carl G., 109
hermeneutics, xxiii, 14, 74ff., 83ff., 211, 238n. 87
Hinkelammert, Franz, 16n. 21, 116, 201n. 74, 219, 235n. 50
Hirschmann, A. O., 179
Hurtienne, Thomas, 179
Husserl, Edmund, 3, 13, 38n. 19, 74–75.

illocutory, xxiii, 26, 32ff., 39n. 27, 84, 139
interpellation, ix, xxiii, 19ff., 31, 32, 39n. 25, 53

James, William, 108
Jervolino, Domenico, viii, 206, 211
Jevons, W. S., 226
Jonas, Hans, 32, 49, 69

Kant, Immanuel, 19, 51, 61n. 26, 85, 107, 111, 135, 137, 138–140, 208, 222
Kautsky, Karl, 84
Kierkegaard, Soren, 12, 17n. 25, 108
King, Martin Luther Jr., xix
Kohlberg, Lawrence, 59
Konnick, Charles de, 77
Kosík, Karel, 84
Kuhn, Thomas, 4, 29, 43n. 54, 107

Lacan, Jacques, 9
Laclau, Ernesto, 115–116
Lebenswelt (life-world), 53ff., 104ff., 138
Leibniz, Gottfried Wilhelm, 11, 77
Leonard, S. T. xxviiin. 17
Levinas, Emmanuel, viii, ix, x, xvi, xvii, 3, 4, 12, 17n. 24, 20, 23, 32, 39n. 20, 40n. 27, 42n. 44, 45n. 76, 53, 62n. 41, 64, 67, 68, 77, 79ff., 84, 91, 114, 121n. 25, 147, 169, 212
liberation ethics, xxiii
Liberation Theology, xx, xxi, 212
Life community (*Lebensgemeinschaft*) 49, 54, 88, 184
life-world. See *Lebenswelt*
linguistic turn, xviii, xxi, xxiii, 20, 49, 103, 106, 107
Locke, John, 117, 131
Lugones, Maria, 124n. 87
Luhmann, Niklas, 7, 72n. 20, 156n. 90, 201n. 59
Lukács, Georg, 54, 84
Lyotard, Jean-Francois. xxii, 4, 20

MacKinnon, Catherine, 113
Marcuse, Herbert, 3, 5, 7, 15n. 6, 38n. 19, 54, 67, 81, 84
Mariategui, José Carlos, 2
Maritain, Jacques, 77
Marx, Karl, vii, x, xiii, xvii, xviii, xxv, 6, 7, 8, 12, 13, 14, 17n. 25, 23, 24, 34–36, 38n. 12, 39n. 20, 45n. 65, 46n. 84, 47n. 86, 53, 55ff., 61n. 39, 81, 83, 84, 85, 88ff., 107, 116, 118,

Index

127n. 110, 147, 164, 166, 168, 185ff., 189ff., 193, 219ff.
Menger, K., 226
Merleau-Ponty, Maurice, 3
Modernity, xviii, xxii, xxiv, 3, 4, 5, 20–21, 50, 51ff., 131ff., 152n. 40
Montesinos, Antón de xviii, xxii, 135
Morris, C. W., 19, 85
Mounier, Emmanuel, 77

Nabert, Jean, 74, 76
Nietzsche, Friedrich, 6, 16n. 20, 67, 108, 109, 110

ontological, 14
Ortega y Gasset, José, xv
Other xvi, xvii, xviii, xxii, 3, 6, 7, 10, 11, 13, 14, 21, 24, 27ff., 33, 35, 36, 39n. 20, 50, 53ff., 66, 82, 136, 138, 144, 146

Parsons, Talcott, xxii
Peirce, Charles Sanders, xiii, xxi, 4, 19, 27, 85
perlocutory, xxii, 22
phenomenological, 14
phenomenology, 32, 74
Pizarro, 20
Plato, 33, 107, 130–131, 144
Popol-Vuh, 86
Popper, Karl, 4, 16n. 21, 65, 67
postmodernity, xviii, xxii, 14, 20, 21
pragmatic turn, 19
pragmatics, 85, 87, 220
prima philosophia (first philosophy), xvi, xvii, 7, 149
proximity, 6, 17n. 24, 22, 39n. 26, 84, 169
Putnam, Hilary, 107

Quine, W. V. O., 107, 109

Rawls, John, 7, 8, 17n. 29, 35, 40n. 29, 42n. 45, 44n. 60, 47n. 90, 70, 87, 89, 117, 208, 210, 236n. 59
Reformation, xxiv
Reichenbach, H., 109
Renaissance, xxiv
Ribeiro, Darcy, 178

Ricoeur, Paul, vii, ix, x, xv, xviii, xxi, xxii, xxiii, xxv, xxvi, 3, 11, 12, 74ff., 131, 213ff., 228, 231n. 11, 238n. 87
Rorty, Richard, viii, ix, x, xviii, xxii, xxiv, 4, 6, 16n. 13, 20, 25, 31, 44n. 54, 58, 66ff., 70, 103ff.
Rosenzweig, Franz, xvii, 17n. 25, 78
Royce, Josiah, xiii, 108

Sabet, Hafez, 182–83
Santander, Francisco de Paula, xviii
Santayana, George, 108
Sartre, Jean-Paul, 3
Scannone, Juan Carlos, xxi
Scheler, Max, 77
Schelling, F. W. J., xvii, 3, 6, 12, 17n. 25, 81, 147
Schiller, F., 56, 140
Schleiermacher, F. 12
Searle, John, xxi, 19, 23, 26, 32, 37n. 9, 65, 84
Seel, Martin, xxiii
Sellars, Wilfrid, 107–109
Sepúlveda, Ginés de, 52–53, 60n. 22, 217
Shaw, G. H., 192
Sloterdijk, Peter, 72n. 18
Smith, Adam, 144, 227
Socrates, 10
speech-act, xxii, 21ff., 139ff.
Spinoza, Benedictus de, 205, 207

Taylor, Charles, viii, xviii, xxii, xxiii, xxiv, xxv, 129ff.
Totality, ix, xvii, 6, 7, 13, 17n. 24, 20, 24, 53ff., 67, 82, 114ff., 144
trans-modernity, xxii, 14, 152n. 40
transcendental economics, xviii, xxiii, 4, 14, 34. *See also* economics
transcendental pragmatics, 4, 14, 19, 27, 34, 164
Tupac Amaru, 24

universal pragmatics, 27

validity claims, 24ff., 65ff. *See also* speech act
Vatican II xix, xx
Vattimo, Gianni, 4, 16n. 13
Vitoria, Francisco de, xxii, 135

Waldras, L. 226
Wallerstein, E. xxi
Weber, Max, xxii, 67, 70, 133, 134, 172, 177, 193
Weil, Eric, 209
Weizsäcker, Ernst-Ulrich von, 182–184
Wellmer, Albrecht, 147
Welterschließung (world-system), xviii, xxiii, 132ff., 213ff., 231n. 10. *See also* E. Wallerstein

West, Cornel, xin. 2, xiii, xviii
Wittgenstein, Ludwig, xxi, 4, 19, 20, 64, 107, 108, 109
world-disclosure (*Welterschließung*) xxiii, xxixn. 24
world-system. *See Welterschließung*

Zea, Leopoldo, xvi, xix, xx, xxi, 77
Zubiri, Xavier, xv, 81

GENERAL THEOLOGICAL SEMINARY
NEW YORK

DATE DUE